# Installations

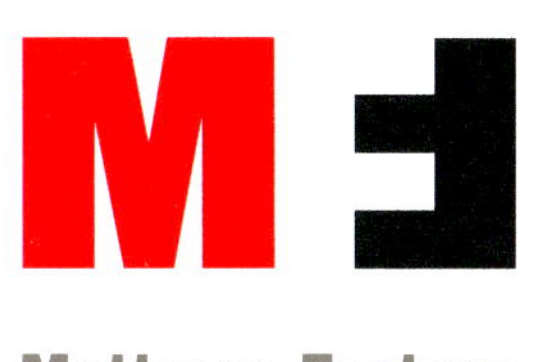

Mattress Factory

1990 | 1999

# Installations

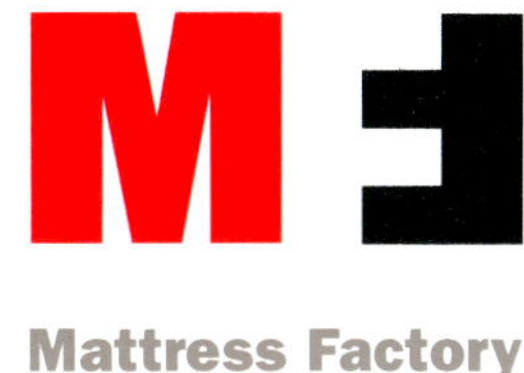

Mattress Factory

1990 | 1999

Michael Olijnyk, Curator of Exhibitions
Barbara Luderowski, Executive/Artistic Director
Claudia Giannini, Editor

Mattress Factory
Pittsburgh, Pennsylvania

University of Pittsburgh Press
Pittsburgh, Pennsylvania

Published by Mattress Factory, Pittsburgh, Pa., 15212
and University of Pittsburgh Press, Pittsburgh, Pa., 15261


Manufactured in the United States of America
10 9 8 7 6 5 4 3 2 1

ISBN (cloth) 0-8229-4169-4
ISBN (paper) 0-8229-5771-X

Funding provided by
The Andy Warhol Foundation for the Visual Arts
National Endowment for the Arts
Pennsylvania Historical and Museum Commission
The Buhl Foundation

Photo credits
Except for the image listed below, the photographs in this volume are the property of the Mattress Factory and were taken by Michael Olijnyk, John Charley, Sonia Yoon, Barbara Runnette, Annie O'Neill, and Joanna Michaelides.

Tracey Emin, *There's a Lot of Money in Chairs*, page 67, courtesy of Jay Jopling/White Cube, London.

CONTENTS

## Ahead of the Curve

Sheena Wagstaff
Tate—Britain, London

My first experience of the Mattress Factory in the winter of 1988–89 was through encountering the works of William Anastasi, Kathy Montgomery, Jessica Stockholder and Cady Noland. I remember clearly the high gloss splatterings and bodily parameters of Anastasi's gestural drawings; Stockholder's cacophony of artifacts and materials —a dazzlingly rich multitude of textures, resonant equally with the real world as they were with a constructed world; the sensual depths of graphic darkness set against corresponding translucent sandblasted glass of Montgomery's meditations on the nature of light and its opposite; Noland's wall of carefully stacked and scaffolded beer cans—their red, white and blue celebratory colors punctured by a note of disquiet with a pair of handcuffs indicating the darker implications of the patriotic bunting. It was immediately obvious that each artist's work was the result of a deeply thoughtful response to its immediate place.

It is tempting to equate the Mattress Factory's importance to making art with its bygone function as a building in which groups of people worked together to produce goods to the highest standard of production. It is true that both types of factory often operate as laboratories, where design ideas are refined and a variety of different means of production are used to make a product—mattresses aren't necessarily comfortable if they are posture-enhancing.

But this dry wadding-and-mattress-ticking analogy gives only a partial account of the Mattress Factory's operation and no hint whatsoever of the intelligent and single-minded development of the Mattress Factory as a unique place where some great art is made.

For it is the freshness and clarity of vision with which Barbara Luderowski and Michael Olijnyk have guided the Mattress Factory that have given rise during nearly a quarter of a century to some remarkable artists' projects. It is these in their turn which have generated and maintained the international reputation of the Mattress Factory. Artists such as Charles Ray, Bill Woodrow, James Turrell, Ann Hamilton, Damien Hirst and the aforementioned Noland and Stockholder were all invited to make exhibitions at the Mattress Factory significantly in advance of their work being recognized on the larger, national stage.

Over the years I became very familiar with the way in which Luderowski and Olijnyk work. They begin with respect for the artist. A conversation follows, often in a room at the top of the Mattress Factory overlooking the Mexican War Streets and beyond to the opposite shores of the Ohio and Monongahela Rivers in one direction and the Allegheny River in the other. For any artist invited to make art by the Mattress Factory, it is the opportunity to stretch one's horizon, to have a broader view of ways to create art, to explore potential directions which hitherto have presented logistical difficulties and which never fail to be enticing. This, and the emphatic assertion by both Barbara and Michael that "nothing is impossible," have become the *leitmotifs* of the Mattress Factory.

Most artists who have shown work at the Mattress Factory in the last decade of the twentieth century have their own versions of heroic stories, epic accounts of how the resourcefulness and energy of the Mattress Factory staff enabled difficult works to be realized. From finding relatively prosaic items like large quantities of sea salt and honey, Edwardian copper baths, or live canaries, to engaging legions of seamstresses to piece together silk-screened blankets, or sourcing fresh fly eggs—each sleuthing venture as an integral part of the process of making art is regarded by the Mattress Factory as every bit as significant as the final artwork.

Essentially, the Mattress Factory facilitates the making of art. Luderowski and Olijnyk, as curatorial guides to artists, act as mediums between the ideas of artists and their realizations in the world. They help to enable ideas to take form. It is also true for a number of artists, such as Turrell, that the expert mediating function of the Mattress Factory has allowed them to work through ideas and move forward in the development of their art more easily and more rapidly than they would otherwise have done.

There has been much discussion recently in the halls of the art kingdom about the curator becoming as significant as the artist in making visual culture. While the role of the curator has traditionally been that of a guardian as well as an interpreter of works of art in a museum collection or in temporary exhibitions, the parameters of the curator's function over the past couple of decades have widened from focusing on a work of art to include a relationship with the artist and the process of production.

Thus, in response to the fact that a great deal of art today is created in relation to—as opposed to separate from—the world it inhabits, so the relationship of the artist to the curator as well as to the exhibiting institution has shifted. As demonstrated by the host of projects described in this book, and by the role of the staff, the Mattress Factory has long been ahead of this curve of curatorial practice. It is a practice, nonetheless, in which the artist, not the curator, is central.

Many projects at the Mattress Factory have resulted in profoundly memorable installations, from the obsessional, mirrored, performative rooms of Yayoi Kusama to the flagellated canvases, pierced sculptures, and devotional spaces of Michael Tracy's paean to the bleeding and thwarted desires of Christ-made-man. The intensity of individual experience, as iterated in the emptied morphine syringes, medication vials, fetishistic Raggedy Ann dolls and devotional images of Patti Smith and Candy Darling in Greer Lankton's recreation of the place of her healing, reached a tragic apotheosis through her subsequent death. Her work, *It's all about ME, not You*, became her ultimate triumph and poignant legacy.

The Mattress Factory buildings themselves, and the surrounding environment, embody many other less personal histories, palimpsests of individual and collective stories. In *Garden*, Winifred Lutz has literally peeled back these physical layers of architectural accretions to expose the old dust and traces of previous lives and other times. Artists such as Buzz Spector have consciously responded to reverberations of memory held within the actual site—in his case by metaphorically winding back the clock to evoke a suspended instant of an earlier period. A further imaginative translation of the historical process was Christian Boltanski's archive, stacked in boxes like a crematorium's "memory wall", of artists who had been included in a century of *Carnegie International* exhibitions. Not only was it a moving memorial to a multitude of artists who have since disappeared from history, but it was also a sobering reminder of the simultaneous power of the museum to chart the history of other artists. Above all, it reminded the viewer of the almost fickle arbitrariness of the historical process itself.

In all these instances, artists have gone to different extents of engagement with or habitation of the site—thus making very different ways of transforming its meanings, some of which have been controversial. While the Mattress Factory has never feared contention—indeed, it encourages artists to take risks—neither has it consciously sought opprobrium or censure. Its reputation is notable as much for the quality and range of artworks produced as for its high regard by other international project spaces such as ArtPace (San Antonio), Artangel (London), Capp Street Project (San Francisco), P.S. 1 (New York) or Portikus (Frankfurt).

While the Mattress Factory attracts an enlightened following in the immediate Pittsburgh and Allegheny County communities, it has also reached a wide circle of supporters beyond. A scan of the Mattress Factory membership list reveals an astonishing array of supporters, extending from Pittsburgh to cities in China, the Czech Republic, England, France and Japan, including as well a wide range of professional interests, from sports lawyers to politicians. All are part of a group utterly devoted to supporting the Mattress Factory's aspirations for both its local and international programs and its tireless efforts in furthering access to and love of art.

Luderowski describes the genesis of the Mattress Factory years ago through the creation of a café where people traded ideas and bought soup for each other. In many respects, the way in which the Mattress Factory operates today does not depart from its original and essential notion of social and intellectual debate, generosity of spirit and the provision of necessary—though not always easily digested or palatable—sustenance for ourselves and others. In bringing together artists of many generations and persuasions to make work, the Mattress Factory privileges us with revelations about a multitude of different creative processes and the deep pleasure of indulging in questions with many answers.

In this respect, it would be appropriate to recall one of the greatest artists of this century, John Cage, whose ever-shifting installation of light, color and chance at the Mattress Factory affected more artists than just those such as Mary Jean Kenton with whom he collaborated. Just as he responded to Spector's awed homily described elsewhere in this book, Cage would have recommended the Mattress Factory in the same modest yet wonderfully evocative terms: "It's just something that happened."

# Installations

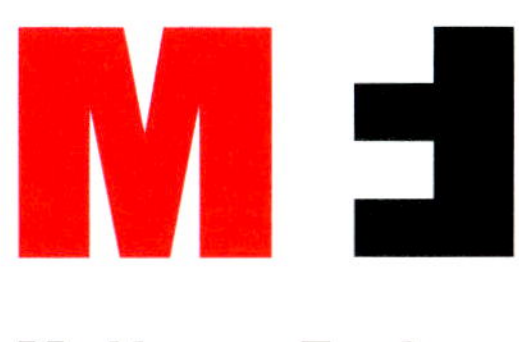

**Mattress Factory**

1990 | 1999

# Introduction

Claudia T. Giannini

One of the most highly valued attributes of western culture is creativity, even though it seems that its practice is often relegated to the fringes of society. Guided by a remarkable vision, the Mattress Factory is a museum where the artist's creative process as he or she constructs installation works is supported by the entire organization.

The Mattress Factory's mission is to provide an unfettered and supportive environment where artists are free to explore new ideas or expand their own work in the process of creating site-specific installations. The museum plays a unique role in the art world by providing artists with the means, space and freedom to create new works they might otherwise be unable to execute.

The Mattress Factory was founded by artists in 1977 in an abandoned Stearns and Foster warehouse on Pittsburgh's North Side. The first five years were a ferment of activities that included space for artists to work, live and exhibit, a children's theater, a dance studio, and a co-op vegetarian restaurant. Then in 1982, three artists—Michael Olijnyk, Athena Tacha and Diane Samuels—presented installation works in an exhibition entitled *Factory Installed*. This marked the turning point toward what the Mattress Factory has become today: a museum of contemporary art that commissions and supports the creation of site-specific installation art. This was followed in 1983 by an invitation to James Turrell to come to Pittsburgh to create a new work at the Mattress Factory. He ended up making two works which were the start of new series for him and which also became the first works in the permanent collection. These two works defined the Mattress Factory as a museum and focused its energy further on installation art.

From its beginnings, the Mattress Factory was a force for community revitalization. In 1986, the Board and staff worked with the local neighborhood council and the Urban Redevelopment Authority to rehabilitate several properties in the community. They converted a nuisance bar at the corner of Monterey and Jacksonia Streets into an exhibition space for both temporary and permanent works, as well as Allan Wexler's *Bed Sitting Rooms for an Artist in Residence*—both a work of art and lodging for artists working on site. Two more properties acquired in this transaction were restored to house six artists in 2000. Over a period of ten years, artist Winifred Lutz transformed a vacant city lot into her work called *Garden*, which combines the remains of the burned-down Stewart Paper Company with indigenous plants. Dedicated in 1997, the Mattress Factory's *Garden* is Lutz's most ambitious outdoor work and continues to evolve as the museum expands. In recent years, the Mattress Factory has been undergoing another expansion that incorporates two adjacent row houses on Jacksonia Street and a three-story structure that connects to the main facility to house educational and administrative spaces.

*Installations, Mattress Factory, 1990–1999* will examine installation art and the process that artists undertake at the Mattress Factory from different points of view in order to explore the creative thinking that goes into making an installation. In a 1998 article in the *New York Times*, Michael Kimmelman tried to define installation art but left the reader feeling as if he were trying to nail Jello to the wall. However, it is just these qualities of indefinability and open-endedness that make installation art such a potent medium for creativity. The creative process undertaken to make large-scale installations is often transformative to both the artists and the viewers, because it makes us see our world in fresh, invigorating, and often transcendent ways. The essays included in this volume are authored by experts from different disciplines, such as art and science. They illuminate the *experience* of installation art and the value of the creative process for both the artist creating the work and the viewer engaging with it.

This retrospective catalogue is a document of such creative activity during the last decade of the twentieth century. Although the Mattress Factory has been focusing on installation art since 1982, it was during the '90s that installation flowered as an artistic genre. This occurred not only in western art capitals but, literally, all over the world. *Installations by Asian Artists in Residence*, 1999–2000, the Mattress Factory's exhibition of new works by artists who had never before shown in the United States, was a testament to the dissolution of old artistic boundaries between east and west.

The realization of this catalogue was a team effort and the result of the hard work and contributions of many individuals. Michael Olijnyk and

Barbara Luderowski provided not only the vision that makes the Mattress Factory possible, but the guidance to steer this particular project to fruition. Cynthia Miller and her able staff at the University of Pittsburgh Press were infinitely patient and helpful with the publication process, and Mark Power, Matthew Wensel, and the staff of Kendra Power Design and Communication are responsible for the stunning design and production of this catalogue. We would like to extend our thanks to the authors of the essays—Buzz Spector, Rita Carter, and Robert Hobbs, who helped us to explore installation art from a variety of perspectives.

Owen Smith and Sonia Yoon, both assistants to the Curator, helped to organize the extensive documentation that accompanies each artist's section in the catalogue. A dedicated group of interns and volunteers helped with research, writing, and organizing photographs. They include Savanah Schroll, Marla Stayduhar, Robert Paul, Sarah Steiner, Jennifer Quinio, and Emily Trice.

Funding for this project was generously provided by the Pennsylvania Historical and Museum Commission, the Andy Warhol Foundation for the Visual Arts, and the National Endowment for the Arts.

Additional funding has been provided by AT&T, Alexander & Tillie Speyer Foundation, the *Pittsburgh Post-Gazette*, and the *Pittsburgh Tribune-Review*.

Finally, I would like to thank all of the artists included in the catalogue, who make our work so interesting and exciting, and whose creative thinking guides us all to new possibilities.

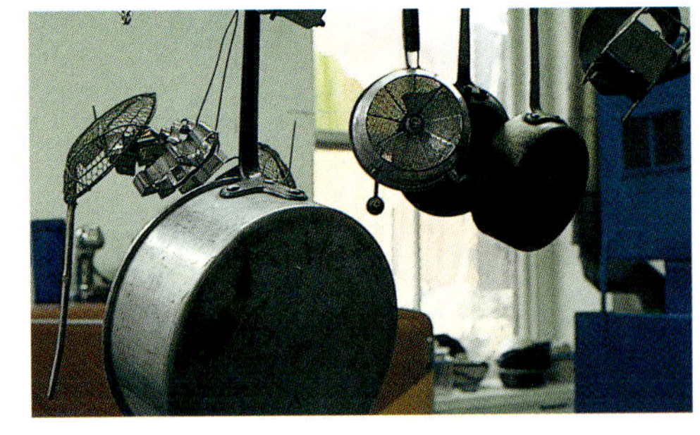

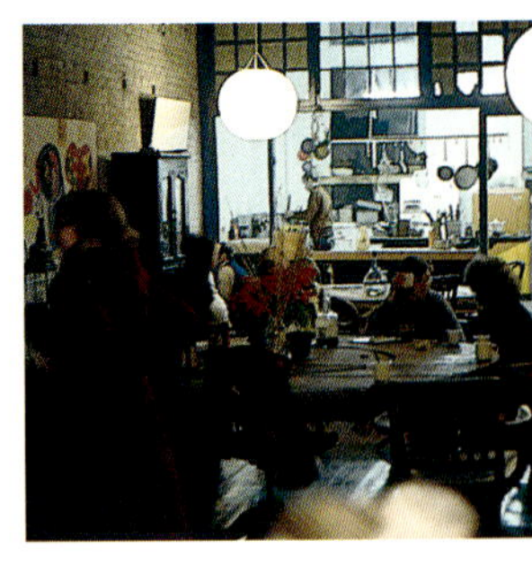

## Statement from the Executive/Artistic Director

Barbara Luderowski

The origin of the Mattress Factory was basically self serving, in that I as an artist wanted to be surrounded by artists who did things other than what I did—which was to make sculpture. I wanted to be around and have in the building different ideas, different approaches to things, different disciplines, and different ways of thinking. This creates an atmosphere where things are going on and discussions take place in a natural way.

The co-op restaurant that we had in the beginning was a great forum for discussion and the exchange of ideas. People came and went, but Michael and I were the ones who stuck with it. It gradually evolved into something that needed more structure and became an organization. I stopped doing my own work because I think that the kind of dedication that artists have for their work is so all-encompassing that it was either do the art work or do this work—which essentially I now view as my artistic process.

If you look at my work in sculpture, it consists of pieces of wood that fit together in a particular way to make a particular outcome. I view what I'm doing here as the same kind of thing. We pick the right people to work in this environment, which is made up of people from different disciplines with different points of view coming together to help artists do their thing.

I like the world of ideas. I like the fact that the Mattress Factory—because of its uniqueness both in Pittsburgh and in the nation—does not follow any prototypes in terms of programming. For instance, our education program is not about making cute things to bring home to mother. We deal with kids or people of any age in terms of the ideas that are going on here. It is about the art but it's also more than the art—it's about an attitude. There's an environment here that hopefully makes you think and explore within yourself the ideas in the work and how they relate to your own life. When it's really working, the art makes you think about the world in a different way or your immediate environment in a different way.

People might think of installation art as an esoteric medium that you have to approach with a major education in order to understand. But I don't think that's true. The phrase that expresses this is, "leave your art baggage at the door. Come in and give it a chance." Our education program tries to encourage this open attitude. The goal is to help children and adults articulate their ideas about creativity and embrace it in some way. I think we have been somewhat successful, because people, at least in our community, have come to be more comfortable with installation art.

Looking back on the twenty-four years we've been in existence, the changes have been enormous: in the physical facilities, in the number of works we've been able to accommodate, and in the number of artists we can invite to work here. The physical changes have hopefully complemented the expanded programs, so that growth occurs not for its own sake but is related to what's happening with programs. That refers again to the pieces and parts thing. If we are creating something that is permanent, not temporary, I hope we've made an organization that is flexible enough to make choices based on opportunity, our relationship to the community, and our relationship to the arts. Specifically, the question should always be: does it make the core issue—which is support of the artist—a more easily executed thing?

I find the interaction with artists really stimulating to my own way of thinking. We came to acquire James Turrell's dark piece *Pleiades* because he wanted two pieces of huge machinery that I had in my wood shop. There was a band saw that was about six or seven feet tall and a big wood joiner about eight feet long and weighing thousands of pounds that I got out of Mercy Hospital's wood shop. He wanted those and my whole pile of aged and beautiful black walnut. So he came and put it all into a U-Haul. He, Michael, and I drove to Arizona, and it was a great trip. I kind of miss those things now because I'm more an executive officer rather than a participant in the process.

I love Turrell's *Roden Crater Project* because I love someone thinking bigger and broader and more extensively than I have ever thought. People think that I've taken on a huge project here, which I suppose I have, but his is just monumental. So it was a reinforcement of the "think big" attitude. It is not just his work, it is his whole persona that is fun to think about. The idiosyncrasies of every one of the artists who has ever been here are interesting eye-openers in many ways.

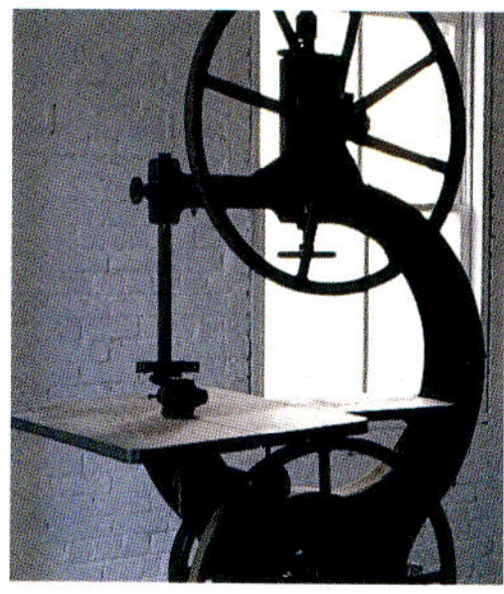

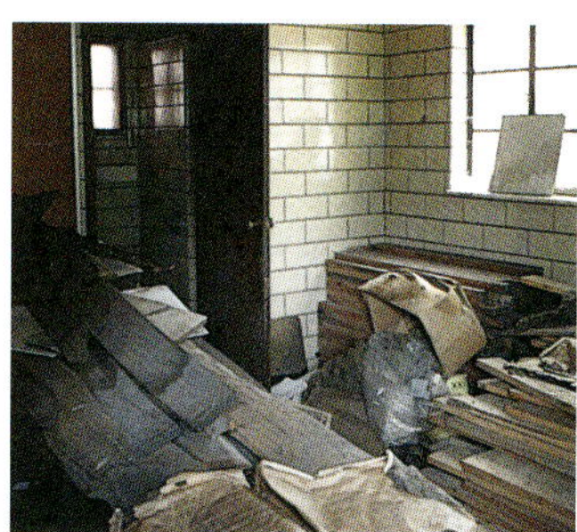

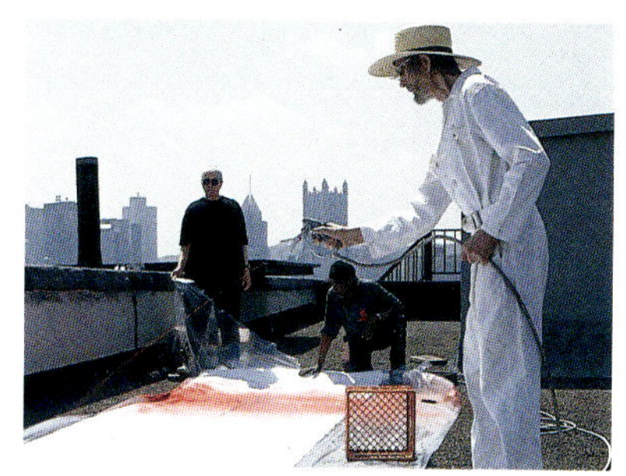

Co-op restaurant on the first floor of 500 Sampsonia Way, c. 1978

Band saw and black walnut traded for James Turrell's *Pleiades*, 1983

John Latham spray painting canvas on the roof of 500 Sampsonia Way for *Long Painting*, 1996

All of the artists have been absolutely identifiable coming off the plane, because they never quite look like everybody else. When we first met John Latham at the airport, he had on a pair of flaming pink sneakers. Latham, who is close to 80, is wonderfully creative and energetic and not afraid to be himself at all times. He got to Pittsburgh late at night and started talking about the process of science and art and astronomy. I know he was saying very important things but I found him very difficult to follow. However, when we sat down to dinner the next night, his conversation was perfectly mundane. I love the fact that he painted his canvases on the roof of the building with a paint compressor and got totally carried away with the process because of his enthusiasm.

The creative part of me is stimulated by challenge. In other words, I get irritated with things that don't quite work right, and I have this strong desire to correct them. Artists are not supported in the outside world, so the Mattress Factory is some small attempt to correct that situation and to provide opportunities for them.

An exhibition is a chaotic situation. The creative process is a messy process. Whoever thinks that the creative process in any form, any artist, any place is neat or orderly is off base. The architecture at the Mattress Factory allows for this disorderly process. At other museums, you need to go through the bureaucracy to get anything, which is frustrating. When you compare that to the Mattress Factory, where anybody and everybody help to get things done, it's much more fun. The fact is that artists overtake the office and use everything and get help from everybody. The staff are all in a state of near dizziness to accommodate the artists and to get the work accomplished. For artists, the Mattress Factory is like working at home—with help. It also gives them an opportunity to do something fresh. They're not carrying something from somewhere else. Turrell's *Pleiades* was one work that he had never actually built before. He was working out something in that piece that he wanted to do at Roden Crater.

I want to work my way in a full circle, by making a communal area where people eat together and discuss ideas, like we had in the co-op restaurant. That is what we are doing with the new artists' living space on Taylor Avenue—designing a communal area where ideas and communication are generated. I would like to have a residency program that is not necessarily aimed at creating a piece but at thinking about things without having to come up with a product.

One of my objectives is to stimulate people to include art in their lives. I want people to realize that art is not unrelated. It's related to sciences, as we are trying to illustrate in this book, and it's related to life. Artists can't live without it, and we would like it if everybody else would not live without it. When you buy a painting or a sculpture, you buy it because it gives you pleasure to look at, and you want to be around it. You visit it periodically in your house, you look at it and it means something to you because it touches some part of you. I think that wanting to be around art or to own art whether it works in your living room or not is a very important thing.

Not feeling a strong urge toward something or a passion for something is a real life lost. If you have a passion for something and you haven't been successful executing it, it's a frustration but I don't think it really matters. You've had that direction, that passion, and it's guided your life in some way. If the Mattress Factory fell apart tomorrow, I would at least feel that the attempt had been made. And I think it's important to make attempts.

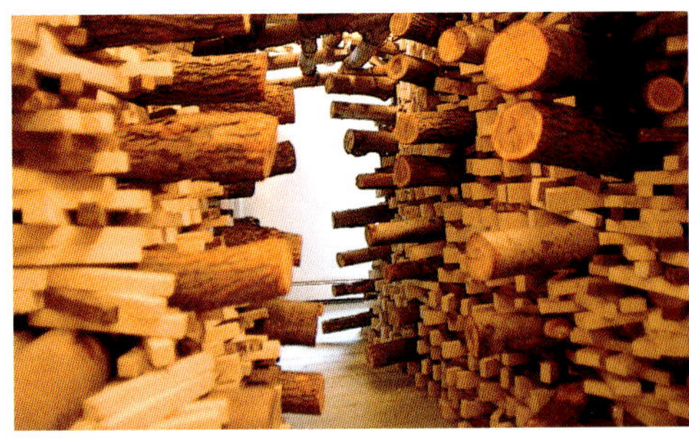

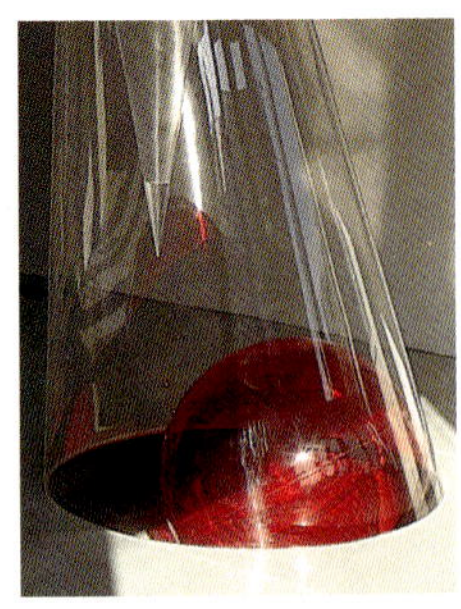

## Statement from the Curator of Exhibitions

Michael Olijnyk

Barbara Luderowski and I were both artists, and we wanted to create a space for other artists to live, work, and exchange ideas. Our goal was, and is, to help artists with projects that they would not be able to produce otherwise. Installations are expensive to make, and even well-known artists need help to push their work to the next level. They have to see the piece before they can understand if they want to continue in that same vein or not. We take that chance.

The Mattress Factory doesn't ask artists to show something that was a previous success. We don't look at proposals for pieces. We choose artists from their previous work; however, we want the actual ideas and working process to happen on site. We try to be as non-bureaucratic as possible, letting artists change their minds or change the direction of a piece. We want to partner with the artist in creating new work.

Basically, the reason that we do what we do is for the opportunity to work with individual artists: as they're making up their minds, as they're making mistakes, as they're trying to figure something out. The issue is not whether the finished work is a great installation but rather supporting artists while they're thinking about the work and going through the process with them. This includes all the mundane things, like picking the artist up at the airport, having the artist live here, and finding the materials he or she needs.

Even though my title is Curator of Exhibitions, my role here is very different from the typical museum curator. I function more like a chameleon. When I initially talk with artists I try to understand what they are trying to achieve conceptually and why they are choosing to work with certain materials. I have to understand what the end product is supposed to be, because in a sense, I'm becoming that artist when I'm looking for materials. I'm scouting and making decisions as if the artist is scouting and making decisions. Being able to understand an artist's visual and conceptual intentions only comes from the experience of having done this for so long. It is essential to understand why the look of something is important to the concept of the piece.

Before artists come to Pittsburgh, we ask them to give us a list of materials that they think they may need, particularly if they are not standard building materials. This process is often more than just a trip to Home Depot. When we work with artists we can end up in oddball places and unusual situations, which makes the whole experience more interesting. For her 1990 work *Plain Air*, Dove Bradshaw wanted a particular breed of pigeons called American Rollers. I normally start investigating materials by going through the phone book, so I called pet shops and breeders. We found this man who lived outside of Pittsburgh in a kind of zoo. From the outside, his house looked like a standard suburban tract house, but when you went inside, he had monkeys, birds, lizards, and outside he had donkeys and llamas and goats, along with dogs and cats everywhere.

The challenge is figuring out how to do what the artist wants and still stay within the amount of money that we have for the exhibition. In order to save money, staff and volunteers put in a lot of time to accomplish what needs to be done. When Takamasa Kuniyasu created his installation, *Return to Self*, 1991, he needed 16,000 bricks of a particular size and color, and it would have been far too expensive to have them custom-made. Instead, we bought soft fire bricks and cut each brick into 6 pieces. We rented a diamond saw and set up a workshop in the small building in the parking lot. Cutting all of those bricks seemed like an endless, hideous process because we were always wet from the spray that kept the blade cool. He also wanted the bricks to be in particular colors. Using concrete pigment, we soaked the cut bricks in buckets of ochre, red, and curry pigment in the parking lot.

John Cage's work, *changing installation at the mattress factory*, for our collaboration with the 1991 *Carnegie International*, actually incorporated this idea of partnership into the work. He used the fourth floor at 500 Sampsonia, which was then a work space, and gathered chairs and twelve art works each from four artists. He assigned a number to each chair and artwork, and the numbers were entered into a computer program, creating an arrangement for every day of the exhibition. Every morning for 103 days, I would get up at 5:00 a.m., walk downstairs from where I live on the 6th floor, take down the works from the previous day, and put in place the new arrangement of chairs and artwork. I would photograph the space each day as well. We had a cat

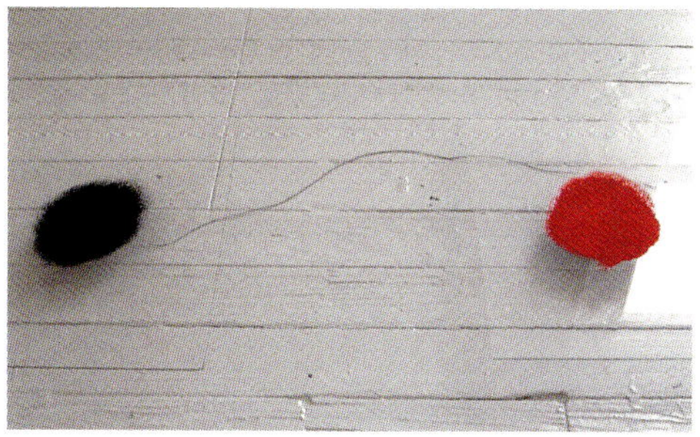

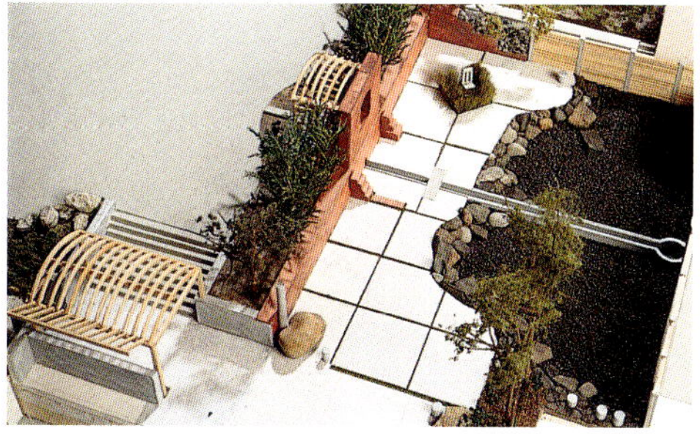

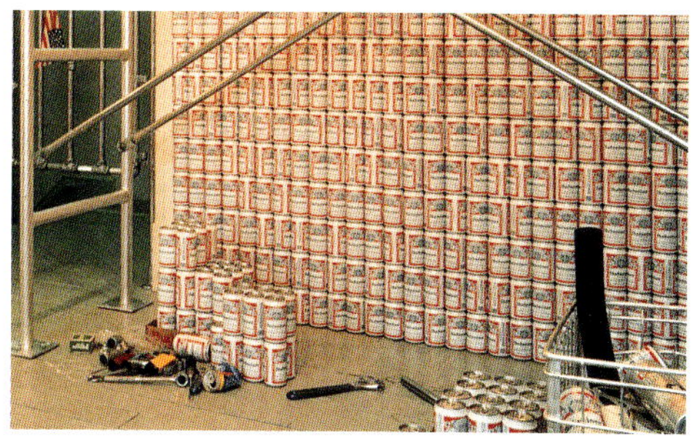

that would always go downstairs with me. As I photographed the pieces for 103 days, you can see that there's a cat in the center of the photographs. The cat placed itself between the camera and what I was photographing, so it appears to be in the center of the space. This was in complete accord with Cage's concept of incorporating random sounds and occurrences into his work.

Sometimes the process is not so smooth. In 1993, Alison Wilding proposed a piece that appeared to be a simple project of fabricating an eight-foot high Plexiglas cone with another inverted cone inside of it. This turned out to be more technically challenging than we thought. We started working with a fabricator here in Pittsburgh, and everything seemed to be going well. But as the opening approached, we went to see how the work was going, and it was a disaster. The cone wasn't geometrically correct, and it was impossible to use what he had made. This was one of the few times that we did not have a piece ready for the opening. For the exhibition, which included six other artists at 1414 Monterey Street, we put up a small sign inside the front door, explaining that when working with a living artist, sometimes things don't work out. We ended up working with a company in New York that had huge roll-in ovens that could hold a large sheet of Plexiglas with a mold. We showed Wilding's work in 1994.

This was a learning process for all of us. Neither we nor Alison Wilding knew what fabricating such a large piece of Plexiglas entailed. Glitches can occur when we are working with an artist and trying something completely new. She had never done that kind of piece before and didn't know what it meant to work with Plexiglas that size.

Because artists live here while they're making their work, we get to know them, and in some cases, form long-term relationships. They send us pictures of their children and we visit them when we're near where they live. Many artists come back to visit us. This fosters long-term artistic collaborations as well. In 1998, Rolf Julius called us to ask if he could work something out with a project he had in progress. We had a gallery free at the time and his project became *Black Listens to Red*, which we exhibited at 1414 Monterey Street in the summer of 1998.

Things can happen at the Mattress Factory without being scheduled on a calendar. We can change things around. We don't plan too far ahead, so things can happen spontaneously. Julius's *Black Listens to Red* turned out to be an interesting piece, and when he was here, we started talking about the *Visual Sound* exhibition for fall 2000. This all came about from having a long-term relationship. Julius came here in 1988 for the first time, and several projects and a major exhibition have slowly progressed from this relationship with him.

We started talking to Winifred Lutz in 1985, before we even owned the property where her *Garden* is now. Barbara and I liked her work, and we started a dialogue with her. She came up with an idea to make a small moss garden behind the main building, because that was the only property we had at the time. You would only see it from the windows inside. This never materialized, but eventually we purchased the vacant lots adjacent to our building. Our first discussions with her were about creating a space that could also be used by other artists. The more we looked at it, however, the more we saw that this would not work.

Lutz made many drawings and took a lot of photographs, formulating the initial idea of the garden space in the late 1980s. It wasn't until we started digging that the present conception of the *Garden* actually evolved. Originally, the *Garden* was going to be a flat, open area with slate, but when we started digging, we found these great foundations from the old Stewart Paper Company, which had burned down in 1963. It turned out that there were basement spaces and some architectural elements that she could work with. She went back to Philadelphia, rethought her original conception, and redesigned the project to incorporate these different materials.

Probably the worst way to do a big building project is in small steps, making decisions as you go along. The *Garden* has taken longer to complete because of that, but we never thought of it as an exhibition with an opening date. We are basically working with an artist whose material happens to be the outdoors, so we wanted to give her the same freedom and support that

Takamasa Kuniyasu, *Return to Self*, 1991, 16,000 fire bricks, 700 logs, steel wire

Alison Wilding, *Ambit*, 1994, Plexiglas

Rolf Julius, *Black Listens to Red (Piano Concerto)*, 1998

Winifred Lutz, Model for the *Garden*, 1993

Cady Noland, *This piece doesn't have a title yet*, 1989, beer cans, scaffolding, cloth and vinyl flags, hand tools we give artists who work inside—even though we were using heavy machinery. In spite of having taken a slower route, the *Garden* as it is now is a much more interesting project than if we had stuck with the original model. This is a very good example of our non-bureaucratic way of doing things, where the artists and their concepts are what lead the project. The *Garden* is still in progress.

Looking back at the history of the organization, you can understand what it means to help an individual artist get to the next step in his or her work. Sometimes we work with an artist to create a piece that isn't well understood because the work is completely new. Artists feel free enough here to try something that they themselves might not understand yet. They might be working with an idea that is five years ahead of its time. But when you look at the work over the course of time, it has become part of art history.

Many of the installations have had a life after the Mattress Factory, through inclusion in catalogues or periodicals or, in rarer cases, because they continue to be exhibited. Charles Ray's *35 x 33 x 32=35 x 33 x 34*, 1989, a 400-pound aluminum box sunk into the floor, was shown at his 1998 retrospective at the Whitney Museum of American Art in New York. He mentioned to us that we were the first to allow him to cut into the floor. Yayoi Kusama created her first balloon piece, *Dots Obsession*, here in 1996, and it then traveled to Rice University in Houston and the Serpentine Gallery in London. Cady Noland's *this piece doesn' t have a title yet*, 1989, continues to be reproduced in major art magazines, was shown at the Whitney, and is now in the Rubell Collection in Miami. At the time that she worked with us, she didn't have a New York gallery. The work was hard to understand then, but it fits into what has developed in the art world since. The Mattress Factory exists to provide artists with the support and freedom to take risks—which is a rare thing in our culture today.

# Installing at the Mattress Factory: a reminiscence

Buzz Spector

Michael Olijnyk and I watched as the technician from Allegheny Refrigeration Sales finished adjusting the freezer unit in the fireplace. Hunched in front of the white, painted mantelpiece he looked, from behind, like he was starting a fire. Instead he flipped a switch and the portable freezer started up with a low hum. We stood for a while as the room began to cool. Michael left to attend to other opening day matters and the technician crouched to make a final turn of the thermostat. I asked him what temperature he'd set it. "It should get down to around twenty degrees Fahrenheit," he replied.

My installation, *Cold Fashioned Room*, was one of four projects that opened in the Mattress Factory's satellite exhibition space at 1414 Monterey Street on Saturday, October 5, 1991. Along with Diana Burgoyne, Patty Martori, and Bogdan Perzynski, I had been contacted by Michael in the spring of that year and invited to make an installation. It was particularly pleasing to me that the invitation was to do something in the building on Monterey. I'd first visited the Mattress Factory in 1986 as a National Endowment for the Arts site reviewer, and Barbara Luderowski had taken me on a tour of the then recently acquired turn-of-the-century structure. The Monterey building was originally a street-level storefront with two floors of apartments above, and I remembered my delight in seeing the illusory golden flood and cut sheet metal objects of Bill Woodrow's *Ship of Fools: Discovery of Time*, 1986–1988, in what had once been a kitchen on the third floor.

The site designated for my project was a former third-floor bedroom. My first thought was to build a stack of found books there, in line with my ongoing work concerning the library as a metaphor for individual memory and public history. The effect of such a form, however, seemed to go against the previous domestic function of the space. I'm not sure when I decided to use coldness as an aspect of my Mattress Factory project, but I had previously made several works consisting of frozen objects displayed in modified commercial freezer cabinets. I know that my idea for a frozen room was influenced to some degree by the sense of stopped time I'd encountered in the Woodrow installation, but I was also intrigued by the resistance to documentation posed by the use of an invisible condition whose presence nevertheless articulated the meaning of the site. But how much would it cost to convert the room into what amounted to a gigantic walk-in freezer? On the telephone with Michael I tentatively broached my idea. There was only the slightest pause before he reassured me that, indeed, it could be done.

Over the summer we had numerous telephone conversations and exchanges of faxes about the design of the project. The details included constructing a wall with a doorway to completely enclose the space, lining the walls with Styrofoam board insulation, placing more Styrofoam on the floor and covering it with wooden planking, including period furnishings to give the room the appearance of a late-nineteenth-century home library, and, crucially, obtaining the equipment necessary to make the environment freezing cold. The room's original fireplace had been removed and the flue sealed during the renovation, but Michael brought the mantelpiece up from storage in the basement and mounted it on a temporary wall that both sealed off a window and provided concealed ventilation space for the freezing equipment.

September 1991 was an eventful month for the Mattress Factory. Besides the projects at 1414 Monterey Street, the organization had agreed to host several site-specific installations, including works by Christian Boltanski, John Cage, Ann Hamilton, and Tatsuo Miyajima, in partnership with the 1991 *Carnegie International*, opening October 17 at the Carnegie Museum of Art. It was also a busy time for me, and I scheduled my set-up visit to Pittsburgh between trips to San Antonio, Texas (for a lecture and panel discussion), and Boca Raton, Florida (another panel and the opening of a group show). I flew to Pittsburgh on Monday, September 16, arriving late in the evening. After a casual dinner with Michael and Barbara in their apartment in the main building, Michael took me over to the Monterey space to see how the room was being readied for my work. I had hoped to stay in Allan Wexler's *Bed Sitting Rooms for an Artist in Residence* but Michael informed me that John Cage was in residence there while he developed his installation for the *International*. Instead I stayed in Barbara and Michael's guest room on the sixth floor of the main building.

The next morning after breakfast, I rode the elevator with Michael down to the fourth floor and met Cage, already at work. Discomfited by

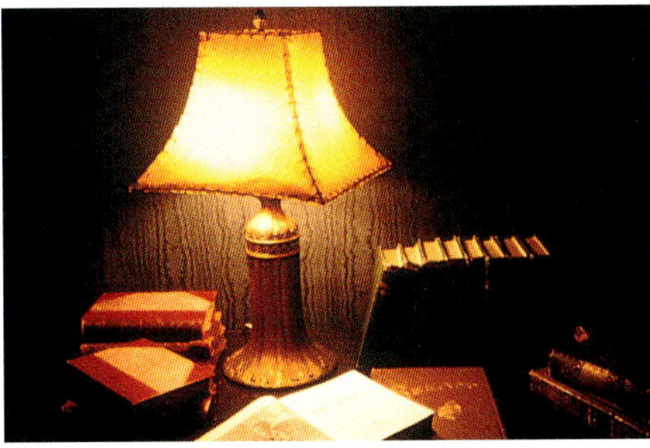

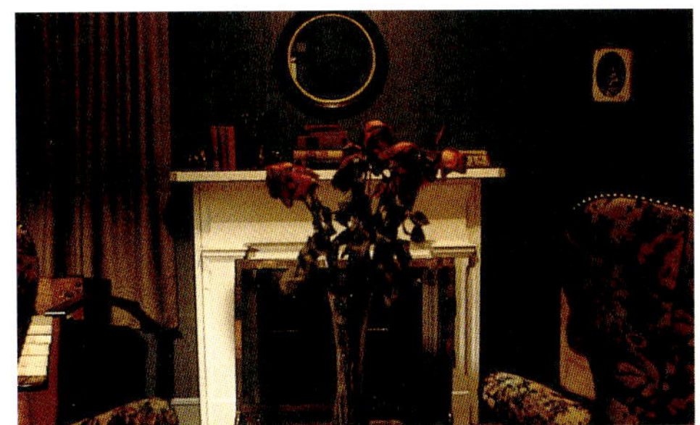

Buzz Spector, *Cold Fashioned Room*, 1991, freezer unit, Victorian furnishings, books

the thrill of meeting one of my intellectual heroes I exclaimed, "Mr. Cage, it's an honor to meet you." "No, it's not," he replied, smiling, "it's just something that happened." Cage's installation was to be a constant work in progress, changing daily according to a protocol of chance operations (compiled using the *I Ching*) that dictated the placement and orientation of seven chairs and fifteen artworks from a selection of forty-eight (twelve each by Cage, Dove Bradshaw, Mary Jean Kenton, and Marsha Skinner). I scribbled a calculation on a piece of paper: "That means Michael will have to hang or reposition 3,366 works during the run of the *International*." "Actually," replied Michael, "it'll be a few less than that because some things on some days will stay in the same place."

It was time to shop, so Michael and I went out in search of wallpaper and paint. By the end of the day we had found an elegant dark green silk moiré paper for the walls of my room and a warm gray low gloss enamel, "Misty Moors" by Pratt and Lambert, at a nearby paint store. The paint was for the interior side of the door and the decorative moldings lining the walls. In addition to those color and material choices, I picked through Barbara and Michael's collection of Victorian furniture, selecting a pair of elegant wingback chairs, writing desk, small table, bookcase, tobacco humidor, and wooden bench. The chairs needed recovering so Barbara's daughter, Taya Ross, drove me over to Gene Sanes, a local furniture upholsterer, where we settled on an attractive paisley.

I accompanied Barbara to the open air market in the Strip District on Wednesday morning, buying Roma tomatoes, lettuce, garlic, and a bag full of tart little Clapp pears. At lunch later I gave one of the pears to Cage with the punning question, "What is the sound of one Clapp handing?" The basic arrangement of my room was set, but there still remained the selection of accessories. In the afternoon I looked through local antique shops, finding an elegant cut glass inkwell for the writing desk and a dark oak framed print of a pastoral painting by Corot. Back at the Mattress Factory, Michael and Barbara supplied me with a suite of nineteenth-century engravings of birds, a lamp for the table, a Persian rug for the floor, a wood and metal dictionary stand, and an old stereoscopic viewer which I later placed on the mantel.

A dinner party was planned for Thursday evening, also my last evening in Pittsburgh, and at breakfast in the morning Cage proposed to search for edible mushrooms in the Allegheny Cemetery. He led a group that included Barbara, Taya, and Pittsburgh artists Kathleen Montgomery and Diane Samuels on the search while Michael and I picked a bagful of lambs' quarters along the weed-lined fences on Sampsonia Way, to supplement whatever mushrooms were harvested. We were quite willing to taste the cooked leaves of this common weed, for which Cage provided us the cooking instructions, but confined our picking to those leaves growing, as Michael put it, "above dog knee level."

There were fourteen of us for dinner: Barbara and Michael, Taya, Cage, Montgomery, Samuels, Dove Bradshaw and her husband, the artist William Anastasi, Mary Jean Kenton and her husband, Jim Rosenberg, Marcia Skinner, the art critic Robert Raczka and his wife, Belinda, and myself. Taya supplied the main course, Colonel Sanchez Chicken Tamales, from a local health food store, while Cage cooked several types of mushrooms, sauteing some and baking the others. I rinsed and steamed the lambs' quarters, which turned out to taste like spinach.

Bob Raczka had once written about my work for the *New Art Examiner*, a magazine for which I also used to write exhibit reviews and essays, and we exchanged stories about the tribulations of writing art criticism. Samuels had also spent time in Chicago, and we reminisced about our experiences of the Chicago art scene. At one point someone asked Cage why he'd included chairs in his installation and not simply the works of art on the wall. "We expect to be able to sit in chairs," he responded, "but not all of the chairs [in the installation] can be sat upon on any particular day. Seeing the chairs in unexpected positions may remind viewers to see the artworks a little differently as well." Cage offered a toast to the resourcefulness and energy of our hosts and we cheerfully raised our glasses despite Barbara's objection to such tributes.

When I left for Florida the next day, my room was not yet finished. The selection of its accoutrements was largely completed but neither the insulation nor the freezing equipment was yet in place. I apologized to Michael profusely for leaving him with so much construction and assembly still to be done, but he told me not to worry, as he was very used to providing the fabrication expertise for Mattress Factory projects.

Indeed, when I returned to Pittsburgh on Friday, October 4, the room was immaculately readied. The green silk wallpaper glowed in the lamplight, and the freshly painted molding looked as if it had always been there. The freezer unit was also in place, with its cooling element and controls in the fireplace and the compressor behind the false wall. It was the task of an hour to move the furnishings into position, and Michael and I finished up the acquisitions for the room with a visit to a used book shop in the Oakland neighborhood, near the Carnegie Museum, where I found the seventeen-volume set of the Lady Burton edition of *1,001 Arabian Nights* and a French-language edition of arctic explorer Fritjof Nansen's memoir, *Vers la Pole* (To the Pole). These supplemented the several cartons of old books lent by Taya and her husband, Michael Ross. I also purchased a dozen red roses and placed them in a crystal vase on top of the humidor.

Besides the four artists in the Monterey space exhibition, Ann Hamilton was also at the Mattress Factory, working on *offerings*, her contribution to the *Carnegie International*. Ann and I had become good friends when we'd taught together at the University of California, Santa Barbara in 1988–89, and I'd subsequently written about her work during my days as a correspondent for *Artforum*. It was an extra pleasure, then, to visit with her the morning of the opening in another Mattress Factory satellite space, the gutted interior of a three-story row house at 412 Sampsonia Way.

Ann showed me a box of cast wax human heads she'd been making from molds of similar castings she'd found during her recent trip to Brazil to make an installation for the *Sao Paulo Bienal*. In Brazil, heads like these (as well as wax arms, legs, and other body parts) were solid wax candles, burned in churches by people praying for divine cures of various physical or psychological problems. Ann's heads were hollow, and they were being made to be placed in a tabletop vitrine on the top floor of the otherwise empty row house. The vitrine was fitted with heating elements so that over the course of a day the heads would melt and the wax would drip through openings in the base onto the rough-hewn wood plank floor below. More heating elements were situated between the planks, so that the drippings would seep through to the second floor, falling onto a table there, also equipped with heat. In this fashion the wax would flow all the way down to street level, so that visitors to the building could see the heaps of congealed drippings as they climbed the stairs. Since the melting process was to occur on a daily basis, Ann and a group of volunteers were hard at work casting a very large number of heads. I smiled at the mental image of Michael starting each day with the reinstallation of Cage's chairs and pictures, then running over to the row house to reload Ann's vitrine.

Two of the other artists installing in the Monterey space, Bogdan Perzynski and Diana Burgoyne, were each making a few last adjustments to their work when I returned. (Patty Martori had finished putting together her installation, *Lovehouse*, a few days earlier and was not able to attend the opening.) Bogdan's installation, *All at the Same Time*, filled the large first-floor gallery with all manner of stuff including, notably, an upright player piano modified so as to read photographic enlargements of fingerprints as if they were sheet music. The deliberately "work in progress" appearance of the room was less an invitation for visitors to help finish the piece than to make the incomplete fabrication understandable as a narrative of creative action. The player piano's "performance" was a kind of model for the deducings invited of its audience. Diana fitted me up in the perambulatory apparatus that activated her video and electronic piece. The tripodal device was rigged with headphones in order to function as a kind of receiver. Wearing it, the viewer could find the "missing" words of the persons whose lips were moving silently on the screens of four video monitors placed on chairs around a table in the next room. Those voices were being broadcast from wire loops mounted to the walls. I walked around the room, snagging electronic traces of the conversation while reflecting on the longing at the heart of the work, that yearning to have again all those discursive moments that, in recounting later, we so often apologize for by saying, "you had to be there."

Less than an hour before the official start of the opening Michael tapped me on the shoulder to anxiously inform me that the freezer in my installation seemed to have stopped working. Sure enough, the room felt merely cool and clammy when I entered. The freezer was still humming, but apparently to no effect. Michael and I bent over the controls, moving the thermostat downward in an attempt to restart it. Nothing happened. I turned to Michael and said, "I'll stay up here and tell people how it's supposed to work. You call Allegheny Refrigeration and see if they can send someone over." I spent the next three hours explaining to visitors that the visual warmth of my Victorian replica was supposed to be accompanied by intense cold. It wasn't until the next morning that we discovered the refrigeration technician had inadvertently set the defrost cycle on the compressor for 4:00–7:00 p.m. instead of a.m.

In retrospect those hours of explanation helped me to better understand the essential problem addressed in *Cold Fashioned Room*. I was able to provide opening night visitors with a reasonable description of the effect of the work. In fact, my story became better through repetition as the night wore on, but its words never actually chilled anybody. It is in the ineluctable zone between the recognitions inspired by language and the real experience of the world that what makes sense to us becomes a matter of faith as much as knowledge. The Mattress Factory continues to operate in this domain.

***Buzz Spector is an artist and writer whose objects and installations have been shown in museums and galleries throughout the world, including* Cold Fashioned Room*, 1991, at the Mattress Factory. He is professor and chair of the painting program in the School of Art and Design at the University of Illinois at Urbana-Champaign and has written extensively on topics in contemporary art and culture.***

# The Creative Mind

Rita Carter

Art and science are after the same thing. Both are means by which we explore and experiment with the world and our relationship to it, and both aim to increase meaning and understanding. But people understand things in two distinct ways. One is irreducible intuition: the automatic recognition of a familiar face; the immediate realization that a particular form is "right"; the flash of insight that tells you that you have fallen in love. The other is the knowledge that comes from formal education or step-by-step analysis: the answer to a sum you have laboriously added up, or the knowledge that the earth goes around the sun. Full understanding requires that these two ways of knowing are integrated, and this was reflected in the ancient disciplines of natural philosophy and aesthetics. But in the twentieth century the two strands became separated. Artists were expected to deal exclusively in the first kind while scientists were limited to the second. The two stood almost in opposition, and sometimes sneered at one another across the divide.

This damaging apartheid is at last ending. The turn of the millennium has brought art and science back together in an occasionally clumsy, but increasingly ardent, embrace. Scientists are acknowledging the beauty and wonder inherent in their work, and artists are incorporating recent scientific discoveries into theirs. Some of the most fertile intermingling is that of conceptual art and my own professional passion, brain science.

Certain installations in the Mattress Factory seem to me to go further than any other form in trying to bring about this synthesis. Like traditional art, the works here produce an immediate emotional impact brought about by sensory stimulation. But they also stimulate active intellectual engagement. In some of the works, knowingly or not, the artists explore neurological processes directly. Rolf Julius's combined sound and visual works, for example, have intriguing connections with synaesthesia, a curious condition in which people "see" sound and "hear" visual images. Synaesthesia comes about when—due to eccentric brain "wiring"—the brain cells that usually produce vision in response to stimulation by information from the eyes, react instead to stimuli coming from the ears. Julius has described his own experience of synaesthesia thus: "The senses of listening, looking, touching, feeling and smelling are, for me, all very close together. I can look at a Beethoven symphony. You know why? Because I am confronted with the surface texture of the music." Only a tiny number of adults experience this sort of blending of sensory experience, but Julius's work gives some idea of what it must feel like.

The scientific study of the brain is especially illuminating in regard to art because it throws light on the very processes of creativity and artistic invention. These rather high-flown accomplishments seemed, until recently, to be beyond the scope of science—a mystery of the spirit rather than a puzzle of biology. But neuropsychology is fast revealing the mechanisms that underlie even the most complex of human feelings, thoughts and behaviors.

Brain scanning studies using imaging techniques such as the PET and the functional MRI show that every subjective experience, whether it is a bodily sensation, a frisson of pleasure, a visual perception, a fleeting memory, or some complicated train of thought, is brought about by patterns of electrical activity in different parts of the brain. Visual information, for example, is processed at the very back, sound in the sides, spatial information in the back crown area, bodily sensations and movement in a V-shaped band, pointing front and located toward the back, and complex thoughts and conscious emotions in the frontal lobes behind the forehead. By watching the patterns created as people undertake various mental tasks, researchers are building a detailed picture of how our brains produce perceptions, thoughts, and behaviors.

So what is going on in an artist's brain when he or she creates a new work? How does it differ from the brain function of, say, a mathematician? Is scientific and artistic creativity the same thing, or are there essential differences? And how does artistic skill relate to creativity?

We are still a long way from having comprehensive answers to these questions, but there are some intriguing pointers.

One clue to the cerebral mechanics underlying creativity comes from observing autistic savant artists—that rare group of people who have stunning islands of ability despite a very low level of general intelligence. Autistic savants who work with images typically make drawings or paintings which are near-perfect in terms of proportion,

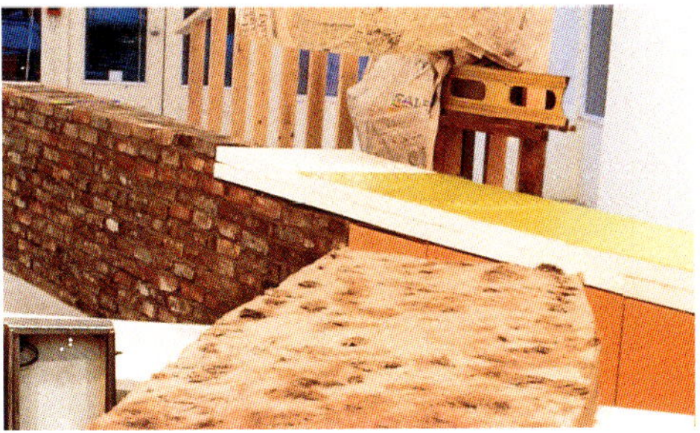

Rolf Julius, *Red*, 1996, speakers, amplifier, CD, red pigment, wire (long-term loan)

Jessica Stockholder, *Mixing food with the bed*, 1989, appliances, wood, newspaper, bricks, concrete, and paint

perspective, and accuracy. The British artist Stephen Wiltshire, for example, could draw phenomenally complex buildings with utter precision at the age of nine.

But autistic artists do not introduce ideas into their work. They usually stick obsessively to the same subject matter and rarely develop or alter their style. They have skill of a high order, but little or no creativity. It may seem strange that these two things can be uncoupled, but in fact it may be that creativity, far from being a component of skill, is in some ways its enemy.

To understand why, it is necessary to know a little about how our brains construct normal, everyday concepts. We are constantly bombarded with billions of fragments of information which pour in through our sensory organs. Normal brains junk the vast majority of this information before it reaches consciousness, but the important bits are extracted and integrated to form meaningful concepts. Concepts are not the same as concrete memories. A concept of a building, for example, is rather like a Platonic ideal—an amorphous mental construct which contains the building from every angle and in every light rather than the particular view that you might have of it from a specific location at a certain time of day. So when normal people look at a building, they take from the visual onslaught only the salient information: it's an office block (or a church); it's beautiful (or ugly); it's big (or small); modern (or old) and so on. If we turned away after a quick glance and tried to draw it, we would certainly not be able to put in every brick or shadow because our mental concept of the building would not contain such detailed information.

The brain of an autistic artist is different. One glance, and every tiny crack and glimmer of reflected light is branded on the mind's eye as clearly as the overall form. Furthermore, he does not seem to see that one is more, or less, important than the other. This gives him the extraordinary ability to reproduce an image accurately and in detail, but it prevents him from seeing through the detail to the essence of the thing. His overstuffed memory gets in the way.

A prerequisite of creativity, then, seems to be the automatic editing out of inessentials and the integration of what's left. This, put crudely, is the process of conceptualizing—a process described almost exactly by the artist Jessica Stockholder, another Mattress Factory artist. "My work is a struggle" she says, "to make order and cohesion consistent with the heap of chaotic information in which we exist."

Conceptual thought is a function of the frontal lobes of the brain, the area behind the forehead. Human frontal lobes are far bigger than those of other animals and they were the latest parts of our brains to evolve. Conceptualizing, therefore, seems likely to be a fairly recently evolved function, and animals, with the possible exception of some higher primates, do not seem to be capable of it. Frontal lobe dysfunction seems likely to be the element of autism which creates autistic savants. There are even cases of people suddenly developing autistic-like savant skills after their frontal lobes were put out of action by brain injury.

Conceptualizing itself is hardly an act of startling creativity, however. It is merely part of normal brain function. Most of the concepts we derive are, anyway, necessarily similar from person to person. If my fundamental concept of a cat was radically unusual, for example, I would be unable to recognize a real one, and any conversation about cats would soon founder. So to be creative requires that we go one step further. I would suggest that this involves taking fundamental concepts and juxtaposing them with others to create new and unique configurations.

This juggling act also takes place in the frontal lobes. When people are asked to come up with new ideas during a brain-scanning study—to think of as many ways as possible to use a rope, say—it is this bit of brain which lights up. It also sparks when they are asked to make choices. One region of the frontal cortex has become known as the central executive, because it selects one course of action over another and, thus, gives us a sense of self-determination without which we would probably have little or no sense of "I".

The creative process as described is not intrinsically artistic—it is essentially the same whether one is dealing with concepts derived from visual imagery or from mathematical equations. "Doing" science and "doing" art are, to that extent, the same. So what is the difference between artistic creation and scientific invention?

I believe it comes back to the two ways of understanding. Non-conceptual art is primarily concerned with bringing about emotional affect—the holistic, intuitive form of understanding. The work may convey intellectual ideas, but they are secondary to the feelings evoked by the work. Neuropsychologist V. S. Ramachandran, of the University of California, San Diego, has suggested that art, almost by definition, is that which creates an abnormally excessive reaction in parts of the brain which are "hard-wired" to generate emotion. Semir Zeki, a pioneer of visual neurology, pinpoints it even more precisely. He has shown that works by some of the abstract masters selectively excite specific cells in the visual cortex. Each subset of cells (those that react to edges, for instance, or to a specific color) produces a different emotional reaction. Red-reactive cells, for example, trigger excitement in a whole batch of other cells, while blue-reactive cells are more calming. Hence, a single line of a particular color can produce a profound and specific effect, even though it may be extremely difficult for the viewers to explain why they are moved. Artists need not understand why their works achieve their effect—they know which color to use and which angle to draw, and most arrive at this only after years of apprenticeship and practice. But they don't necessarily know how they know.

Science, on the other hand, must be transparent to consciousness. There is no point in a mathematician simply declaring the truth of a statement—her work involves providing a step-by-step, objective proof. The two endeavors, art and science, therefore involve dealing with concepts arrived at through, on the one hand, intuition, and on the other, deduction. Each type of understanding comes about by a different neurological process, and it is the distinction between the two which, I believe, distinguishes scientific creativity from art.

Even this distinction, though, breaks down in some of the Mattress Factory projects. James Turrell, for example, a former perceptual psychologist, arrives at his creations through a process almost identical to scientific enquiry. In earlier works, Turrell posed precise questions about the nature of perception: e.g., what kind of aural stimulation is necessary to maintain a sense of physical well-being? How much sound is needed? Does it have to be interrupted periodically? Are "natural environmental noises" necessary for normal functioning? How is sound involved in the maintenance of circadian rhythms? What visual stimuli are required for maintaining attention and orientation? From these questions, Turrell derived new insights into the nature of human perception, and from that he began to explore the nature of illusion. His Mattress Factory installations illuminate the tricky nature of image construction within the human brain and force us to attend to the process of vision as well as its end result.

Other artists explore the nature of unconscious brain processes, especially those concerned in emotion. These processes take place in the deeper reaches of the brain. Beneath the gray, corrugated cortex lies a cluster of oddly-shaped organs connected to the surface by long white strands of connective tissue. These nuclei are collectively known as the limbic system, and it is here that emotions are generated.

We think of emotions as conscious feelings, but in essence they are mere physical survival mechanisms—automatic reflexes that trigger the body to act appropriately when something important comes along. When the brain receives information that something dangerous is about, for example, one particular part of the limbic system, the amygdala, sends messages to the body to get ready to run. A waft of sex pheromones stirs part of the hypothalamus to produce an urge to move in on the target; the smell of food triggers a grasping reaction; and a rage-inducing stimulus produces a compulsion to strike out.

None of this is, of itself, conscious. But if the limbic system becomes highly activated, its messages spread up through the connective tissue to the frontal cortex, where they are experienced as fear, attraction, or anger. The accompanying physical changes in the body feed up to the cortex and manifest as emotional markers,

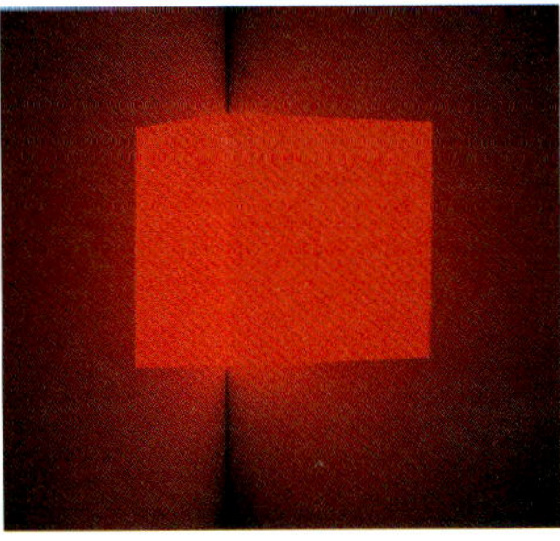

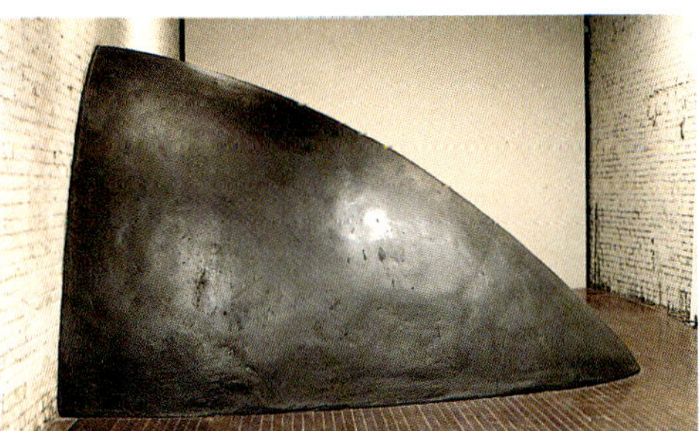

James Turrell, *Catso, Red*, 1994, drywall, paint, xenon projector

Jene Highstein, *Buttresses*, 1985, concrete over wood and wire armature, paint

like butterflies in the stomach or weak knees.

This route to consciousness—via the unconscious and in the wake of bodily changes—results in understanding that is instantly complete and emotionally charged. We cannot explain how we achieve it because the processes that led to it were unconscious. This, I believe, is the understanding that informs traditional artists and allows others to appreciate their works. It also has a role in conceptual art. The power inherent in the massive sculptural works of Jene Highstein, for example, arises largely from the harnessing of unconscious brain function. By placing a large object in a small space, he creates what he describes as "contradictory impulses to either push or be pushed." These impulses spring directly from the amygdala, one part of which creates the urge to hit out and another to flee or appease. Highstein has produced a work which—for some at least—stimulates the amygdala in such a way that these competing urges are held in unstable equilibrium, a state of mind rarely encountered in everyday life.

The essential ambiguities of Highstein's work also highlight another of the brain's built-in unconscious functions—the imposing of patterns on novel sensory stimuli. When we encounter something new, or are confronted with sensory information that does not immediately make sense, the brain scours its memory banks for things which seem similar. If a perfect match is not available, it will make do with the next best thing. Hence when people look at Highstein's work, they invariably come up with descriptions which accord with their own experience. Describing visitors' reactions to one of his installations, Highstein says: "Usually people say 'Oh, that's a mound', or, 'Oh no, that's a breast—he's made a breast you know.' Everybody is sure what it is I've made. In this case they're sure I've made a bean pot. Because there is a Mexican bean pot which is, I'm sure, not anything like these forms, but to people who are used to seeing them they liken it to these things."

Bill Woodrow's work also exploits the brain's capacity for pulling on disparate memories to make sense of things that at first sight may seem senseless. In his untitled lithograph, which is part of the Mattress Factory's Limited Edition Project, a ship "floats" on two serrated hand-saws. Thus, a seemingly incongruous object, like the handsaw, serves as a hook for memories and ideas of choppiness, danger and damage, fear and cruelty—a device more effective than an accurate drawing of waves.

Art which uses intellectual hooks such as these is, for some, more accessible than that which depends solely on emotional effect. Although we all have the capacity to understand in both ways, intuitively and rationally, some brains are constructed in such a way that information flows more freely along the intellectual route, while others grasp emotional truths more easily. Art in the twenty-first century will, I hope, succeed in fusing both forms of understanding. The Mattress Factory shows how it can be done.

*Rita Carter is the author of the critically acclaimed best seller,* **Mapping the Mind,** *which charts how human behavior and culture have been molded by the landscape of the brain. For the past ten years, she has been an award-winning medical and science writer, contributing to newspapers and magazines such as the* **Independent, New Science,** *and* **Daily Mail and Telegraph.**

# Merleau-Ponty's Phenomenology and Installation Art

Robert Hobbs

Most scholars focusing on installation art have exhibited a common desire to understand its post mid-twentieth-century currency through carefully tracing its genealogy.[1] In their efforts to comprehend its distinctness, they cite a range of disparate sources, including such genres as the decorous art of the tableau vivant and the improvisational outdoor environments of self-taught artists. They have also referred to such acclaimed works as the post–World War I Merzbau constructions of Hanover Dadaist Kurt Schwitters, Marcel Duchamp's *One Mile of String* for the First Papers of Surrealism exhibition in 1942, Frederick Kiesler's 1954 piece entitled *Galaxies* for the Sidney Janis Gallery in New York, Louise Nevelson's many black wall environments initiated in the decade of the fifties, Yves Klein's contemporaneous empty galleries evoking the Void, and Allan Kaprow's events, environments, and happenings that were developed around this same time. Scholars undertaking these studies have been assiduous in acknowledging legitimate and distinctly different threads leading to the widespread efflorescence of installation art that began in the late 1950s and early 1960s and has continued to the present. Their histories are careful and rewarding descriptions of *effects* based on mosaics of related phenomena that assume the force of a *raison d'etre* when viewed together. Because these studies have been particularly conscientious in detailing installation art's serendipitous beginnings, this essay will explore specific *causes* leading to its accepted significance in the second half of the twentieth century by considering installation art a specific genre. It will concentrate on likely intellectual sources for this new form category by looking first at Maurice Merleau-Ponty's phenomenology, which examines embodied, interactive perception in which the "see-er" becomes one with what is seen. It will then consider the relevancy of westernized Zen and, after a brief detour introducing the concept of "suture" from psychoanalytic film theory, it will show how installation art incorporates viewers into itself, thus cementing Merleau-Ponty's emphasis on the enmeshing of see-er and seen that constitutes preconscious perception, or what Merleau-Ponty refers to as preobjective vision.

## Harold Rosenberg and Phenomenology

In her 1983 catalogue essay for Richard Serra's exhibition at the Musée National d'Art Moderne, Centre Georges Pompidou, Rosalind Krauss proposed that the initial French reading of Merleau-Ponty's *The Phenomenology of Perception* differs from the American understanding of it in the 1960s. She pointed out that soon after the publication of Merleau-Ponty's book in 1945, Giacometti's figures were regarded as particularly apt illustrations of its theories. The reason for this is that they seem to be " . . . forever caught in the aureole of the beholder's look, bearing forever the trace of what it means to be seen *by* another *from* the place from which he views."[2] Because Merleau-Ponty's work was not translated into English until 1962, Krauss assumed an existential reading of his theories to have been unavailable to minimalists in the United States, consequently leaving them free to approach his preobjective experience in a radically new way.[3] While Krauss's comments are appropriate and useful given the received wisdom regarding Merleau-Ponty's impact on American art at the time of her writing, my recent research on the American post–World War II response to his thought has uncovered his important discussions and correspondence with critic Harold Rosenberg. The Rosenberg/Merleau-Ponty connection shows that the latter's ideas were a direct influence on American art well before the first English translation of his work became available in 1962.

Rosenberg read many of Merleau-Ponty's major phenomenological studies in French and used them in 1952 to develop his concept "action painting,"[4] a special existential/phenomenological reading of abstract expressionism in terms of its improvisational means. Rosenberg's famous essay, "The American Action Painters," in which he first developed the term, "action painting," was in fact written for the journal *Les Temps modernes*, edited by Merleau-Ponty and his longtime friend Jean-Paul Sartre. Most likely Rosenberg did not submit it to them for publication because Merleau-Ponty had resigned from the editorial board at this time.

Merleau-Ponty's phenomenological explication of action served as a background to Rosenberg's explanation of the way that action works. The French philosopher's ideas are useful in explaining why this New York critic was content to focus on the generative aspects of art rather than attend only to finished pieces as did his major competitor, critic Clement Greenberg. Merleau-Ponty asserted, " . . . painting does not exist before painting . . . style is an exigency. . . ."[5] And he commented, "A vision or an action that is finally free throws out of focus and regroups objects of

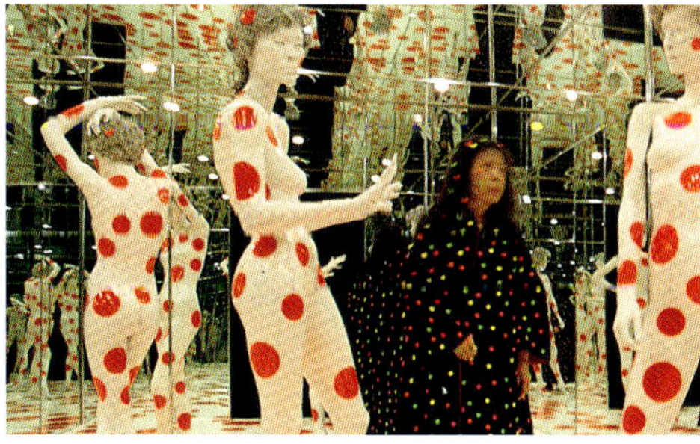

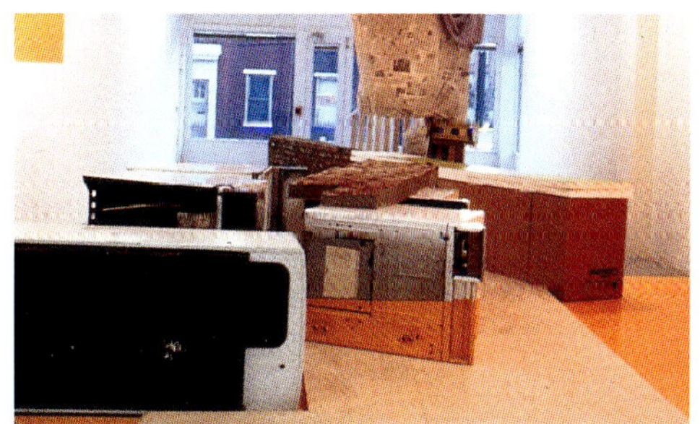

Yayoi Kusama, the artist in her work, *Repetitive Vision*, 1996, Formica, adhesive dots, mannequins, mirrors

Jessica Stockholder, *Mixing food with the bed*, 1989, appliances, wood, newspaper, bricks, concrete, and paint

the world for the painter and words for the poet."[6] We might compare Merleau-Ponty's observations with Rosenberg's claim in "The American Action Painters" that "The new American painting is not 'pure art,' since the extrusion of the object was not for the sake of the aesthetic. The apples weren't brushed off the table in order to make room for perfect relations of space and color. They had to go so that nothing would get in the way of the act of painting."[7]

Merleau-Ponty's philosophy might be summarized as a reworking of the idea of phenomenological reduction, which is Edmund Husserl's *époché*, or bracketing of everyday phenomena from that which is known. This serves as a method for becoming aware of one's initial relationship to the world, and as a means of coming to terms with consciousness through one's own acts rather than from a preconceived perspective or a later reflection. Merleau-Ponty's emphasis on the primordial territoriality of the body that comes before thought and conditions it is no doubt one reason that Rosenberg, in "The American Action Painters," preferred the preobjective world of action to the nonobjective world of formalist art.

While Merleau-Ponty's (and Rosenberg's) discussions are confined to painting, we do not need to look far afield to see how this philosopher's ideas could be interpreted by artists wishing to break away from painting's confines to environmentally-based art. A notable example from his *Phenomenology of Perception* is the introduction to Part Two, subtitled "The World as Perceived," with the heading, "The theory of the body is already a theory of perception." This section begins with the engaging analogy, "Our own body is in the world as the heart is in the organism. . . ." And it continues with the following speculation regarding the dynamics of Merleau-Ponty's body as a sensate organ:

> *When I walk round my flat, the various aspects in which it presents itself to me could not possibly appear as views of one and the same thing if I did not know that each of them represents the flat seen from one spot or another, and if I were unaware of my own movements, and of my body as retaining its identity through the stages of those movements.*[8]

Although several steps ahead of our narrative, this example suggests at the outset the relevancy of Merleau-Ponty's thought for installation art.

## Allan Kaprow

Merleau-Ponty's name would most likely not even have been known by Allan Kaprow in the 1950s, but he nonetheless served as the unknown bearer of the philosopher's ideas. Over the years Kaprow has repeatedly credited Rosenberg's action painting[9] and Jackson Pollock's fields of dripped paint as sources for the events and happenings he initiated, without ever mentioning Merleau-Ponty's ideas. Kaprow's lack of familiarity with this French phenomenologist's thought is all the more remarkable when one considers the following passage from his 1958 essay "The Legacy of Jackson Pollock" that seems to have been inspired by it:

> *I am convinced that to grasp Pollock's impact properly, we must be acrobats, constantly shuttling between an identification with the hands and body that flung the paint and stood "in" the canvas and submission to the objective markings, allowing them to entangle and assault us. This instability is indeed far from the idea of a "complete" painting. The artist, the spectator, and the outer world are much too interchangeably involved here.*[10]

We can compare this prescient statement with Merleau-Ponty's observation:

> *In short, he [Cézanne] wanted to understand what inner force holds the world together and causes the proliferation of visible forms. [Balzac's] Frenhofer had the same idea about the meaning of painting: "A hand is not simply part of the body, but the expression and continuation of a thought which must be captured and conveyed. . . . That is the real struggle!"*[11]

The major difference between these two approaches is that Merleau-Ponty remains convinced of paint's ability to communicate the uncertainty of

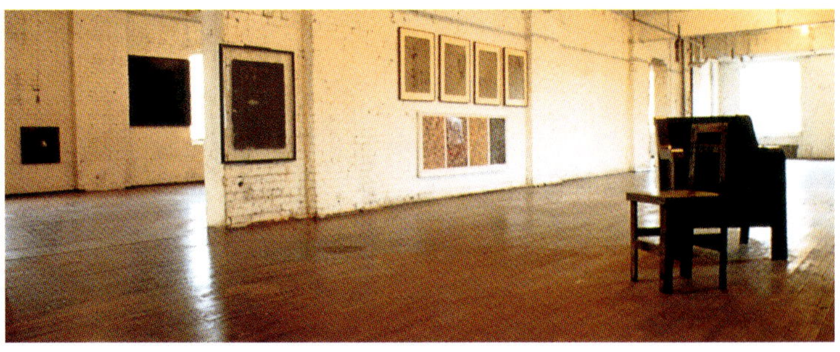

preobjective vision, while Kaprow determines in this essay that Pollock "destroyed painting."[12] Kaprow looked further afield for a new type of art that was consonant with his thinking, and, as a result, developed events and happenings, which were crucial precursors to installation art.

While Kaprow was to serve as an unwitting carrier of the phenomenological strain that would proliferate widely in the 1960s, a number of artists—such as Robert Morris in his early Green Gallery installations and Bruce Nauman in his series of corridor pieces—knowingly embraced Merleau-Ponty's thought. What made his brand of phenomenology so seductive was its apparent ability to release artists from the stranglehold of feeling that was one of abstract expressionism's major legacies. It did this by dispelling the concept that sensations might reside in objects (like paintings). Instead of accepting the idea that feelings inhere in the objective world, Merleau-Ponty suggested that they are twice-removed from reality. First they must be abstracted from human consciousness in order to be ascribed to objects that in turn are assumed to embody them. This enables them to be projected back on the consciousness that conceived them in the first place. In addition to undermining sensations, Merleau-Ponty's phenomenology promised a release from the twin pitfalls of empiricism and intellectualism that forced people to choose between a world that imposed its reality on them, making them its subject, and a world that was forced to accommodate itself to their thought.

In place of empiricism and intellectualism, Merleau-Ponty's philosophy offered installation artists a primal vision lurking beneath their personal subjectivities. It claimed, in fact, to create a ground zero realm predicated on the dialectics of being structured by their actual bodies at the same time they were apprehending it. This doubly-viewed realm of the see-er becoming the seen was emphatically consecrated through Merleau-Ponty's citation of Cézanne's observation, "In a forest, I have felt many times over that it was not I who looked at the forest. Some days I felt that the trees were looking at me, were speaking to me." It made the creation of art a collaborative proposition between artist and material, thus getting rid of the idea (grounded in the so-called "intentional fallacy") that artists' intentions might simply determine the work. Even more importantly, it transformed the viewer's role so that looking became a dynamic and ongoing pursuit. We might say that in installation art, the role of the viewer is enhanced as never before, and it is this role that needs to be understood if we are to appreciate the important contributions that this recently developed genre offers to our way of knowing the world.

### Brian O'Doherty's Spectator

In his notable series of *Artforum* essays entitled "Inside the White Cube" (published in 1976 and 1986), the critic Brian O'Doherty explores the subject of the modern art gallery as an intelligible space informing and providing permission for new art. While he does not directly refer to phenomenology, his essay "The Eye and the Spectator," included in this series, is a witty treatment of phenomenological themes. O'Doherty characterizes the Spectator (also referred to as the Viewer and Perceiver in the Merleau-Pontian terms of embodied perception) as possessing a "slightly clumsy" mien, an appearance of being "a little dumb," and the habit of "stagger[ing] into place before every new work that requires his presence."[13] In contrast to the Spectator, O'Doherty views the Eye as aristocratic, highly sensitive, disembodied, and necessary to the smooth operation of modernist painting when he notes:

> *The Eye is the only inhabitant of the sanitized installation shot. The Spectator is not present. Installation shots are generally of* abstract *works; realists don't go in for them much. . . . The art the Eye is brought to bear on almost exclusively is that which preserves the picture plane—mainstream modernism. The Eye maintains the seamless gallery space, its walls swept by flat planes of duck. Everything else—all things impure, including collage—favors the Spectator. The Spectator stands in space broken up by the consequences of collage, the second great force that altered the gallery space.*[14]

Although O'Doherty is referring to the early modernist period in this passage, his analysis is

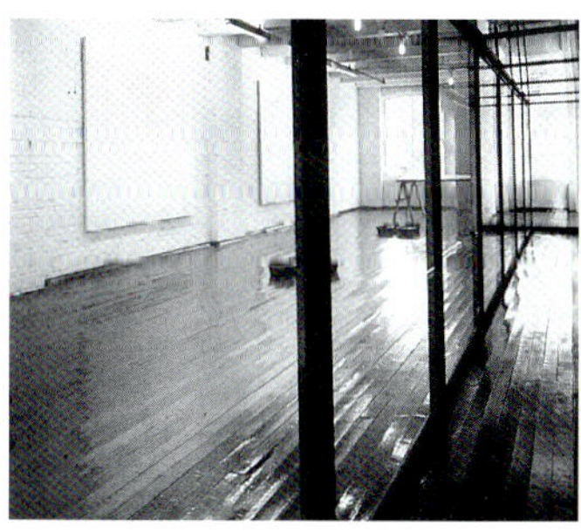

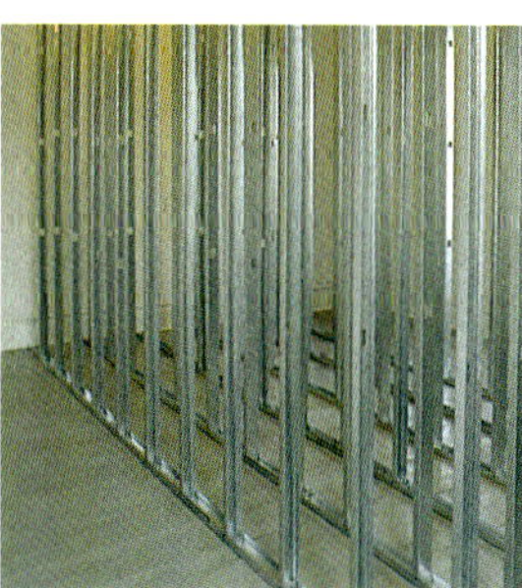

John Cage, *changing exhibition at the mattress factory*, 1991, chairs and art works

Damien Hirst, *Bad Environment for White Monochrome Paintings*, 1994, steel, glass, acrylic on canvas, plastic containers of food and water, sarcophaga, and musca domestica

Matthew McCaslin, *16 On Center*, 1990, metal studs, electric cable, light bulb

rooted in the assumptions of his time, particularly his acceptance of a phenomenological mode of perception for works of art in which the contiguities of daily life play significant roles. This interpretation is confirmed by O'Doherty's analysis of the Spectator approaching Schwitters's *Merzbau* when he cryptically writes, "Both space and artist—we tend to think of them together—exchanged identities and masks."[15]

These words are not far removed from Merleau-Ponty's ideas, particularly his exegesis on the role of the mirror image in his essay "Eye and Mind":

> . . . *the mirror image anticipates, within things, the labor of vision. Like all other technical objects . . . the mirror arises upon the open circuit [that goes] from seeing body to visible body. . . . The mirror itself is the instrument of a universal magic that changes things into a spectacle, spectacles into things, myself into another, and another into myself.*[16]

Just as it is a short distance from O'Doherty's sentence to Merleau-Ponty's statement, so it is also a brief move from Merleau-Ponty's ideas to installation works incorporating mirrors, such as the Mattress Factory's two mirrored chambers *Repetitive Vision* and *Infinity Dots Mirrored Room* (both 1996) by Yayoi Kusama. In them, participants' identities are multiplied as they seem to be reflected into infinity, presenting them with both literal and multiple instances of viewers becoming the viewed. Although we enter Kusama's special terrain in these mirrored rooms, we also take over this realm, making it our own, through the series of ongoing exchanges—seeing ourselves being seen—that Merleau-Ponty has described as an inherently phenomenological activity.

## Zen and the Everyday

Installation art's ready acceptance of the quotidian, ranging from the everyday materials used for building and for furnishing public and private interiors to the ephemera of daily living, can be considered a natural extension of phenomenology. In addition, this art can be regarded as an appreciation of the significance of everyday reality that is one of Zen's major contributions. Admittedly, post–World War II Zen in the West is different from its Japanese counterpart. Chiefly promulgated by D. T. Suzuki, who employed such terms as *keiken* and *taiken* (which are rarely found in pre–twentieth-century religious literature) to connote direct experience, western post-war Zen was far more pragmatic and far less doctrinal than its eastern counterpart.[17] Suzuki's early introduction to western thinking while he was still living in Japan, in addition to his later self-appointed role as the Japanese spokesperson for Zen in the West, made him susceptible to its desire for a life-changing form of enlightenment. *Satori* (meaning sudden understanding) and *kensho* (coming to terms with one's original face) seemed to fill a western desire for unmediated experience in an overly mediated world. Such terms as *satori* and *kensho* are consistent with Merleau-Ponty's concept of preobjective vision. In addition to these interpretations of *kensho* and *satori*, which incorporate western ideology within a distinctly eastern orientation, this hybridized form of Zen shares with its eastern counterpart an interest in embodied perception that has made it particularly appealing to both installation artists and phenomenologists. Zen's emphasis on integrating the body with the mind and spirit is evident in the types of pursuits undertaken by initiates who often choose to learn this belief system indirectly as part of their training in archery, calligraphy, and flower arranging. In undertaking these activities, they seek an inner harmony between themselves and their acts, so that the limitations of the ego are surmounted and an indefinable "it" that superintends the archer, the bow, the arrow, and the target takes over when the bull's eye is hit time after time.[18] Such transcendence of the self is akin to Merleau-Ponty's desire to move beyond personal subjectivity and find a pre-personal—and even anonymous—being. As he pointed out in his preface to *Phenomenology of Perception*, "The world is not what I think, but what I live through."[19]

Similar to phenomenologically based art, the understated character of Zen art traditionally depends on both artists' and viewers' participation. Nowhere is this participation more evident than in traditional tea ceremonies, where visitors are immersed in a range of sensory experiences. They might begin with the smells of the garden itself, the tactile sensation of washing their hands, the physical involvement of stooping to enter a rustic tea house, as well as the sounds of the water boiling and the tea bowls being washed. The visual beauty of the appurtenances of the entire tea ceremony, including the choice of painted scroll and special flower arrangement made to commemorate the fleeting sensations of the season and day on which it occurs, solemnizes the entire ritual, underscoring its ephemerality.

If we subtract from this entire ritual its precious refinements, including its highly developed nostalgia and its emphasis on nature, and replace it with western building traditions and manufactured objects, we begin to approximate aspects of installation art. Ridding ourselves of the Japanese connoisseur's over-refinement, this idea of immersion in sensory stimuli prepares us for the headlong encounters with the mounting detritus of western planned obsolescence that is an important component of much installation art. By doing so we come even closer to an entire group of installation works focusing on the diurnal. In these works, the Japanese appreciation of the simple presence of things finds its western equivalence in a frank acceptance of materiality. Such a transposition of commonplace elements into artificial components appears in Jessica Stockholder's 1989 installation at the Mattress Factory entitled *Mixing food with the bed*. In this piece, discarded appliances turned on their sides, building fragments, and a bathtub half-submerged in the wall were arranged in the gallery and partially painted with bright colors. In Stockholder's words, "The real elements and the painted elements are of equal value. . . . Mixing things which feel as if they are immiscible causes doors to open where there were none before. How we see informs how we are."[20]

Although we must rethink Japanese Zen in order to appreciate the innovations of its American counterpart, we need to remember that eastern as well as western types of works are the result of affluent times. The seemingly egalitarian Zen art originally created by tea masters and shoguns can be compared to post-1950 vanguard works that were made in the West at a time when artists, intellectuals, and thoughtful collectors wished to separate themselves, at least aesthetically, from the rampant materialism embraced by the rest of their culture. This anti-materialist approach is the basis for John Cage's 1991 *changing installation at the mattress factory*, in which both everyday objects and works of art were subsumed under subject of daily changing installations over the 103 days comprising the exhibition.

Both phenomenology and Zen supported the development of new art forms predicated first on multisensory perceptions that involve the human body and its surroundings. Most importantly, both of these theoretical constructs diminish the role of the artist's ego in support of a new type of interactive looking that synthesizes the viewer and the view. The possibilities of this new mode of perception have been of the utmost importance to installation artists since it has enabled them: (1) to reject the intentional fallacy and counter the residual romantic belief that works of art are mere bridges connecting the minds/spirits of artists with those of viewers, (2) to invoke a new directness in line with a rapidly changing, media-dominated world, (3) to develop the theoretical basis for an open-ended art capable of responding to these changes, and (4) to create new forms of interactive works, combining aspects of painting, sculpture, and architecture without being bound to elitist canons that channel looking along predetermined lines.

A number of these criteria are evident in Damien Hirst's *Bad Environment for White Monochrome Paintings* (1994). In this piece, Hirst uses the life cycle of ordinary house flies (musca domestica) to create, during the course of the exhibition, interactions with four pristine, white, seven-foot by seven-foot monochrome paintings. In front of each painting he places a black bowl. The first is filled with powdered sugar and powdered milk; the second, which is covered with gauze, holds water; and the third and fourth contain a recipe of molasses, wheat germ, yeast and water that provides sustenance for the maggots that are hatched from flies' eggs that have been laid there. Three of the paintings, which have been positioned vertically, have been sprayed with sugar water. During the exhibition, they are sullied by flies feasting on their surfaces. The fourth painting, positioned horizontally, is sprayed with a clear adhesive that will not dry, so that it becomes a graveyard for these insects. Although the general trajectory of this piece might be predicted, its specific outcome depends on life itself. This new approach to art, which is inextricably connected with the changing world, has made artists less dependent on modes of perception that assume that viewers are firmly rooted in traditional culture and will use it as a diagnostic tool to interpret new art.

Differing from Zen but remaining firmly within the purview of Merleau-Pontian phenomenology, viewers who are apprehending particularly successful pieces of installation art for the first time need to respond to the question of whether the constructions before them should or should not be considered art. If they are works of art, these viewers must confront their own assumptions and prejudices regarding art even as they are viewing a particular work. Thus, looking is transformed from a passive acceptance of given objects in a known world (Merleau-Ponty's "act intentionality") to an understanding of unknowns (his "operative intentionality").

## Suture

In order to comprehend more clearly the persuasiveness of installation works and their mode of implicating viewers, it helps to recognize the usefulness of the term "suture," which Jacques-Alain Miller originated in the late 1970s, and which has since become an accepted mode of interpretation in film criticism.[21] If one thinks of suturing in its surgical sense of stitching together the two sides of a wound or incision, one comes close to Miller's use of the term. Suturing is not only a means by which a viewer identifies with a given work of art, it is the agency by which an onlooker is called into being as a subject so that he or she assumes a subjective role through it. As Merleau-Ponty pointed out, "Seeing is not a certain mode of thought or presence to self; it is the means given me for being absent from myself. . . ."[22] We might think of this absence as analogous to a viewer's wound or a break in identity which the subjectivity of a given work of art both catalyzes and also helps to heal, even if only briefly. In this way, viewers are induced to undergo the experience offered by the work in order to come to terms with the new identity it holds out to them. Sometimes installation art, in a similar way to classic film, assumes a coercive stance in relation to its viewers. In installation art, a variety of provisional and discontinuous subjectivities await viewers: in this genre viewers may be recruited as subjects, but their roles depend on the dynamics resulting from a synthesis formed between themselves and the special environment awaiting them.[23] These subjectivities are even more discontinuous than in classic films: they are negotiated and then renegotiated in the time necessary to move through the installation. Matthew McCaslin pointed out in his statement for *16 On Center* (a 1990 installation at the Mattress Factory), "The inbetween, to be somewhere, to be in a room, to be in a wall, to be in your mind, to be in my mind. A work place. A domestic place, any place, every place. The journey, the continual, letting go to find out from within."

***Robert Hobbs, Ph.D., holds the Rhoda Thalhimer Chair of Art History at Virginia Commonwealth University, Richmond. He has published extensively in the areas of modern and contemporary art and has curated exhibitions throughout the world, including a retrospective of the work of Robert Smithson at the American Pavilion of the 1982 Venice Biennale.***

## Notes

1. Important recent summaries of the genre include: Julie H. Reiss, *From Margin to Center: The Spaces of Installation Art* (Cambridge and London: The MIT Press, 1999) and Hugh M. Davies and Ronald J. Onorato, *Blurring the Boundaries; Installation Art 1969–1996* (San Diego: Museum of Contemporary Art, 1997).
2. Rosalind E. Krauss, "Richard Serra, a Translation," in *Originality of the Avant-Garde and Other Modernist Myths* (Cambridge and London: The MIT Press, 1986), 263.
3. Their interest in straightforward description and desire to avoid emotions stems not only from the excesses of abstract expressionism but also from the literary precedence of French New Wave novelist Alain Robbe-Grillet, who wished to look at the world through an objective lens. In such novels as *Jealousie*, he plays with the limits of objectivity and suggests that it can serve as the mask of paranoia. But even this rationality gone awry appealed to the American artists who wished to rid themselves of the excesses of the romantic ego.
4. Robert Hobbs, "Rosenberg's 'The American Action Painters' and Merleau-Ponty's Phenomenology," (paper presented to the 1999 College Art Association Annual Meeting, New York City).
5. Merleau-Ponty, "Indirect Language and the Voices of Silence," in *Signs*, trans. Richard C. McCleary (Evanston: Northwestern University Press, 1964), 54.
6. Ibid., 56.
7. Harold Rosenberg, "The American Action Painters," *ARTnews* 51, no. 8 (December 1952): 50.
8. Merleau-Ponty, *Phenomenology of Perception*, trans. Colin Smith (London and New York: Routledge & Kegan Paul Ltd, 1962; rpt. 1996).
9. Elaine O'Brien, "The Art Criticism of Harold Rosenberg: Theaters of Love and Combat" (Ph.D. diss., City University of New York, 1977), 53, note 68. In this footnote, O'Brien refers to her conversation with Allan Kaprow in La Jolla, California, 23 September 1992, as well as correspondence between Kaprow and Rosenberg in the 1960s in the Rosenberg/Takak Papers, now located in the J. Paul Getty Library and Archives.
   Cf. Allan Kaprow, *Assemblage, Environments & Happenings* (New York: Harry N. Abrams, Inc., n.d.) in which he points out the following in the essay "Art and Architecture," written in 1959 and revised in 1961: *Painting, which has been without question the most advanced and experimental of the plastic arts, has over and over provoked the question, "Should the format or field always be the closed, flat rectangle?" by utilizing gestures, scribblings, large scales with no frame, which suggest to the observer that both the physical and metaphysical substance of the work continue indefinitely in all directions beyond the canvas.*
10. Allan Kaprow, "The Legacy of Jackson Pollock." *ARTnews* 57, no. 6: 24–26, 55–57.
11. Merleau-Ponty, "Cézanne's Doubt," in *Sense and Non-Sense*, trans. Hubert L. Dreyfus and Patricia Allen Dreyfus (Evanston: Northwestern University Press, 1964), 18.
12. Kaprow, "The Legacy of Jackson Pollock."
13. Brian O'Doherty, *Inside the White Cube: The Ideology of the Gallery Space*, expanded edition (Berkeley, Los Angeles, London: University of California Press, 1999), 39.
14. Ibid., 42.
15. Ibid., 45.
16. Merleau-Ponty, "Eye and Mind," in *The Primacy of Perception*, trans. James M. Edie (Evanston: Northwestern University Press, 1964).
17. Robert H. Sharf, "The Zen of Japanese Nationalism" in *Curators of the Buddha: The Study of Buddhism under Colonialism*, ed. Donald S. Lopez (Chicago and London: University of Chicago Press, 1995), 107–160.
18. The classic statement on Zen and archery is Eugen Herrigel, *Zen in the Art of Archery* (New York: Pantheon Books, 1953).
19. *Phenomenology of Perception*, xvi–xvii.
20. *Mattress Factory: Installation and Performance 1982–1989*. (Pittsburgh: Mattress Factory, 1991), 202.
21. Jacques-Alain Miller, "Sutures (elements of the logic of the signifier)," *Screen* 18, no. 4 (1977–78): 24–34.
22. Merleau-Ponty, "Eye and Mind," in *The Merleau-Ponty Aesthetics Reader: Philosophy and Painting*, ed. Galen A. Johnson, trans. Michael B. Smith (Evanston: Northwestern University Press, 1993), 146.
23. A good source on this subject is Kaja Silverman, *The Subject of Semiotics* (New York and Oxford: Oxford University Press, 1983).

# Temporary Exhibitions

1990–1999

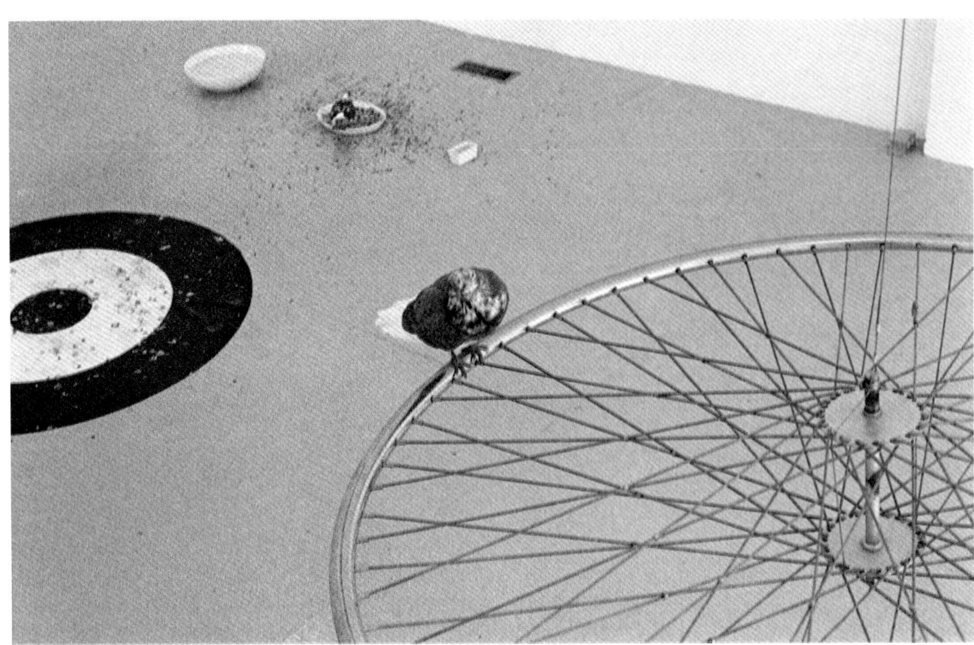

## Dove Bradshaw

American

**Plain Air,** 1990
Birds, mixed media
1414 Monterey Street, 1st floor

The gallery is given over to two brown and white pigeons. The pigeons are provided with nesting materials, food, and a bicycle wheel as a potential roosting spot; they more often roost instead on the ceiling fans.

Targets, placed under the roosting places, accumulate droppings. Windows are frosted with glass wax so that the birds will not fly into them. The pigeons, making immediate use of the materials provided, construct their nests in the soft canvas pouches attached to corner spaces. Visitors to the gallery can walk comfortably through the space, which is large enough to allow pigeons and people to coexist.

Late in July 1990, a pigeon, walking on the keyboard of a computer (Apple Macintosh) located in an office within the space tapped out this message: "]]x xxxxx mp ``````"

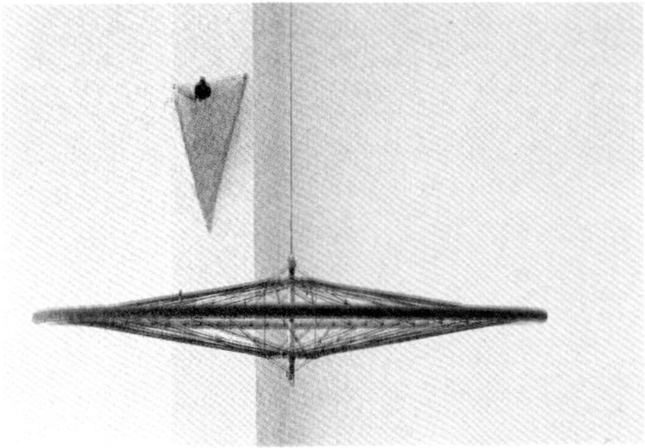

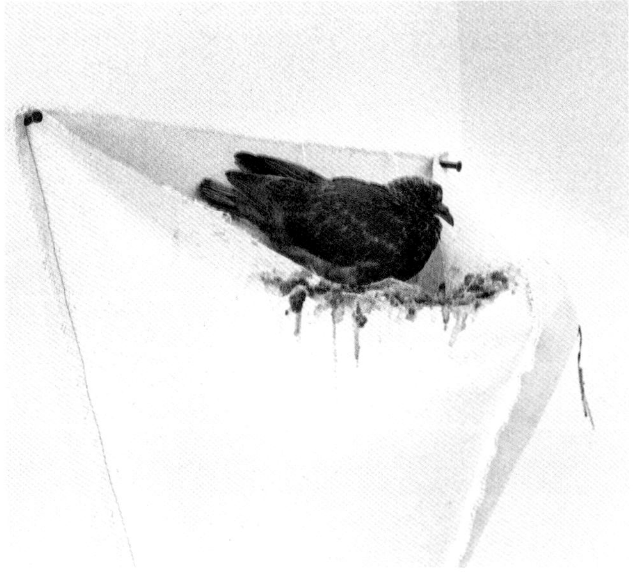

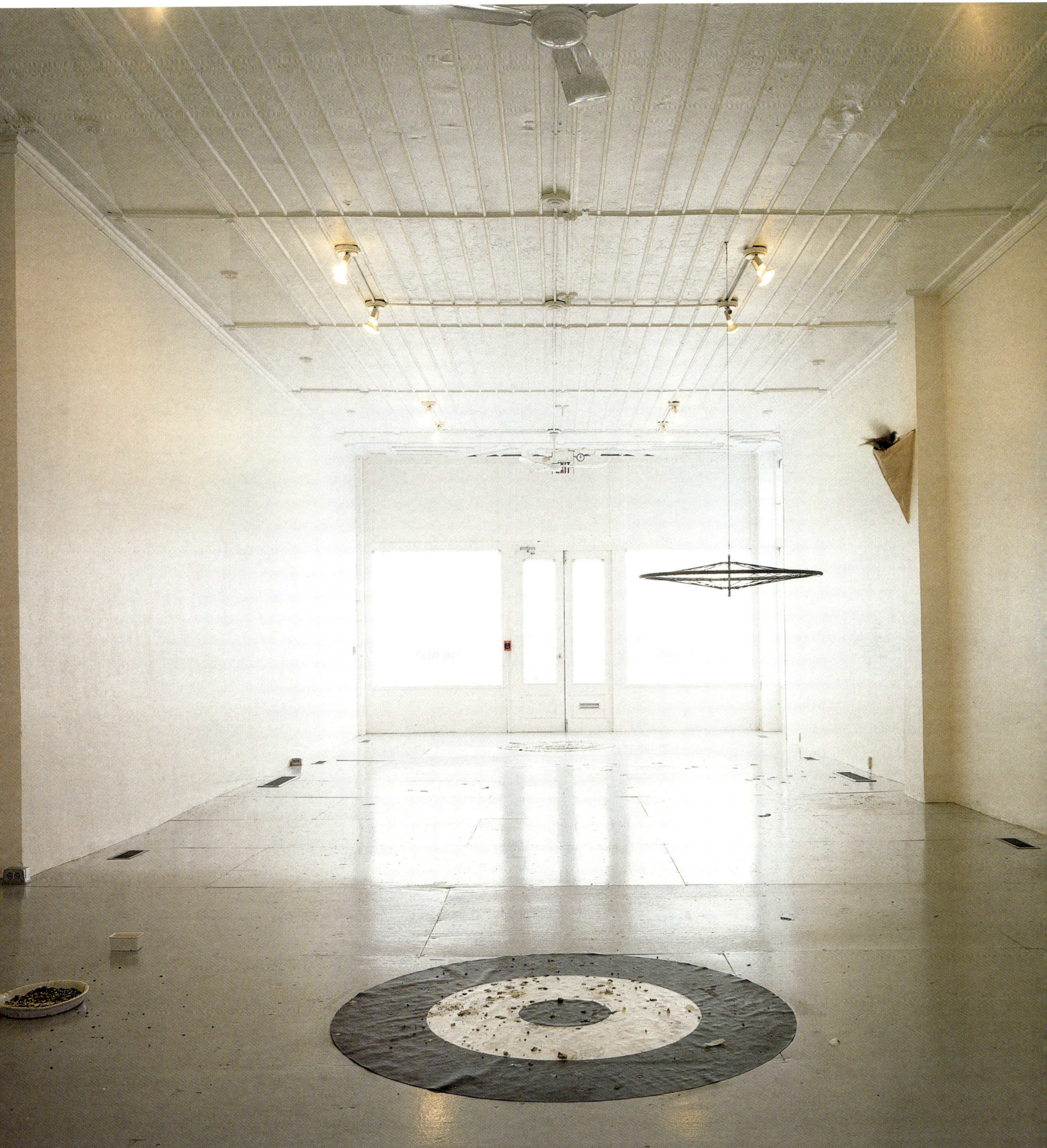

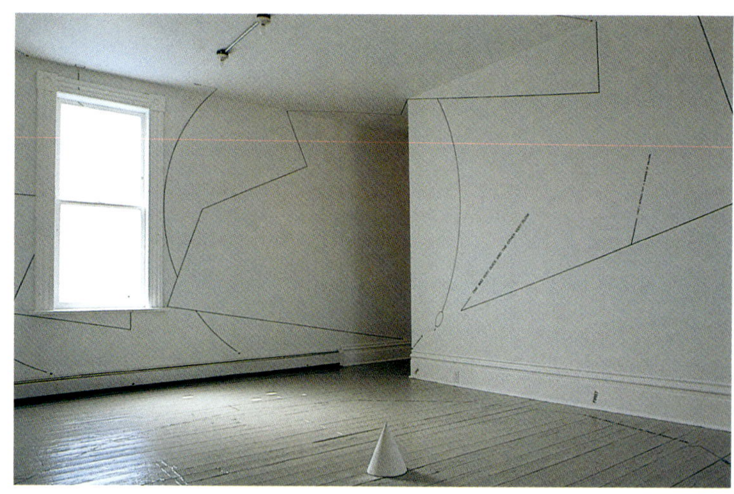

## Paul Glabicki

American, born 1951

**This Is/Just That,** 1990
Ink, vinyl tape, hydrostone
1414 Monterey Street, 3rd floor

Throughout the room, the artist makes connections between geometric drawings within the gallery and the environment outside the gallery. A white cone shape sits at the center of the floor and references a Victorian roof outside. Around the cone, a circle of large circumference has been drawn. Geometric shapes have also been drawn on the room's walls and ceiling. One window in the room is frosted, but tiny openings are outlined to reveal a view of the PPG Tower in downtown Pittsburgh.

For the geometric drawings within the space, the artist uses text written by the acting theorist Stanislavski. The source of this material is Stanislavski's "System" trilogy, which discusses acting technique and focuses on the subjects of observation, objective examination, personal perception, memory, and response.

The circle around the cone reads: "The Circle: I found myself in the center of the medium light circle. In such a small space as in this circle, you can use your concentrated attention to examine various objects in their most intricate details, and also to carry on more complicated activities such as defining shades of feeling and thought."

The text fragments on the frosted windows relate to the shapes and diagrams in the room: "This That." "That was just it . . ." "First." "One 2." "Here." "Over there." "In here." "With this."

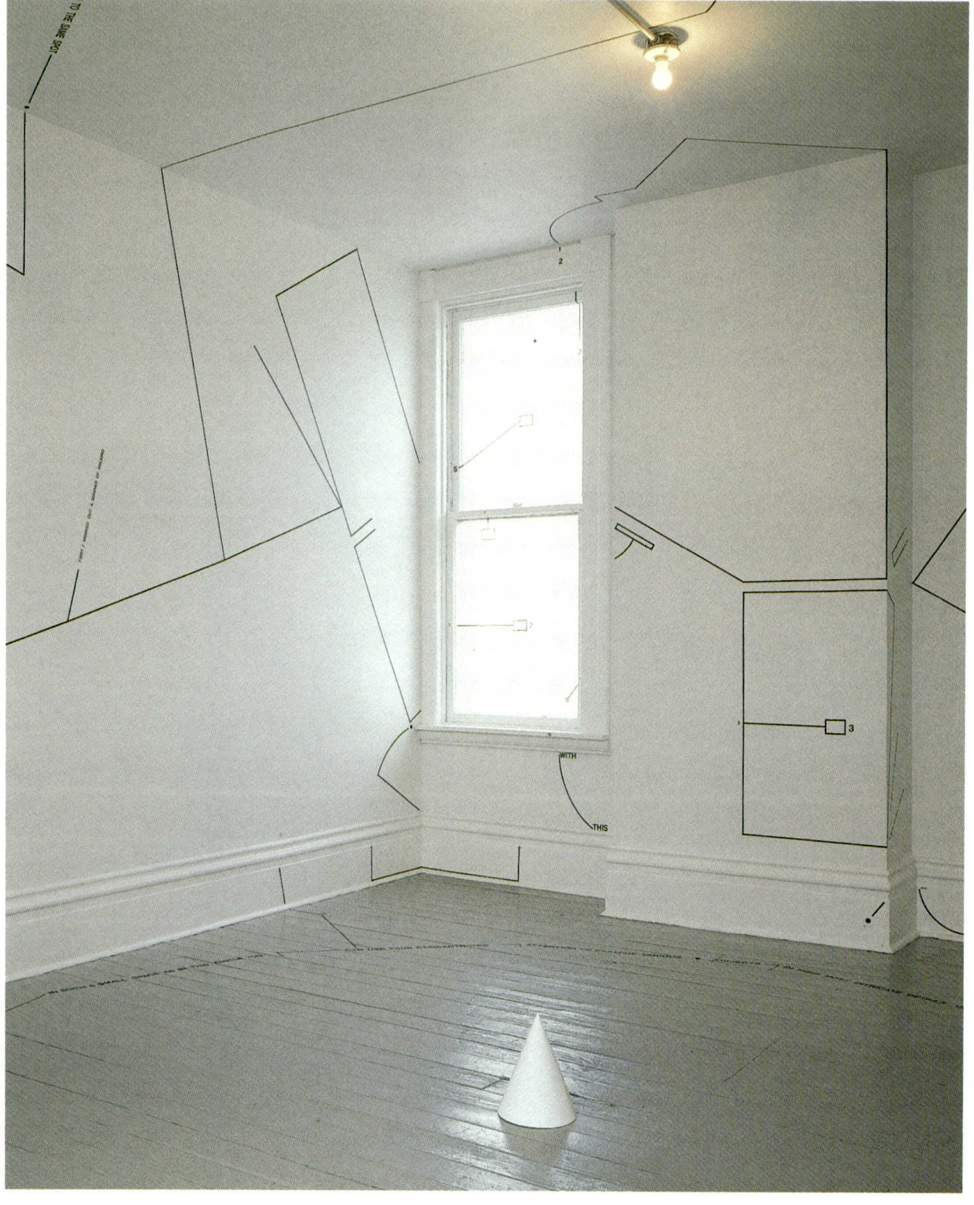

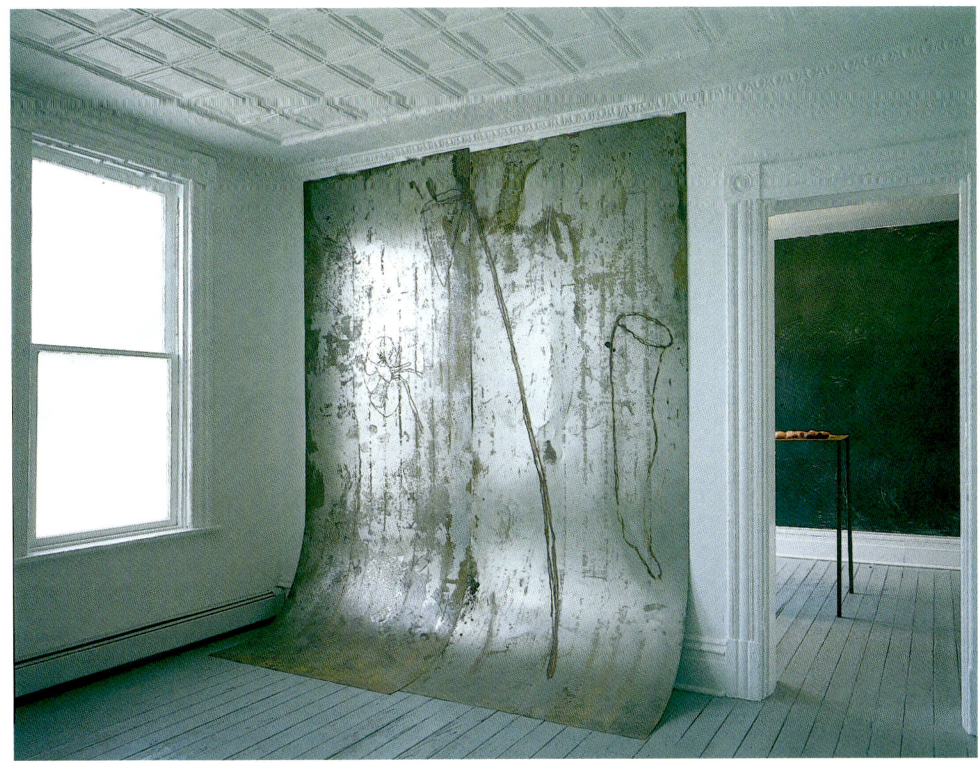

## Shelagh Keeley

American, born 1954

**Flesh of the Body,** 1990
Steel, wax, graphite, pigment, oil stick
1414 Monterey Street, 2nd floor

Seven flexible steel panels cover the walls in the first room. They extend from ceiling to floor. Body organs have been drawn on them with red-brown oil stick. The panels rust around the oily lines, and begin blending with the color of the drawn images.

In an adjacent room, walls are covered with graphite and Vaseline. A tall, rusted table is covered with wax replicas of body parts. They are ex-votos, which are sold outside Spanish and Mexican churches to represent body parts which may be in need of healing. The models include an ear, a hand, a breast, a foot, a tongue, and a heart.

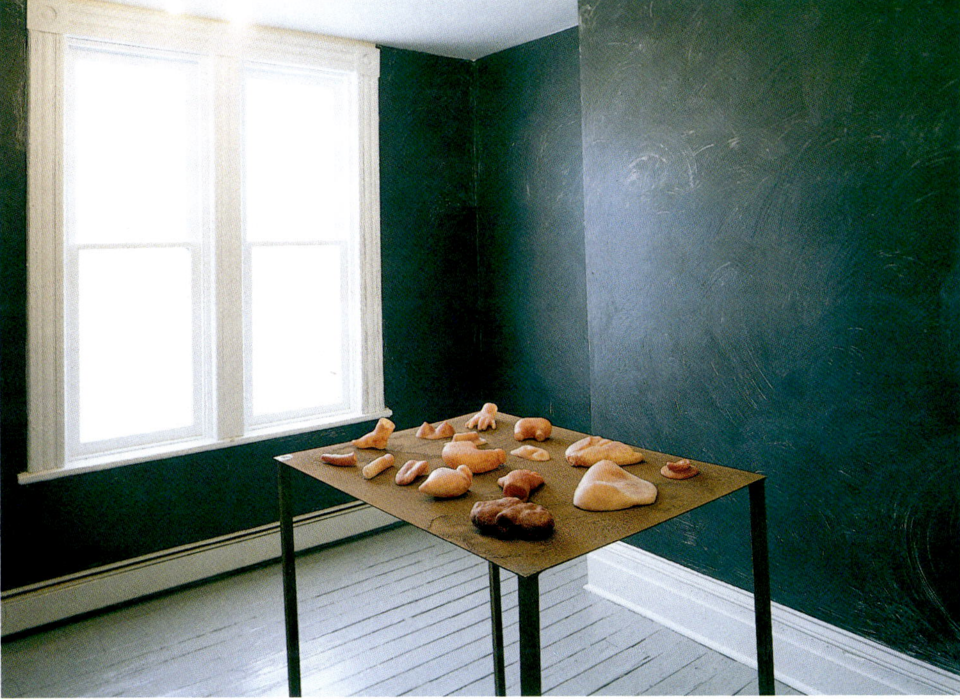

**Artist's Statement**
In my installations I am concerned with the recovery of space through instinctive gesture. The archetypal wall, its structure a monumental act of enclosure, speaks as a refuge of willed silence. The room is a container, as is the body; the walls are its skin. Considering the fragility and vulnerability of our own viscera, the externalization of body organs and bone structure is a revelation—the public display of a private mystery, an emotional landscape.

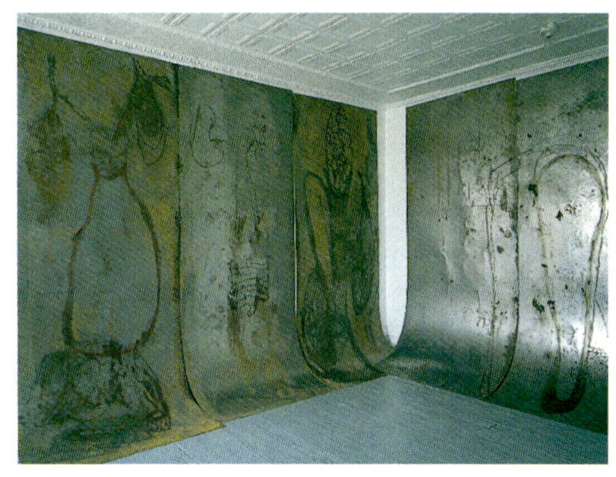

## Matthew McCaslin

American, born 1957

**16 On Center,** 1990
Metal studs, electric cable, light bulb
1414 Monterey Street, 3rd floor

McCaslin installed six walls of metal studs, which are standard building materials. The studs in each wall are sixteen inches apart, and each wall is installed sixteen inches from the next wall. As a group, they separate the room's entrance from its windows. It is possible for a person to slip through the spaces to stand amidst the studs.

At the bottom of the stairs leading to the gallery, a coil of electrical cable with metal covering sits on the floor, encircling an illuminated light bulb.

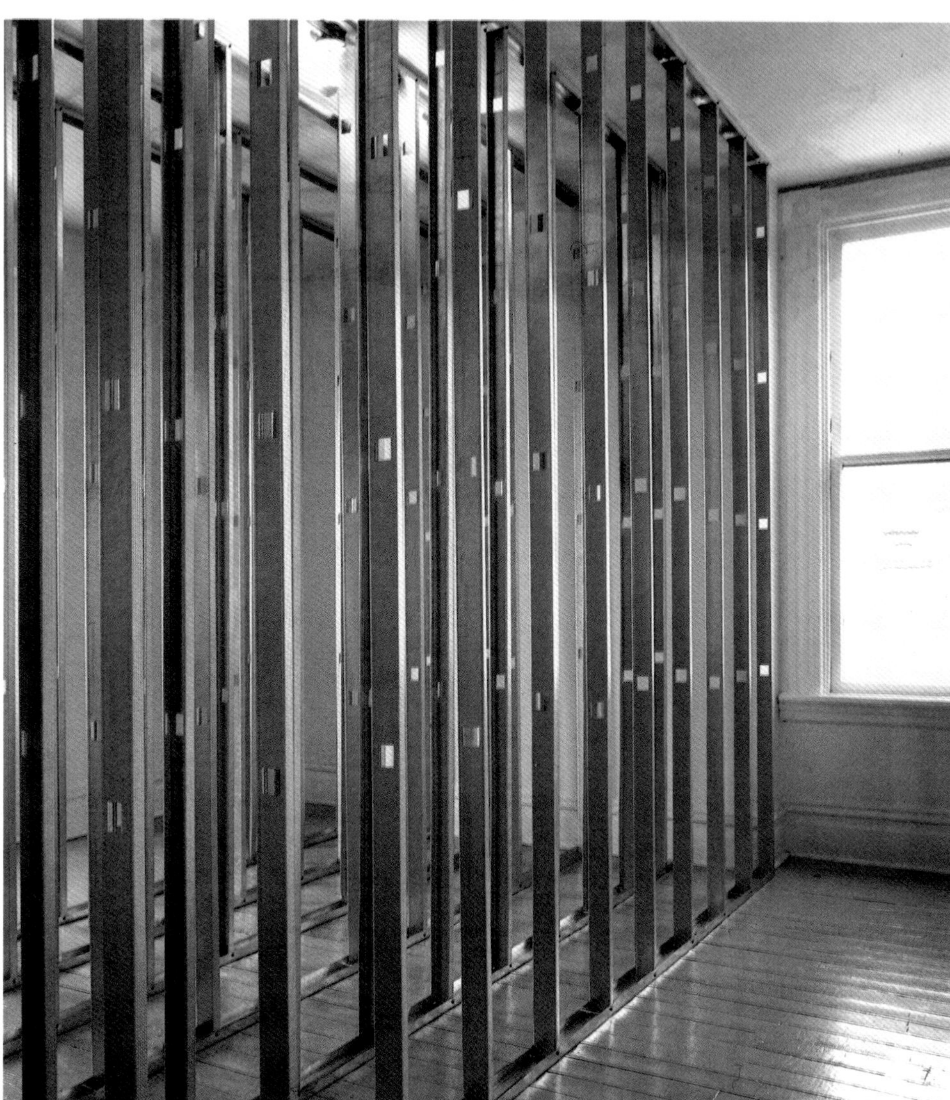

**Artist's Statement**
The inbetween, to be somewhere, to be in a room, to be in a wall, to be in your mind, to be in my mind. A work place, a domestic place, any place, every place. The journey the continual, letting go to find out from within.

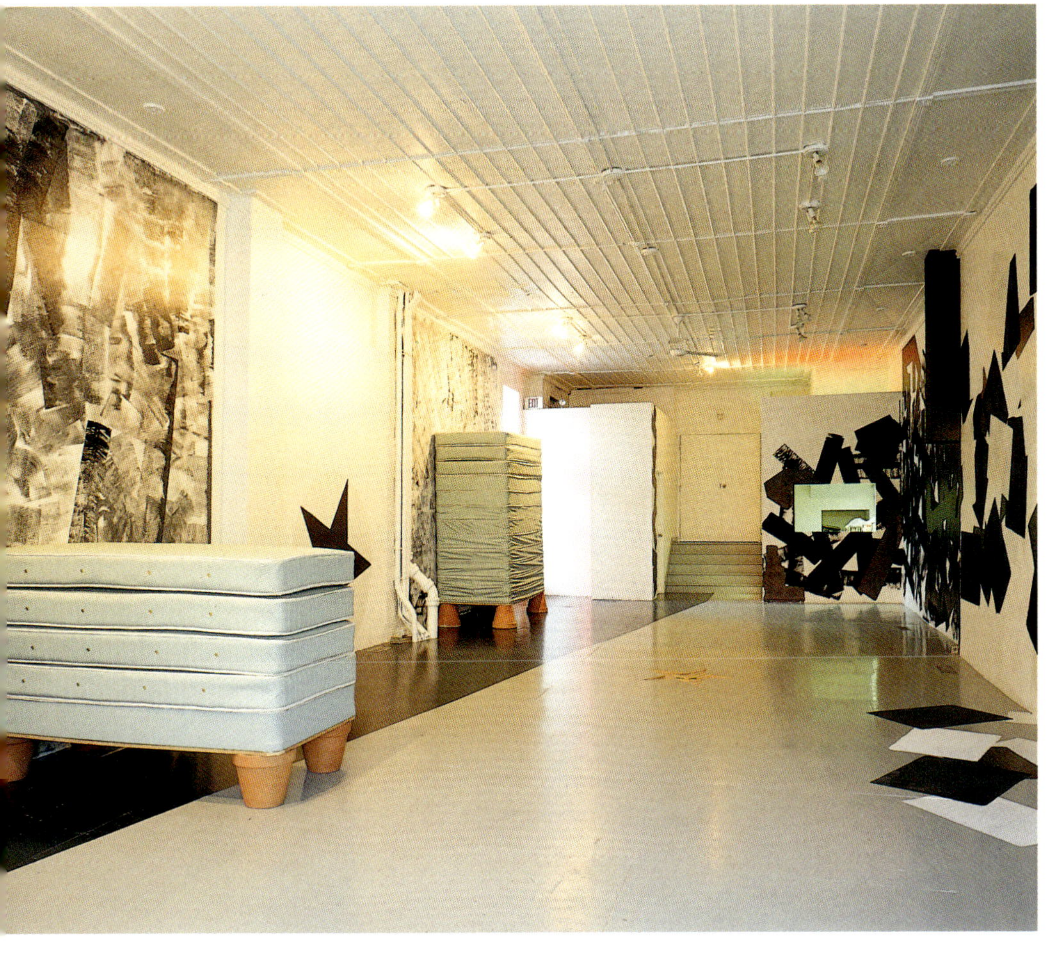



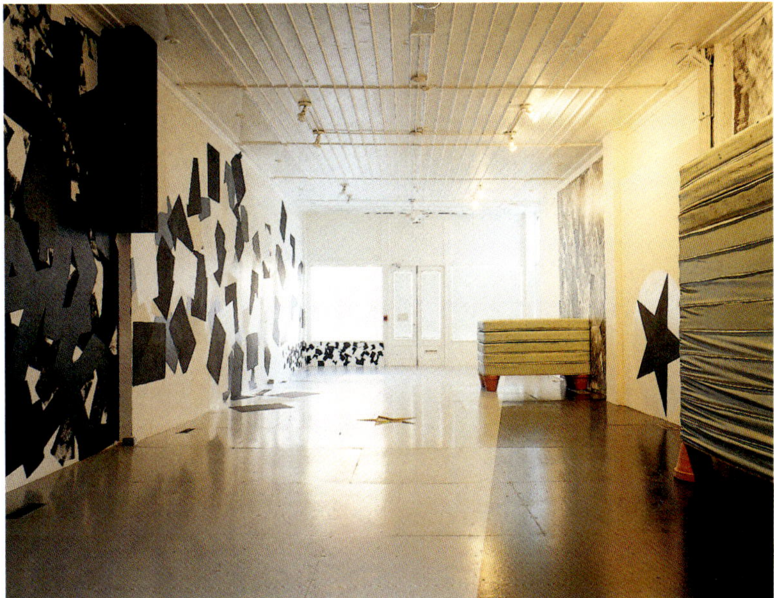

## Stephen Davis

American, born 1945

**Plato's Inn—Zeus Suite,** 1990
Paint, mattresses, terra-cotta pots, wood
1414 Monterey Street, 1st floor

Black and white shapes are arranged along two long walls of the gallery space, clustered tightly in the beginning and more loosely arranged as you proceed. Sometimes these patterns are referenced elsewhere in the space. For example, a star is painted on one wall and another has been cut from the floor. The latter provides a view of the basement, which is illuminated with red light.

Everything in the installation is either black or white with the exception of blue and green mattresses and upturned terra-cotta pots, which support the mattress piles like the legs of bed frames. A red glow on the ceiling at the rear of the installation is actually a reflection from an unseen panel coated with red fluorescent paint.

**Artist's Statement**

Every room harbors a potential ritual. As one works and moves in a room, some of the forces and patterns of energy in that room become available to the participant. This accumulation of these forces begins to take shape and form, culminating in an image. The viewer enters the conversation between the work and the room.

## Kim Jones

American, born 1944

**Untitled Installation/Mudman Performance,**
1990
Paint, sticks, earth, photographs, newspapers
1414 Monterey Street, 2nd floor

Kim Jones's installation occupies two rooms whose floors are covered with mud-splattered newspapers. Spider-like forms made of bare branches hang from the ceiling and lie on the floor. Masses of rats and trees are drawn around the walls of one room.

For the performance within the space, Jones covers his nearly nude body with mud and carries a heavy weight of branches, evoking images of his time spent as a Marine in Vietnam. With his appearance thus altered, he walks about the gallery and talks with visitors in unplanned encounters about whatever topics may arise.

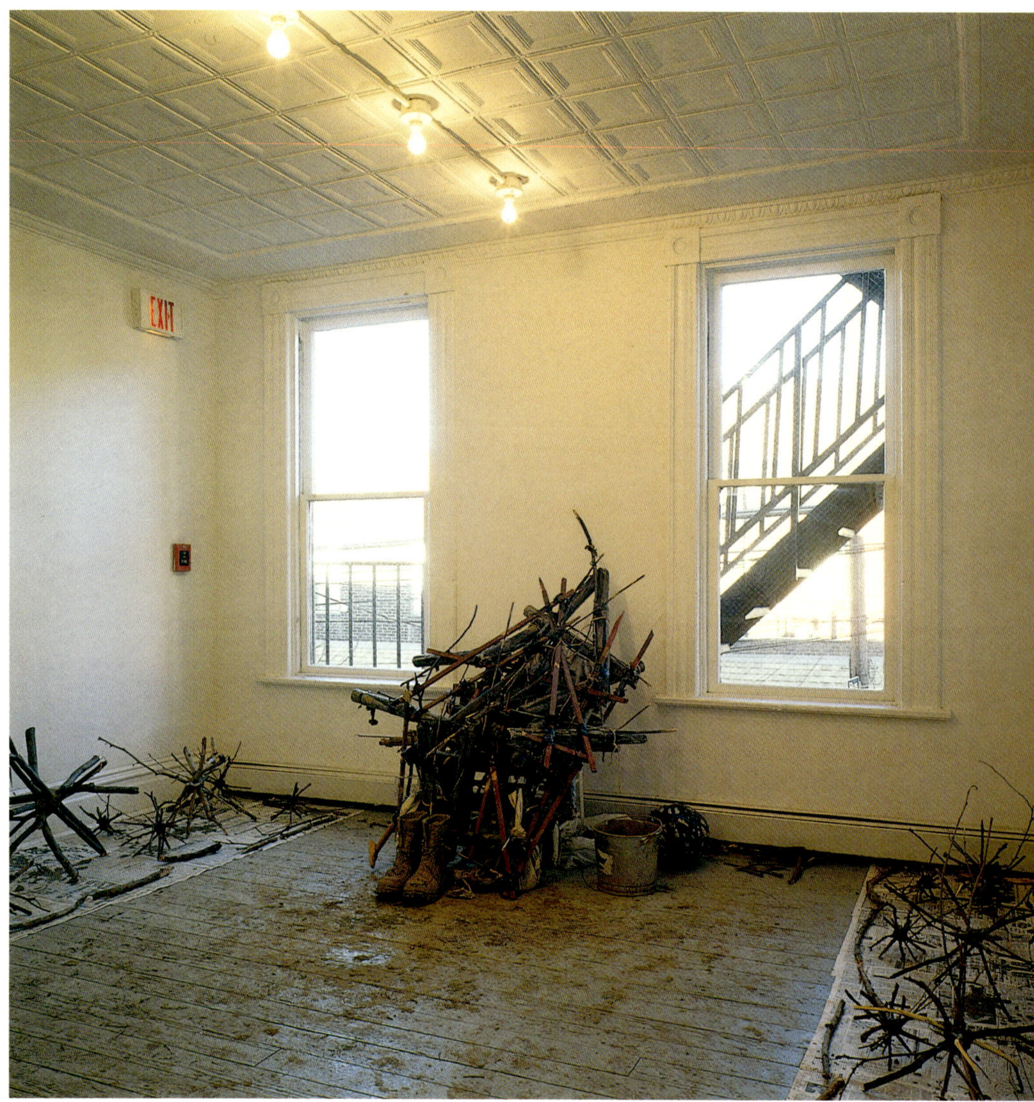


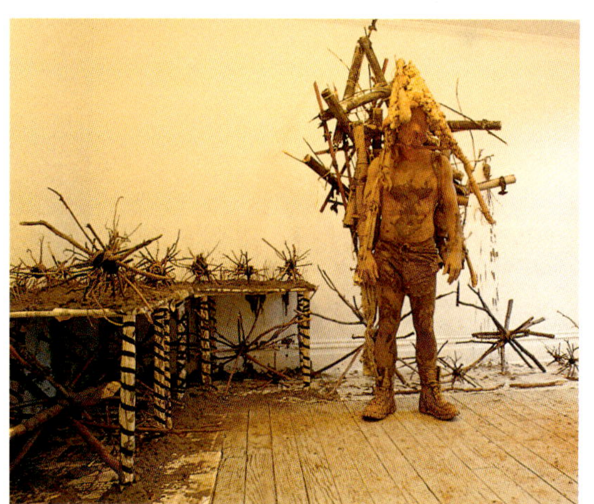

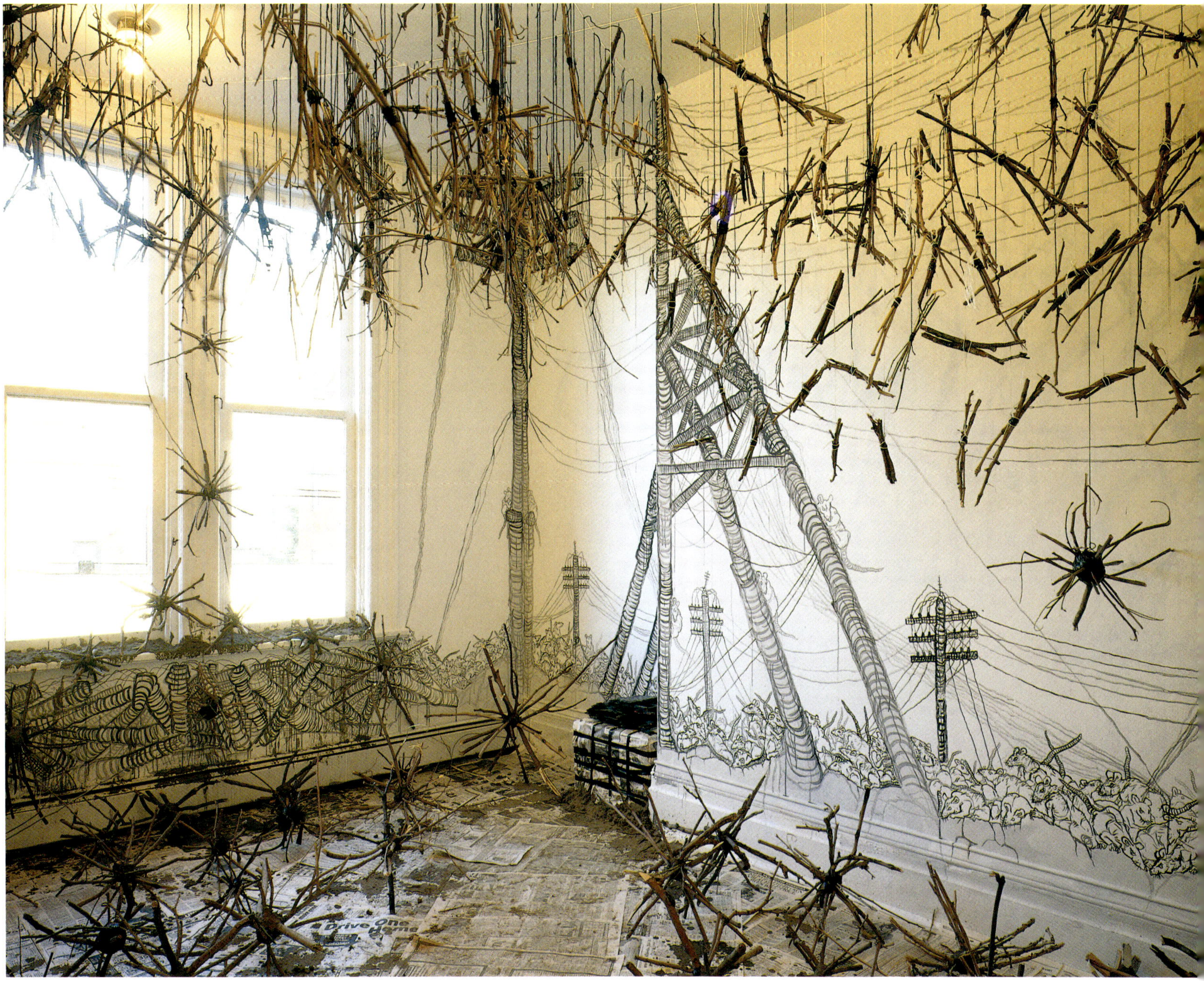

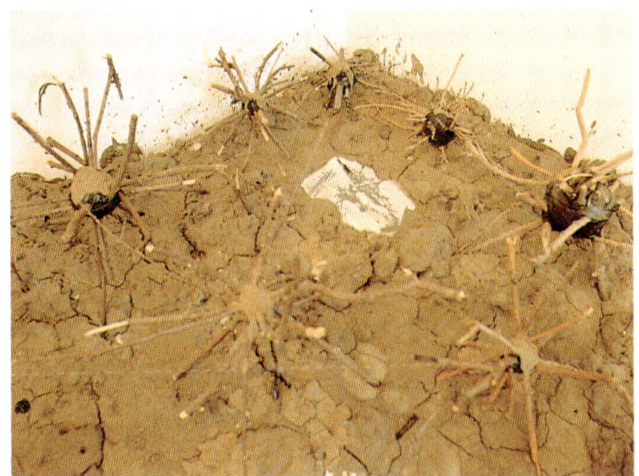

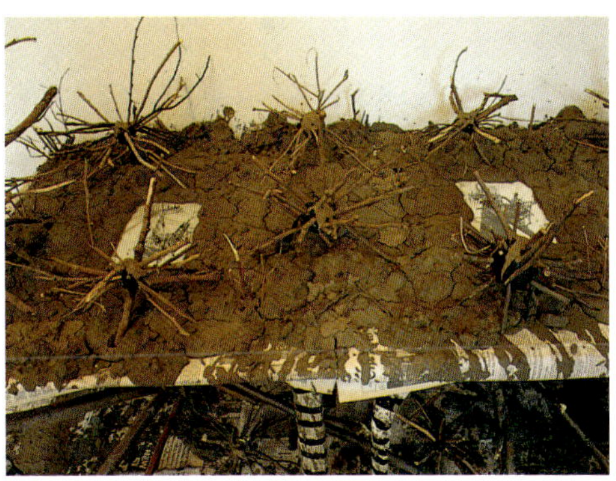

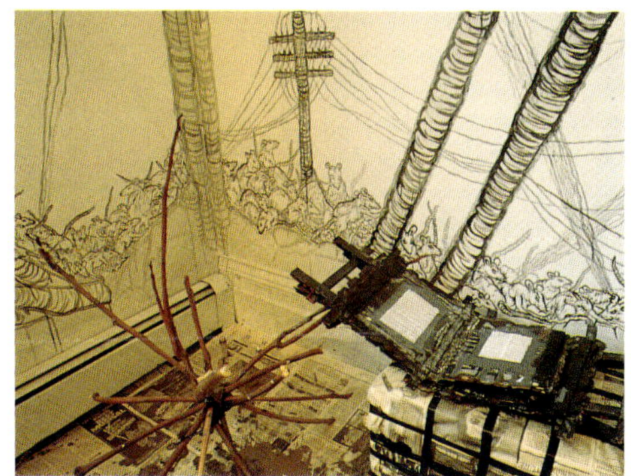

## Valerie Brodar

American, born 1962

**X knows P,** 1990
Drywall, paint, graphite, aluminum and lead triangle, audio from televisions
1414 Monterey, 3rd floor

Brodar constructed a triangular space and painted all the surfaces, including ceiling and floor, white.

Hand-written messages cover the walls, floor and ceiling—even the light bulbs. A partial transcription reads: "female perception male perception sound perception voice perception homosexual perception heterosexual perception sex perception violence perception racism perception sexism perception human perception responsibility perception pornographic perception."

From behind the walls, ten televisions, all tuned to different stations, fill the air with different noises and a jumble of messages. The words and sound are continuous but indiscernible.

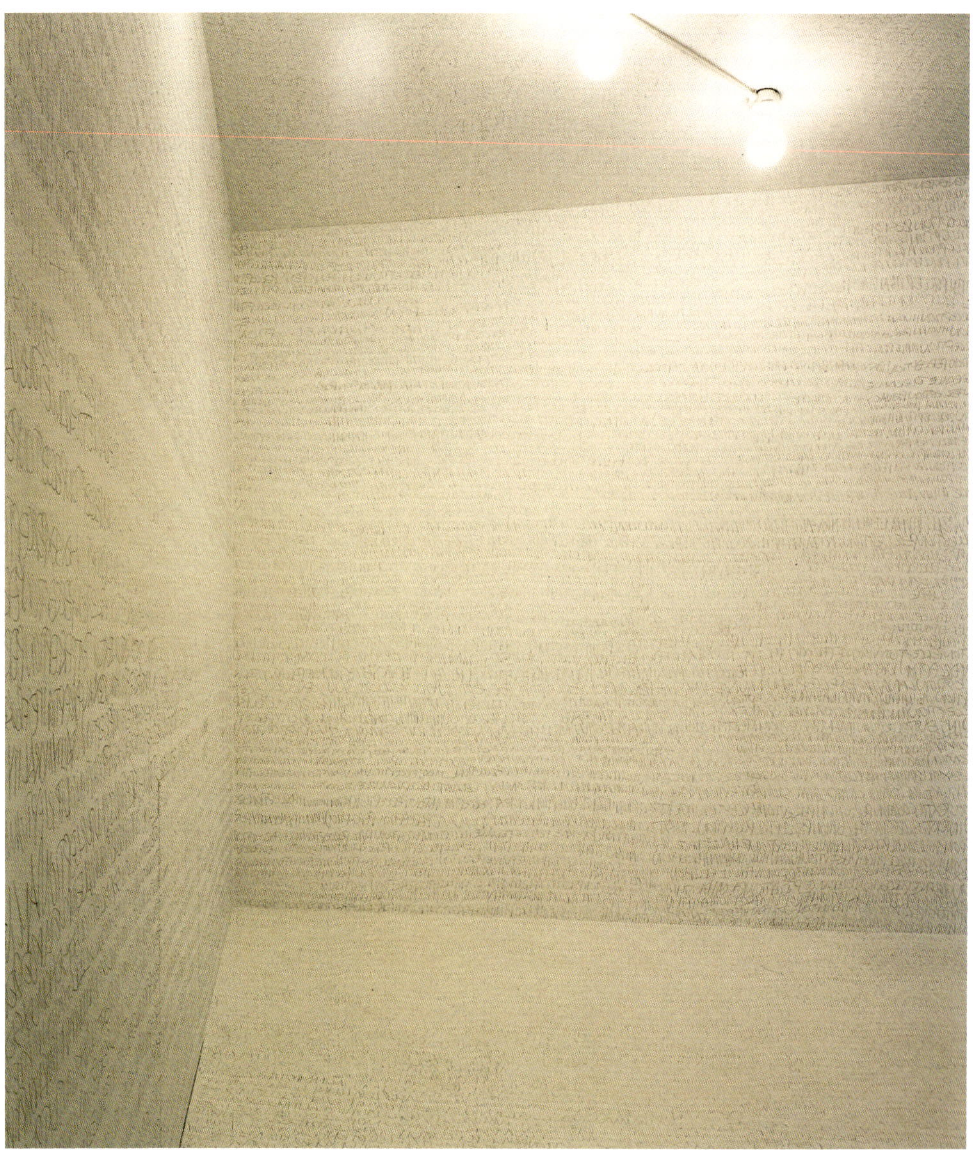

**Artist's Statement**

It is important that my work be accessible to a wide audience. There is at least one level that can be easily discerned, opening a door to an understanding. I want the viewer to slow down and become involved in an internal dialogue with the work, to become isolated from the presence of others and immersed in his or her own memories and thoughts. I wish to create an environment in which the viewer will have a physiological response, not only a cerebral one. The viewer completes the work in an ever changing interaction, reaction, experience. Sharing a multifaceted reality, an internal conversation hidden to the external, a dialogue of memories lost and found.

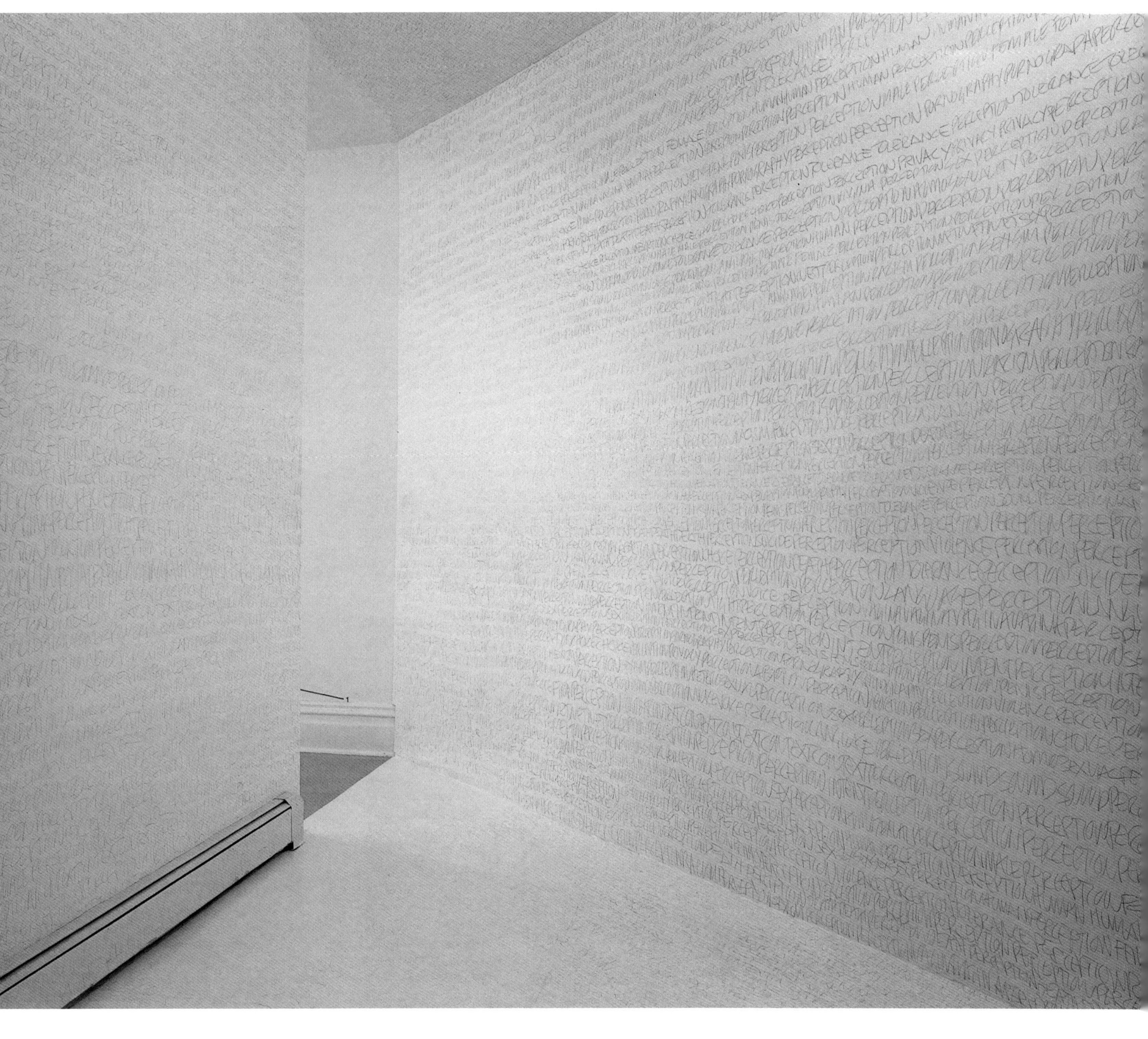

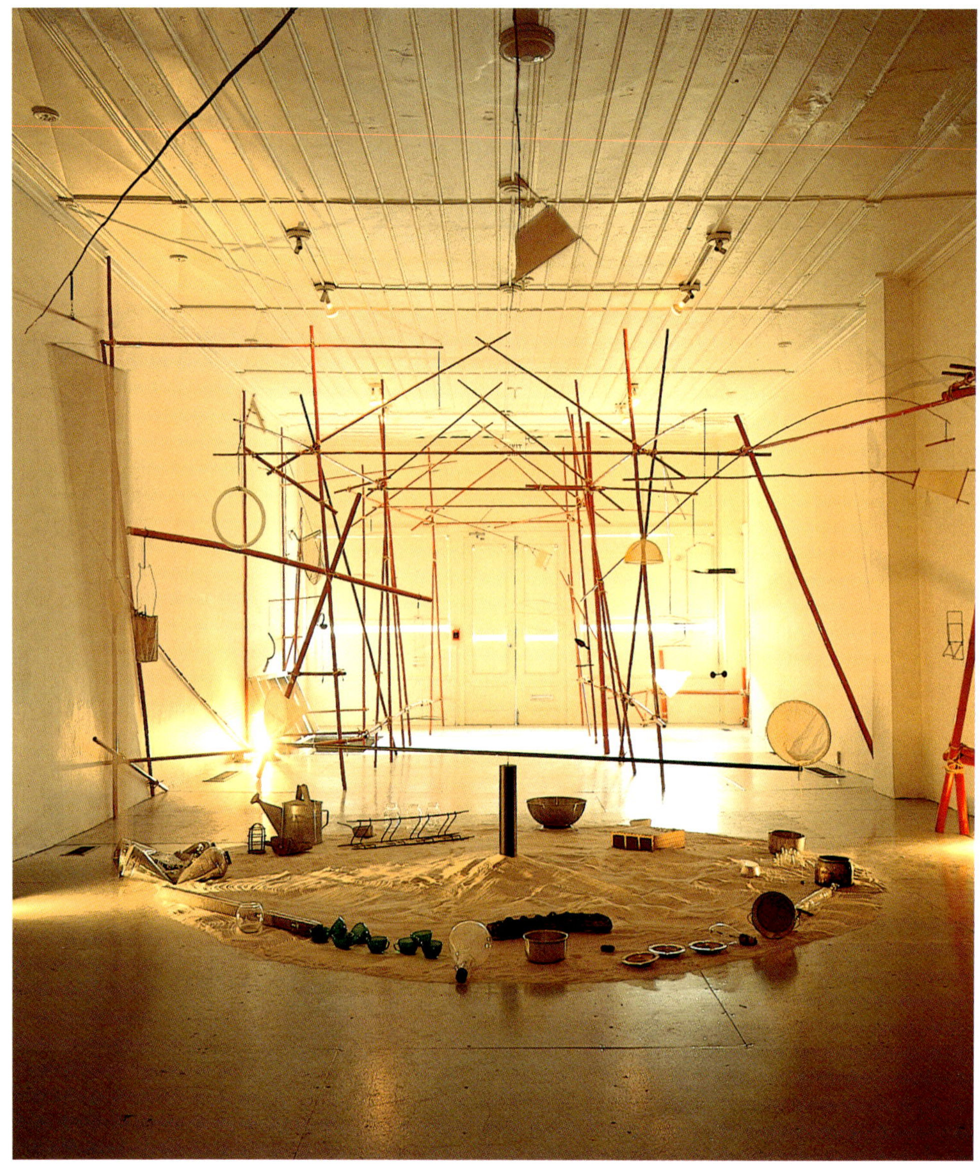

## Yoji Matsumura

Japanese, born 1950

**Celebration,** 1991
Bamboo, lacquer, sand, electric fans, found objects, sound
1414 Monterey Street, 1st floor
(included in *Three Japanese Artists*)

A Japanese gate frames and provides entrance to the space. Like all the parts of the bamboo structure, it is painted with red lacquer. Within the bamboo structure Matsumura collected junk, such as jars, metal parts, doorknobs and crushed fire extinguishers, placing them in a circular area of sand on the floor. Above, a windsock is moved by a fan. A bead hanging on one side of the windsock hits objects with a chime-like effect.

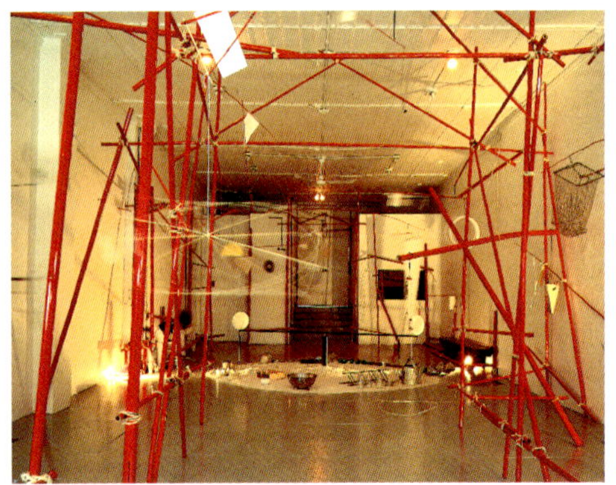

**Artist's Statement**

My main idea developed from "doing sculpture" rather than "making sculpture." I assembled all the natural and man-made elements within a Space and in Time. I could, in this way, put my own concept and expression into my art work by digesting the unlimited power of our natures.

The material I have chosen in my recent works is important because it has given me an opportunity to be aware of my living environment and its elements. I like to discover unique and innovative uses for the common materials that I find. The excitement of finding the alternative meanings for these materials and making use of them is the essence of my art work.

It is also important to me that the audience participates and experiences a new sensitivity beyond the five or six senses given to humans. My works are created to communicate my own anger, sadness, surprise, and joy and share this with others, not only visually, but through sensations of like experience.

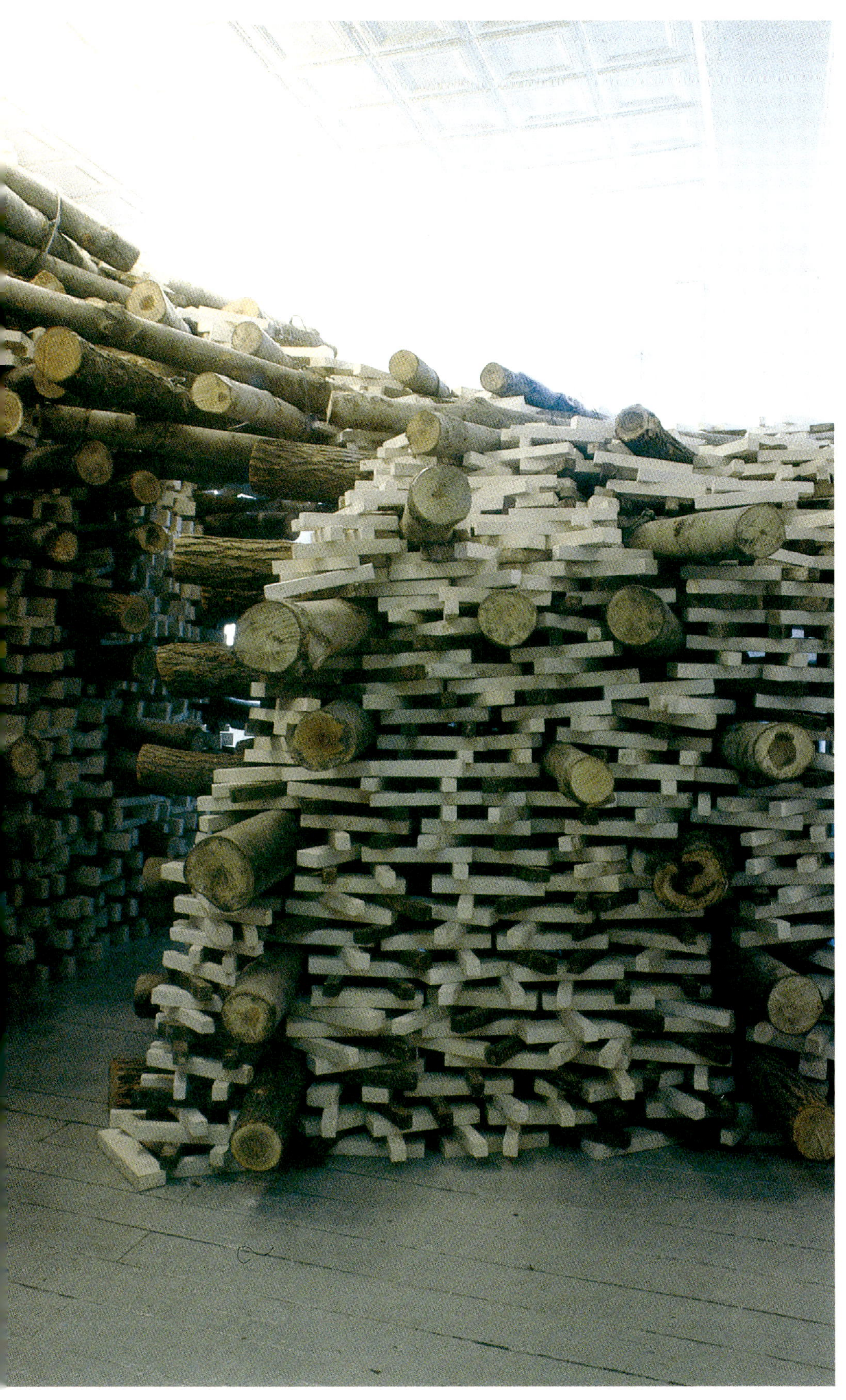

## Takamasa Kuniyasu

Japanese, born 1957

**Return to Self,** 1991
16,000 fire bricks, 700 logs, steel wire
1414 Monterey Street, 2nd floor
(included in *Three Japanese Artists*)

Seven hundred logs and sixteen thousand small bricks are carefully stacked to fill two small galleries. Visitors are able to walk among the dense construction in two rooms. Tight passageways take the viewer past niches, amidst the scent of freshly cut wood and the varying rhythms of stacking patterns.

**Artist's Statement**

FIRST STEP

I sometimes imagine an ancient age when humans did not have words. They probably drew something even in that age.

It is said that the origin of sculpture was the obelisk, which consists of four monoliths facing north, south, east and west. It is also said that a hole appeared in the obelisk, and a movement was born. The hole was space around the human form, the open areas between the fingers, legs, arms. Finally that developed into Greek sculpture. I am not sure if this is true or not. However, the story fascinates me.

I think if the monolith is the origin of art, stacking bricks as I have done is part of the origin. I want to return my thoughts to the starting point by the routine stacking of bricks. Then I want to think about art, about human beings, about nature, and about the world. Moreover, I want to ask "the question of the human" that nobody has found the answer to yet through art.

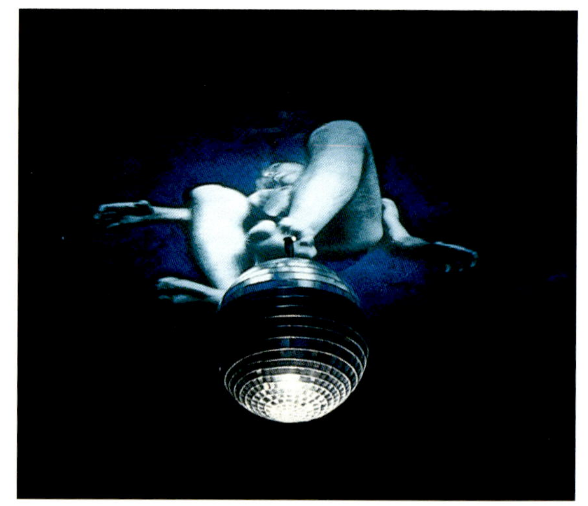

## Tomoaki Ishihara

Japanese, born 1959

**Untitled installation,** 1991
Photo emulsion on canvas, acrylic paint, transparency, mirrored ball
1414 Monterey Street, 3rd floor
(included in *Three Japanese Artists*)

A stacked spiral of canvases is situated in the center of the first room. Each canvas has been painted several times and the various layers have trickled over the sides. The uppermost canvases bear a nude photograph of the artist. The overlapping canvases form three complete figures, each of which appears to rise as the height of the stack increases.

In the second room, a rotating mirrored ball reflects light projected from a spotlight in the floor. The reflections from the rotating ball cover the walls with moving light. A light box above the mirrored ball contains a transparency of the artist's body rising.

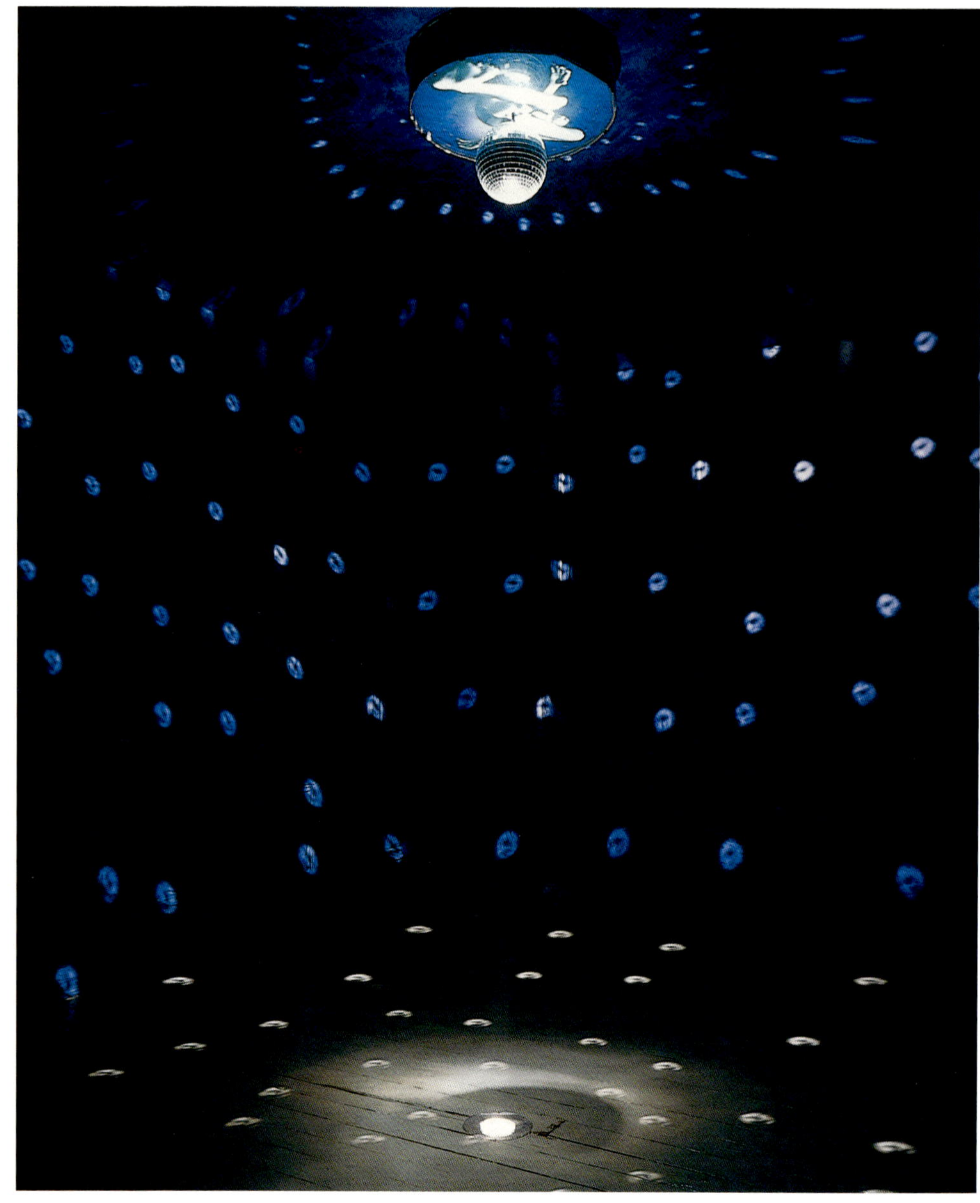

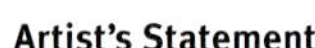

**Artist's Statement**

First, a hypothesis: "I am not a genius." Second, a fact: "I have an ordinary body." Third, a hope: "I wish to change history." Fourth, a determination: "I won't ask God." In this way I create myself and the details of the world working with awareness and love. I'm a common type of person you often come across.

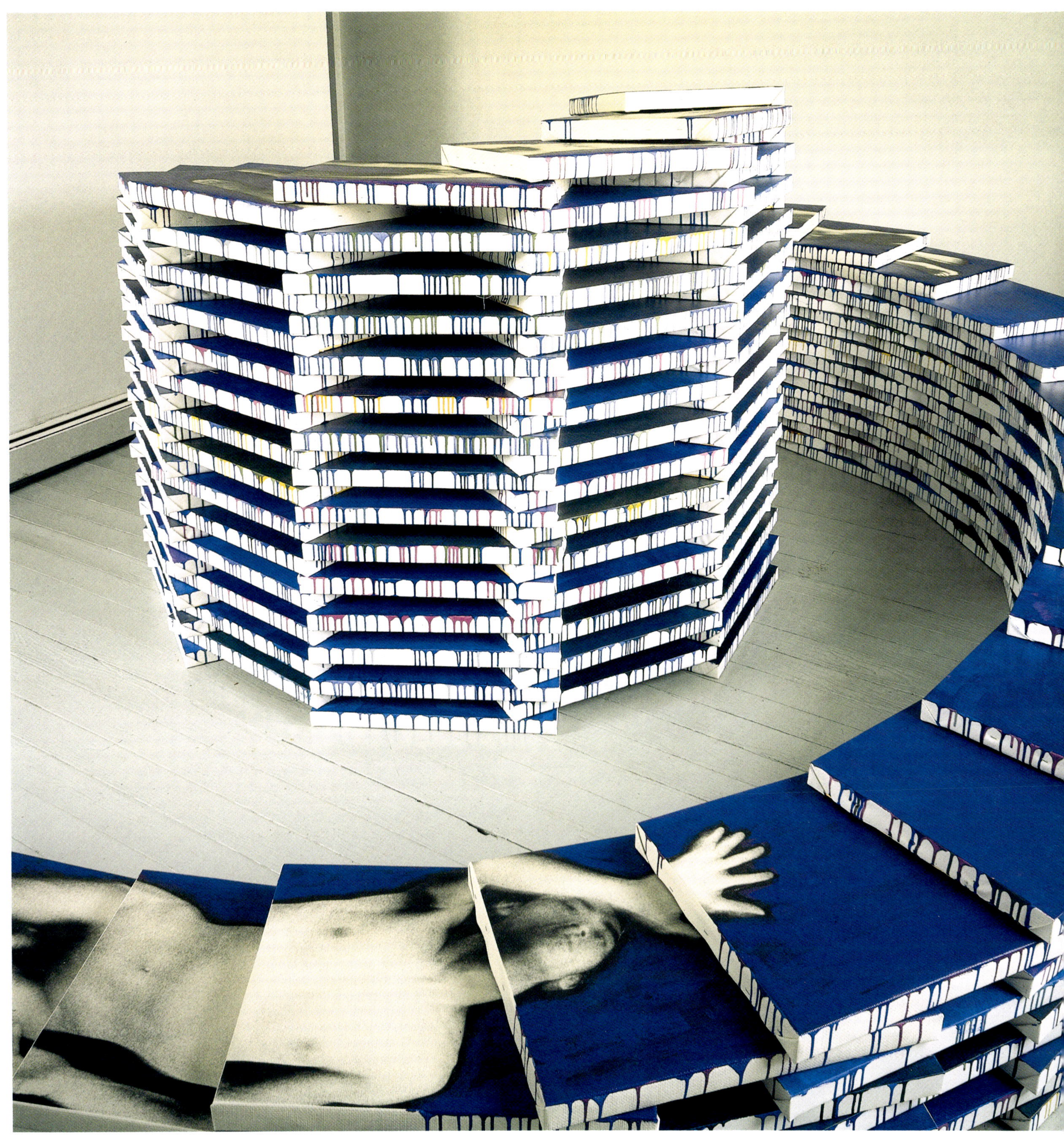

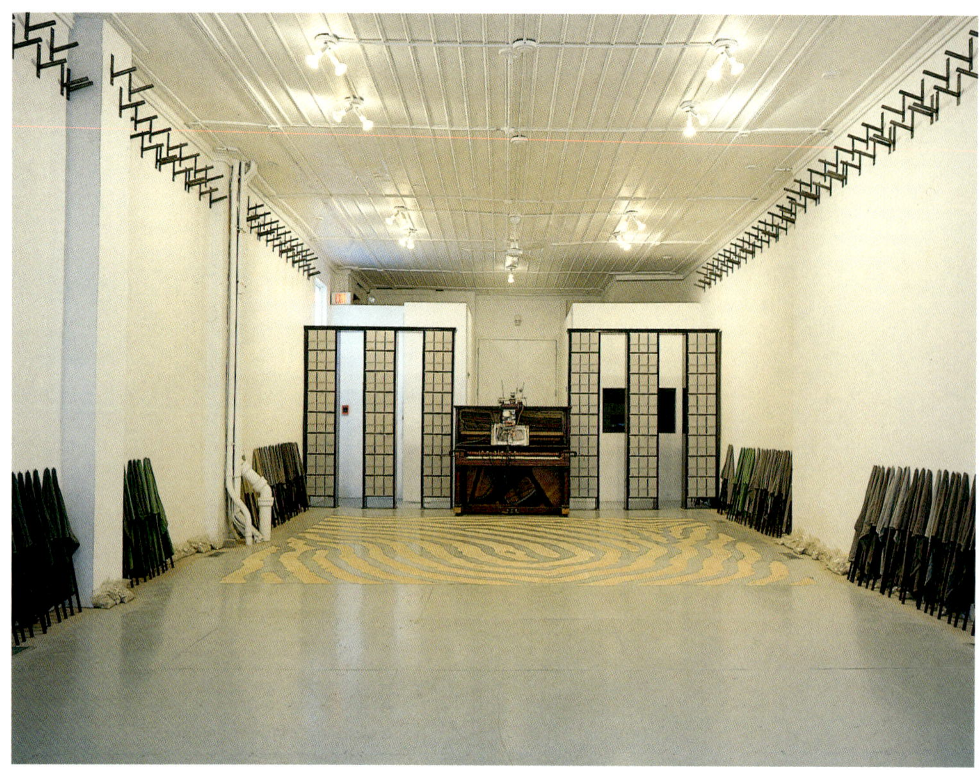

## Bogdan Perzynski

Polish, born 1954

**All at the Same Time,** 1991
Piano, flags, steel, archival boxes, shelves, trees, recorded sound
1414 Monterey, 1st floor

The space is lined on either side with unmounted green flags that lean against the walls below their brackets. Potted trees are placed at the entrance. Large cardboard shipping crates sit near the front door and the walls remain scuffed.

The lines and swirls of a large fingerprint have been sanded into the floor. The sawdust generated by the creation of the fingerprint has been swept neatly into piles or captured in plastic sandwich bags, both of which appear throughout the space.

An old player piano has been rigged with an electronic eye to scan and play music based on an enlarged version of the artist's fingerprint. The piano is flanked by shelves, neatly stacked with unlabeled archival boxes. Recorded sounds can be heard coming from beneath the floor.

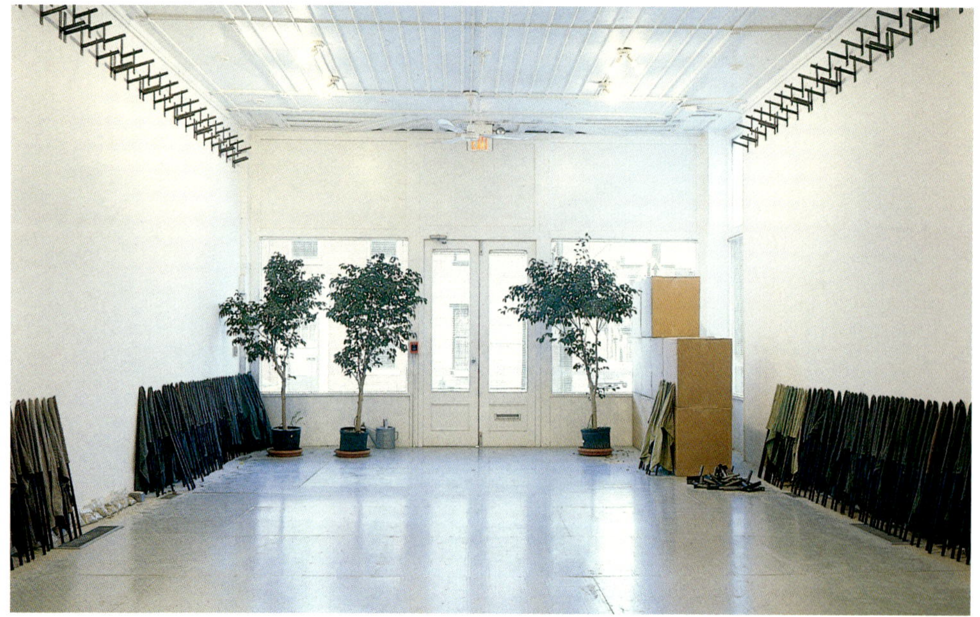

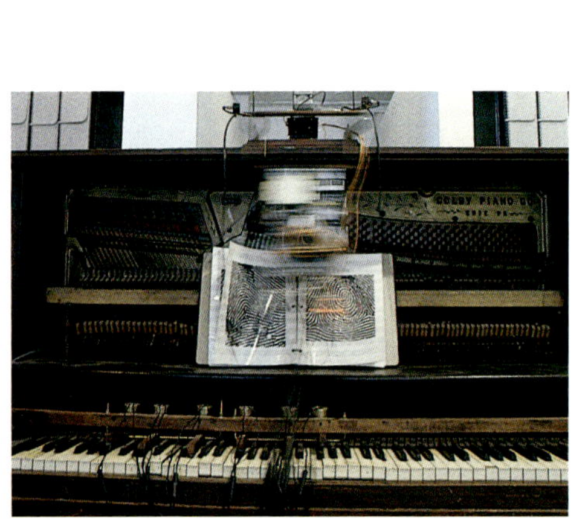

**Artist's Statement**
I enjoy the fact that time seems to run faster than I felt it did just a couple of years ago. I don't mean that I feel fatigued or I am not doing very well. To the contrary, I feel rather happy and my health remains very good. *All at the Same Time* interests me as a work that stays away from dependence on any psychological obsessiveness or the distortion with which so many artists choose to be associated. Also, I was reluctant to employ any systematic aesthetic routine designed to guide me or the audience in search of a central illuminating point. The desire for such a point is nostalgic and corrupts the need for inventiveness and significance. I like the idea that art and culture have nothing in common, that the first must stay independent from the other, which keeps on going thanks to the repetition of its own premises.

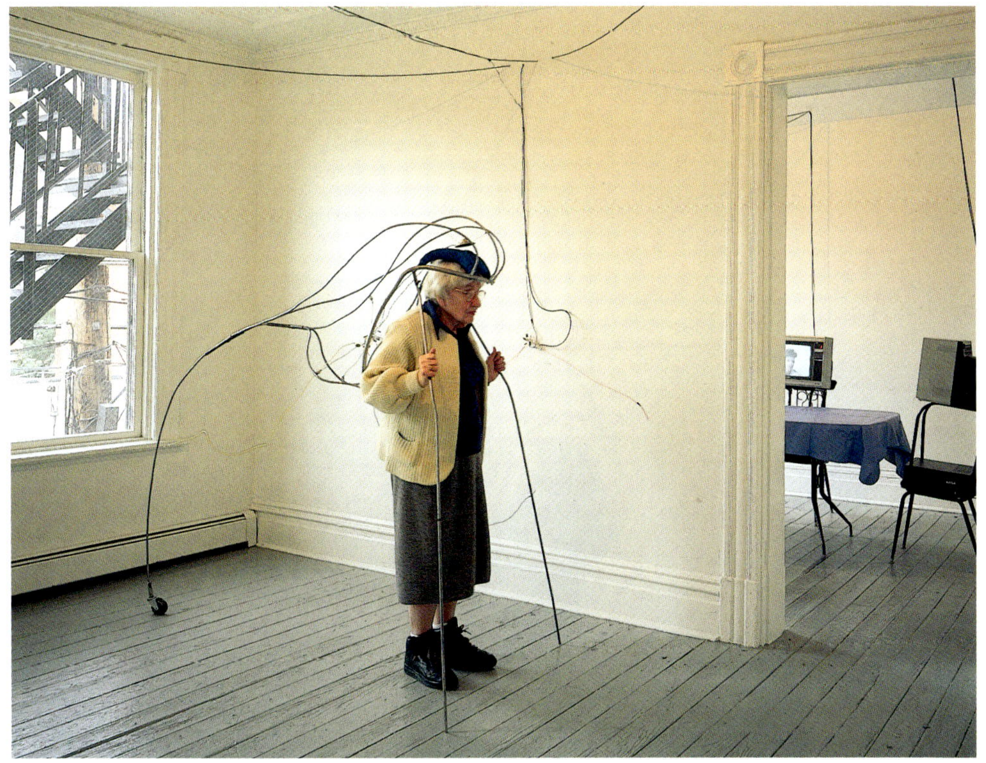

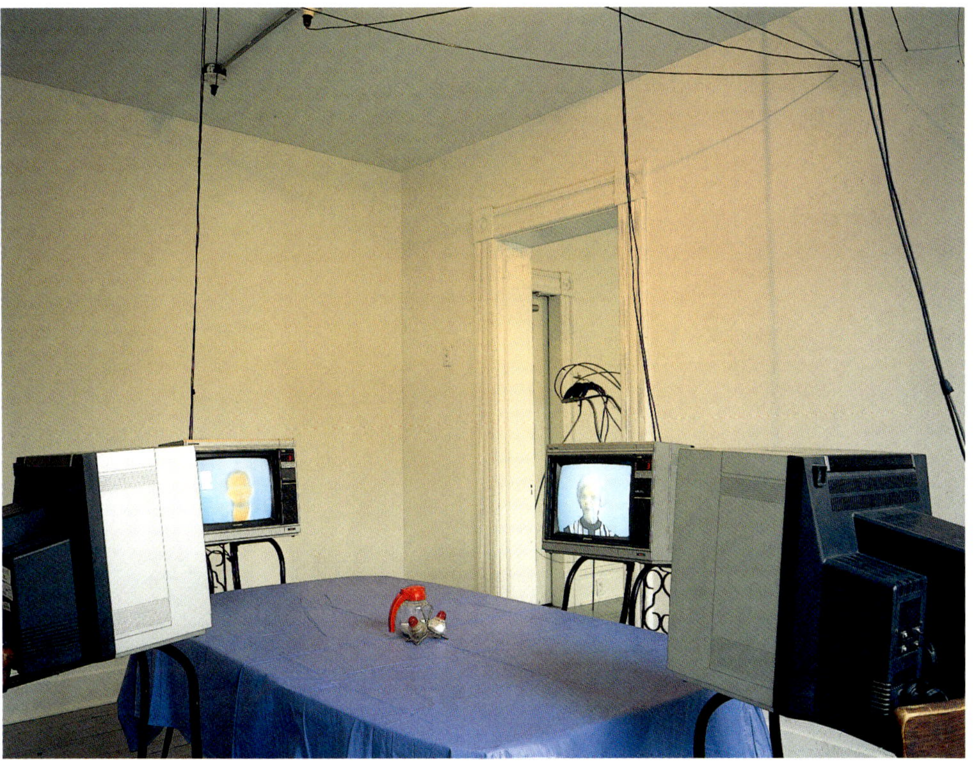

## Diana Burgoyne

Canadian, born 1957

**Untitled,** 1991
Table, chairs, video monitors, electronic apparatus
1414 Monterey Street, 2nd floor

In the center of the first room is a tripod-shaped structure consisting of two legs in front, a leg with a wheel at the rear, and a helmet in the center. Four electronic devices are mounted on each wall of the space.

In an adjacent room, four video monitors sit in chairs around a kitchen table. The monitors carry faces of people from Pittsburgh's North Side neighborhood. Each TV head appears to speak, then to turn and listen to another talking head. However, no sound actually comes from the monitors. In order to hear the faces on the monitors speak, the visitor is forced to go to the first room, put on the helmet, and walk close to the electronic transmitters. The figures can then be heard carrying on a conversation. One of the neighbors recalls that the building now housing the museum was once a candy factory; she remembers that the workers sometimes tossed candy from the windows to neighborhood children. The other faces on the monitors recount similar reminiscences.

**Artist's Statement**

Installation allows me to connect the viewer physically to the piece. Giving the viewer an active role makes him or her part of "the system" referred to in the work.

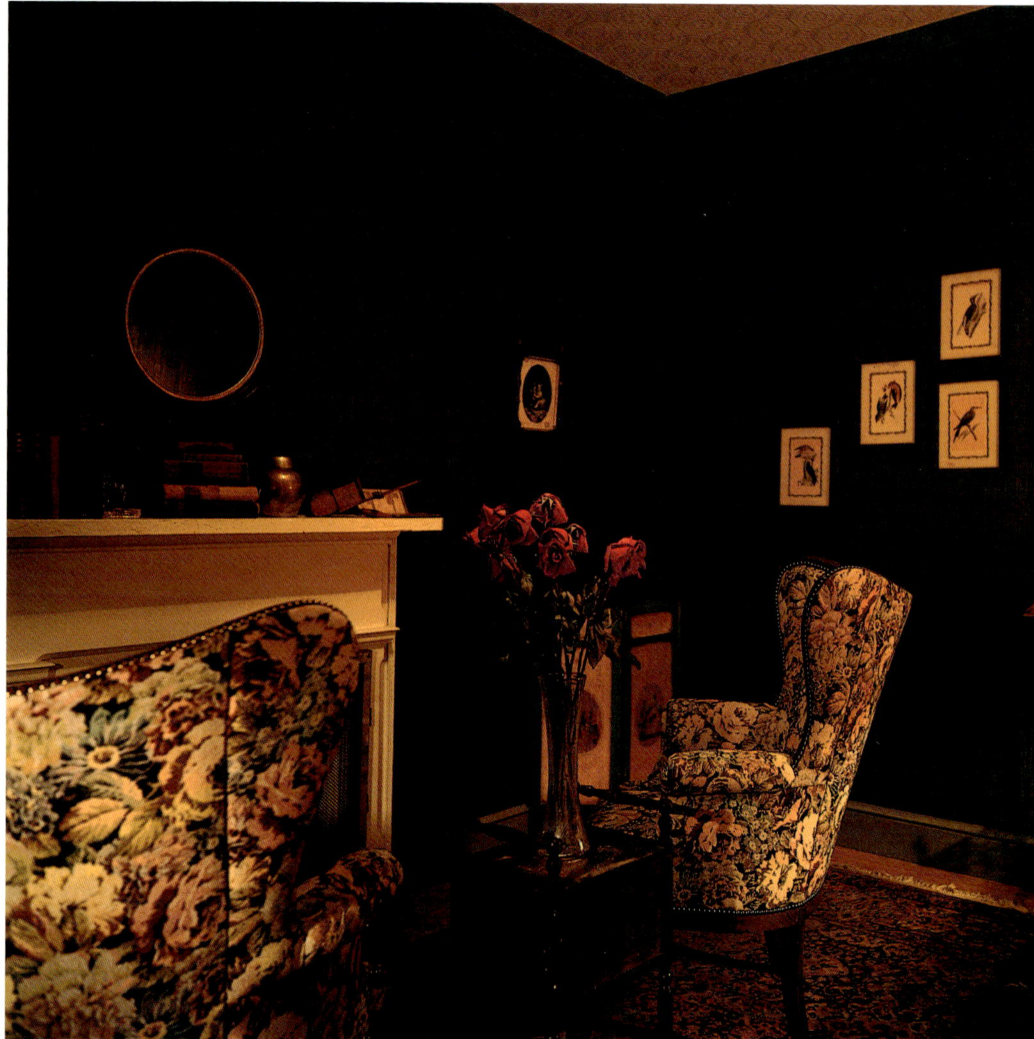

## Buzz Spector

American, born 1948

**Cold Fashioned Room,** 1991
Freezer unit, Victorian furnishings, books
1414 Monterey Street, 3rd floor

Spector furnishes a beautiful parlor with typical Victorian trappings. The temperature is set to twenty-eight degrees. In this environment, the water in the vase of roses is frozen solid and the glass is broken—the only visual clues to the disparity between the visual and physical presence of the room. Books chosen for the room are pertinent to the subject. Some relate to the Victorian history of Pittsburgh, including its steel industry. Others relate to the cold, such as a history of North Pole exploration.

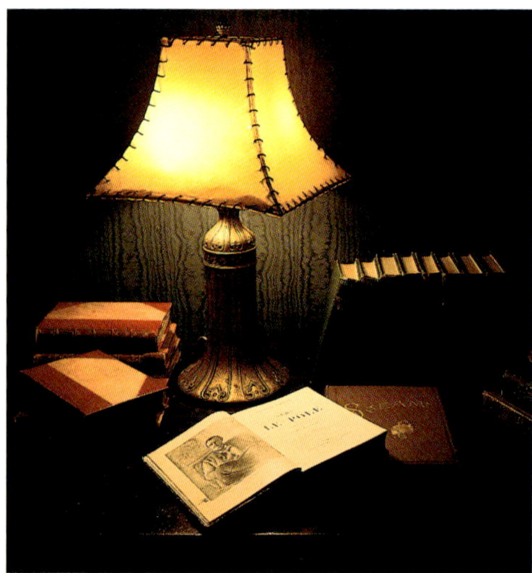

**Artist's Statement**
This room was assembled during August and September of 1991, although it is set within a space constructed almost a century earlier. The building has been rehabilitated and converted into an exhibition space for contemporary art. This room has been restored and decorated so as to simulate its original incarnation. The look of the room is a fiction. It represents an idealized—hence nostalgic—moment of its history as a space. What is impossible to see in photographic reproduction is the coldness of the room. Hidden machines have lowered the temperature below freezing. This effect is physical but invisible. It is the "real" experience here. Frozen, the room becomes another order of representation of itself. Coldness is its inscription.

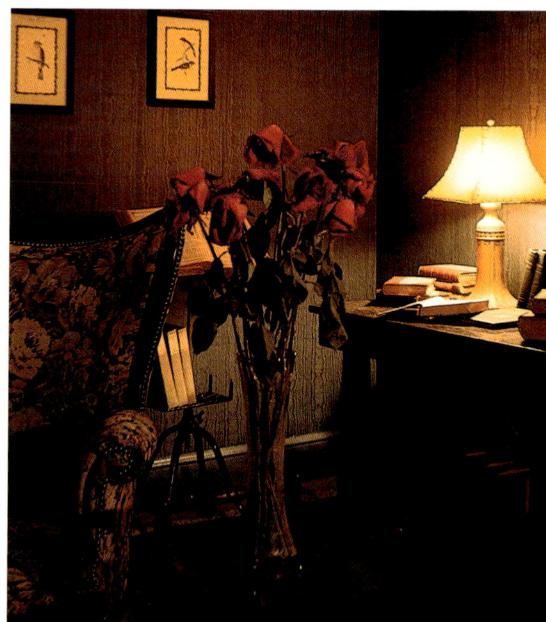

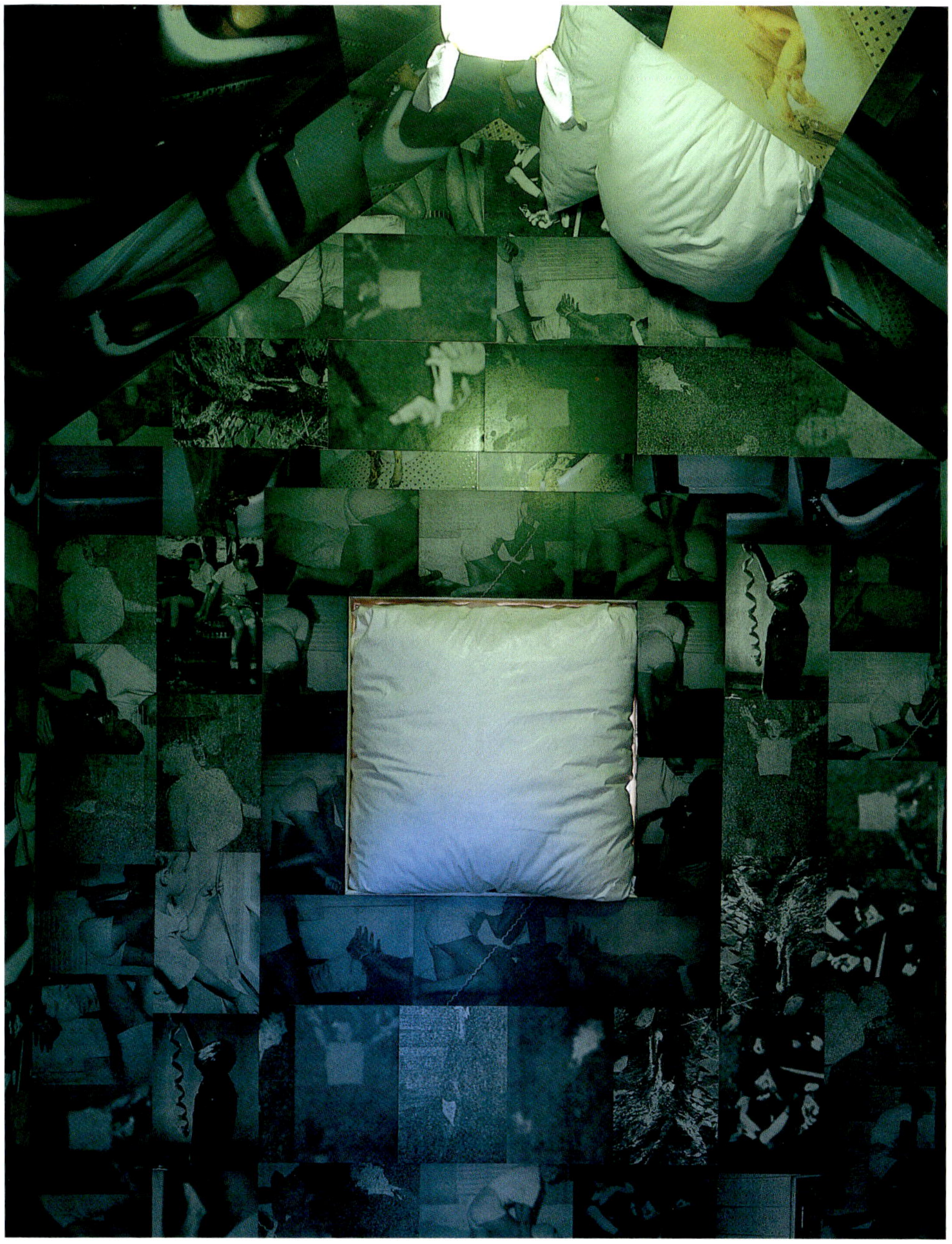

## Patty Martori

American, born 1956

**Love House,** 1991
Drywall, wood, color photocopies, pillows
1414 Monterey Street, 3rd floor

At the center of the room is a drywall construction that resembles a child's playhouse. One can see a view of the interior through the top half of the Dutch door. The inside of the door is papered with color photocopies of a bathtub murder.

On the walls are illustrations from *Popular Mechanics*, which show a father teaching his son how to build something. Juxtaposed with this image is a photograph of a woman smothering a man while she talks on the telephone. White pillows have been stuffed inside both the windows and the chimney of the house.

**Artist's Statement**
Go home.

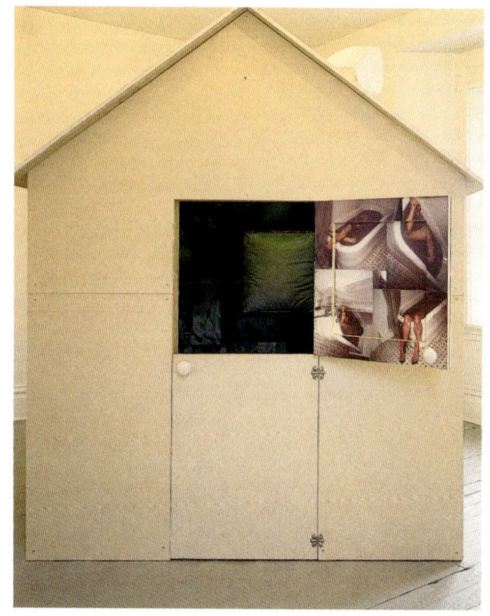

## John Cage

American, 1912–1992

**changing installation at the mattress factory,**
1991
Chairs and art works
500 Sampsonia Way, 4th floor
(included in the 1991 *Carnegie International*)

Cage designed his installation for the fourth floor of the Mattress Factory's main building at 500 Sampsonia Way. The space was raw, unfinished and unchanged from Cage's first view of the room. The installation within the room changes daily. It consists of six chairs and forty-eight wall-hung works, twelve each by Dove Bradshaw, John Cage, Mary Jean Kenton, and Marsha Skinner. Each element in the installation has been assigned a number, which determines whether it will be seen and where it will be positioned in the room. The choice and placement of both works and chairs are determined by a computer-generated formula. Each morning for 103 days, fifteen of the works are hung and one or more chairs are positioned according to their number. Every day a camera, positioned according to another script, made a chronicle of the changing gallery.

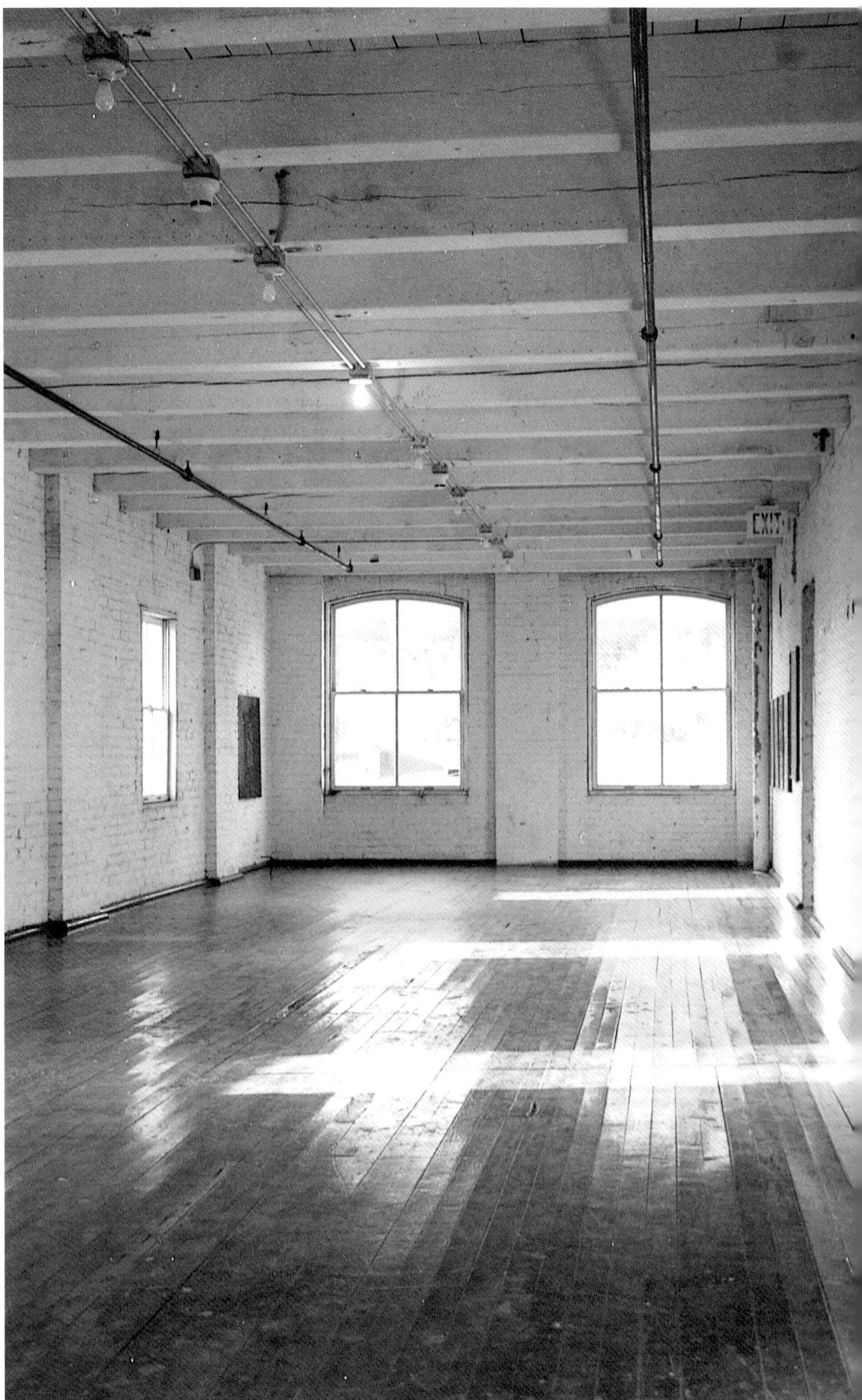

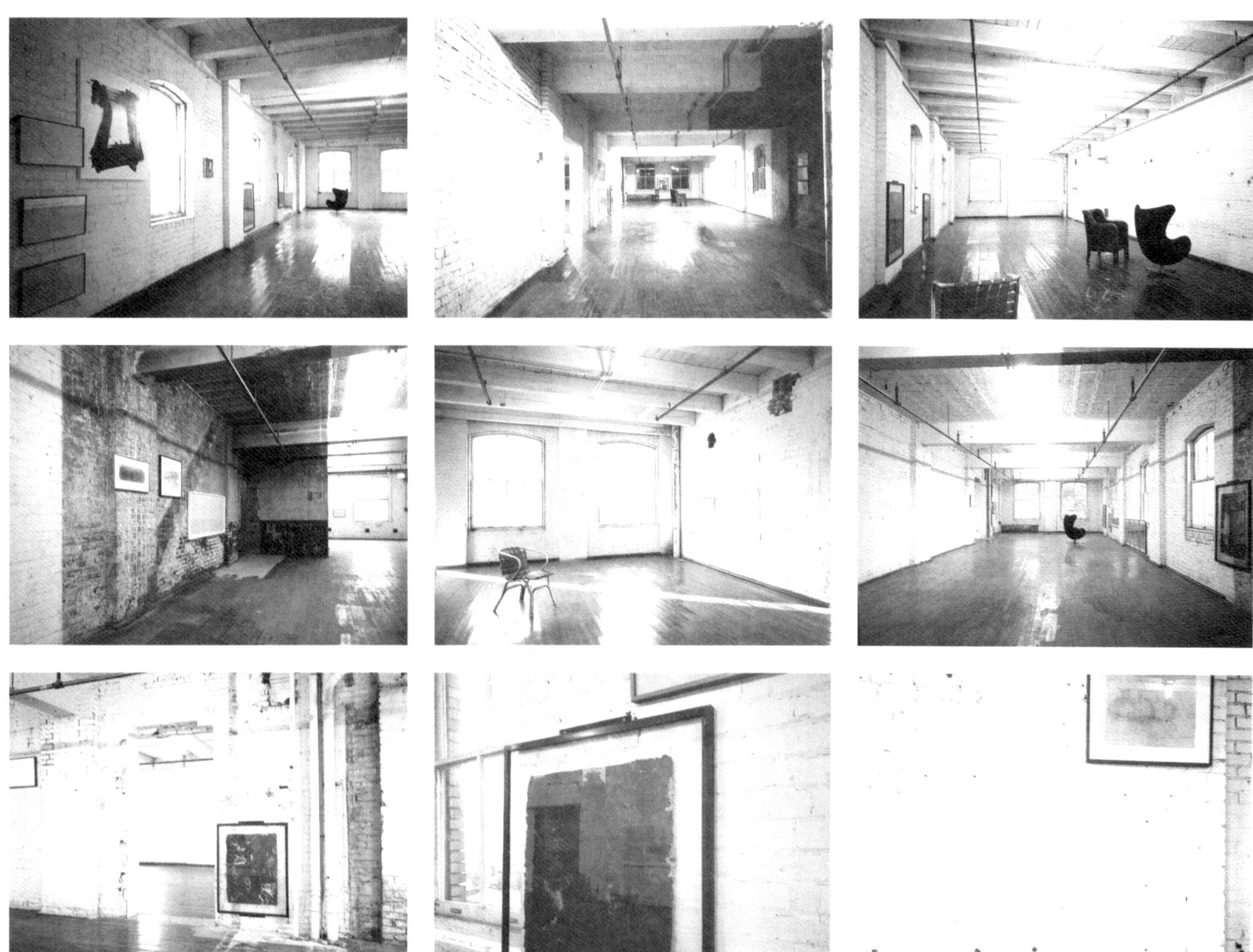

Artist's Statement
(as faxed from John Cage)

in an empty room the chair(s), the walls neither painted nor the paint removed (the walls as they are), the use of chance operations to determine the placement and orientation of the chair(s) and which fifteen of a source of forty-eight works, twelve each by dove bradshaw, john cage, mary jean kenton, marsha skinner are presented each day in which positions

changing installation at the mattress factory

## Tatsuo Miyajima

Japanese, born 1957

**Over the Border,** 1991
Red and green LED numbers
500 Sampsonia Way, 3rd floor
(included in the 1991 *Carnegie International*)

Two galleries, with a brick wall between them, have been painted black and darkened. Inside one gallery, green LEDs run along the left and back walls about one foot above the floor. On the other side of the dividing wall, red LEDs continue the line on the back and right hand walls. In total, the exhibition contains 160 feet of LEDs, which are perceived by the camera to be colored lines. They are actually continually changing strings of numbers.

The sequences of numbers could continue to infinity. They serve as a kind of international language and are almost organic in their continuity.

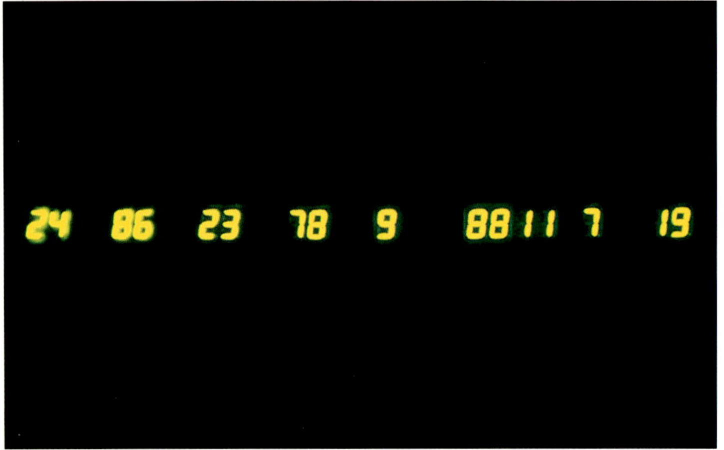


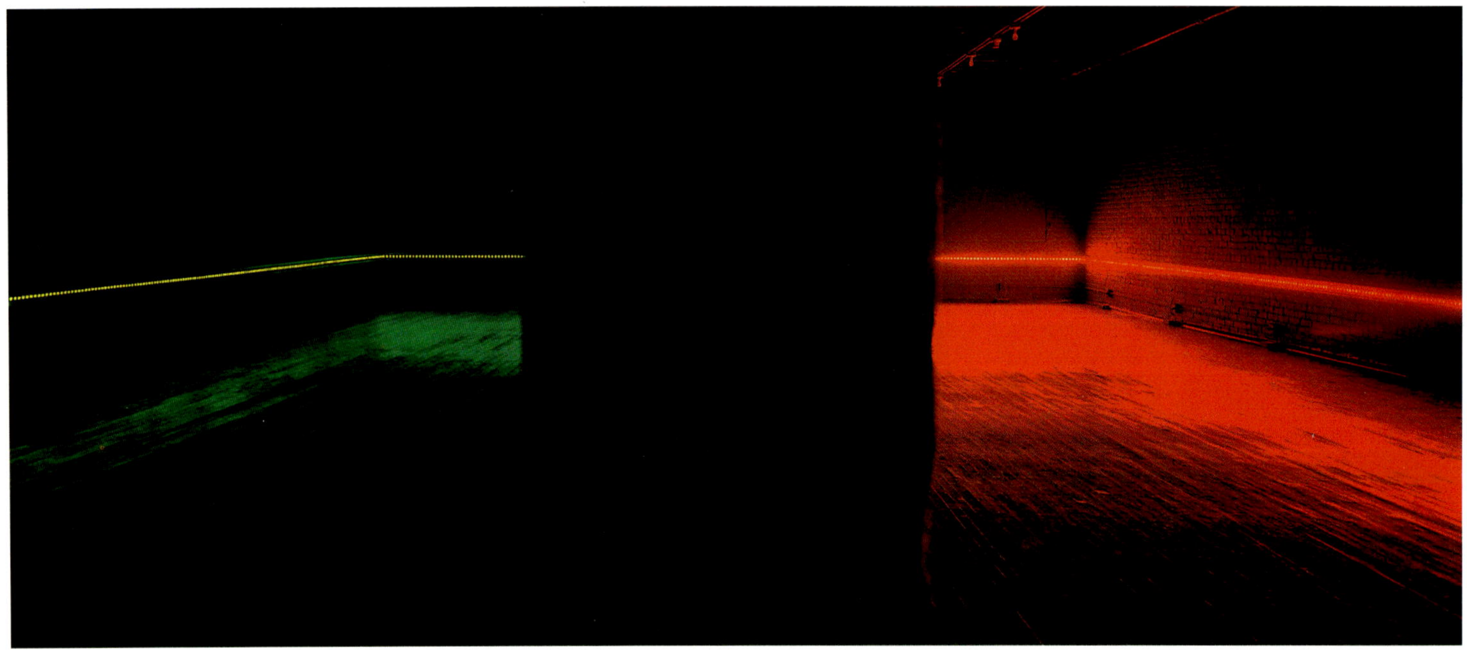

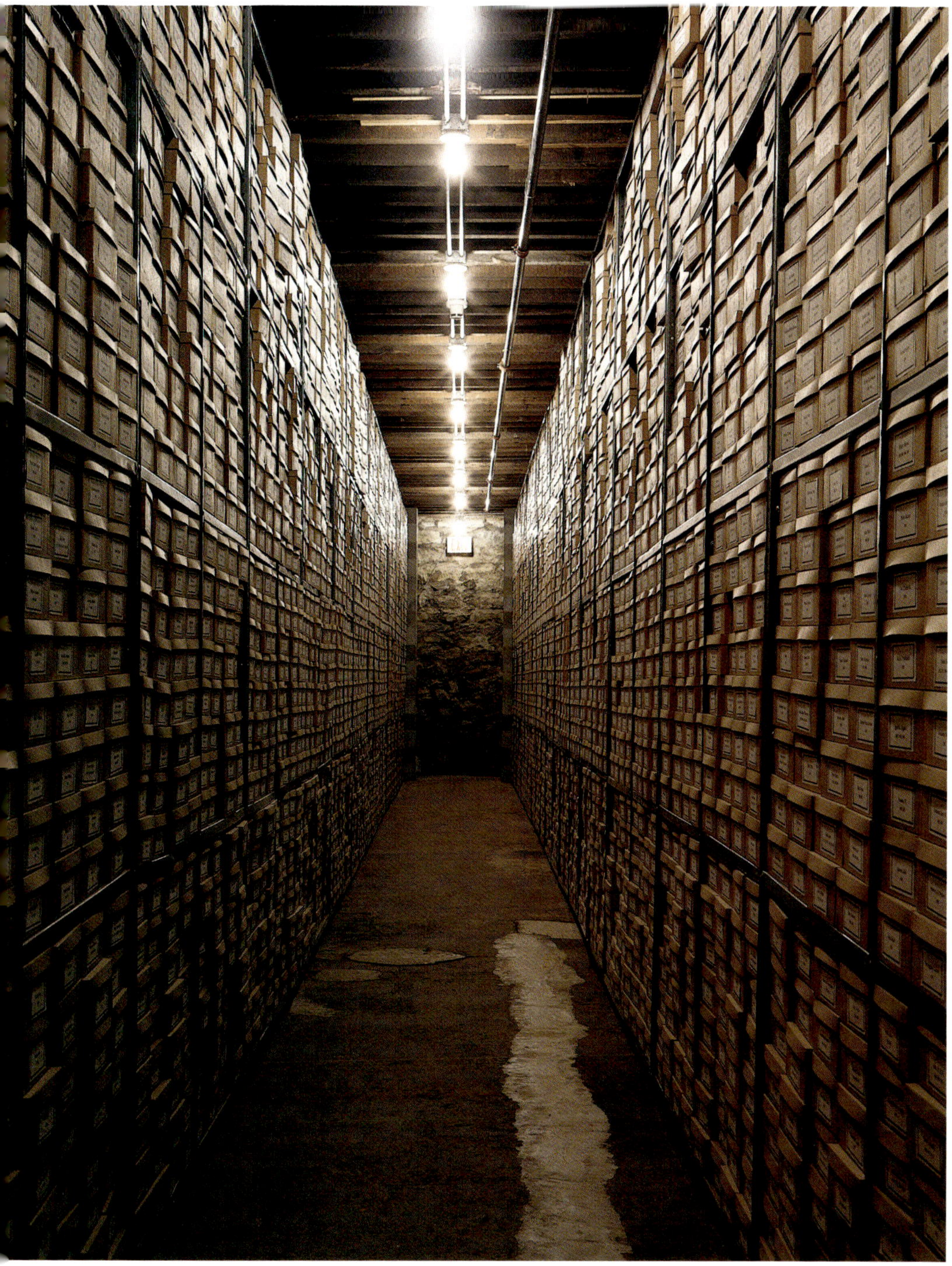

## Christian Boltanski

French, born 1944

**Archives of the *Carnegie International*, 1896–1991,** 1991
5,632 cardboard boxes, metal shelving, labels
500 Sampsonia Way, lower level
(included in the 1991 *Carnegie International*)

Boltanski's installation records the names of each artist whose work has appeared in the fifty-one *Carnegie International* exhibitions since the first in 1896. Gray metal industrial shelves arranged along the walls form a long corridor from the door to the far exit of the gallery. On the shelves are 5,632 cardboard boxes, many bearing the name of an artist and the dates of the *Internationals* in which he or she participated. In order to accommodate future artists, some of the boxes carry blank labels. Boltanski inserted archival material relating to the artists and their exhibits in some of the boxes. Eventually, the public also brought material to include in the archive.

An accompanying book lists all of the artists' names and was created to serve as a directory for previous *Internationals* as well as for the installation itself.

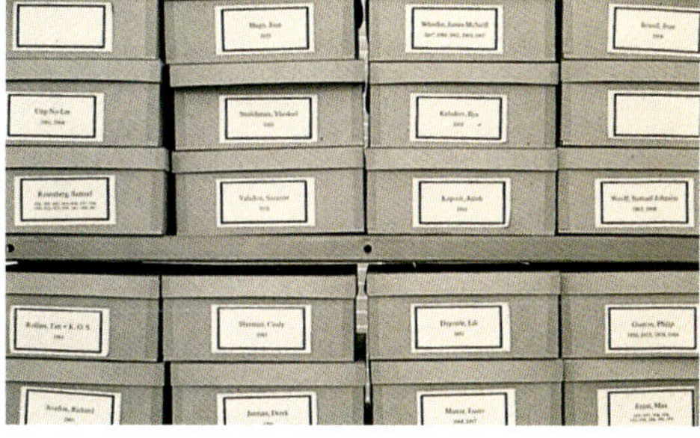

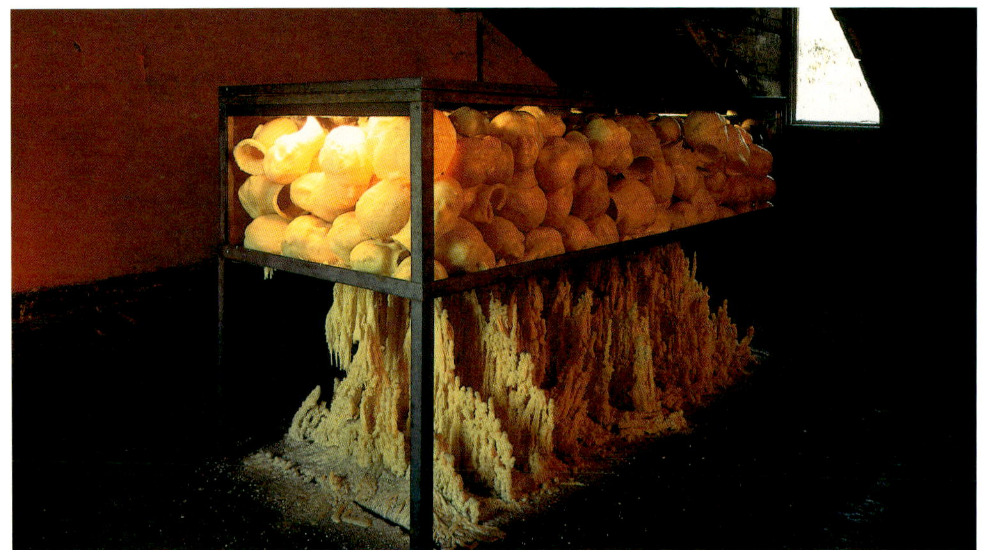

## Ann Hamilton

American, born 1956

**offering,** 1991
Wax ex-voto heads, steel and glass case, heating elements, canaries, steel table, coal miner's ledger
412 Sampsonia Way, 1st, 2nd, and 3rd floors
(included in the 1991 *Carnegie International*)

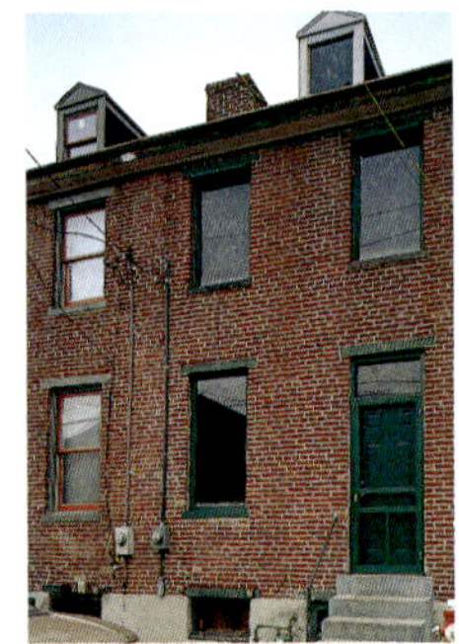

Entering the first floor from street level, the visitor hears noises, smells melting wax, and sees wax stalagmites rising from the floor. The windows have been smoked with candle soot.

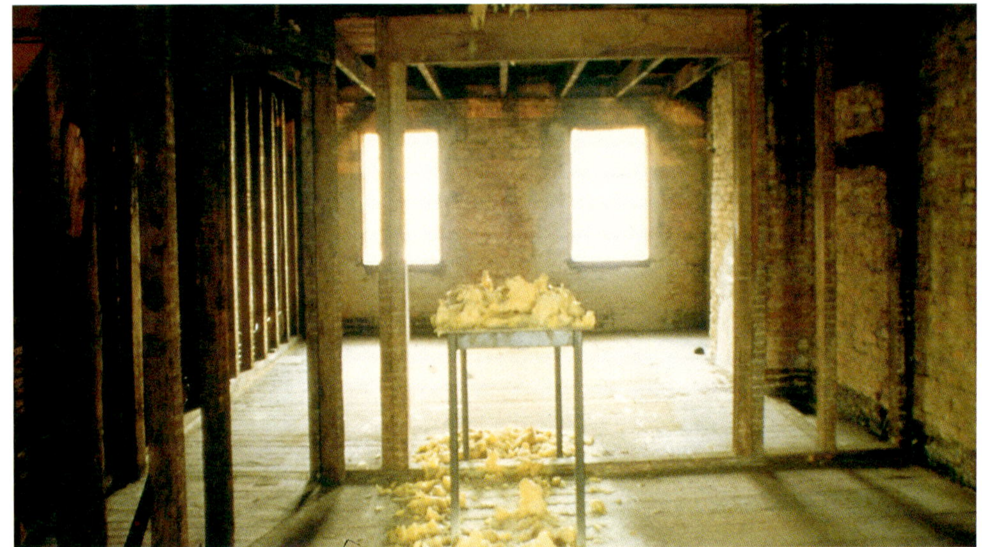

On the second floor, a steel table stands, on which a coal miner's ledger has been placed. Wax, dripping from the ceiling above, slowly covers the ledger.

On the third floor, a steel-framed glass cabinet contains wax heads. A heating system within the case causes the heads to melt, and wax drips to the floor. Another heating element in the floor causes the wax to drip yet farther, to the ledger on the second floor below. Ultimately, the wax from the heads in the case slowly trickles from the third floor to the second floor to the first floor.

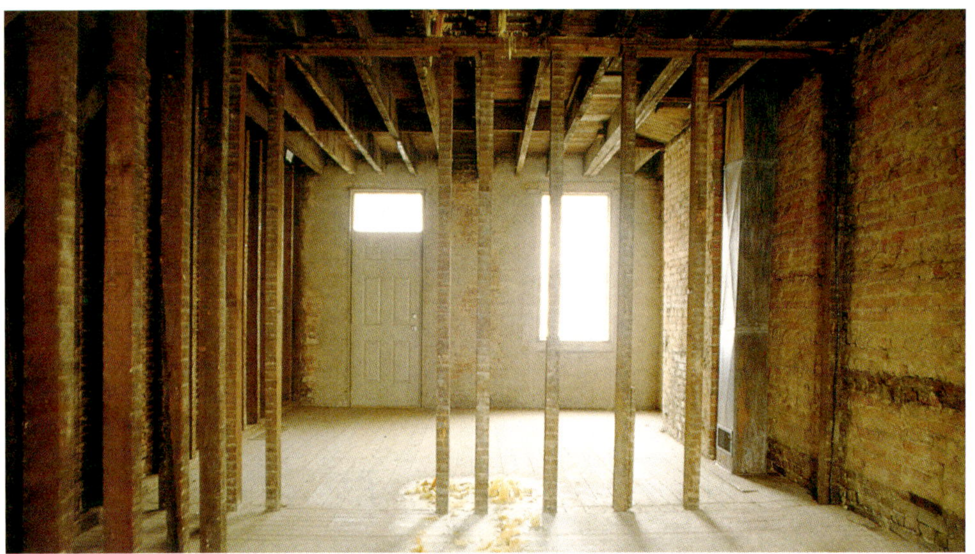

Thirty canaries, American Singers, also inhabit the third floor. The canaries are provided with food, water, perches and nesting material, where they begin to lay eggs.

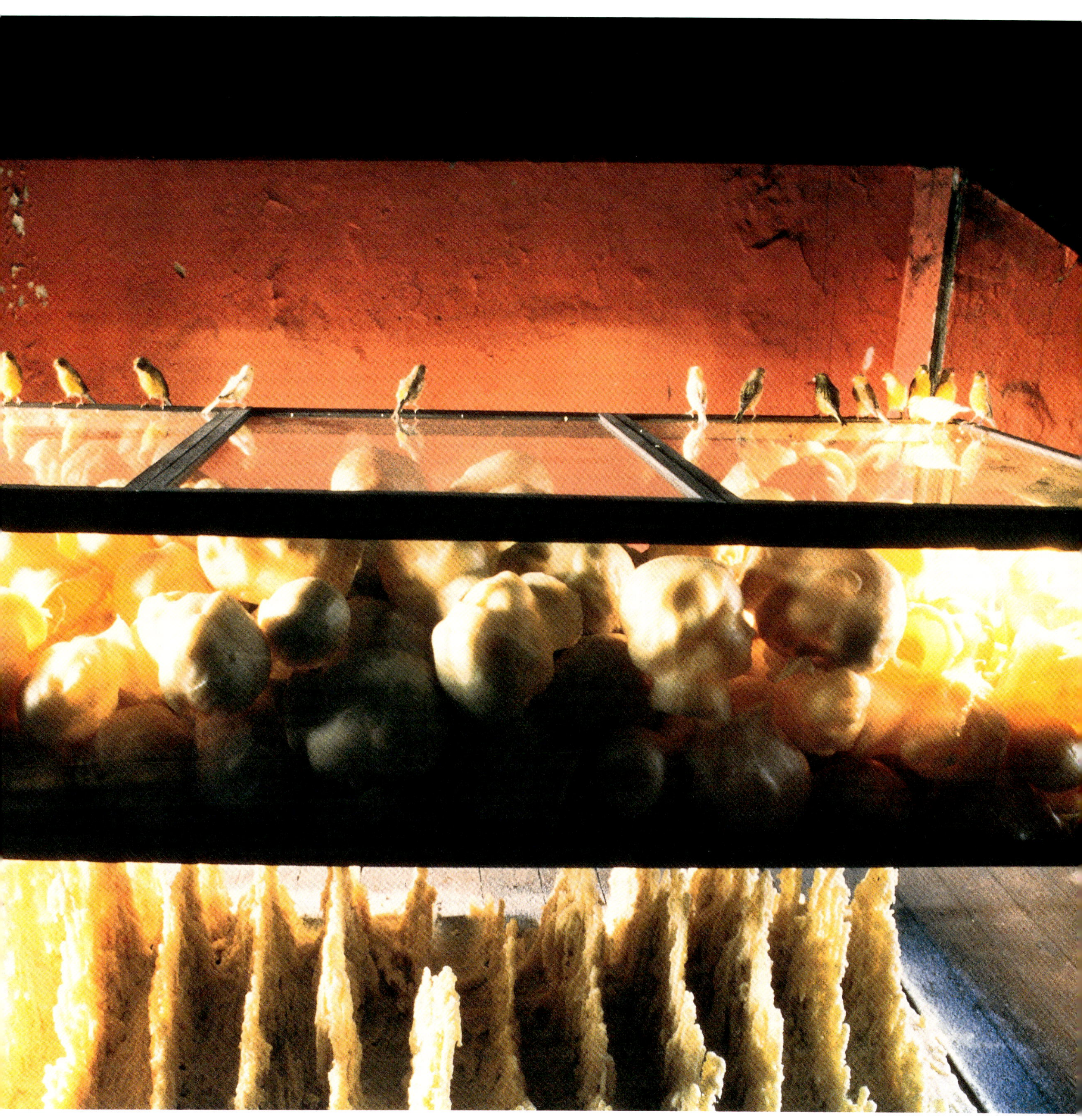

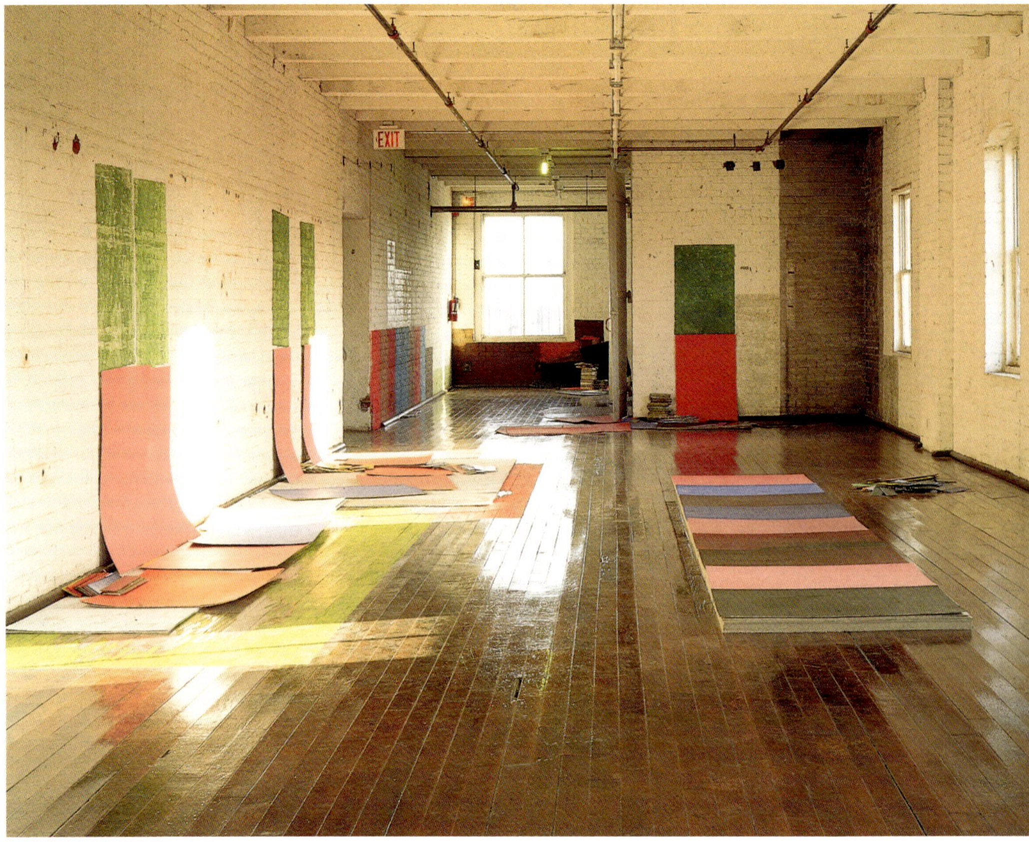


## Mary Jean Kenton

American, born 1946

**The Free Rectangles,** 1973–1992
Cardboard, paint
500 Sampsonia Way, 4th floor

*The Free Rectangles* series is made up of thousands of pieces of a type of cardboard called Davey Board, which has been carefully placed on the floor and mounted on the walls throughout the room. During the course of the exhibition, Kenton regularly rearranged the works.

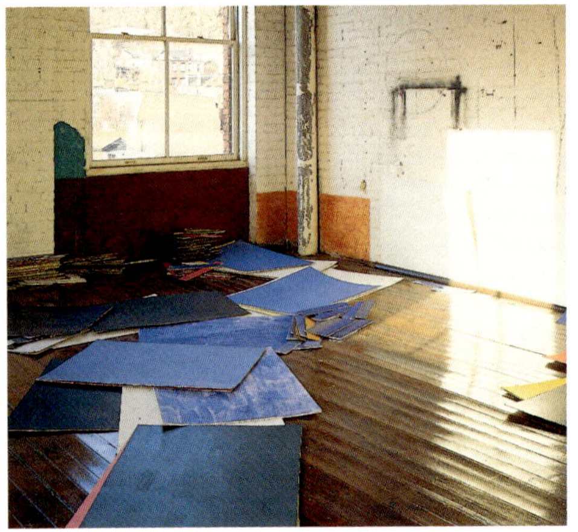

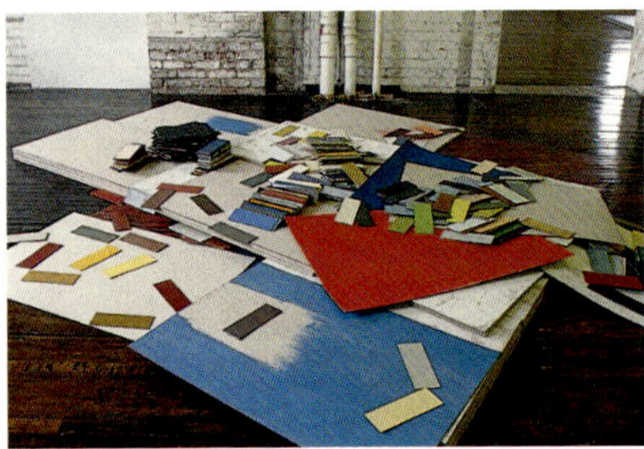

**Artist's Statement**

I began this work in 1973 out of a desire to escape several restrictions intrinsic to painting on canvas. One was the fact that a canvas painting can absorb only so much labor before it becomes overworked. A point arrives at which the painting must either be spoiled or set aside as finished, and at that point the artist's relationship to it changes. I wanted a painting that need never be completed—that could remain in progress for as long as I lived, developing over time and in response to the various locations at which it might appear.

In addition, in keeping with changing notions of what art-making can entail, I wanted to paint in a way that included elements of chance and the haphazard, that resisted commodification and that focused not on the work of art as an end in itself, but on the work of art as a tool by means of which I could continue to refine my sense of line, mass, and most of all, color. These impulses resulted in the work referred to originally as *The Color Cards* and ultimately as *The Free Rectangles*.

I eventually saw that because *The Free Rectangles* constitutes a population with its own patterns of growth and development, its aesthetic implications are not counter to nature, but rather are in accord with her.

Although this exhibition marks the sixth public appearance of *The Free Rectangles* since 1974, it is the first time that I have supplemented them with a painted under-structure that mediates between the individual pieces and the rooms in which they are set out. I will continue to add additional pieces at irregular intervals throughout the duration of the exhibition.

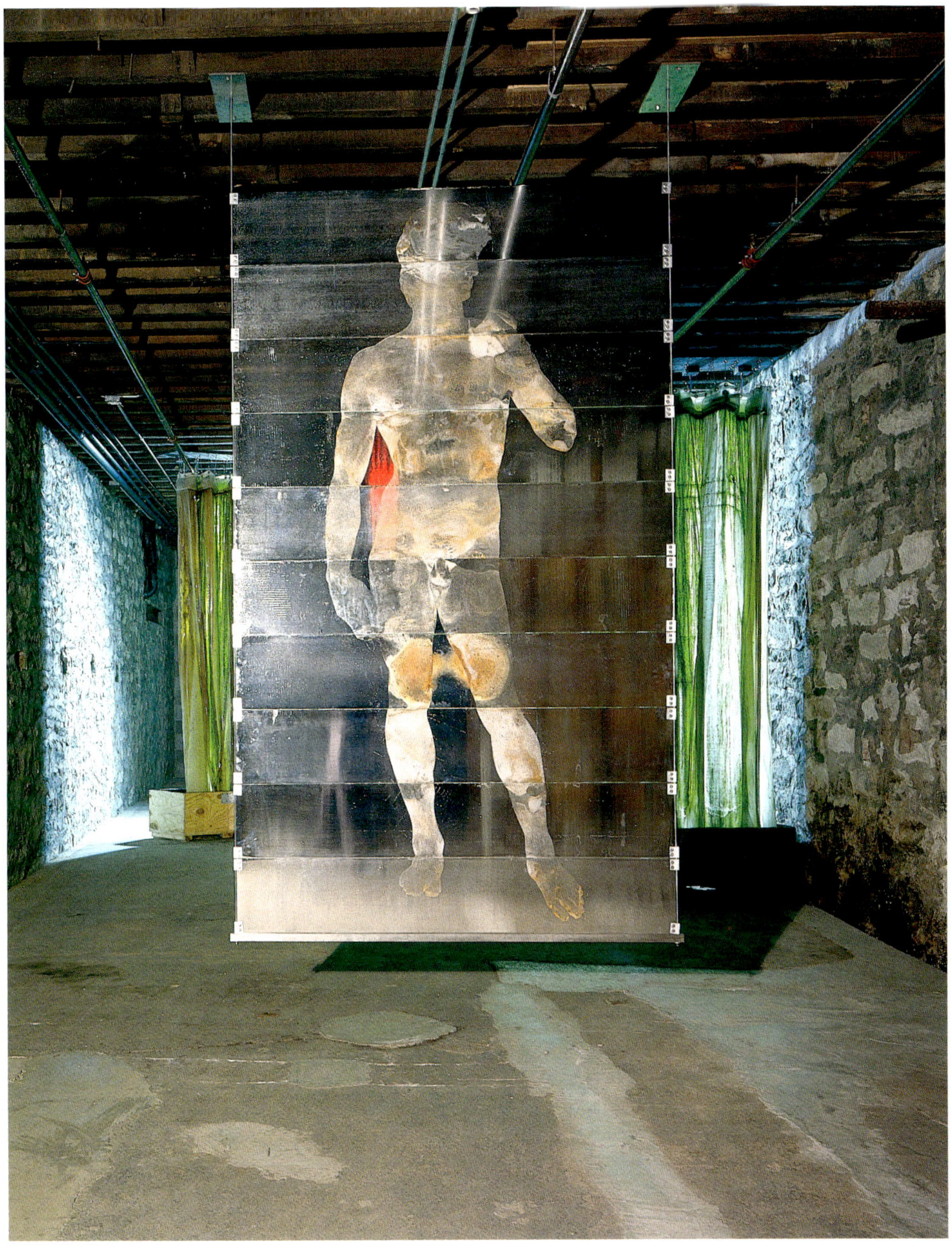

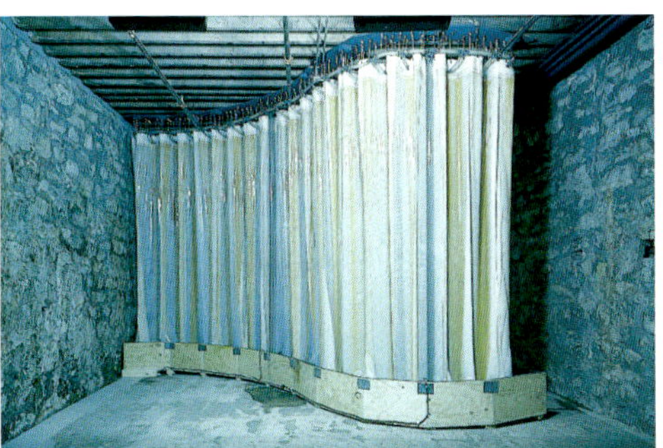

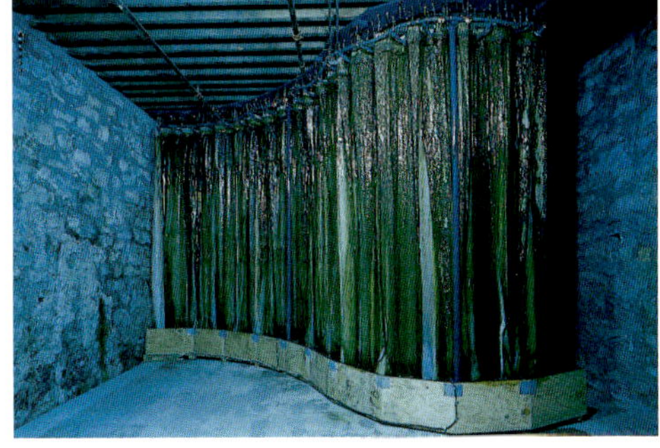

## David Nyzio

American, born 1958

**Observation Platform,** 1992
Steel, polyester curtain, hydraulic pumps, water, algae, quartz lamps
500 Sampsonia Way, lower level

**Artist's Statement**

In *Observation Platform*, I am using two interactive elements to investigate form.

The element "Test" consists of a polyester curtain which functions as a substrate for a garden of algae (Oscillatoria). Nutrient-rich water is pumped from a reservoir in the hem of the curtain. As the water flows down the curtain back into the reservoir below, the conditions within the curtain substrate are almost ideal for a rich culture. With the addition of appropriate light for this species of plant, and the introduction of the plant itself into the system, growth and reproduction will occur.

The second element, "Oxidizing Event," is made of chrome-plated steel, and shares an intimate relationship with "Test." The extremely protective, stable layer of chrome reflects the algae growing on the curtain substrate. The blue-green algae is even more stable than chrome. It is simple, and purged of all flaws, which have frozen its form unchanged for millions of years. Beneath the protection of chrome is steel. It has been partially exposed through the elimination of its protective layer, and now its weakness faces the oxidizing component of "Test." Ultimately, this humid condition will result in the transformation of the exposed form, along with the mirrored image of itself.

Being a good observer, I feel, is of extreme importance. The fact that we can see, however, doesn't necessarily mean that we're good at observing. Our senses are deceptively empowering. We assume them to be extraordinary, when in fact they are mediocre at best. I've discovered, through a history of misidentifications and false correlations, the need for conscious and focused attention to this matter. I've also found that layered observations within varied engaged activity tend to alter my general philosophy about life and morphology. . . . My art-making process takes me through a wide range of experiences. These varied experiences function as a training ground for observation, and a deflocculent for the components of understanding.

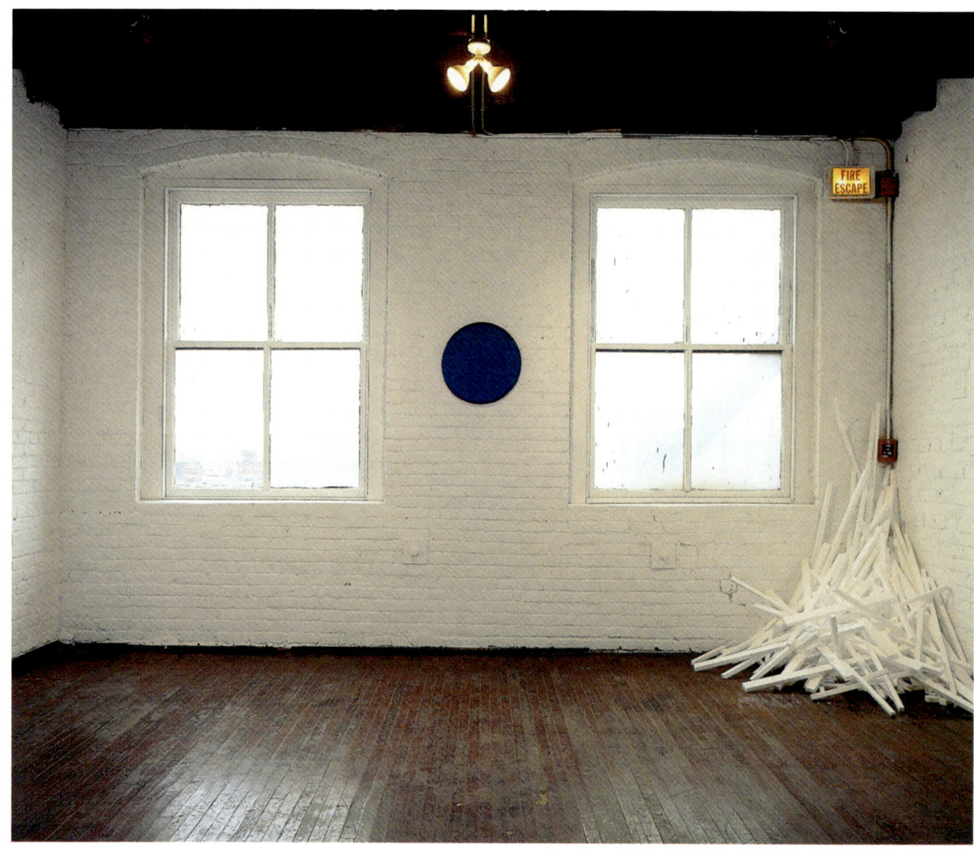


## John Kirchner

American, born 1955

**Faith and Aphasia,** 1992
Polystyrene, 52" waist suit, blue satin, drafting paper, suits
500 Sampsonia Way, 3rd floor

The visitor first sees a stack of Styrofoam chairs and nearby, a pile of business suits in a heap on top of leftover Styrofoam pieces.

Walking into the first of two large spaces, the visitor is at the rear of the room, which is set up like a lecture hall. Folding chairs constructed of Styrofoam face an enormous, size 52 suit with a hole cut out of its chest. The chairs, while completely useless, are visually convincing.

In another gallery are deck chairs constructed of Styrofoam and slings made of architects' drafting paper. Facing is a gigantic, blue, first-place ribbon. The center is cut out of the ribbon, but this time the missing piece has been placed on a back wall of the gallery. A pile of Styrofoam pieces has been swept into a corner.

**Artist's Statement**

I wanted to create an environment of ambiguity by taking the substance out of the form and the soul out of the substance. I decided to use the format of an assembly or lecture hall, then remove the soul from the rooms altogether. I wanted it to be a lecture on nothingness, a forum on the absolute. I used the suits as the international symbol of uniformity and the huge, blue ribbon to play on the notion of honor. I removed the "soul" from both the ribbon and the large suit to create specious objects that would reverberate in the chairs. I guess what I am ultimately questioning is faith: faith in the validity of the repeated experience, faith in tradition, and faith in individual free will. I wanted to fill both rooms but create a void.

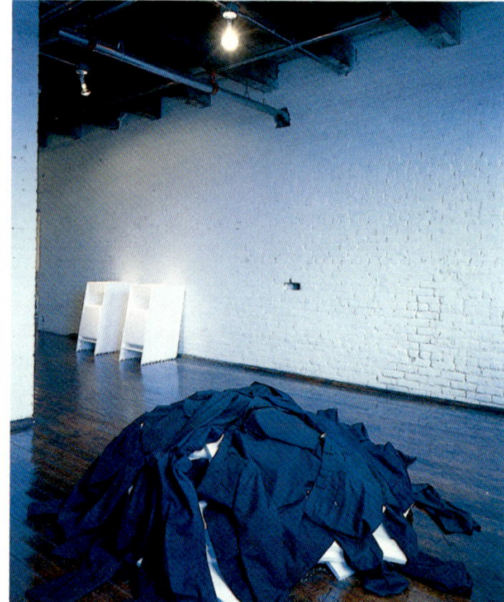

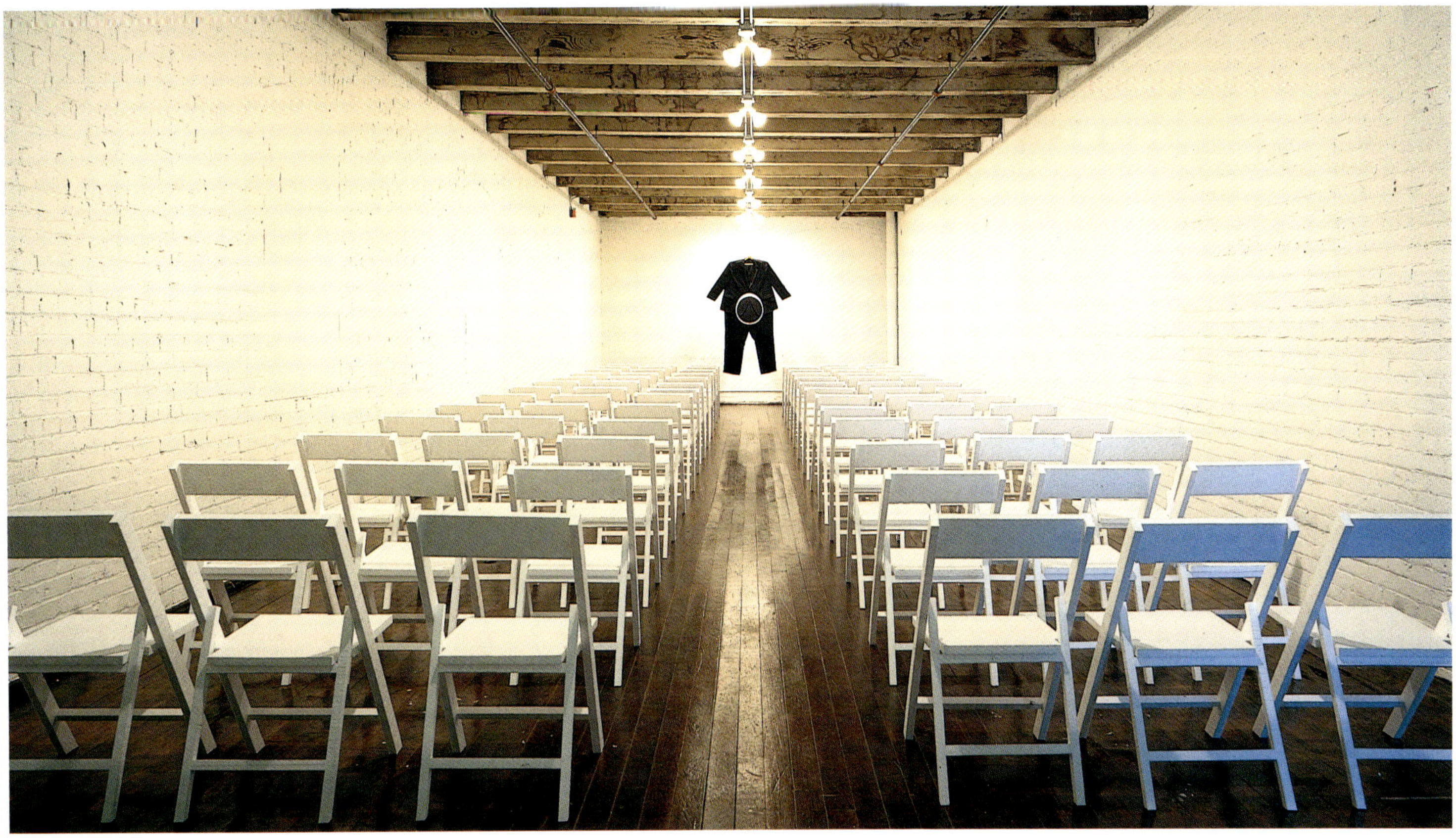

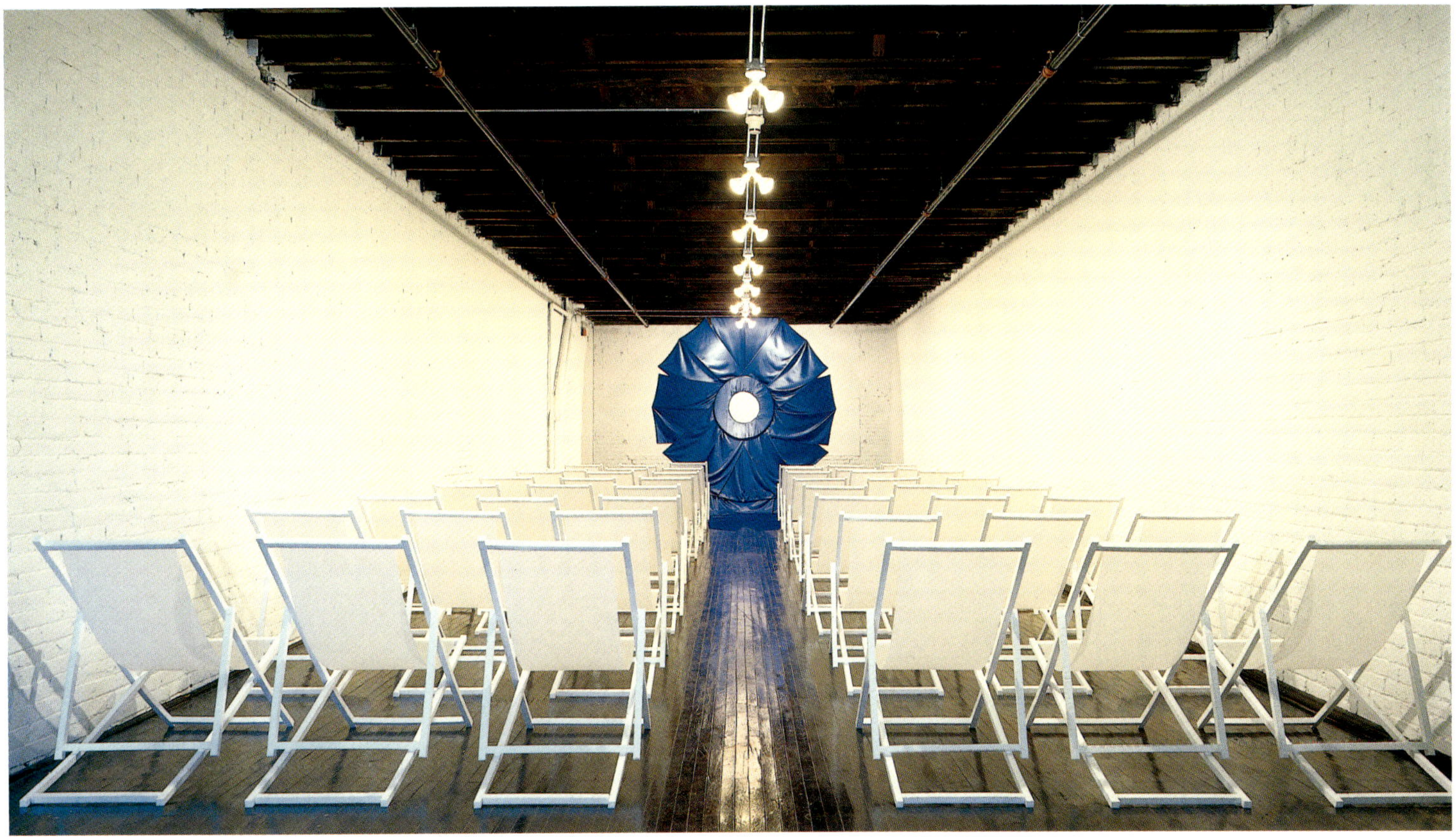

## David Ireland

American, born 1930

**Untitled Installation,** 1993
Cast concrete lawn ornaments, metal cabinet, patio furniture, ficus trees
1414 Monterey Street, 1st, 2nd, and 3rd floors

The installation is built with concrete lawn ornaments. Statues like these were first temple icons, then museum pieces, then lawn ornaments. In Ireland's installation, he returns the lawn ornaments to the museum.

Patio furniture and ficus trees reference the outdoors, and statues in a tight stack emerge from a trap door. They are arranged in a line through the first floor gallery, around the corner and up the stairs. A row of single lights in the ceiling follows the line of statues.

The figures proceed up the steps to the second floor, where they jam the gallery door open. They completely fill the opening, blocking the view. On the third floor, an old metal kitchen cabinet contains the heads of statues and concrete hats, lit by a single bulb.

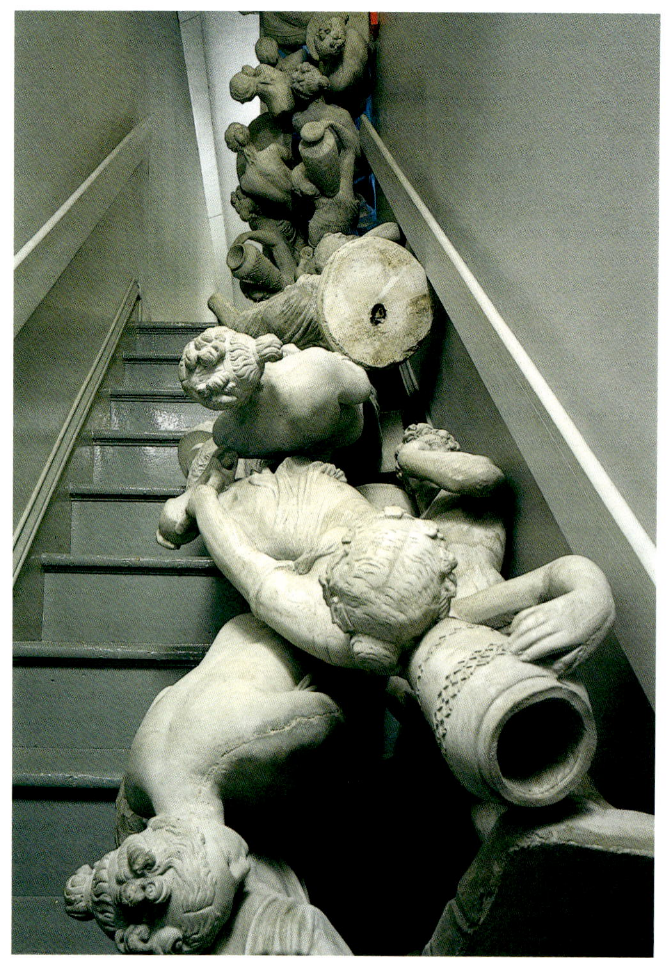

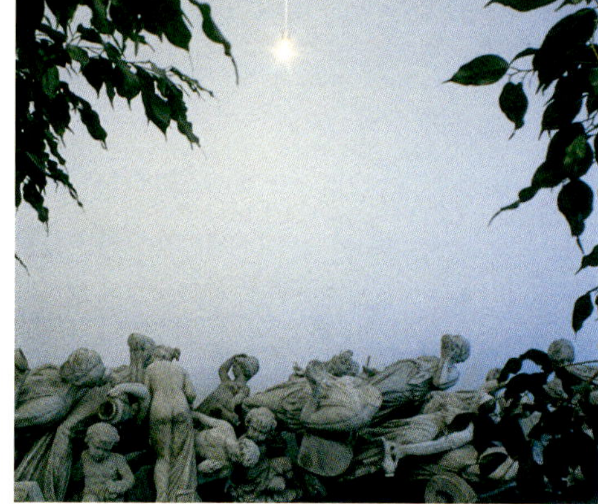

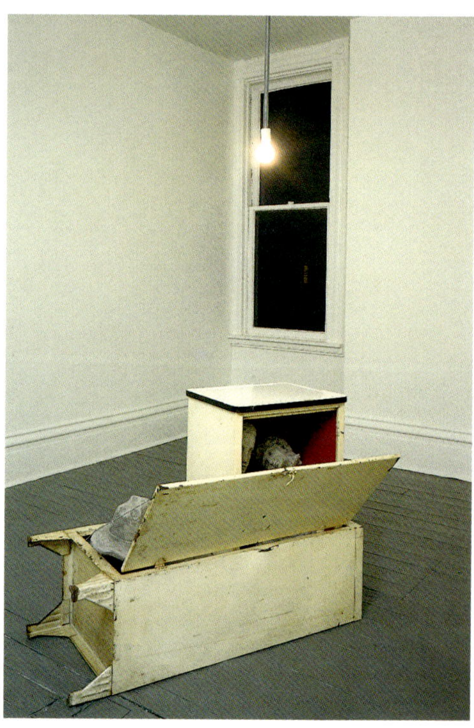

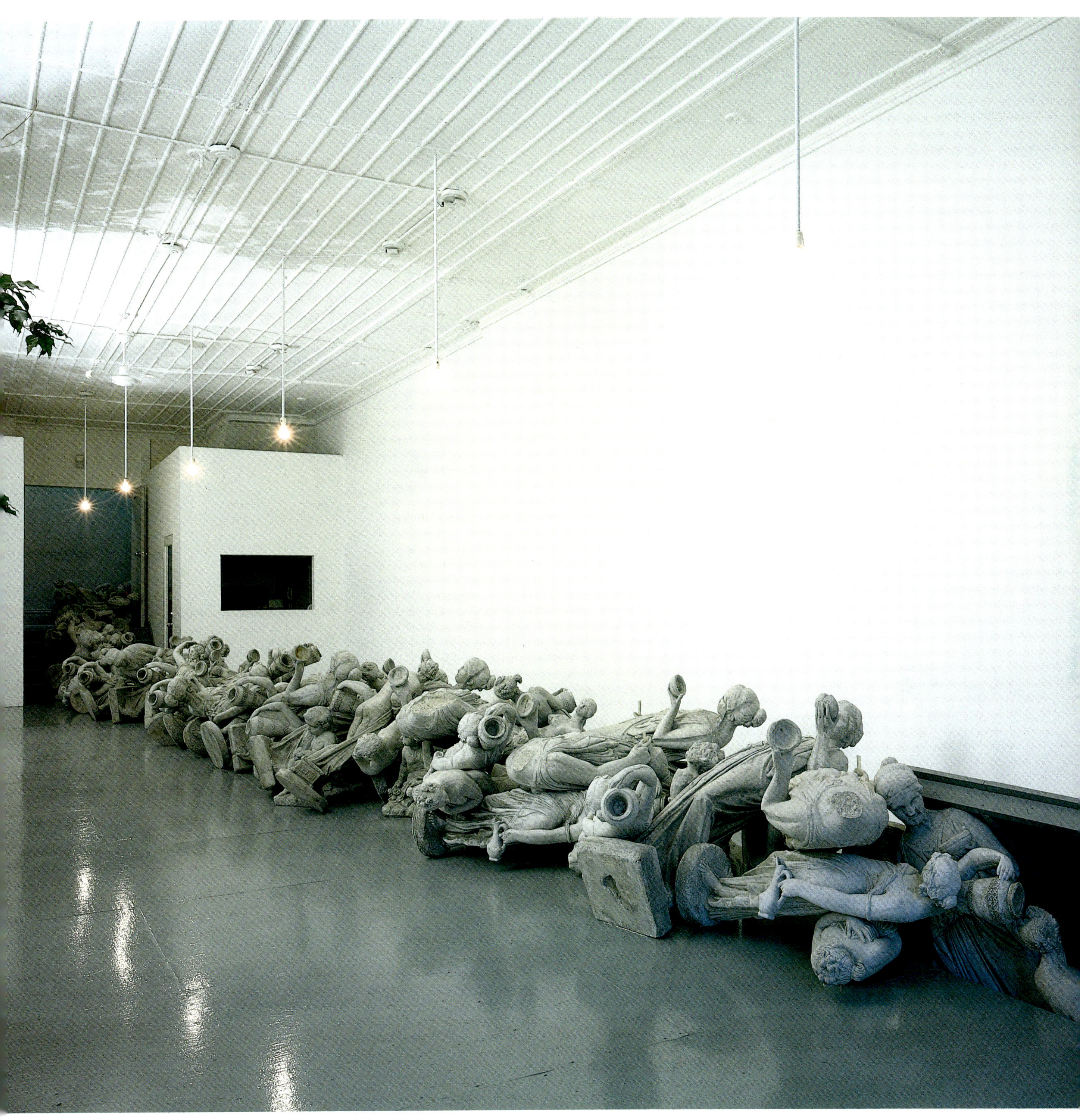

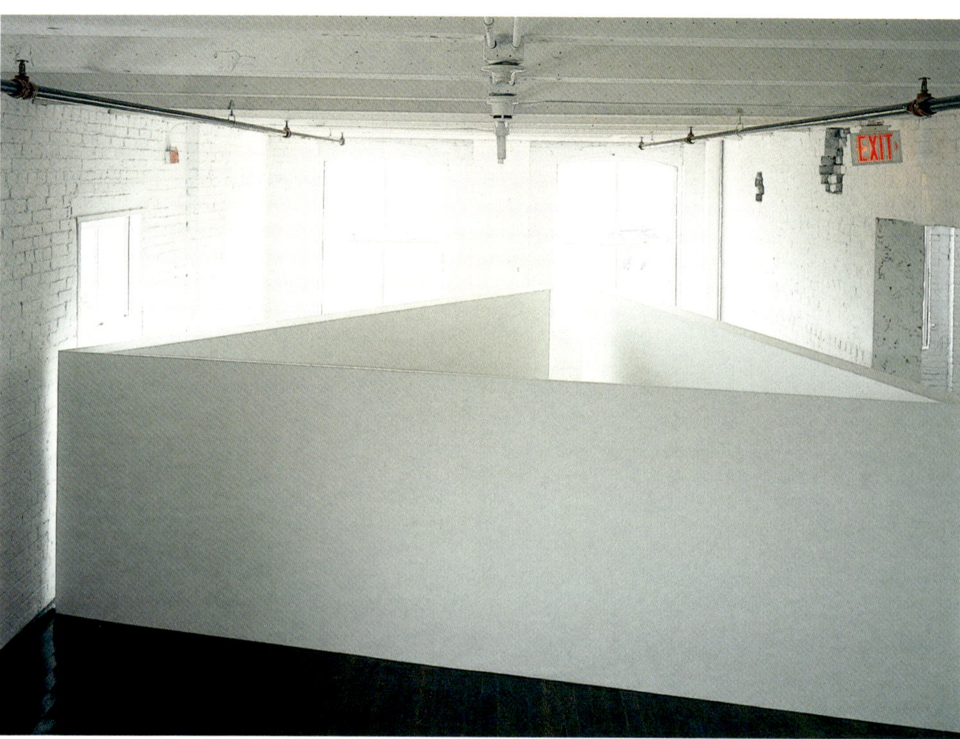


## Peter Lodato

American, born 1946

**Open Triangle 1** and **Open Triangle 2,** 1993
Plaster, wood, paint
500 Sampsonia Way, 4th floor

The artist has created two pure white installations that reflect the light as it changes throughout the day.

In one work, three walls form a triangular enclosure with an opening at one corner. The top of the wall is slightly above eye level, and slants in so that from outside, it appears to have no thickness.

The companion piece is a wall relief that is the floor plan for the enclosure. At certain times of the day, the wall relief, its recessed image three inches deep, appears to be completely flat.

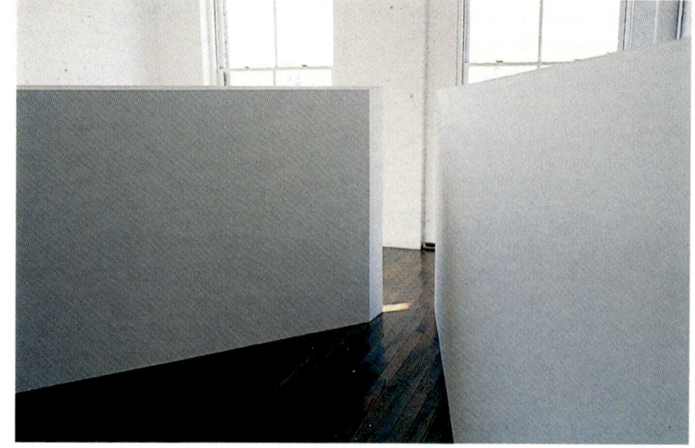

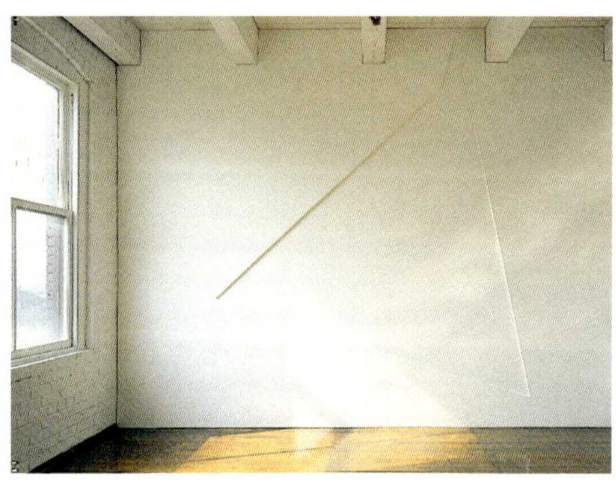

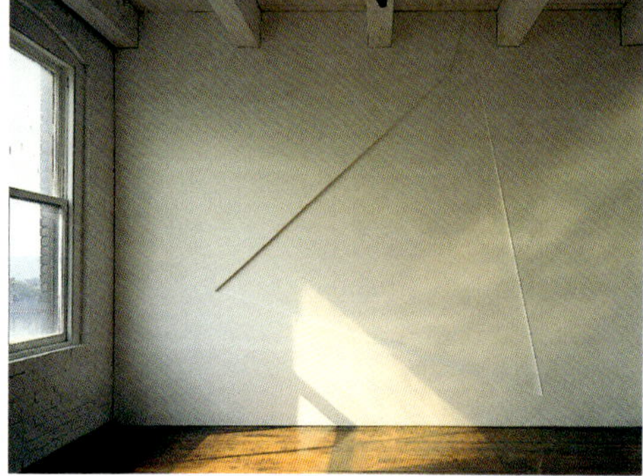

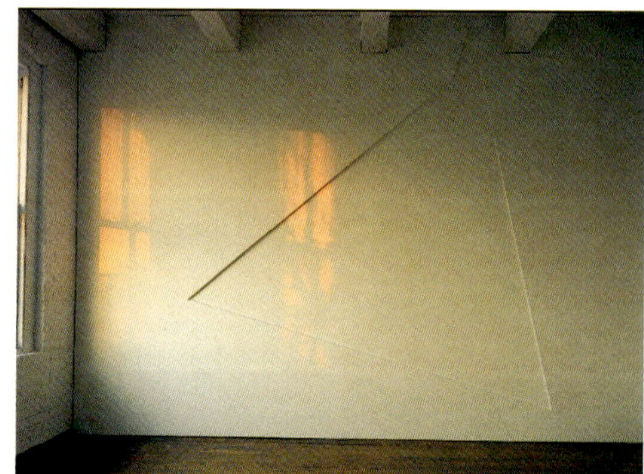

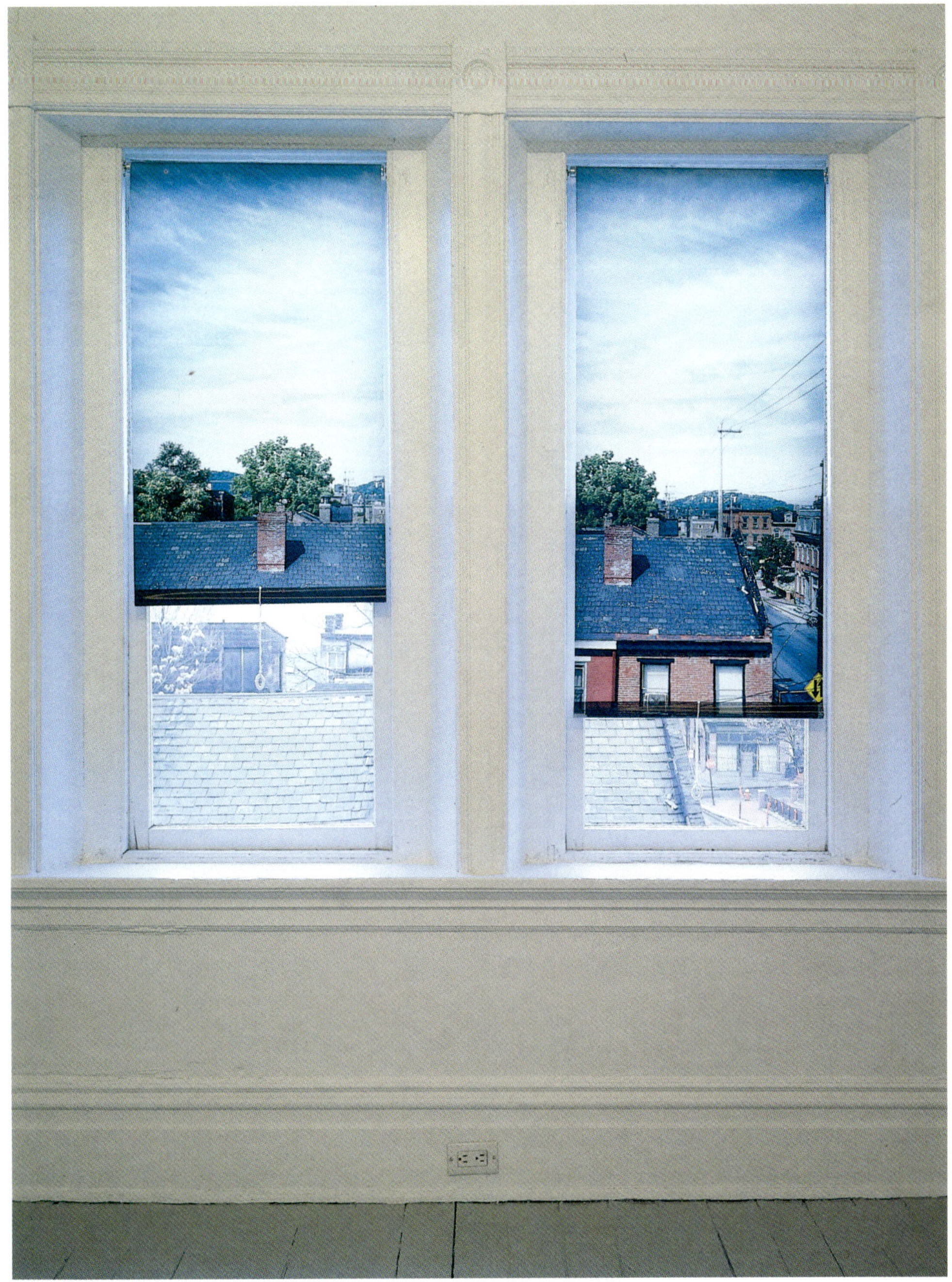

## Monica M. Bock

American, born 1960

## Mary Carlisle

American

## Cathy Lynn Gasser

American, born 1960

## Melissa Goldstein

American, born 1961

## Sandrine Sheon

American, born 1964

## Catherine Smith

American, born 1950

**A Collaboration,** 1993
Periscope, Door, Hand Rail, Window Shade, Closet Door, Balcony, Line of Scent
1414 Monterey Street, outside, and 2nd and 3rd floors

## A Collaboration

continued

Six artists worked together on all parts of this installation. Their work begins outside on the sidewalk.

There is a periscope, built in the same fashion and with the same molding as the building itself. A small binocular eyepiece provides a view to a constantly running video which shows a waterfall. The video can be seen only in this place, but it is the first of a number of references to inside and outside images.

On the second floor, a cast-resin door appears to provide entry to a gallery, but it does not open. Natural light from the windows in a closed-off gallery shines through it. Windows in the accessible gallery are covered with foam core, repeating the pattern of the tin ceiling.

Between the second and third floors, water flows down the stairway's handrails. Upon reaching the third floor, the viewer finds three windows with blinds made out of transparencies. Each is a photograph of the actual scene outside the window, taken on a beautiful, sunny day. The three shades are kept partially pulled down. The scenes may line up perfectly with the outside view, or they may not, depending upon one's height.

Between the two rooms is a small corridor, which contains a miniature version of a normal-sized door. Behind the door, the sound of running water can be heard.

A steel railing in the next gallery guides the viewer's gaze onto a horizon line cut into the wall. From the horizon line comes the scent of fresh grass.

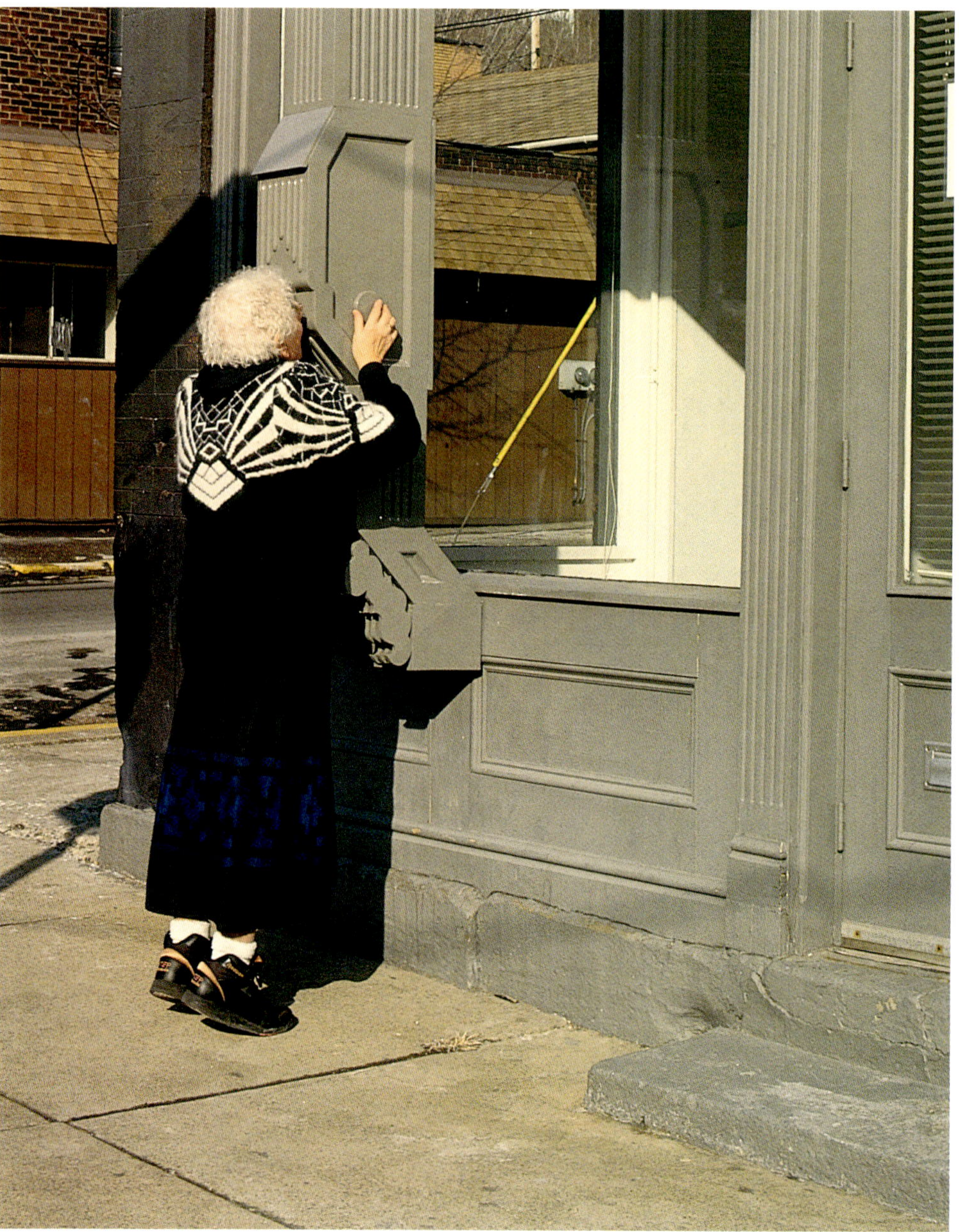

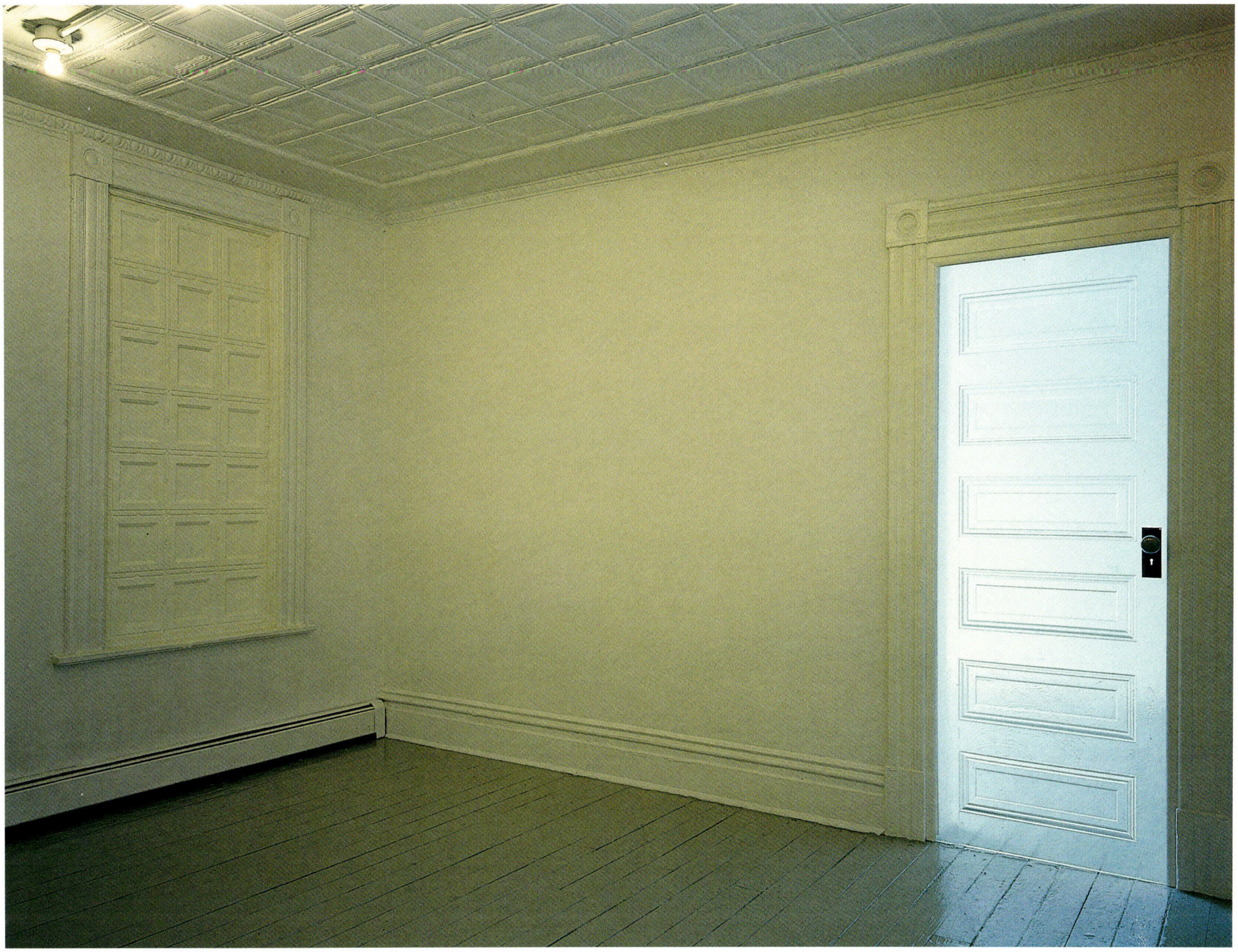

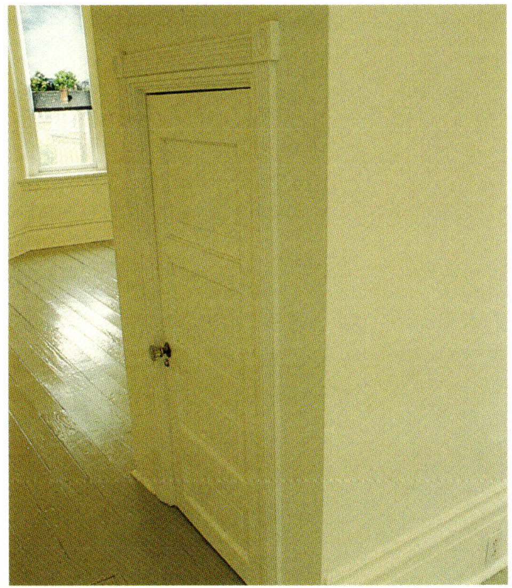

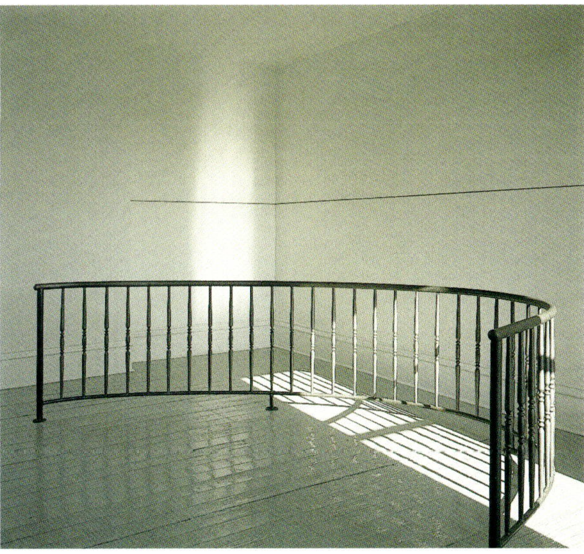

## Alison Wilding

British, born 1948

**Ambit,** 1994
Plexiglas
1414 Monterey Street, 1st floor

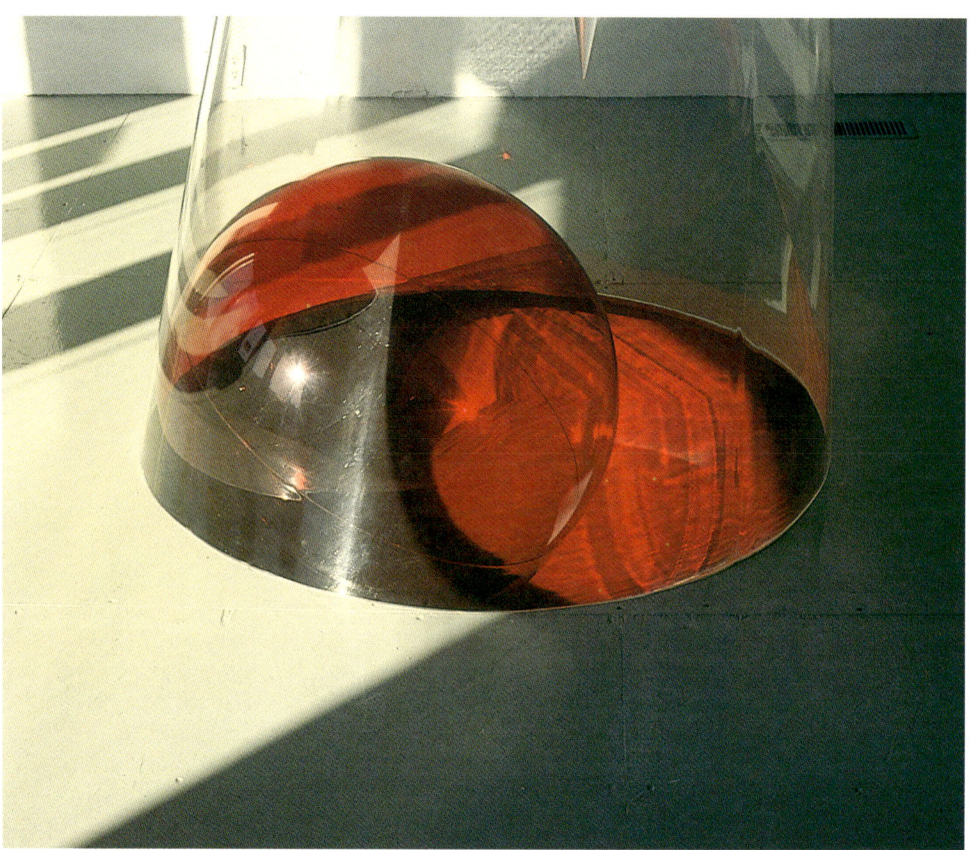

An eight-foot, transparent, Plexiglas cone is set in the middle of the gallery. Inside it, a smaller, inverted cone appears to be suspended from the top of the piece. The smaller cone has been rubbed with pumice, which has resulted in a frosted finish. The large cone also contains a red Plexiglas ball, which sits below floor level on a false floor.

The installation takes advantage of natural light, as the elements look different depending on the viewer's position. At times it seems that the red sphere has been cut off at floor level rather than dropped to a lowered platform. At other times a red glow hits the wall.

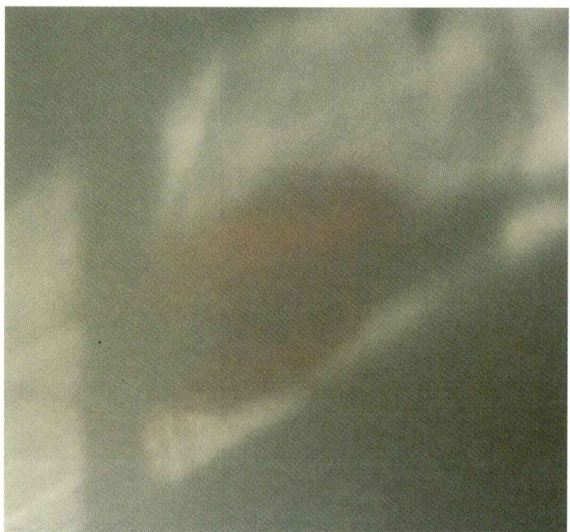

Scale is significant since this is the only element in a large gallery. The title word, "Ambit," means "an area within which something or someone exists, acts, or has influence or power."

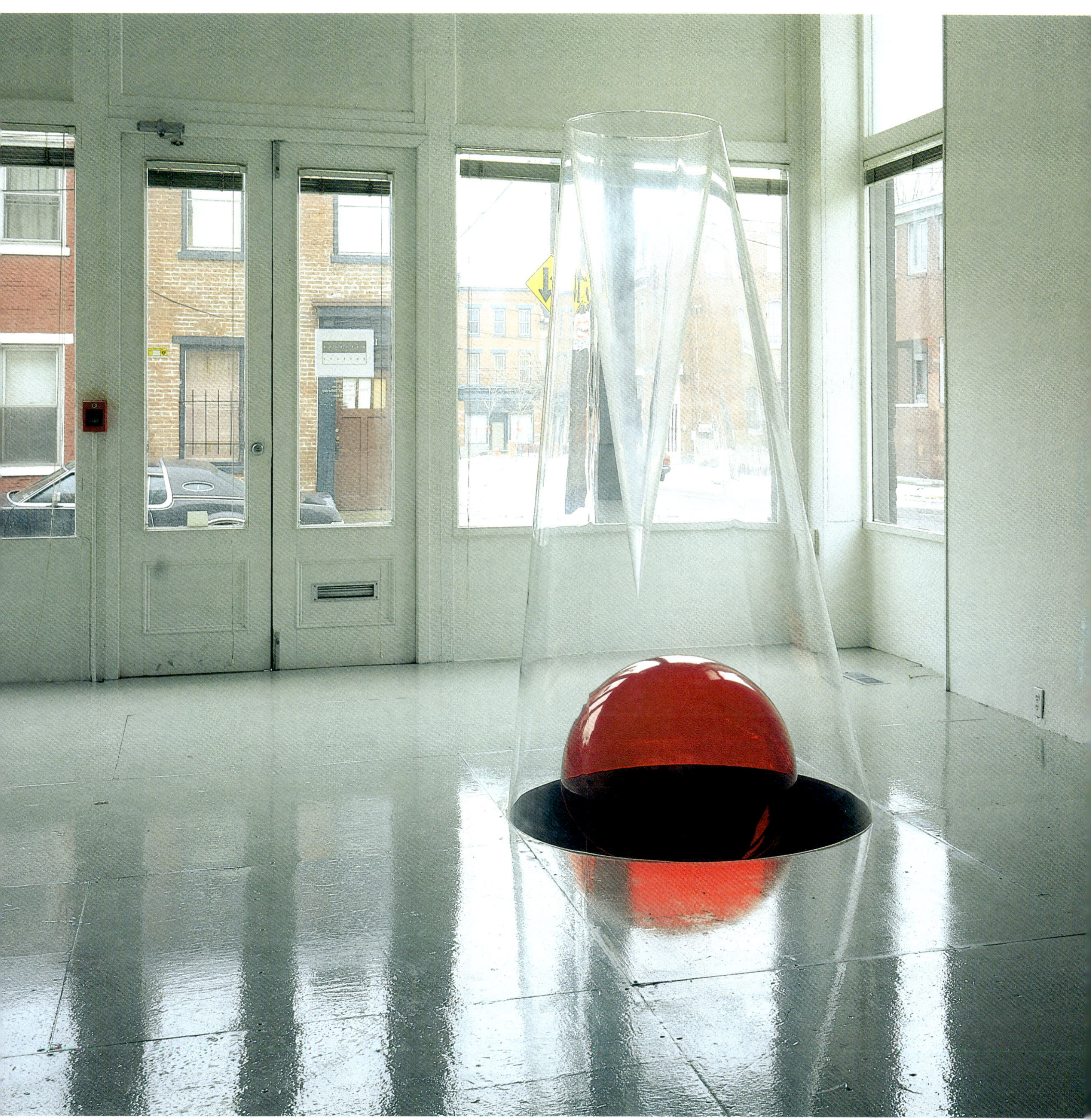

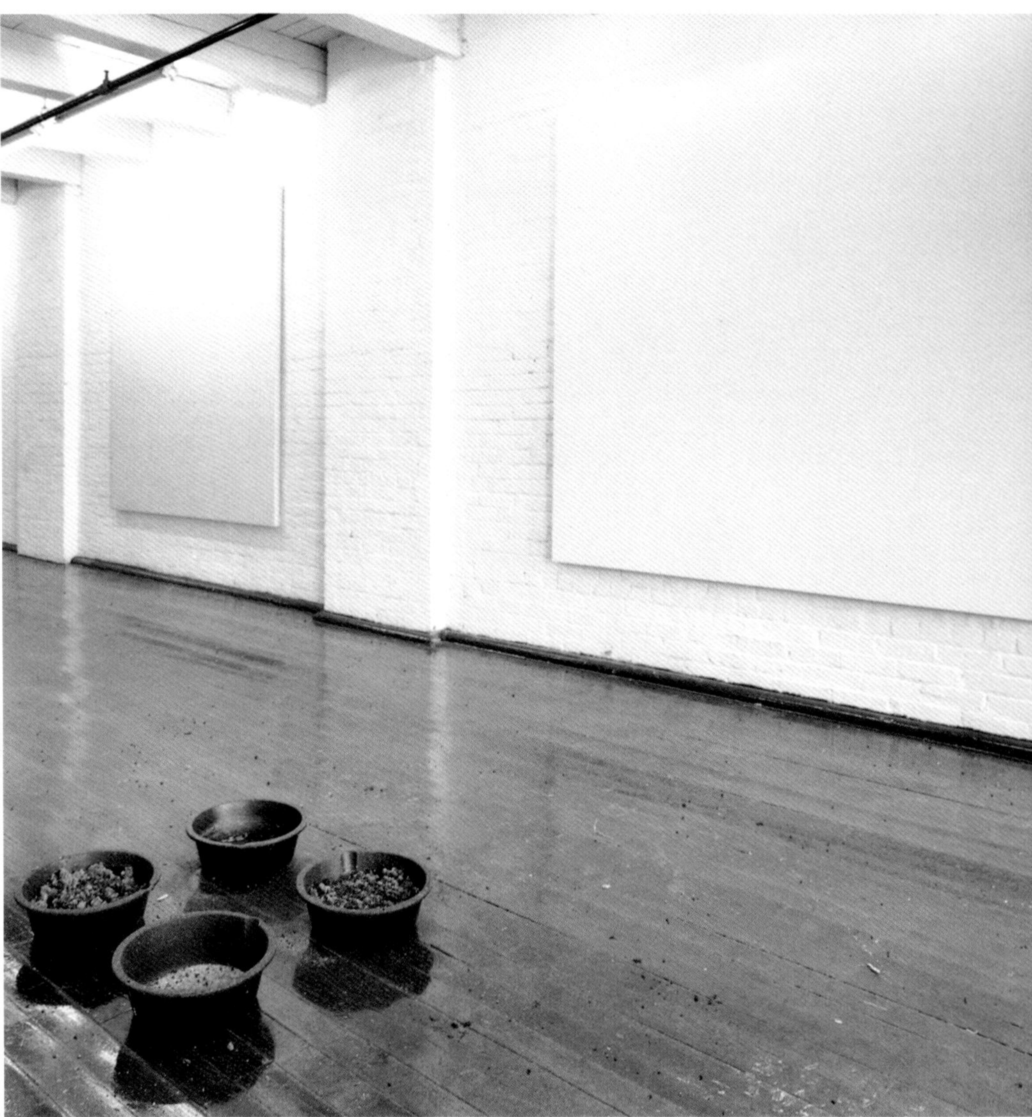

## Damien Hirst

British, born 1965

**Bad Environment for White Monochrome Paintings,** 1994
Steel, glass, acrylic on canvas, plastic containers for food and water, sarchophaga and musca domestica
500 Sampsonia Way, 4th floor
(Sheena Wagstaff, curator)

A fifty-foot corridor of glass and steel separates the viewing public from the gallery. There are four white monochrome paintings, measuring seven feet square, in each of two galleries. Three paintings, hanging on the walls, have been sprayed with sugar water. The fourth, propped horizontally on sawhorses, has been painted with a clear adhesive that never dries.

In front of each painting, four black bowls sit on the floor. In each set of bowls, one contains powdered sugar and powdered milk; another contains water and is covered with gauze; and two contain a mixture of molasses, wheat germ, yeast and water, where flies can lay their eggs. Maggots were initially placed in the medium, to set the natural process in motion. As the maggots become flies, they drink the water and eat the food, which is changed regularly.

The installation opened with pristine cleanliness. As time passes, the flies multiply and die, and the space and the canvases become dirtier.

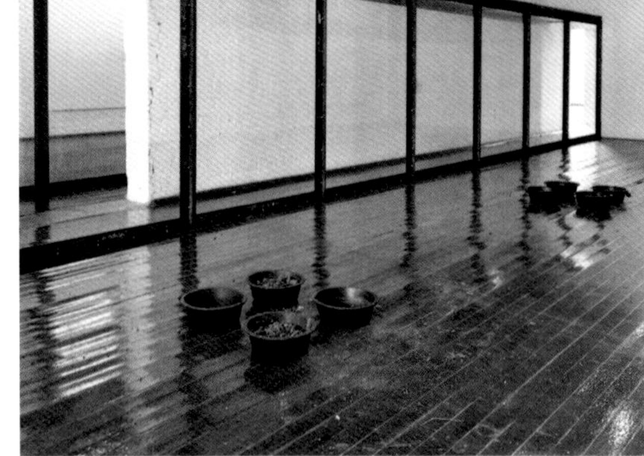

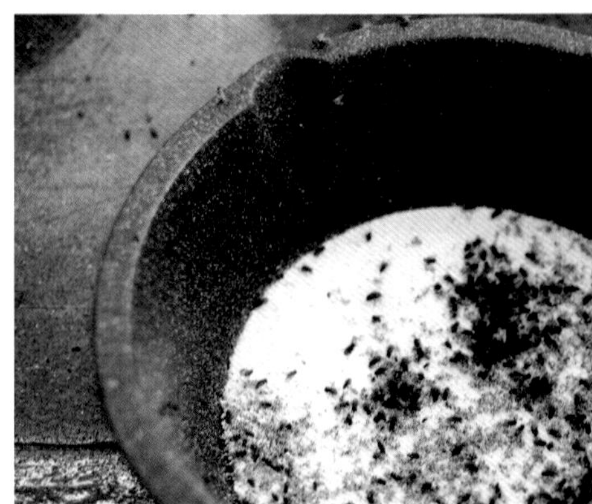

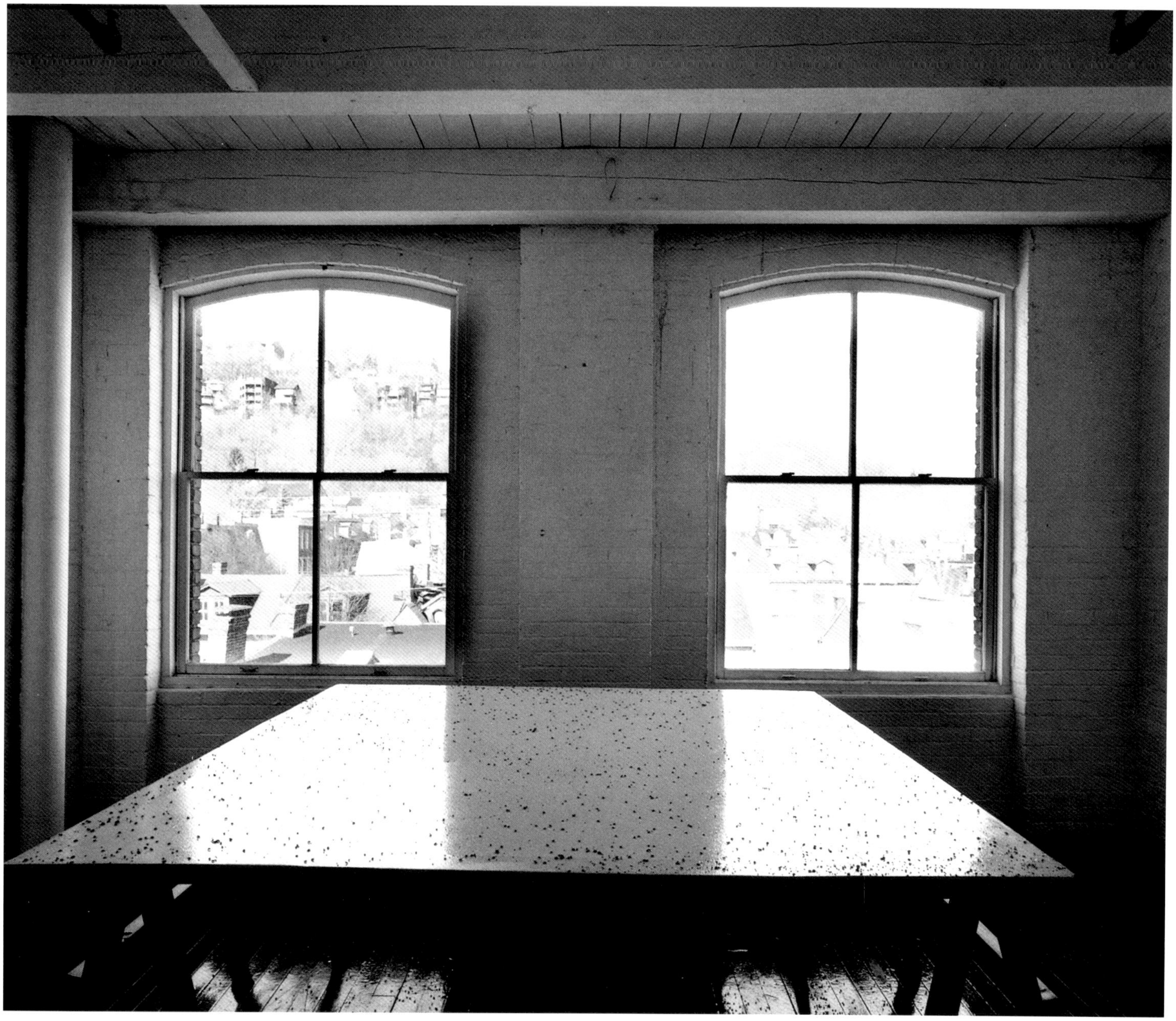

**Artist's Statement**

Art seems to me to be about life. I make art; I try to make it alive.

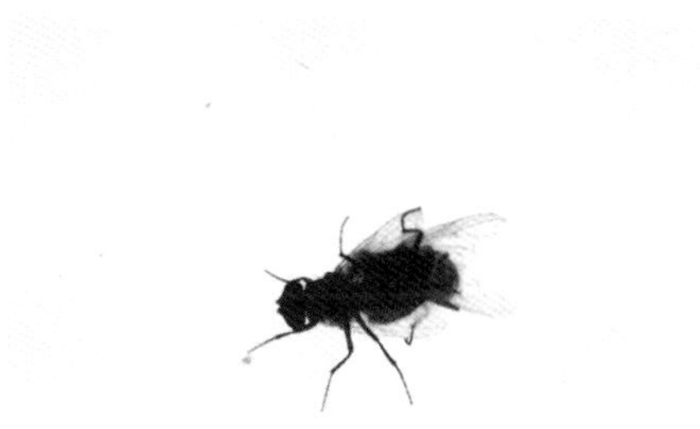

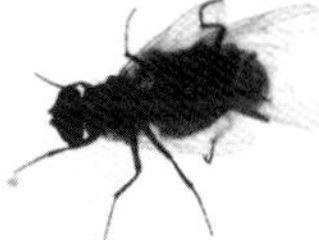

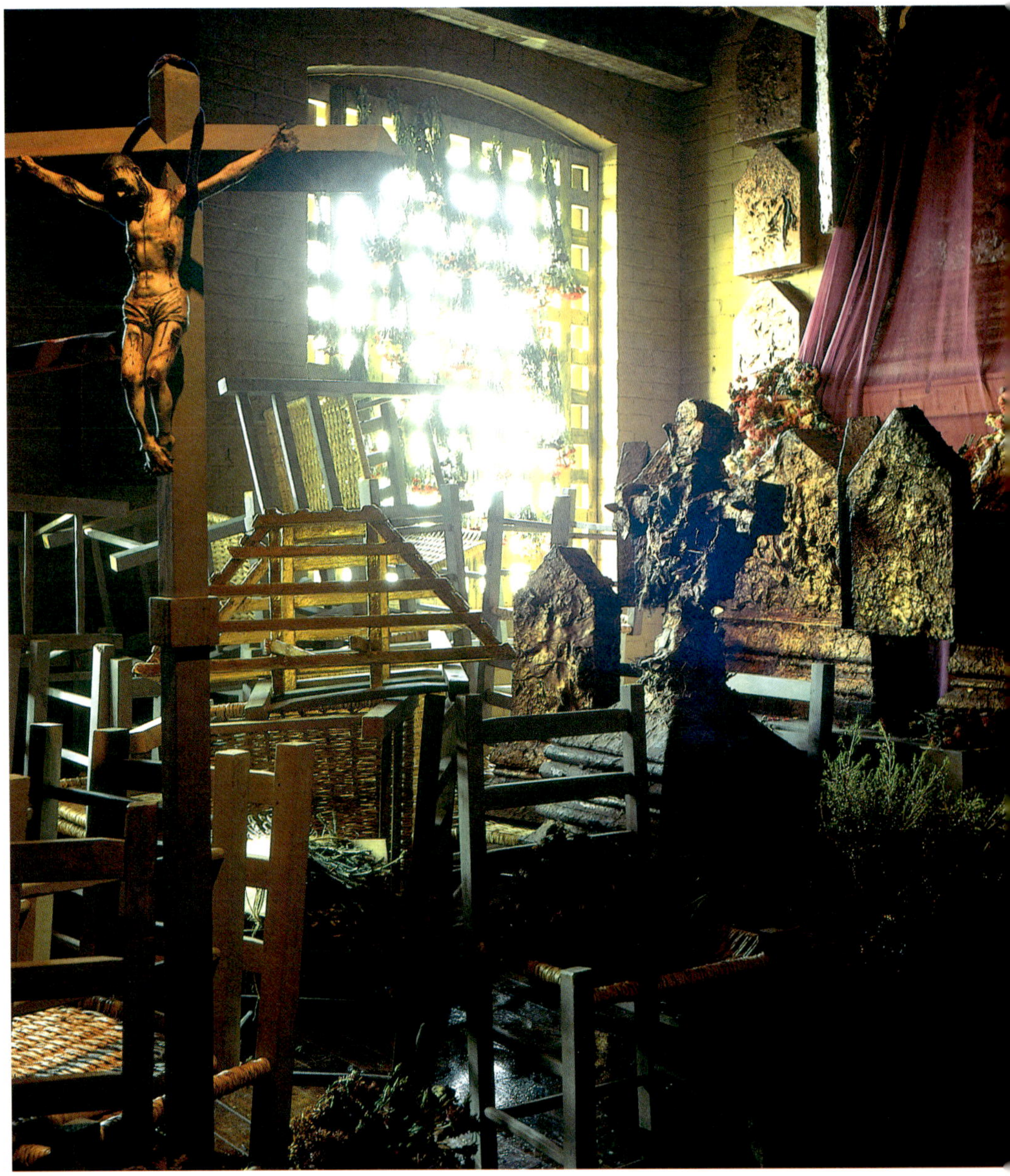

## Michael Tracy

American, born 1943

**Chapel: In the Mexican War Streets,** 1994
Mixed media: 15 years of past work
500 Sampsonia Way, 3rd floor
(Sheena Wagstaff, curator)

The entire installation is arranged and constructed according to the principles of ecclesiastical architecture. The first room, which Tracy describes as the "passive space," is a storage area. A combination of his altarpieces, crosses, tabernacles, and oil paintings are housed there.

The "active space," which consists of an altar to the left and a sacristy to the right, functions as a performance space. This area contains huge, golden triptychs, dark Stations of the Cross, an altar pierced with machetes, and rows of mesquite chairs.

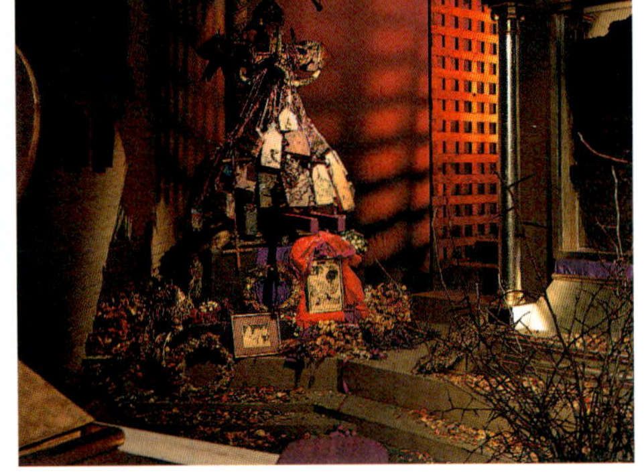

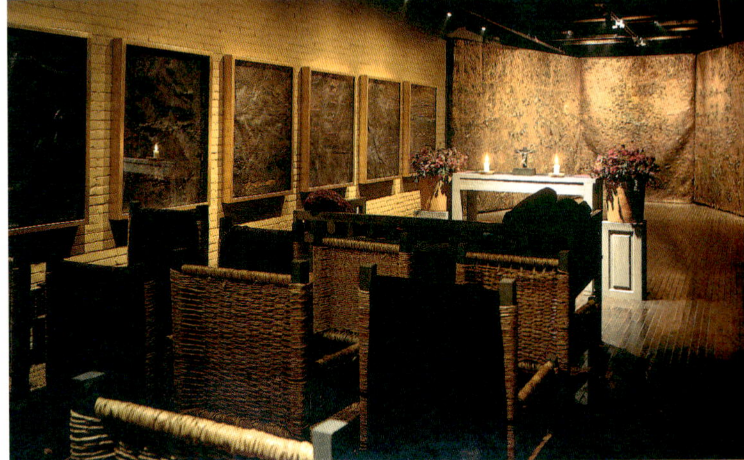

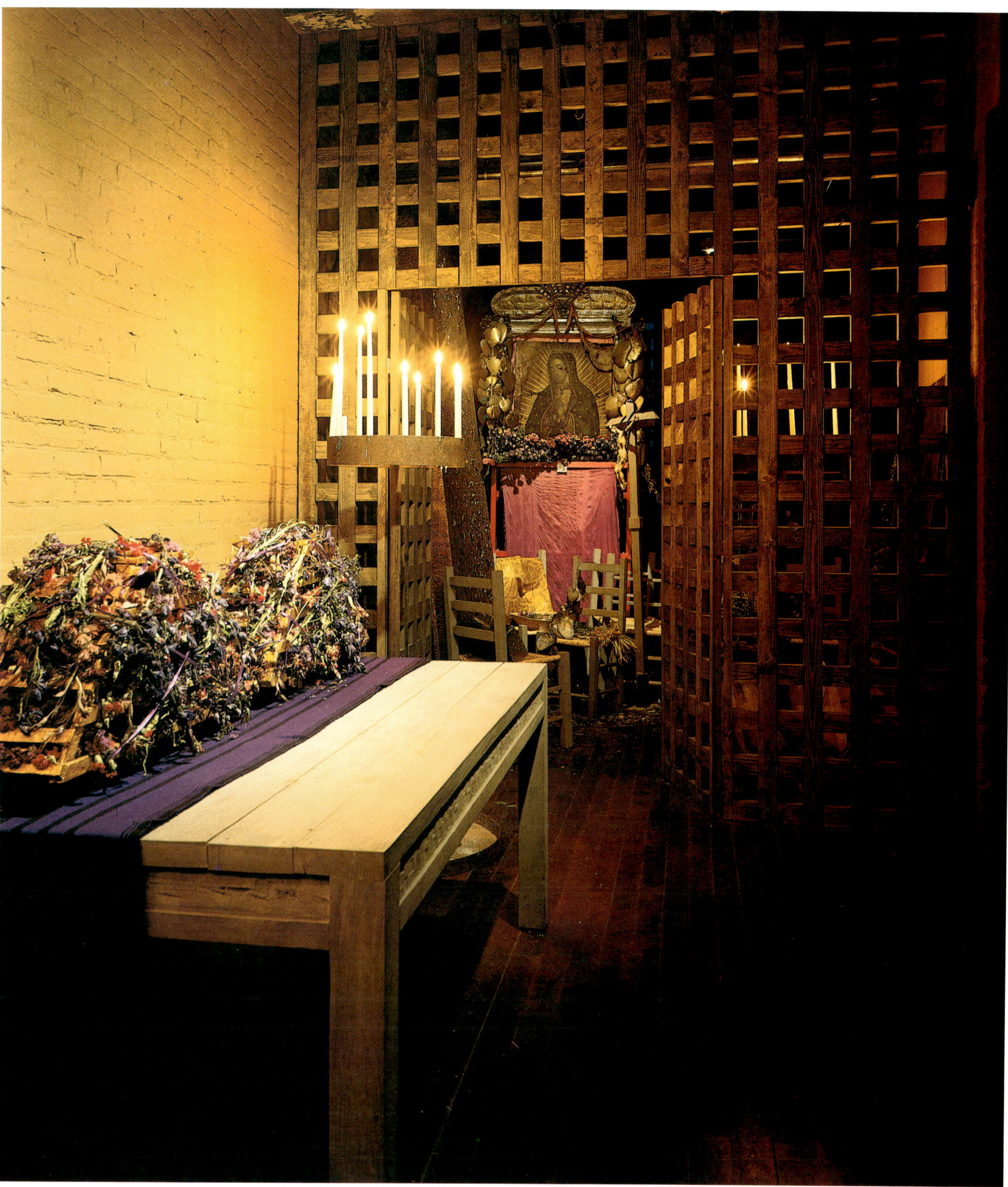

## James Turrell

American, born 1943

**Soft Cell,** 1992 (exhibited 1994)
Aluminum frame, acoustic foam rubber, laser light, carpet, and other materials
500 Sampsonia Way, 1st floor

One viewer at a time walks up carpeted steps and enters the enclosure, which is covered inside and out with soundproof foam. The viewer closes the door and sits down in a chair. A red laser light is reflected off of a white disk on the door. It takes about fifteen minutes for the viewer's eyes to adjust to the dim light.

*Soft Cell* is part of a series of "Perceptual Cells" that the artist has been developing, in different formats, over a number of years. Each is a portable, autonomous unit that encloses the viewer in an environment where perception is altered.

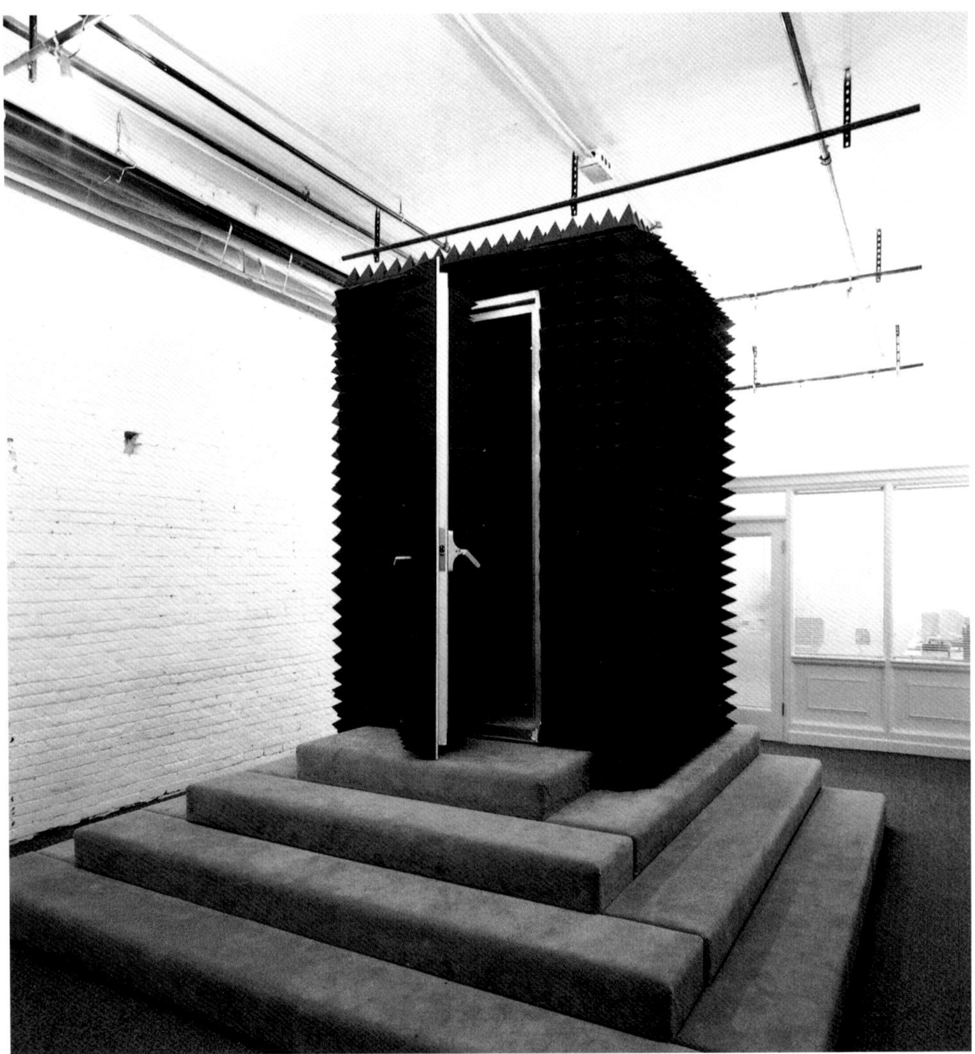

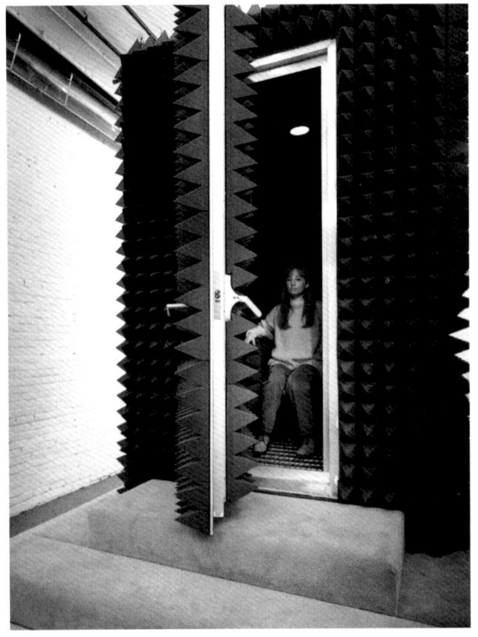

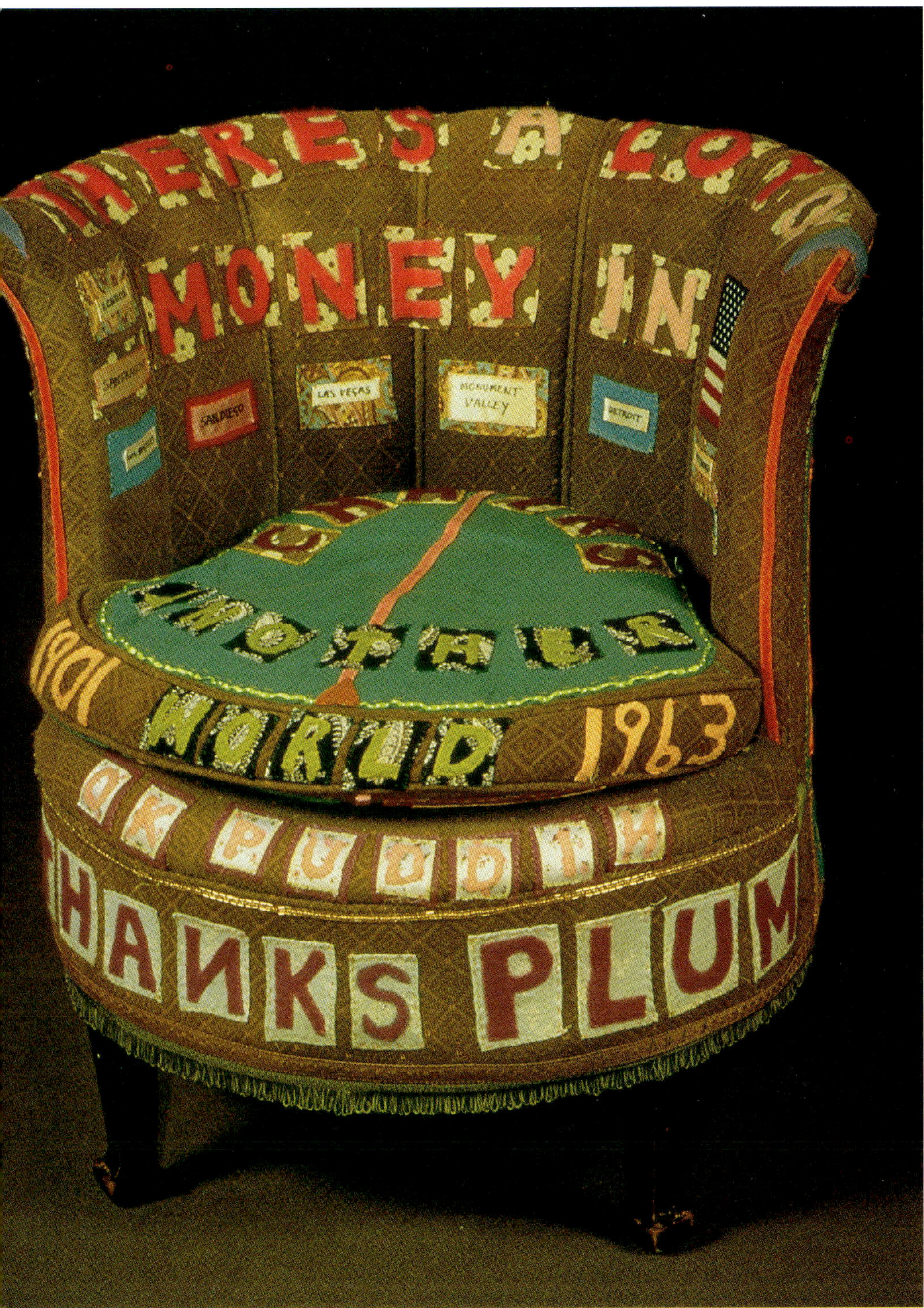


## Tracey Emin

British, born 1963

**Performance,** October 8, 1994
A reading from *Exploration of the Soul—A Journey across America*
500 Sampsonia Way, 1st floor

**Artist's Statement**

A few years ago my Nan gave me a small green bucket-shaped arm chair. It's not that special to look at, in fact, it's a bit shabby. My Nan is ninety-three now and the chair is nearly as old as she is—when she gave me the chair she told me:

> "There's a lot of money in chairs."

I believe that she is right—I've decided that this chair is my inheritance—an inheritance to my future. I have decorated the chair with patchwork, embroidery and appliqué. It tells the story of my life. I've written a book called *Exploration of the Soul* which is about me—my beginning—from the moment of conception to the time I lost my virginity: age 0–13.

I will travel across America by car to San Francisco from New York with the chair and copies of my book. I will be giving one-night performances reading my book in galleries and other venues.

## Robert Beckman

American, born 1958

**Examination,** 1994
Type C photographs, drywall, metal studs, slide projector and video equipment, fabric
1414 Monterey Street, 1st floor

The installation begins behind a blue curtain. The curtain provides an opening to a kind of studio. Tables, fixed walls, and two rolling walls are constructed from metal studs and unfinished drywall. Photos of body parts hang in front of blue fabric curtains. Piles of photos and tracing paper lie carelessly on the tables. The space is always in flux during the exhibition. The artist reorders the layering of information by moving objects around, tracing new images, and putting new images on top of photos.

Two large photographs of a transparent man and woman illustrate human organ systems. Cadaver trays contain similar photos of body parts, and the floor is strewn with other images. Two TV monitors provide yet another layer of information: one monitor displays a live shot of the slide projections being shown as the visitor enters the space, while the other monitor runs a video of slide projections previously shown.

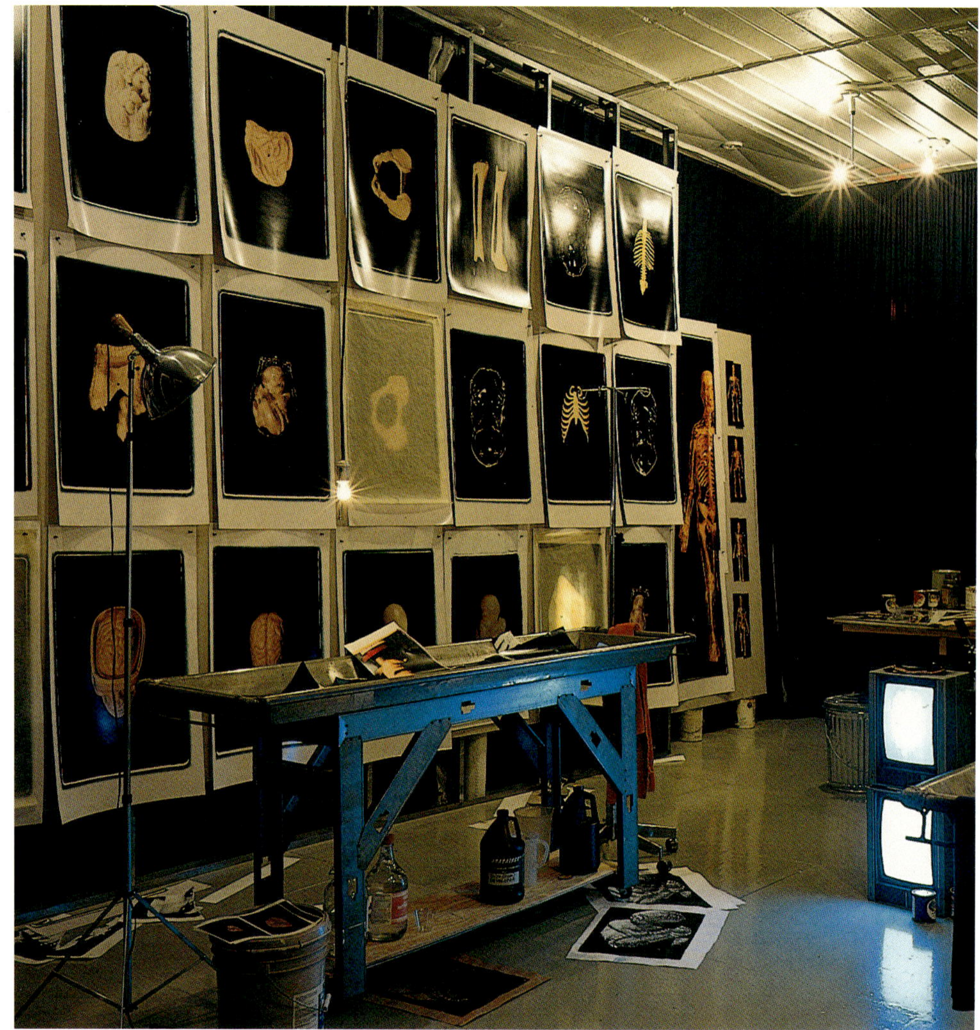

**Artist's Statement**

This installation is an investigation of "other ways of knowing." The basic idea was to create a space where the participant could suspend his or her relationship to the outside world and allow the physical and non-physical residue of an urgent and obsessive activity to determine the significance of the space. . . . Each element was chosen for its implied reference to an idea or activity: blue fabric for its reference to theater, religion, ritual and performance; steel tables for their reference to the clinical, the scientific; a model of the human figure for its reference to the physicality of being human; the clear shell of the human model for its reference to transcendence beyond the physical. . . . Photography was chosen as the means of investigation for its capacity to quickly document material with an implied truthfulness. The fact that these images are of plastic organs and that photography has nothing to do with truth creates tension between what is known and what is understood.

The space is meant to suggest the idea of activity itself rather than the idea of a finished product or position. All of the elements of construction and creation have been left visible and nothing has been made permanent. Every item has been fabricated concentrating on its function or implied function within the space, not its existence as object. This sense of transience and residual activity concentrates our experience on the idea of process rather than outcome.

The process of creating this space has been a dance between the tendency to impose and articulate meaning and the ability to allow meaning and significance to exist in a purer form through activity itself.

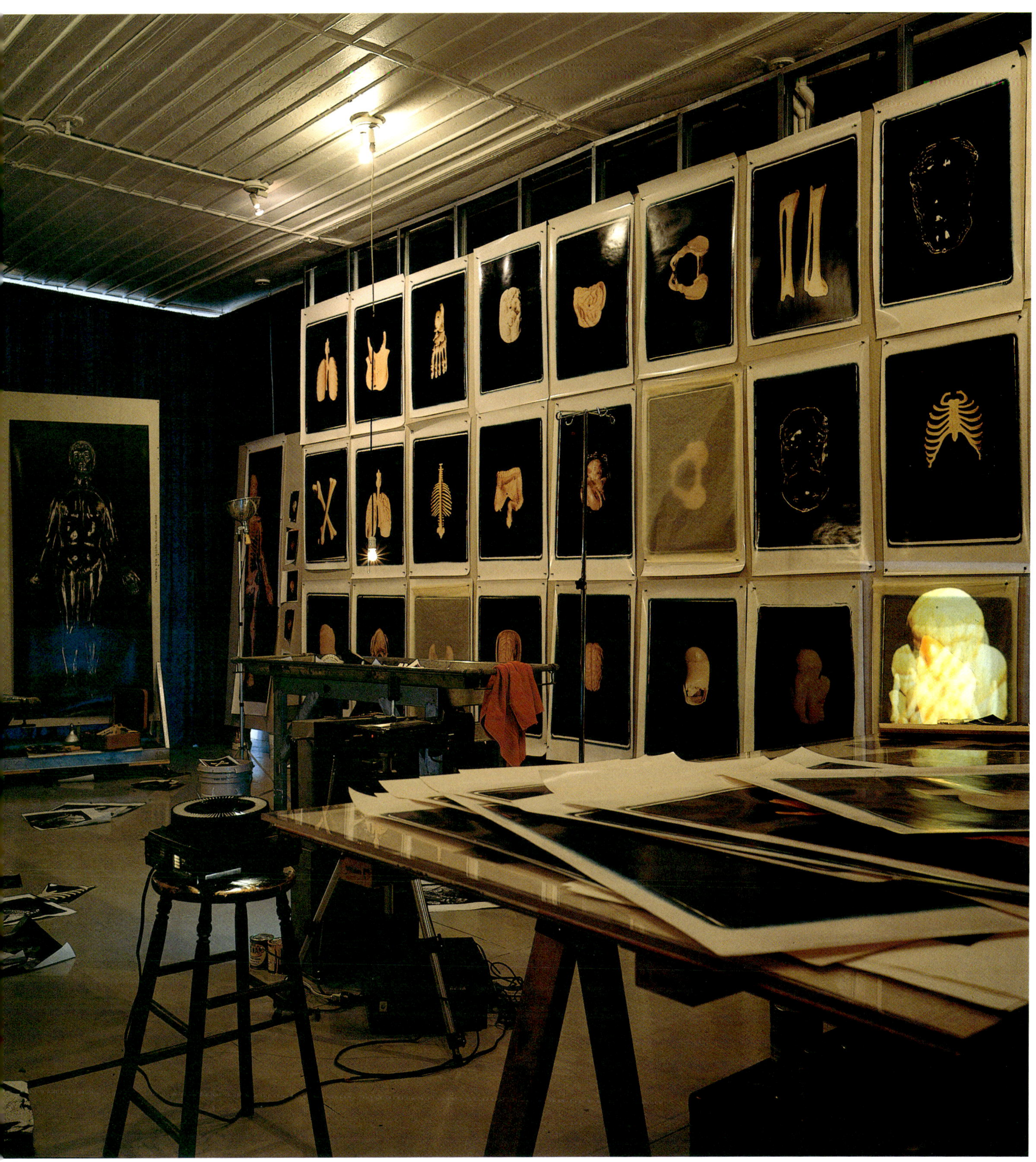

## Bob Karstadt

American

**Raphael (a Healing Machine)** or
**The Humming Bird Waltz,** 1994
**The Seraphim Buoy on Archangel Pond,** 1994
Copper, salt, honey, corn oil, glass, sweet potato, mirror, plant materials, quartz
1414 Monterey Street, 2nd floor

A copper tripod construction made of feathers, wire, and other found objects rests on a circular bed of salt in the center of the first room. In an adjoining room, another copper tripod construction stands on a circular bed of salt. Six ovoid mirrors surround the structure at its base. The two constructions, which according to the artist both produce and absorb energy, are made of materials traditionally regarded as having power: honey, salt, crystals, oil, and copper.

Instructions accompanying the first copper construction direct the viewer to put on a headdress hanging on the wall and to remove a wand with a scoop on the end from the base of the structure. The viewer is then instructed to dip into one of three hanging containers and remove salt, honey, or flour and pour it on the growing material—a sweet potato in a container resting on the bed of salt. The headdress includes orbs filled with honey; thus the person wearing it must look through the honey. The copper structure sits in a circle of rock salt, which turns the copper green. Crystals, placed at the center of glass disks, resemble radar dishes.

With a wand from the wall in the second room, the viewer may pick up a bit of oil at the base of the piece and pour it into a funnel. From there, the oil runs slowly along wires. After it drips, a viewer may use a blade of grass, dipped in the oil, to write his or her name. Barely visible marks on the window result from a drawing made of honey.

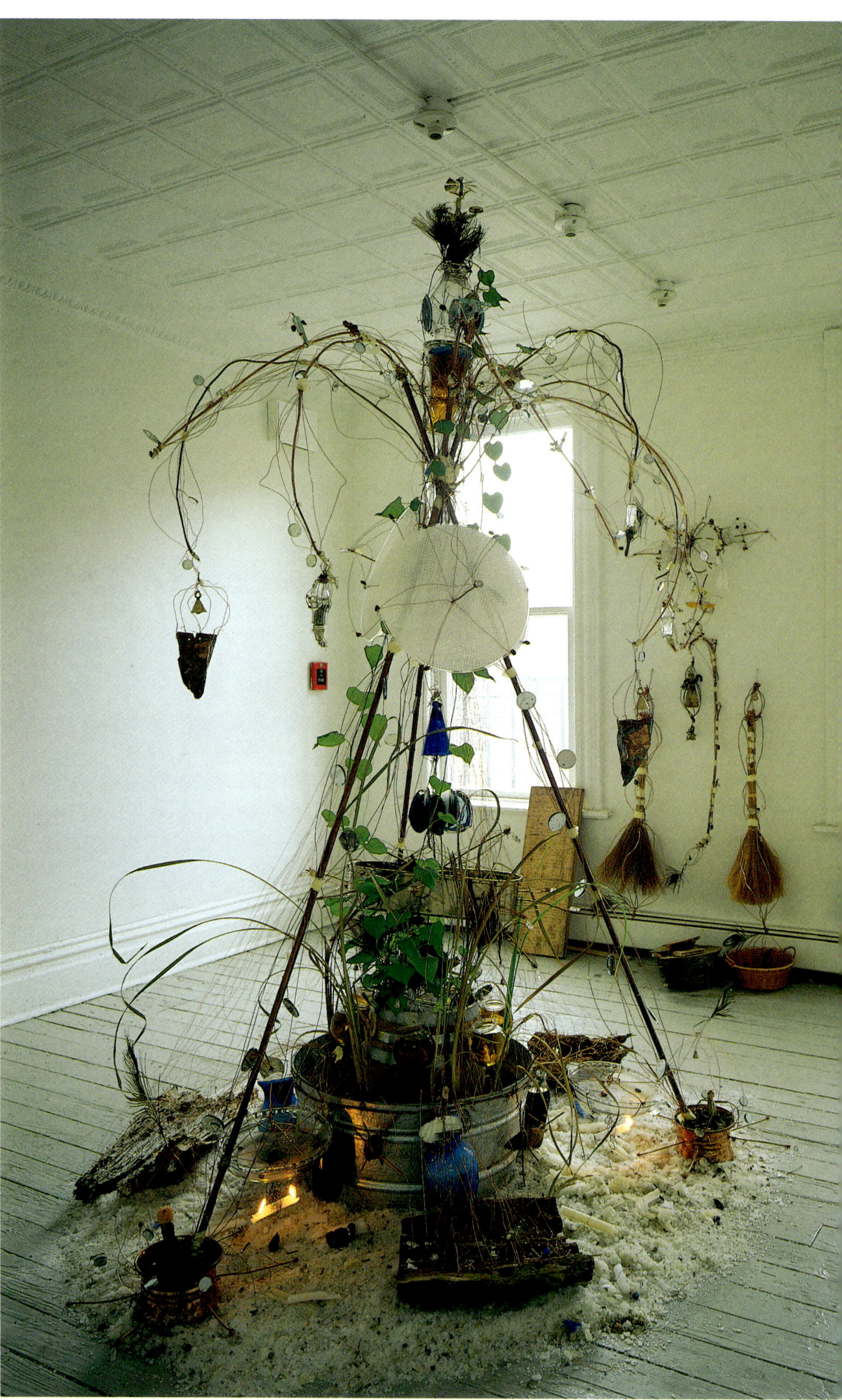

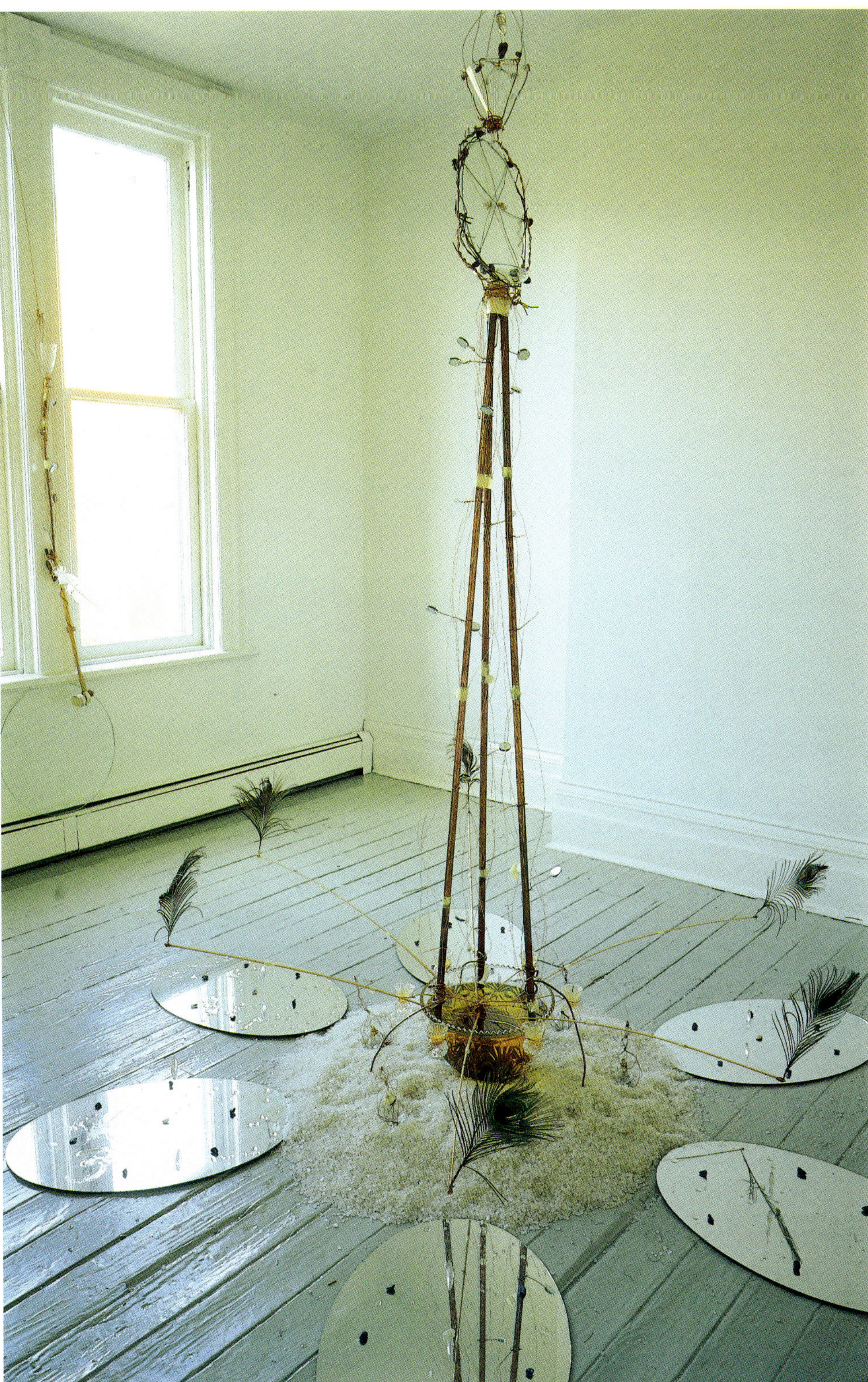

**Artist's Statement**

Blue eye flame spins gold sound, speaks wind
Hummingbird wings kiss blue, dusting Y
Blue light drips to heart root swims sweet gold
Seraphim eyes Ellu
Sifts
Speaks
Copper Cloud
Light
Sifts
Speaks
Ground
Reflect Jasper

Winged community fly sea gold orbs
Ear fixture light hold crystal song, vortex wings
Blue horns six moons sing chest finger waltz
Root center triangle
Ashes spin fish eternal
sifts
wheat
commune
House field seeds
Residue rests home shards
Eye root circle nurtures Book, journeys nestled
on delta growth through Earth white
Spots Leave
Lungs sail clear
Further table spice lights song

Enoch's tree copper words speak, sings
Waves through heart root
Ice grow Lead Vortex
Salt Melts
Double Vortex waltz holds root fruit
Electricity
Home breath through window, spoken name
Book travels wax salt deluge
Spot leaves eye roots
Copper sun pierces Lead door
Dance Dessert yellow
Circle river
Crystal ocean
Two ended flame clots wound
Sweet Enoch's light pierces jasper wall
Names skim light pound
Buoys light guides white ship
Sea both sides
Veil lifts
Ellu

## Kate Temple

American, born 1966

**Elemental Correspondence,** 1994–1995
**Mineral Cycle—October 22, 1994**
Minerals were collected from various states including Vermont, Virginia, Pennsylvania, Oklahoma, Texas, New Mexico, Arizona, and South Dakota.
**Plant Cycle—December 5, 1994**
Vegetable matter, including lily-of-the-valley leaves, goldenrod, chrysanthemum, marigold, zinnia, wild chokecherry, blueberries, black walnuts, and butternuts
**Animal Cycle—January 16, 1995**
Animal matter, including milk, egg yolk, crushed shell, burned bones, cochineal, squid ink, and animal ashes
1414 Monterey Street, 3rd floor

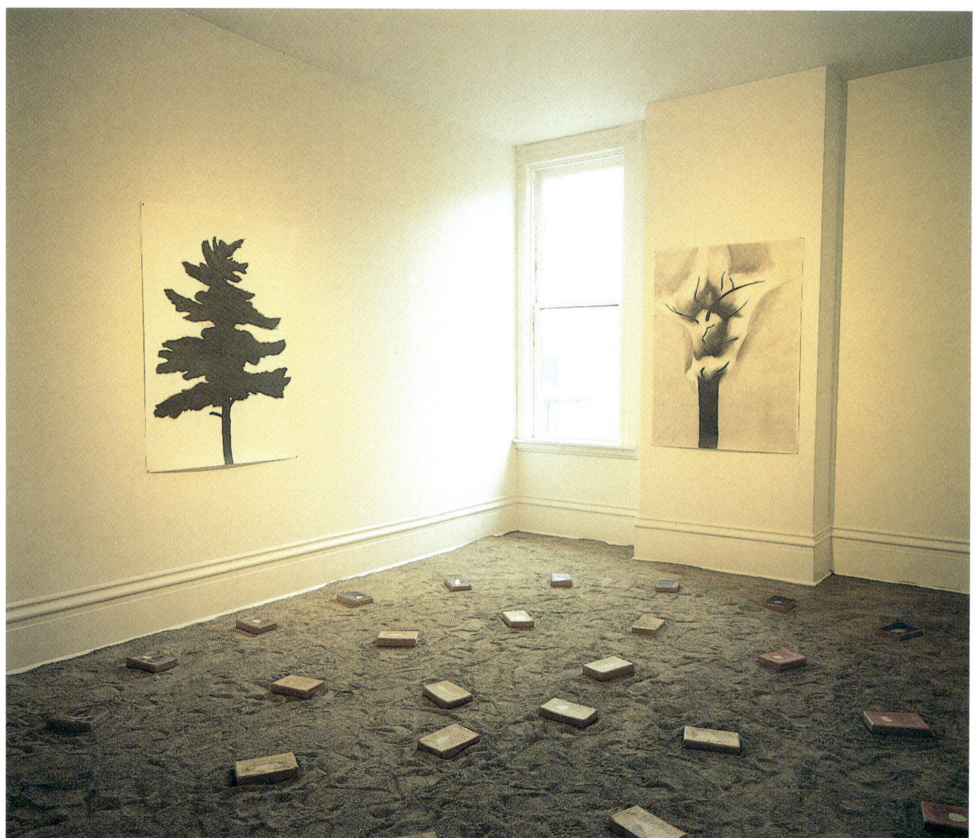

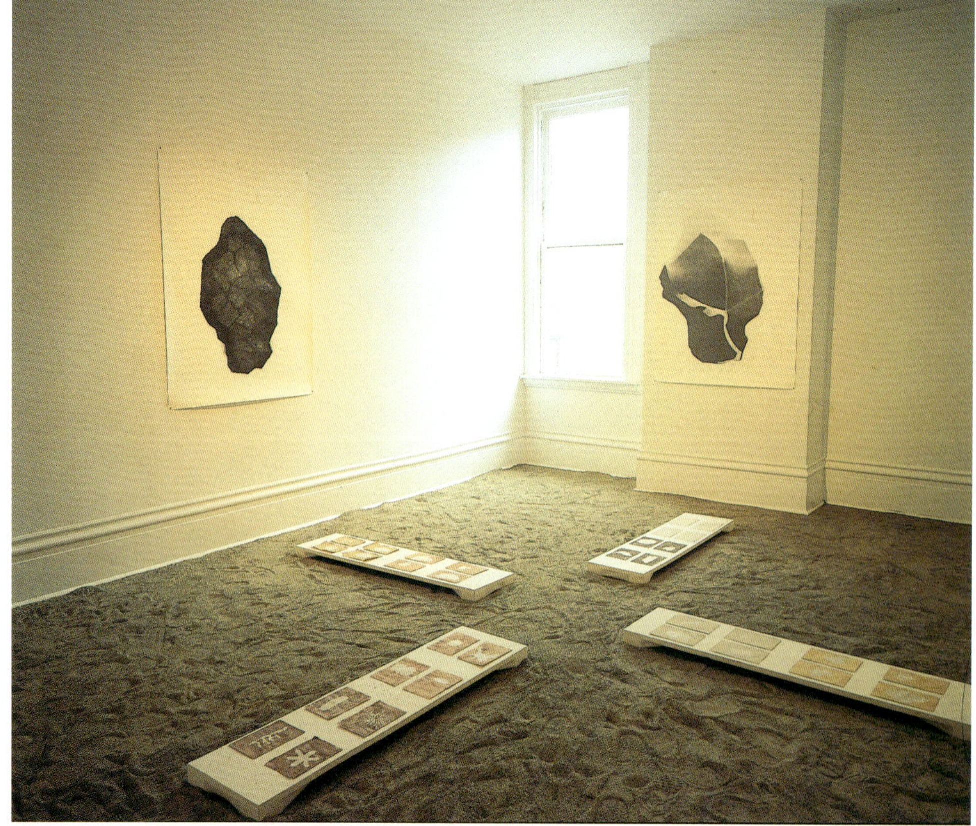

The installation consists of items collected on walks through wooded areas in the U.S. The objects are divided into three categories—mineral, plant, and animal—and arranged throughout two rooms. The piece is presented in cycles, with the artist working in the spaces prior to each cycle. Found objects are arranged on a plaster circle in the center of one room. In the adjoining room, the artist painted with pigment made from animal, plant or mineral material, as appropriate, on pages torn from an Italian edition of Dante's *Inferno.* These paintings were mounted on small canvases and arranged on a bed of sand. Charcoal drawings on the walls correspond to the four cardinal directions.

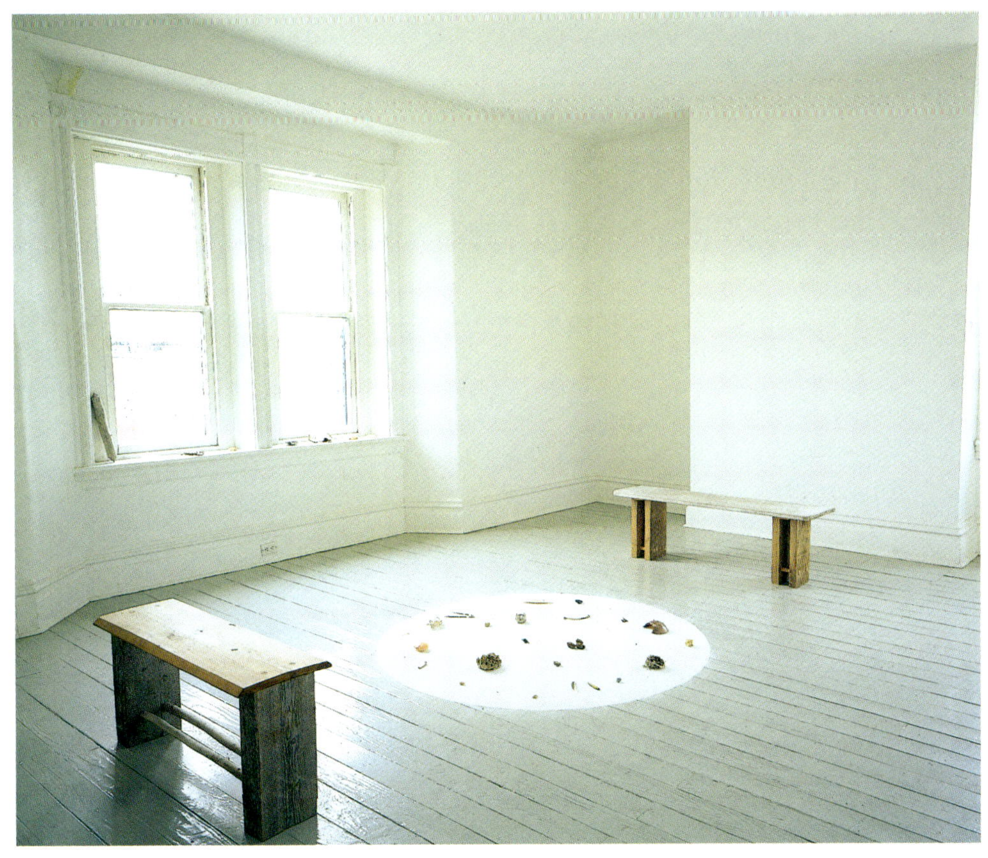

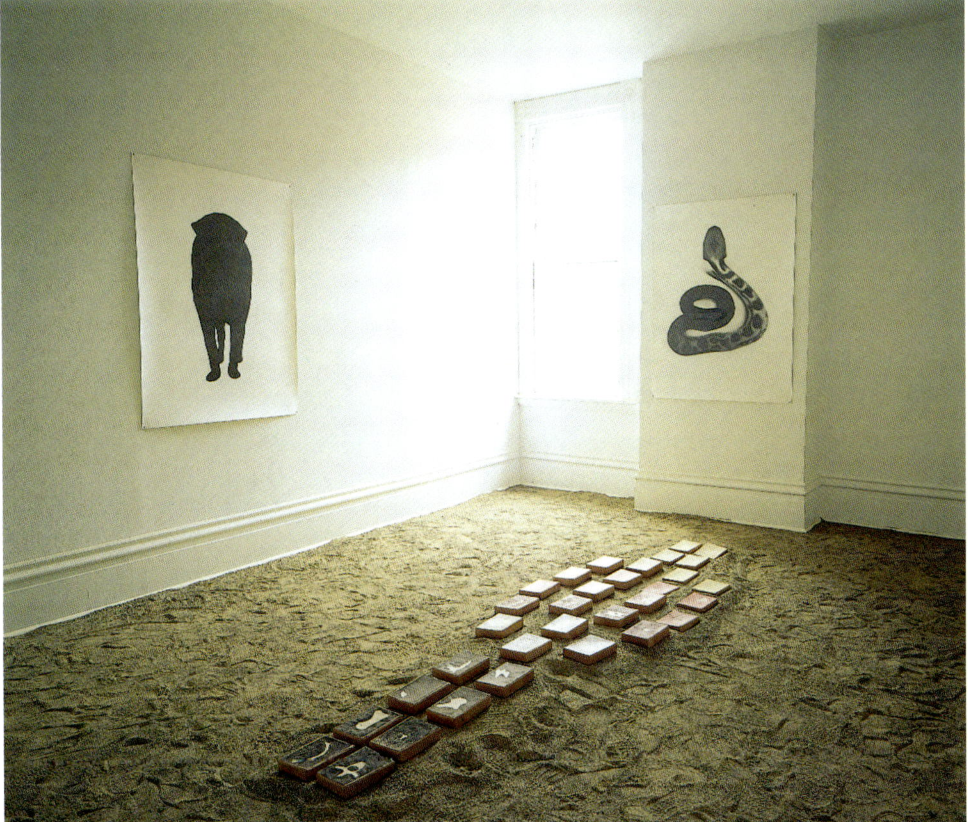

**Artist's Statement**

This work is part of an ongoing exploration into the nature of the elements—air, water, earth, fire—as they move through forms and as they depart, leaving behind their tracks on the dead matter. During the course of several years, in spring, summer, fall, winter, I walked east, south, west, north until a piece of the world spoke to me—animal, plant, mineral. Then, either through its form or substance, the exchange was recorded.

The drawings, executed in graphite, are records of form—found and seen—with the sense of a dominant element at work within the body. The small paintings are tracks of the singular, voices of the world's substance outside of form; the colors are derived from various mineral, vegetable, and animal substances. Assembled in the form of a compass, the singular tracks constitute the beginning of a series of trails, which will move through three separate cycles as time passes.

Each living thing has its own correspondence to the elements, the cardinal directions, the change of seasons, the journey from birth to death. While following one of life's minute particulars, one becomes an active participant, a tracker. The act of tracking involves a keen awareness of place and time, usually informed by the direction of the wind, the flow of bodies of water, the slopes of the earth, and the journey of the sun. Yet at the moment one achieves a certain understanding of the track ahead, a new impression is added to the trail behind, thus we become the track as well as the tracker.

It is within this active mediation that the individual's particular track can contribute to a series of collective trails by which one can resurvey the paths drawn between ourselves and the rest of the living world.

## Alumet

## Astrid Tielemans

Dutch, born 1953

## Aart Elshout

Dutch, born 1947

**Notes Between Heaven and Earth,** 1995
Plastic, canvas, peat moss, candles, crystal, stone, gold leaf, copper
500 Sampsonia Way, lower level

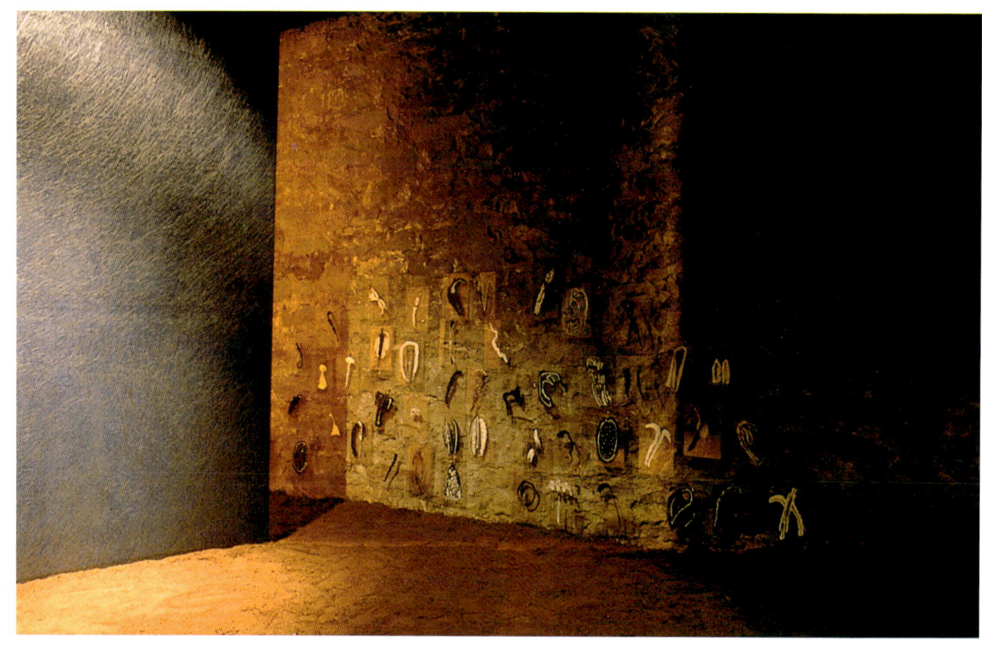

As you enter, peat moss covers the floor, which deadens all sounds. Holes in the stone wall contain candles. The light from these candles passes through crystals, a substance often believed to have power and energy.

A rustic ladder suggests a connection between heaven and earth. The artists cut holes in the concrete, beneath the peat moss, so the feet of the ladder are touching the earth. The top and bottom of the ladder are covered with gold leaf.

A wall has been constructed at the entrance, initially blocking the view of the gallery. The side facing the entrance is painted bright yellow; a human form is faintly discernible on it. The other side, painted navy blue, has silvery writing, layered until it becomes unreadable. Both sides suggest cave paintings.

A canvas book, cut from a painting tarp used often at the Mattress Factory, contains pages with gold leaf markings. These are not actually real words, but, rather, evidence of human tracings. Gold leaf also appears in a circular indentation carved into a large rock. An "X" is carved into the other end of the rock, with its ends oriented toward the four cardinal points. Drawings with such themes as nature, angels, and human forms appear on 1,000 sheets of plastic, and are arranged near the entrance and along the stone walls.

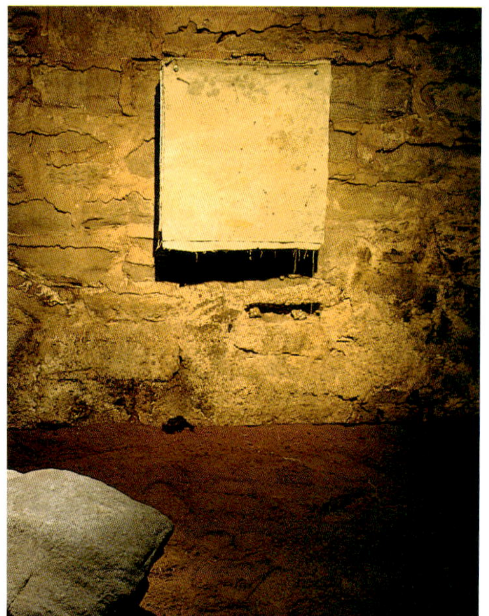

**Artists' Statement**

As Alumet, we make art situations that invite participation in our process of finding roots and powerful sources to continuously recreate and confirm perceptions of ourselves as human beings related to art and nature.

Our work is centered around this relationship and celebrates a growing awareness of mankind as the creature that creates and thus develops its self-consciousness as well as a notion of being part of . . .

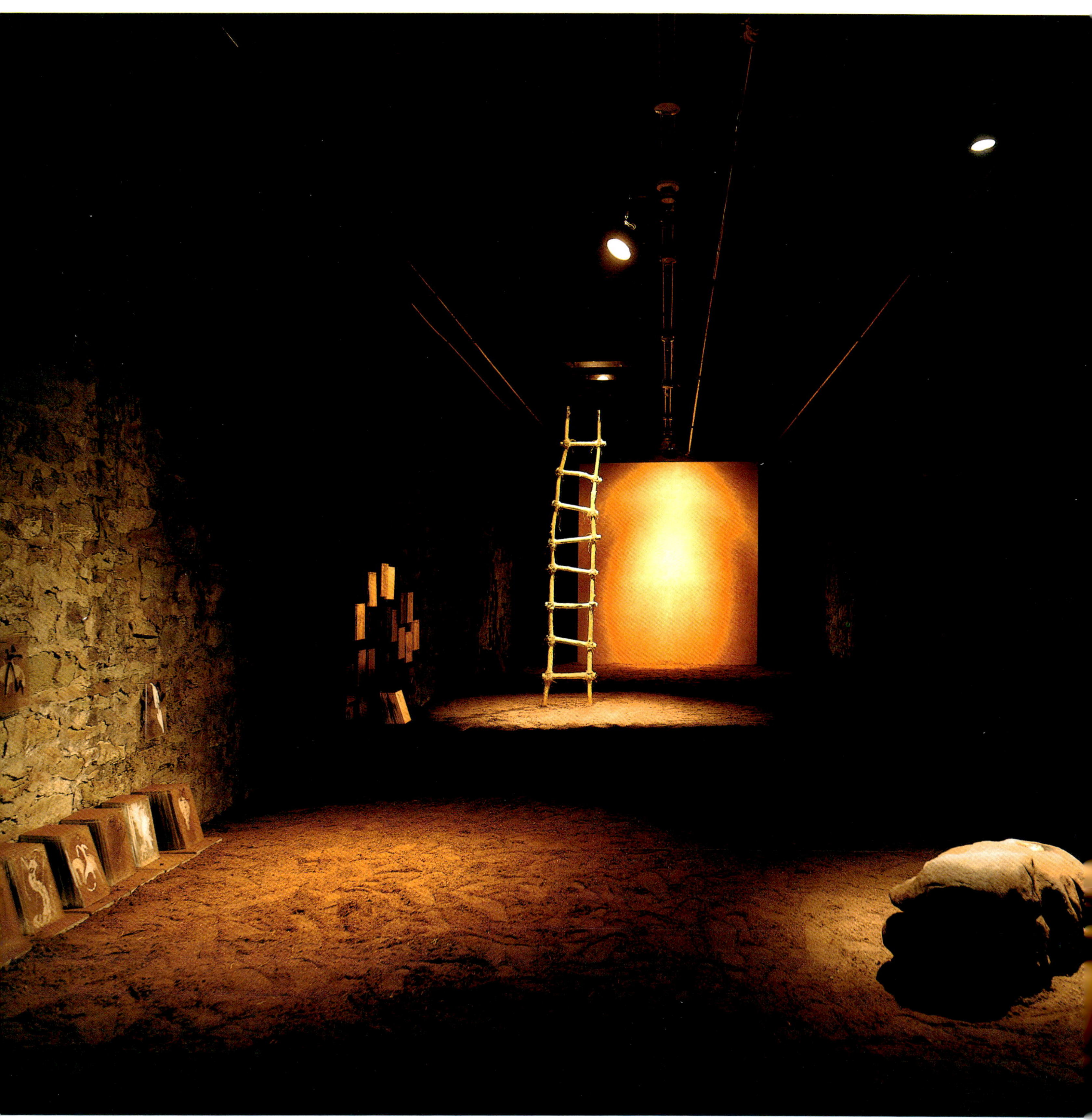

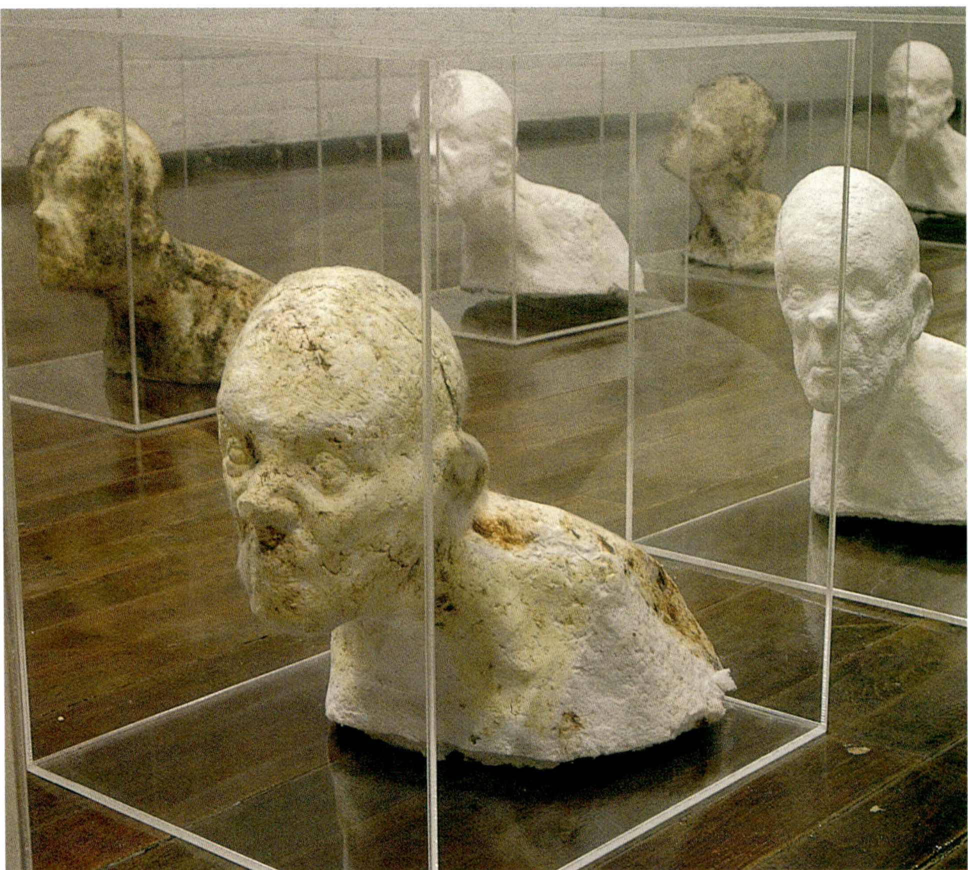

## Ladislav Čarný

Slovakian, born 1949

**Phase of Nigreda,** 1995
Cast paper, Plexiglas, phosphorous, bacteria
500 Sampsonia Way, 3rd floor
(included in *Artists of Central and Eastern Europe*)

Čarný created twenty papier-maché busts, cast from a mold of a marble head, titled *The Stink*, by the eighteenth-century sculptor F. X. Messerschmidt. Intending the heads to decay, he coated them with phosphorus and banana pulp and sealed them in Plexiglas cubes. The heads grew moldy at differing rates, some disintegrating into a heap. The phosphorous in the papier-maché glowed as the light gradually dimmed.

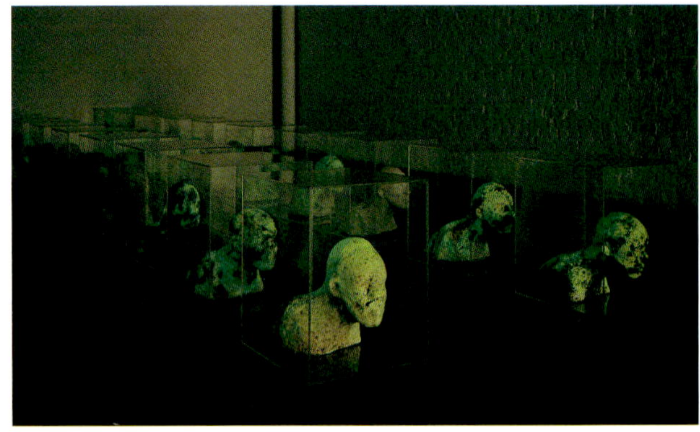

**Artist's Statement**

*Humus* is created by the process of sedimentation of geological and biological layers.

Products of the human spirit (conceptions, artifacts, interpretations . . . ) are created analogously—they create a cultural *humus*. Metabolism makes the recycling of physical life possible.

In alchemy, the teaching of the metamorphosis of the world-putridity (=decomposition) is one of the basic stages of transmutation. The English Franciscan and scholar Roger Bacon (thirteenth century) stated: "Putrefactio est omnium rerum mater."* The primary mass exists [decomposes] in order to enable the development of a new quality.

Analogously, putridity in spiritual alchemy means the transmutation of mystical conditions.

Recycling of the idea means cultural metabolism: reauthorization (reapplication, reactualization and reinterpretation) of the forgotten artifact, conception, symbol . . . in the new context. This form of creativity (creation) works with one's memory.

* "Decomposition is the mother of all things."

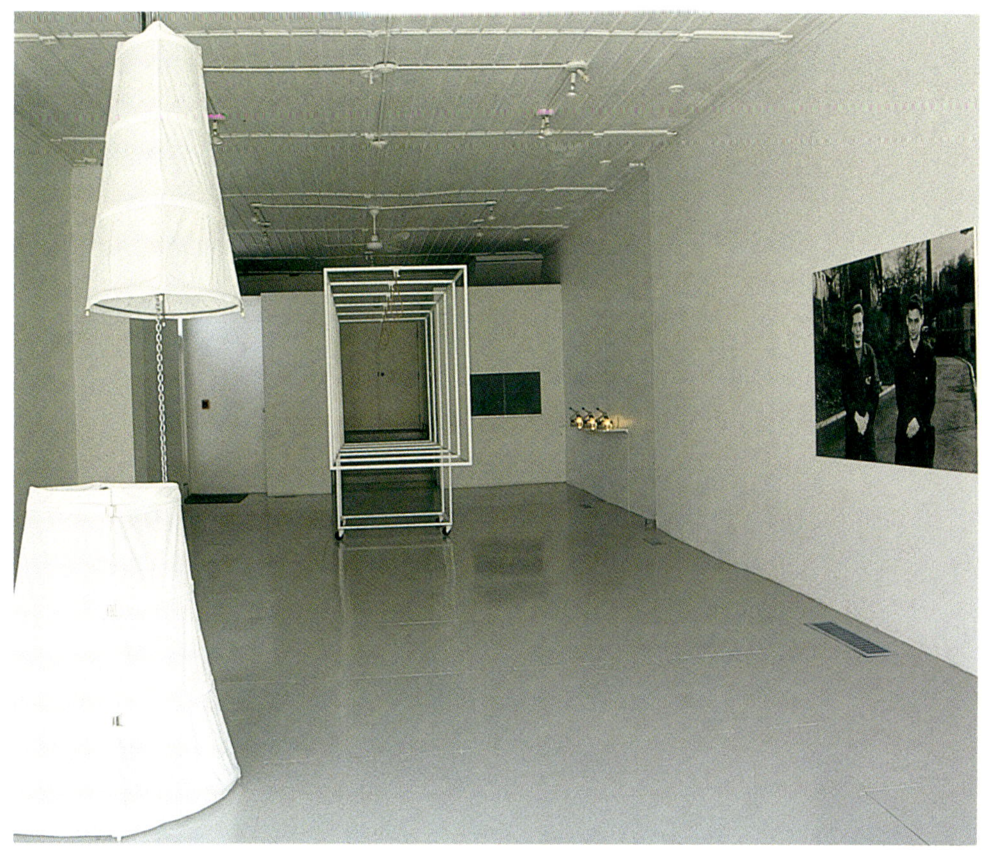

## Milena Dopitová

Czech, born 1963

**Follow Me,** 1995
Steel, photograph, microscopes, transparencies, fabric
1414 Monterey Street, 1st floor
(included in *Artists of Central and Eastern Europe*)

Monochrome and spare, the room in which the installation is situated suggests a clinical environment. A steel structure, painted white, is placed directly in front of the door. It looks like a tunnel, but is inaccessible. Leather handles hang inside this construction. A skirt-shaped construction made of steel and fabric similar to hospital sheeting hangs by a pulley from the ceiling, and another, similar fabric construction rests on the floor. A large photo of two men who work in a hospital morgue is mounted on an adjacent wall. Only their white rubber gloves provide a clue to their occupation. Microscopes sit on a shelf along the wall, providing a view of slides of trophies.

Dopitová's installation is linked to her mother's clinical death while she was in the hospital having surgery. The artist's mother felt herself to be in a tunnel, pulled toward a light at its end, and meeting people already dead. She believed that she had a choice. While she felt attracted to light and wanted to go toward it, she chose instead to come back and return to her family.

**Artist's Statement**

In my work, I would like to reach a certain feeling which will remind the viewer of a situation familiar to him, a situation to which he can relate in his own way. This experience can be different from my first idea, and I find installations where the viewer explores new meanings himself very interesting. I had several opportunities to work on my new installation abroad. This means that the project was created in the context of contact with a different society. I find inspiration in my own experiences or situations I see around me. Lately, the experiences may be seen as moralist commandments. But they come from present interpersonal relations in which an obvious, carefree optimism does not dominate. On the other hand, anxiety, vulnerability, aggressiveness, indifference and dullness have found their place. Seeing the world through pink glasses or serving it on a silver plate is not my cup of tea, because I don't live in such a world.

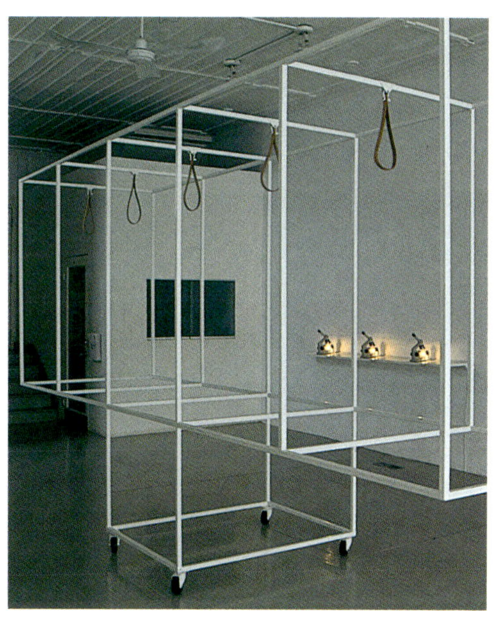

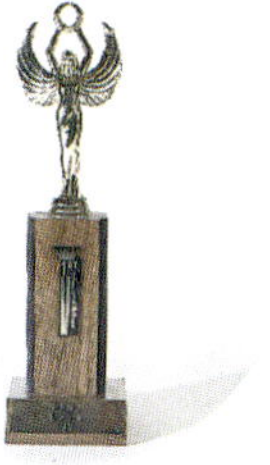

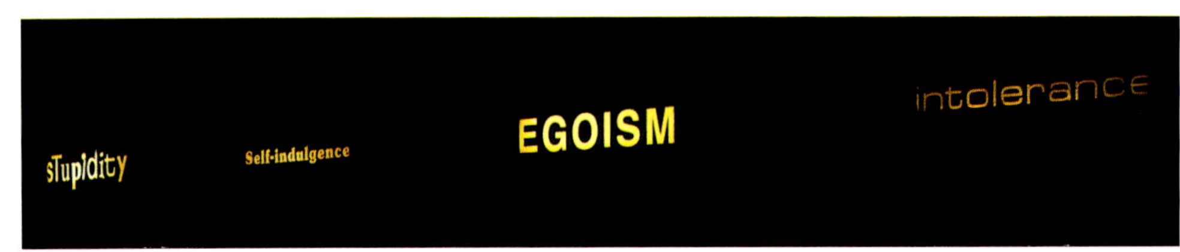


## Daniel Fischer

Slovakian, born 1950

**Memento,** 1995
Polyester, steel, aluminum, rubber, plastic, paint
500 Sampsonia Way, 3rd floor
(included in *Artists of Central and Eastern Europe*)

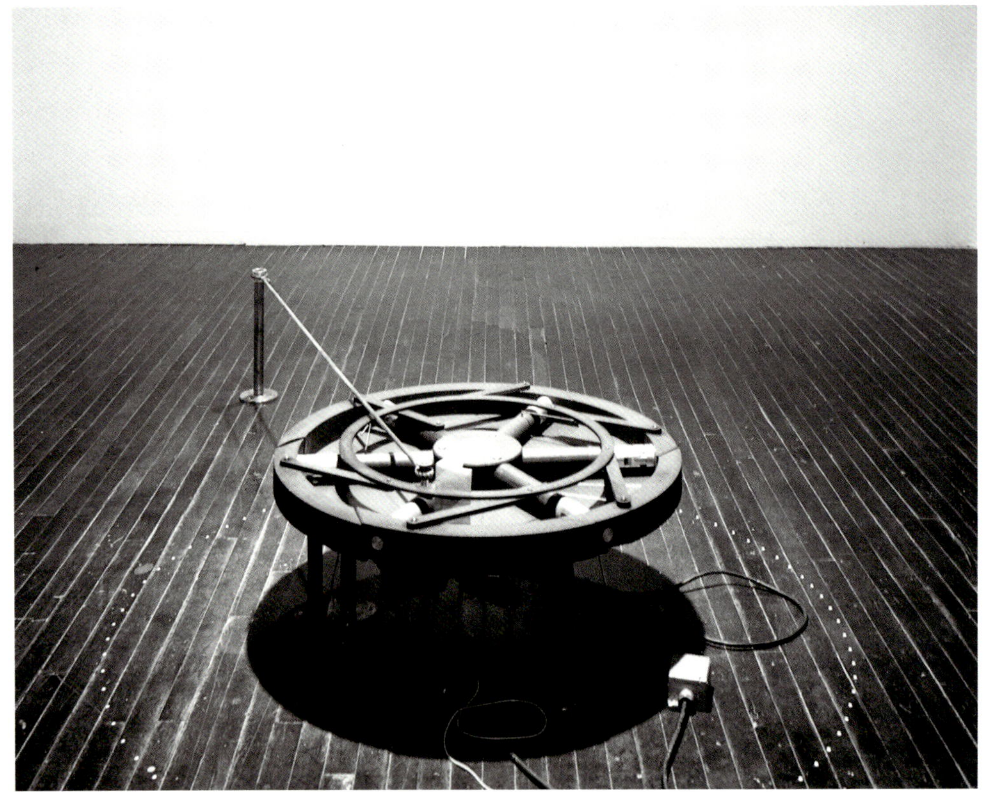

On the floor, in the center of a room, a wheel turns almost imperceptibly. Elastic cords attached to the wheel grow tighter and tighter until sections of the wheel fly outward in a surprising flash of color and burst of noise. The gallery lights go out and ten luminous words become visible on the walls: STUPIDITY SELF INDULGENCE EGOISM INTOLERANCE HATE CRUELTY ENVY PRIDE INDIFFERENCE LAZINESS.

Fischer is influenced by the French mathematician Rene Thom, who theorized that systems will run quietly and effectively until small changes in circumstances or behavior cause a "catastrophe."

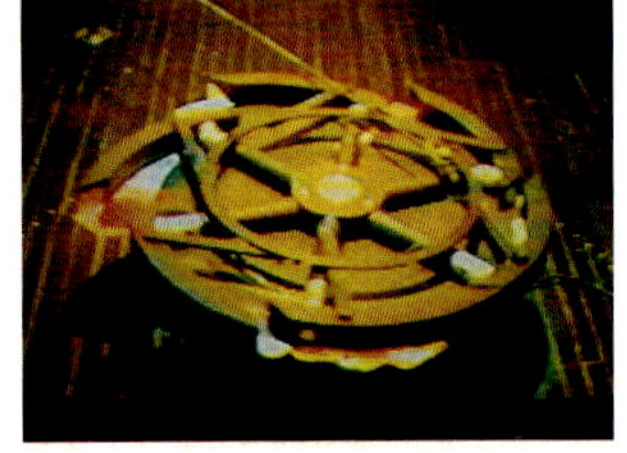

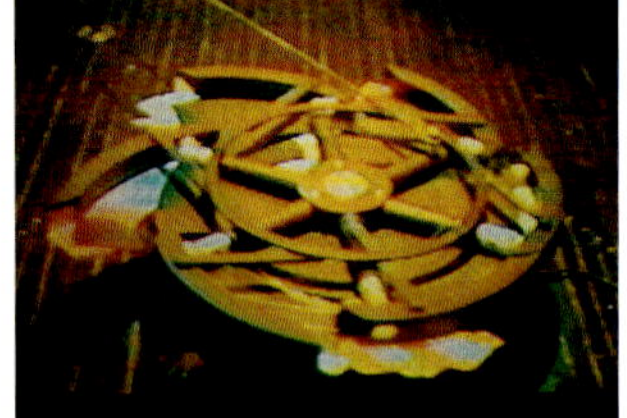

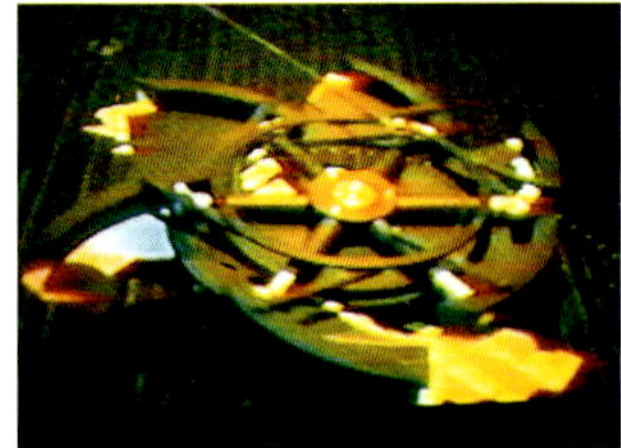

**Artist's Statement**

For my project . . . I have used the so-called Zeeman's machine, through which it is possible to give a concrete demonstration of the *Theory of Catastrophes*. The *Theory of Catastrophes* concerns systems in which continuous and gradual changes in acting forces (in a broader, not only physical sense) cause a sudden great change in the condition of the system. This theory promises to have many potential applications in various real situations in embryology, economics, ecology, psychology, and sociology . . .

Working on my project, I was thinking about various concrete situations, which push me to ask basic questions:
Why?
How is it possible?
Why are people doing this?
What is the reason?
What is the motivation?

And what is—or can be—the psychological regulator?
(Isn't it culture?)
I am trying to find answers on the individual level, knowing how fragile is the balance between good and bad . . . life and death.

My life experience has taught me about the natural overlapping of aesthetics and ethics. I believe that art is a sort of message, an information ( . . . ontological information)—but only in a case of a living complexity of the sensory-intuitive and rational-intellectual, as a correctly chosen-discovered medium in relation to the idea.

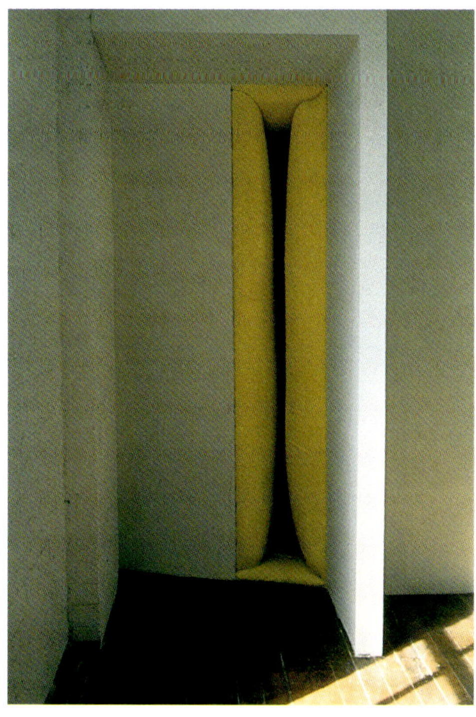

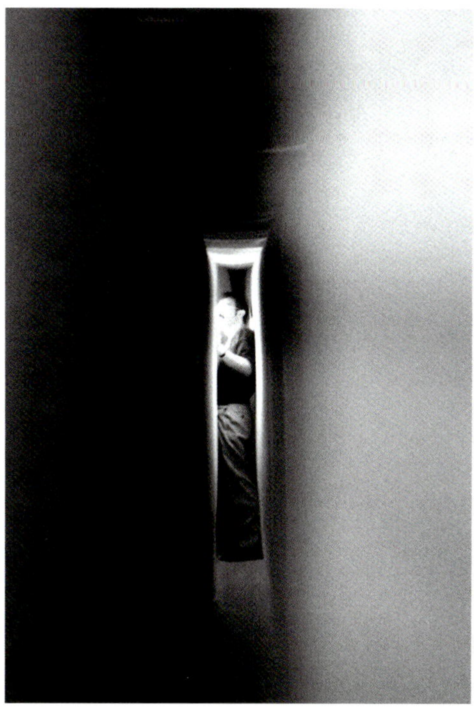

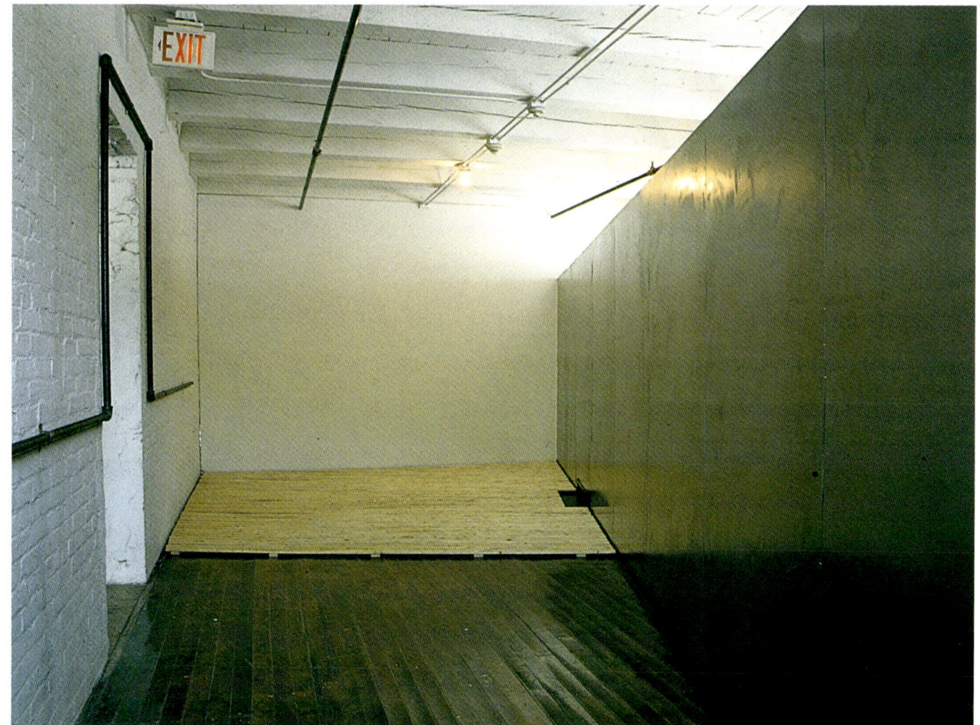


## Jaroslav Hulbój

Polish, born 1969

**Reconstructions for Lazarus's Situation,** 1995
Steel, fabric, foam rubber, wood, drywall, lens, paint
500 Sampsonia Way, 4th floor
(included in *Artists of Central and Eastern Europe*)

A narrow slit admits visitors to a passageway, which grows increasingly confined. The walls and floor of this passage are padded with foam and covered in yellow fabric. A window of thick Plexiglas near the end of the passage provides a distorted view into a well-lit room.

The gallery space itself has been divided into two parts by the passageway. One side of the space refers to the living world and the other, to the realm of the dead. The only way to see the "living" or "risen" side of the space is to squeeze down the passageway. On the "dead" side, steel panels cover the walls. A bed-like construction made of wooden slats and a sheet of steel appears to have sunk beneath the latticed floor.

**Artist's Statement**

The reality of the imagination can change the dimensions of space and move its frontiers.

This possibility has become an obsession with me and it has affected the direction of my explorations.

That is why there appear motives in particular realizations, in different places and spaces, which escape out of the door, windows, or into the void of the wall.

I always feel the necessity of leaving something in my work which could be experienced as present beyond the body of space.

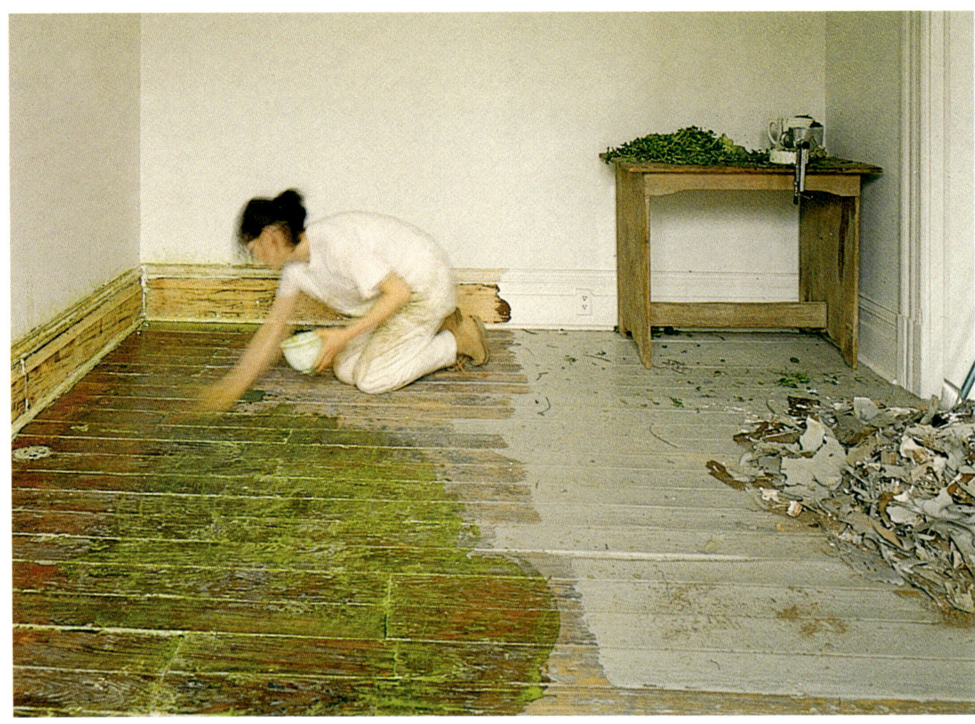

## Monica Kulicka

Polish, born 1963

**RECONSTRUCTIONS,** 1995
Plexiglas, chlorophyll, refrigeration unit, circulating pump, hardware
1414 Monterey Street, 2nd and 3rd floors
(included in *Artists of Central and Eastern Europe*)

Kulicka crushed grass and clover with a meat grinder and extracted chlorophyll. In one room, she scraped the floors by hand and rubbed the chlorophyll into the bare wood, temporarily giving it scent and green color.

On another floor, a refrigerated Plexiglas tank is filled with a mixture of chlorophyll, water and alcohol, and plastic tubing carries the liquid through the walls into an adjacent room. These tubes lead to wooden floorboard in various parts of the room.

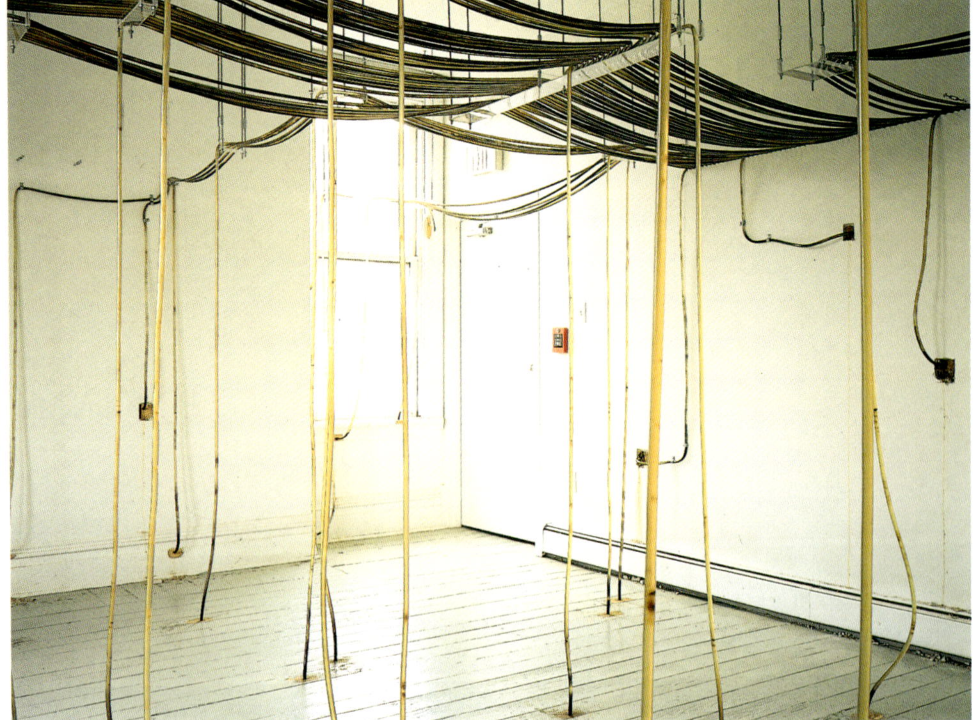

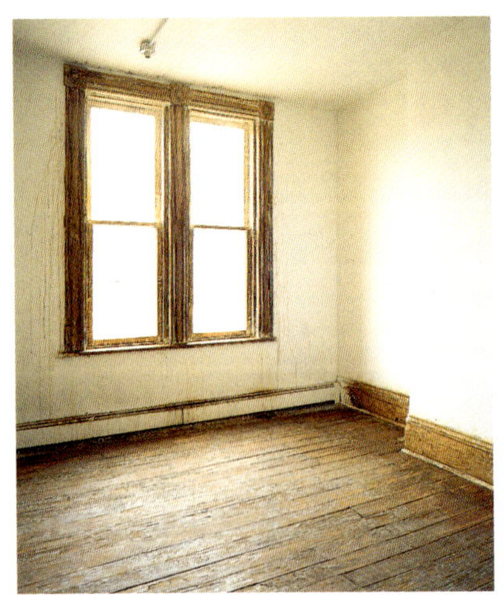

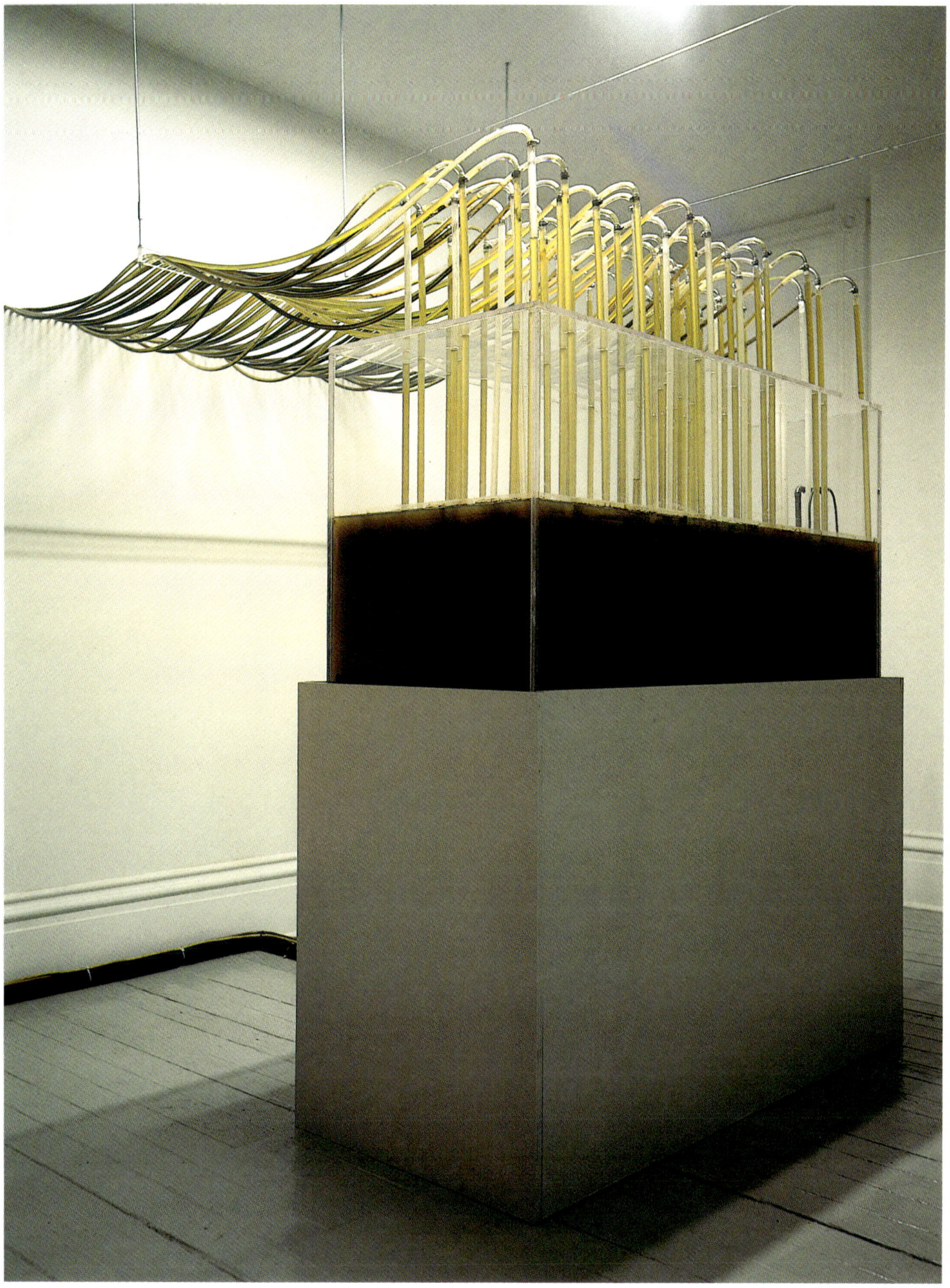

**Artist's Statement**

*RECONSTRUCTIONS* is a continuing series of installation/attempts to bring long-gone life back into wood, to bring wood back into a tree.

The *RECONSTRUCTIONS* at 1414 Monterey consist of two complementing projects. On the third floor, a series of transparent tubing runs from the large tank containing over ninety gallons of chlorophyll. It distributes the liquid into the exposed wood of the window frames, floor, and wall studs. This system is mechanical and engineered, a reminder of industrial civilization.

On the second floor, the chlorophyll is being rubbed into the wooden elements of the architecture with the artist's bare hands—a process that is performed over the weeks, personal and emotional, inspired by spirituality and magic of ancient healers and shamans.

I try to counterbalance the high logic, rationality and effectiveness of technologies around me with irrational, futile gestures—seemingly naïve, foolish acts—and with the emotional and intuitive, sometimes desperate or inadequate.

In *RECONSTRUCTIONS* I build my own machine to give an old, wooden building a (green) blood transfusion; I gently rub fresh chlorophyll into old planks of the floor. It's a mockery of technology, it's a mockery of good intentions. My aim is to stir our hidden appreciation of absurd, to startle minds set by the logic of cause and effect.

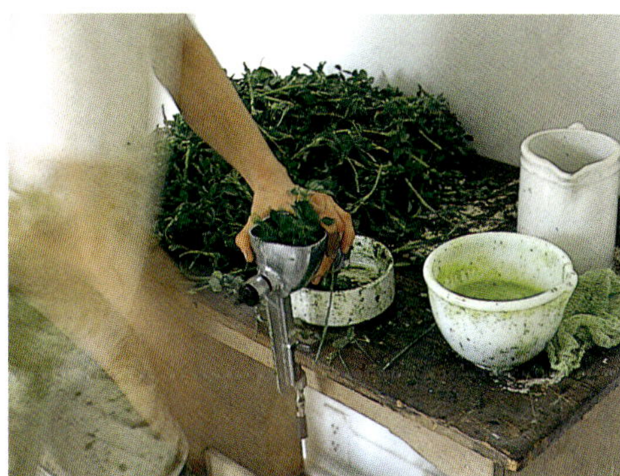

## Otis Laubert

Slovakian, born 1946

**Gastronomic Tapestry,** 1987–1995
Plastic, fruit, string
**Deer,** 1994–1995
from the series ***Animal***
Thumbtacks, stuffed deer head
**Bicycle,** 1995
from the series ***Civilization***
Bicycle and matchsticks
**Stars,** 1995
Polystyrene
**Fire Making Darkness,** 1995
Matchboxes
**Knowing They Are Losing Their Heads,** 1995
from the series ***Animal***
Mirrors, plastic animals, glue
**Stairs,** 1987/1995
from the series ***Civilization***
Shoes, wood, glue
**Connections,** 1995
Wood, dowels
**Bricks,** 1995
Polystyrene
(included in *Artists of Central and Eastern Europe*)
500 Sampsonia Way, 3rd and 4th floors

Laubert created nine separate works. He worked with everyday objects, the materials themselves determining the direction each piece took. Several of his works were inspired by the architectural elements of the gallery, such as the brick walls and star-shaped beam bolts.

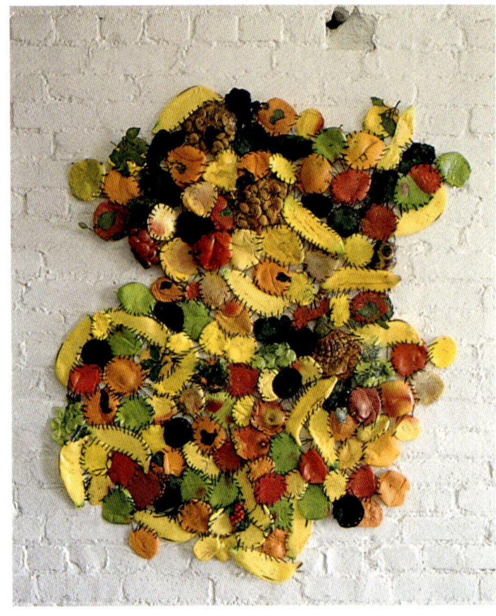
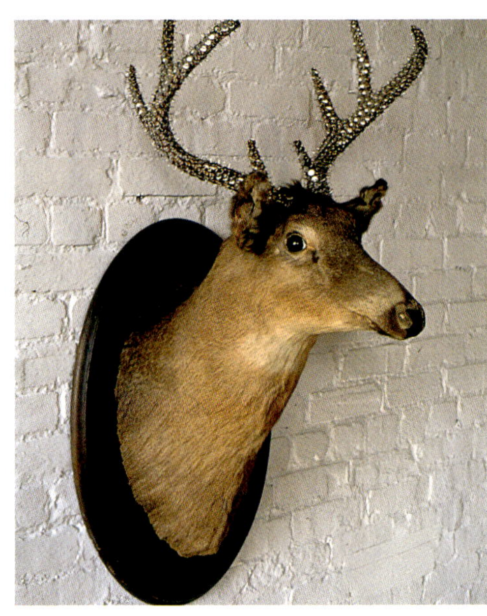
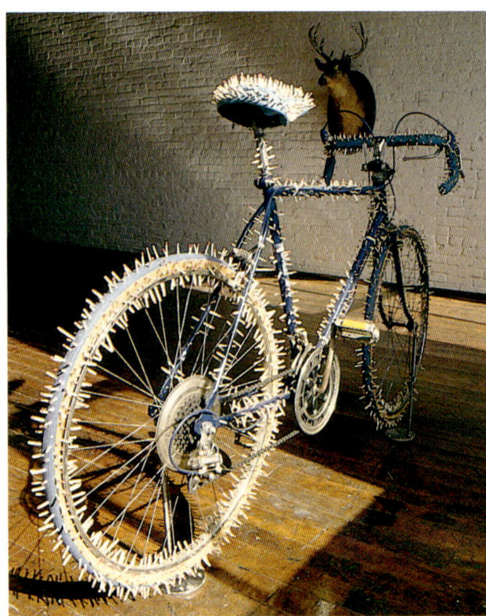
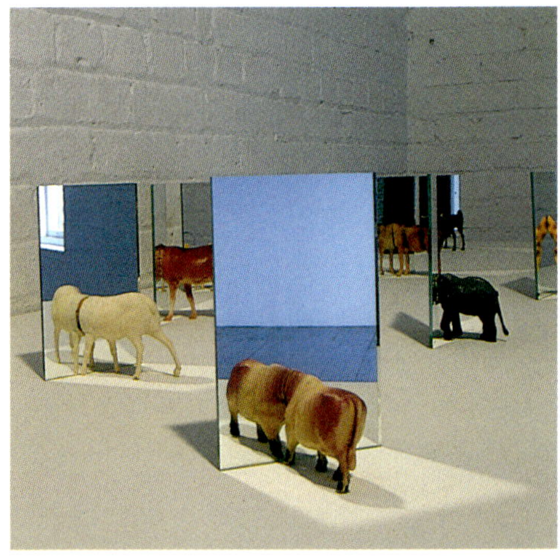
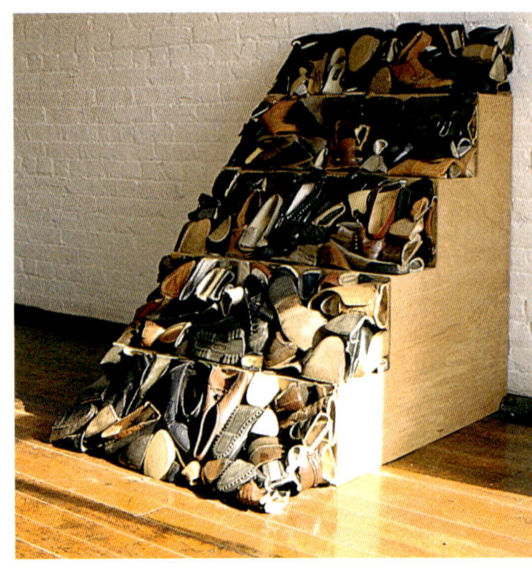
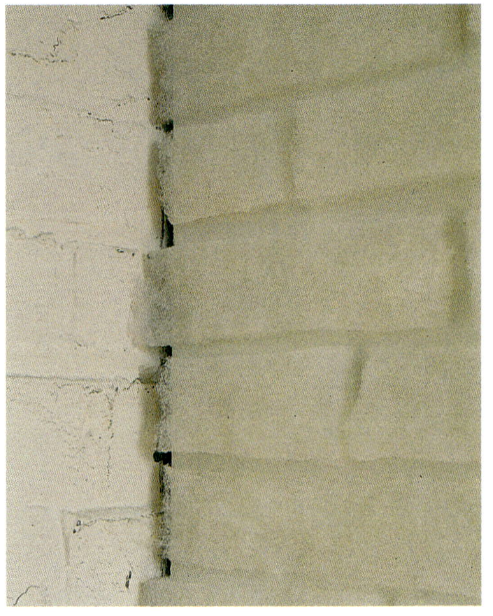

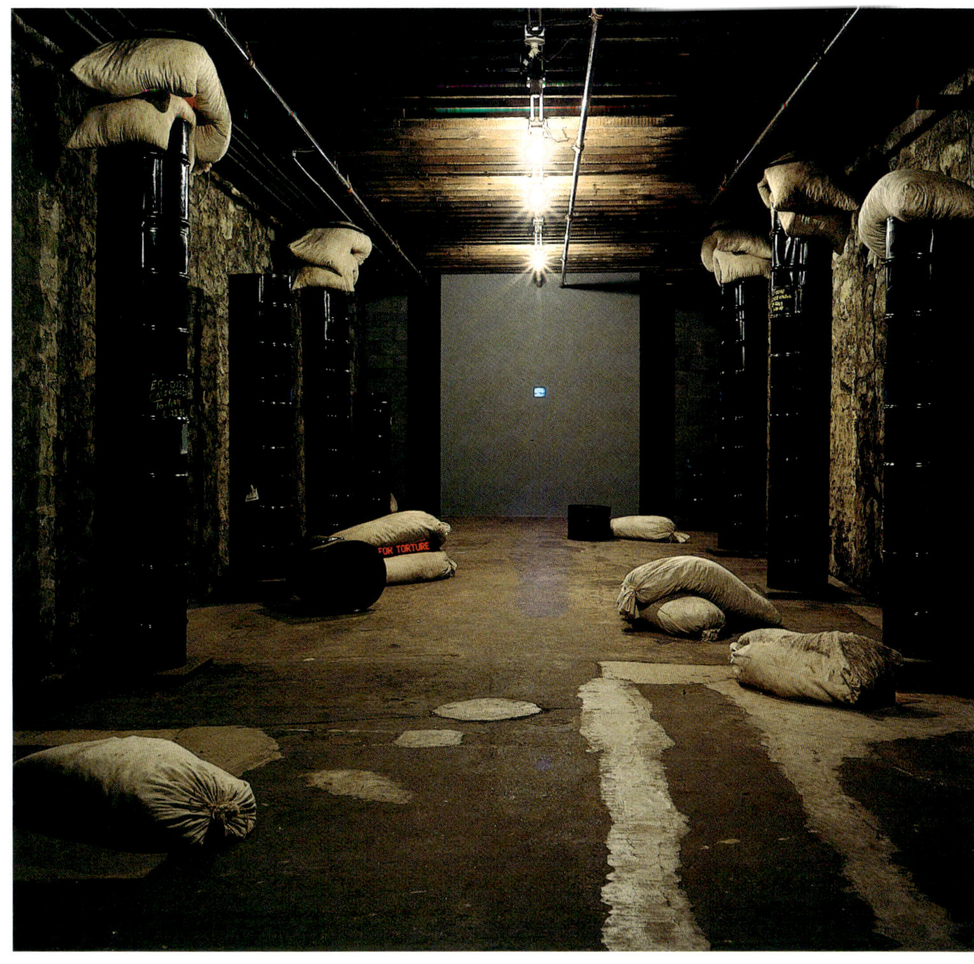


## Peter Meluzin

Slovakian, born 1947

**Wordburger Column,** 1995
Steel drums, ketchup, canvas, LEDs, video
500 Sampsonia Way, lower level
(included in *Artists of Central and Eastern Europe*)

Columns formed from steel drums and topped with sandbags and LEDs are arranged along the stone walls in the basement. The LEDs display text gleaned from local newspaper headlines and advertisements. A steel drum filled with ketchup sits just inside the entrance to the gallery, referring to hamburgers, ketchup as a blood substitute in movies, and the way that blood flows so freely in war. A video at the end of the gallery shows a black and white photograph of a soldier on a bunker in Bosnia. The artist compares the soldier's pose to Michelangelo's *David.* The soldier in the photograph was killed two days after the picture was taken.

**Artist's Statement**

MASS MEDIAL OUTBURSTS AND MASS CONSUMPTION OF WORDBURGERS, SACKS OF EMPTIED WORDS AND SACKS OF AN ARMY BUNKER WHERE WHATEVER WORDS ARE USELESS, HERE AND THERE ROMAN COLUMNS WHICH BEAR THE TRACES OF ANCIENT CULTURE AND SOMEWHERE ELSE ANOTHER PLATFORM MELTING ITSELF INTO RUINS UNDER THE BURDEN OF WORD NONSENSE, SOMEWHERE, SOMETIME, THE KETCHUP IS AN IMITATION OF BLOOD, ANOTHER TIME, ELSEWHERE THE BLOOD IS WORTH NOT MORE THAN KETCHUP (RECYCLING OF KETCHUP AND BLOOD), MICHELANGELO'S DAVID IS IMMORTAL, DAVID OF BOSNIA ON A TREMBLING TV SCREEN IS (EXACTLY) TWO DAYS BEFORE HIS DEATH (RECYCLING OF ART AND LIFE?), MASS MEDIAL OUTBURSTS AND . . .

I'm not sure if this is an artist's statement or just another wordburger. But perhaps the wordburger column has to go on . . .

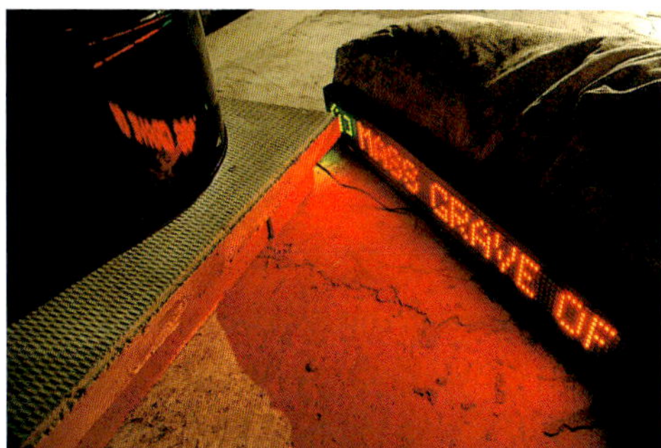


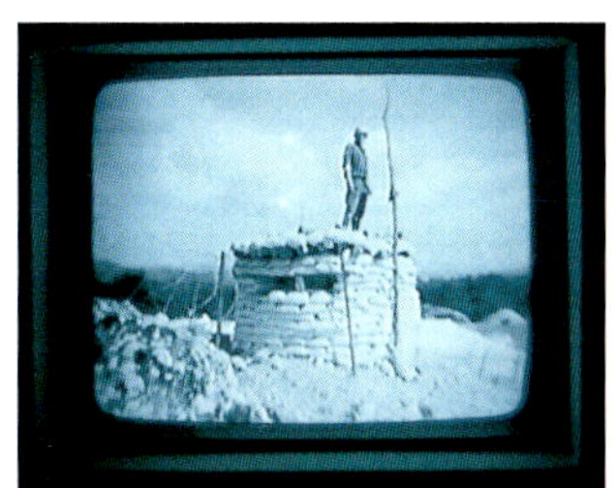

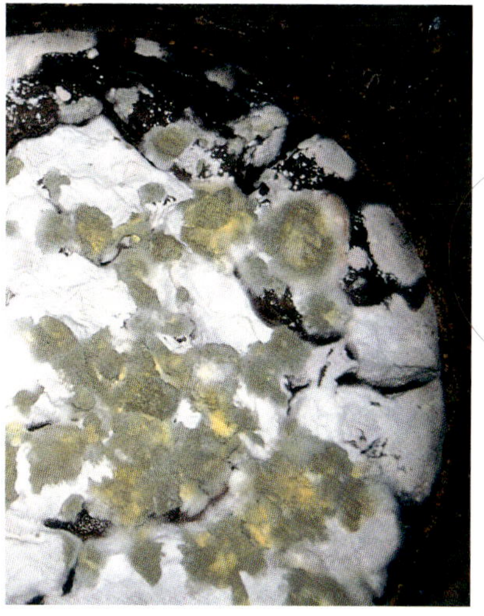

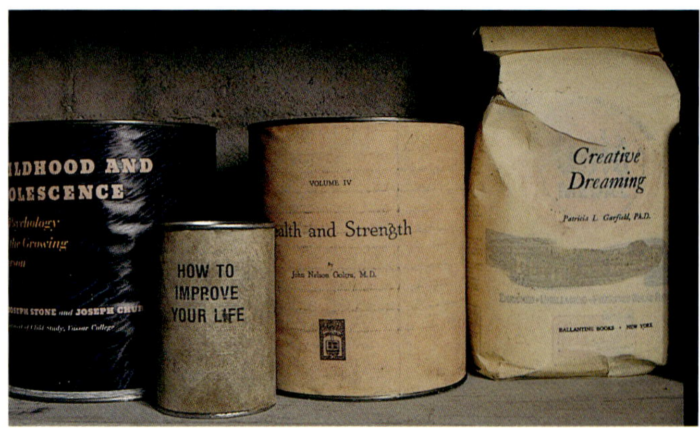


## Roman Ondák

Slovakian, born 1966

**Taste of Thinking,** 1995
Food packages with silk-screened and laser-printed labels, furniture, appliances
505 Jacksonia Street
(included in *Artists of Central and Eastern Europe*)

Using a storage shed adjacent to the Mattress Factory parking lot, Ondák built a sterile and spare living space. He lowered the ceiling, blocked the windows, and added minimal furnishings. Everything that suggested warmth and ease had to be removed in order to evoke the feeling of an occupant whose life is limited and bound. A bookcase is stacked with dry and canned goods. The food labels have been replaced with book covers bearing the titles of psychology textbooks, meditation guides, and other kinds of self-help books.

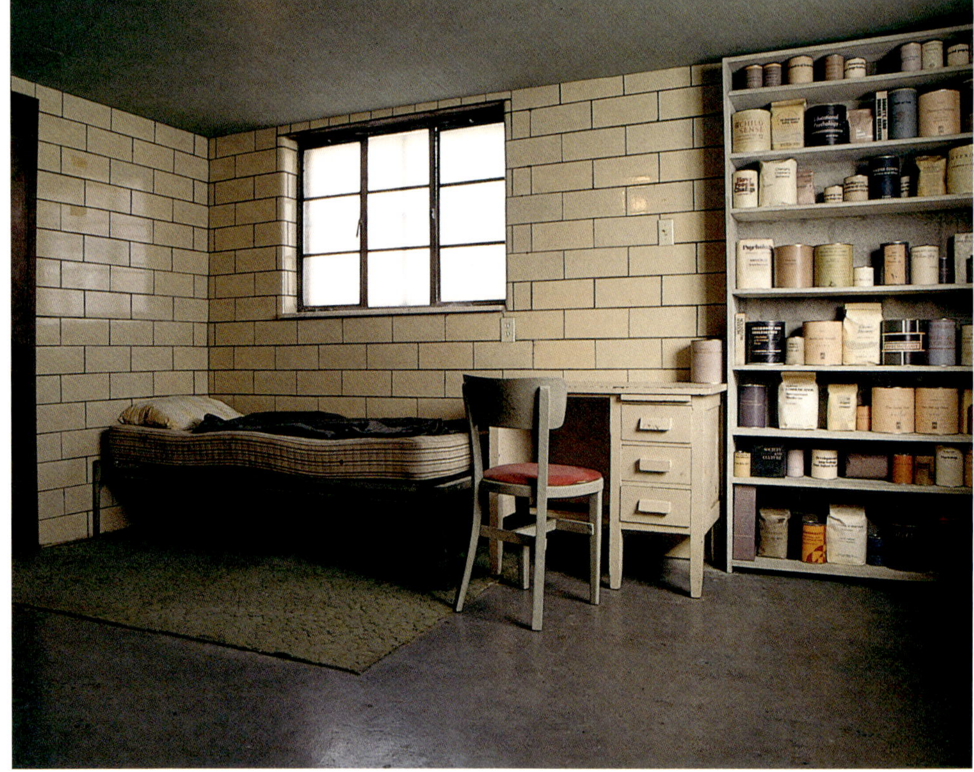

**Artist's Statement**

My interest in working with the subject of abandoned rooms was the reason that I chose this space for the installation. I arranged the room like "the cell for living" with a very reduced amount of furniture and a library in the corner. The contents of the library are dominated by the things in the space, specifying their relations. Books in the library are made up like food cans and packages with the book-like labels on them. I suppose that people will stay in the room longer reading some of the book titles and that way they will absorb the sensation of going into the mind of someone else living there.

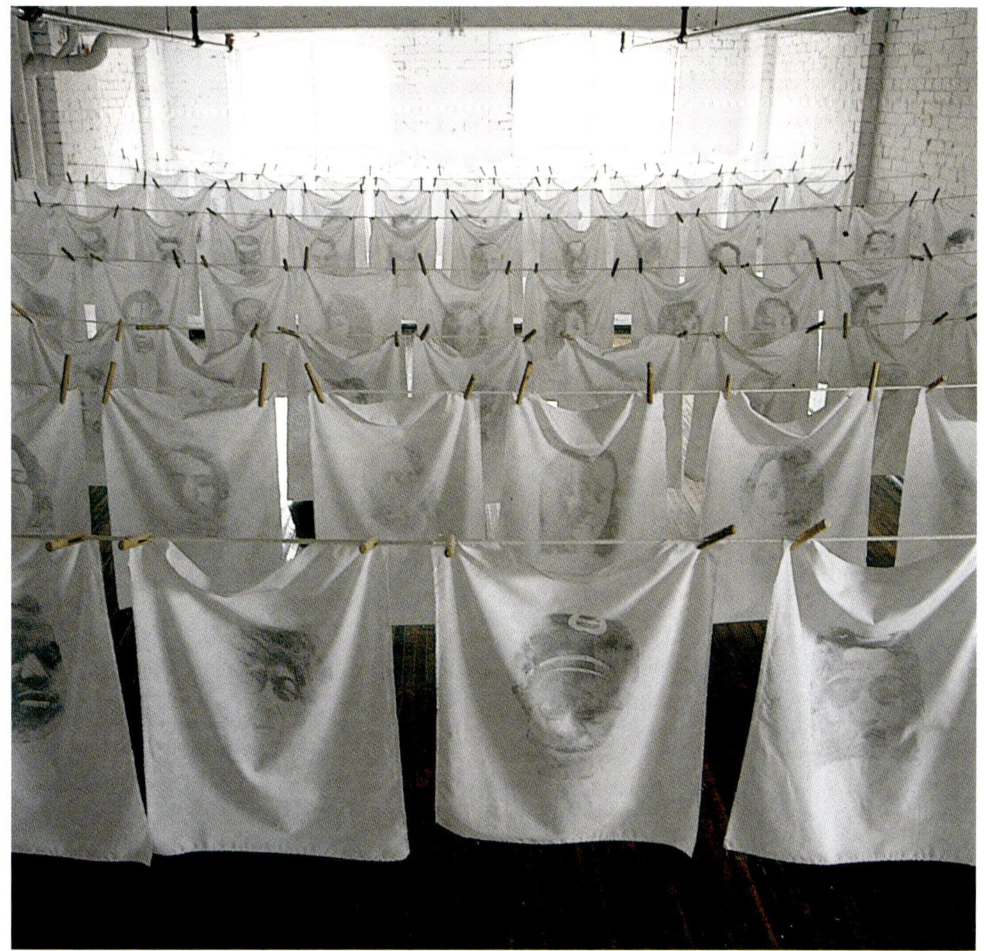

## L'ubo Stacho

Slovakian, born 1953

**Message from Saint Veronica,** 1995
Fabric, clothes line, clothespins, transferred photocopies
500 Sampsonia Way, 4th floor
(included in *Artists of Central and Eastern Europe*)

Stacho was inspired by the legend of Veronica's Veil, on which the face of Jesus is believed to be imprinted. He wanted to achieve the same kind of energy transmission, from face to fabric, to make energy visible in his installation. He photographed a cross section of about 200 people he met in downtown Pittsburgh, requesting each person to pose for two photos—one with eyes open and the second with eyes closed. He then photocopied each of the portraits until he had a fourth or fifth generation print. Each print, faint and indistinct enough to have a mystical quality, was transferred to fabric with a solvent. Dressed in white, Stacho dipped each fabric image into water in the Mattress Factory *Garden*, a process suggesting baptism. The faint portraits queue up on laundry lines in the fourth-floor gallery.

**First Communion,** 1995
Fabric, heat-transferred color photocopies, clothesline and clothespins
500 Sampsonia Way, *Garden*
(included in *Artists of Central and Eastern Europe*)

A companion piece hung in the *Garden*: a clothesline with canvas portraits of young Slovakians, taken before and after their First Communion.

**Artist's Statement**
Spirit.
Secret, Mystery,
Religion.
These are things in which I am interested; what is inside.
I like to balance on the edge. Where is irony, where is truth?
I baptized 200 Americans in my mind.
The shroud of Turin is a print from Christ's face, a photograph is a print from the light. In both cases it is energy transmission. I am interested in this transmission.

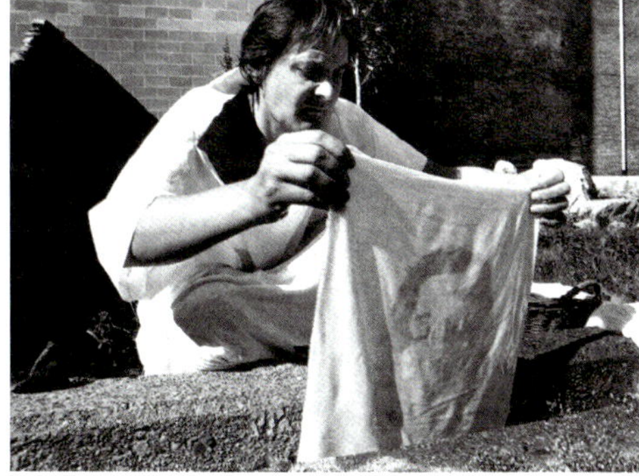

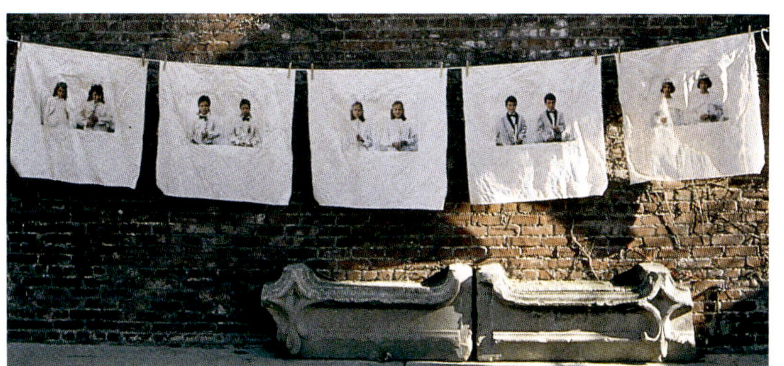

## Dezider Tóth

Slovakian, born 1947

**Reservation,** 1995
51 wooden shelves, books, paint, glue
500 Sampsonia Way, 3rd floor
(included in *Artists of Central and Eastern Europe*)

Tóth worked with cast-off library volumes, cutting, gluing, and painting them. On shelves mounted on the walls of the gallery space, the books were arranged in patterns based on their size, then painted black and glued shut.

**Last Aid,** 1995
Wood, canvas, paint, steel
500 Sampsonia Way, lower level
(included in *Artists of Central and Eastern Europe*)

Tóth constructed twenty Army stretchers made of canvas, painted red. On them he painted yellow letters which spell out a political slogan. The stretchers are stacked casually, almost hidden, in the basement galleries of the Mattress Factory.

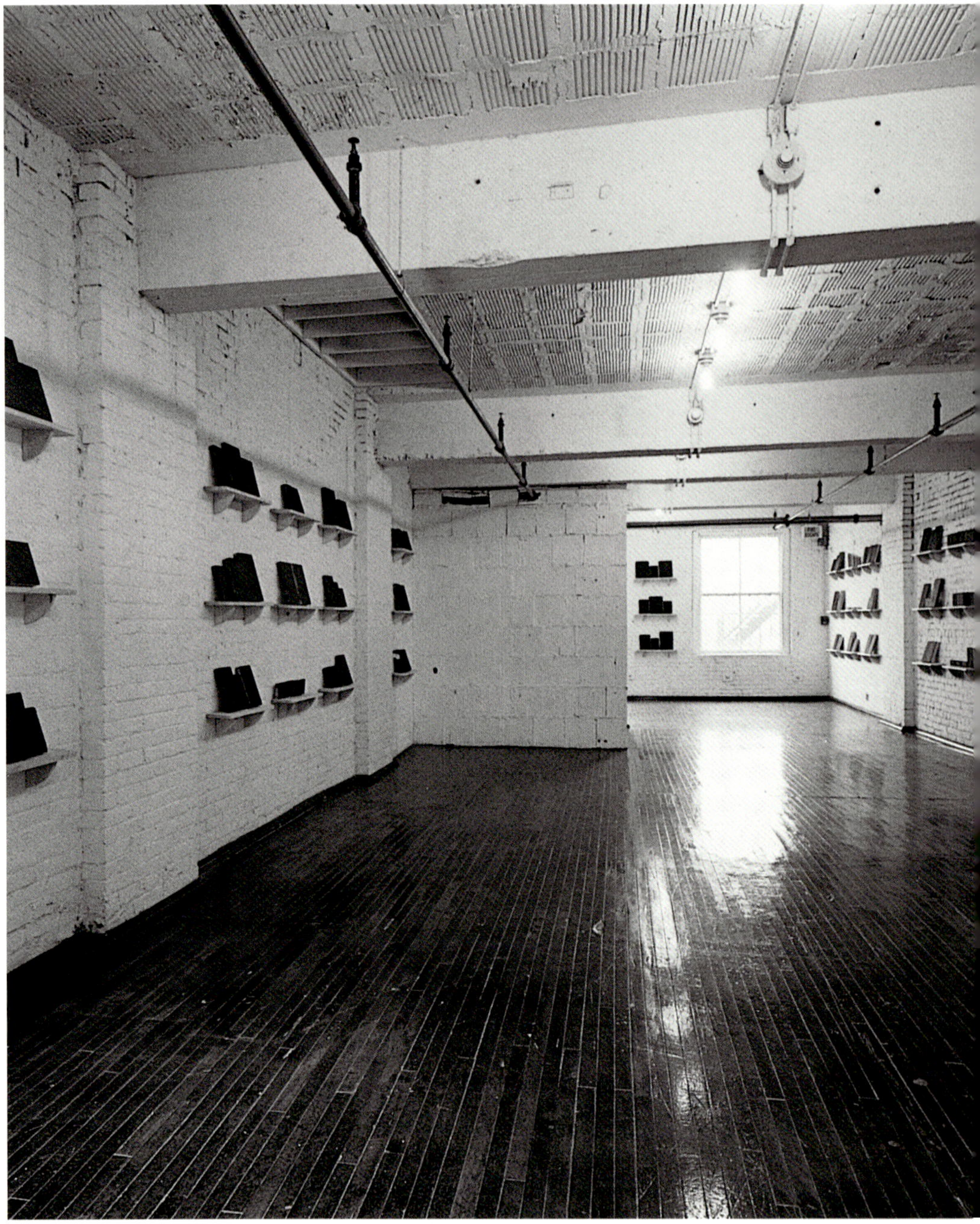

**Artist's Statement**
I group discarded books of various authors . . . into pairs, threes, fours and fives, and on the maps that this makes, with concealed information inside, I paint in black a space for a new meaning. Black icons of emptiness.

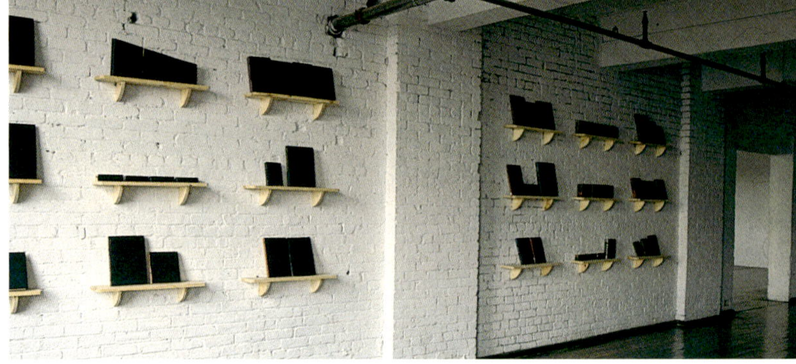

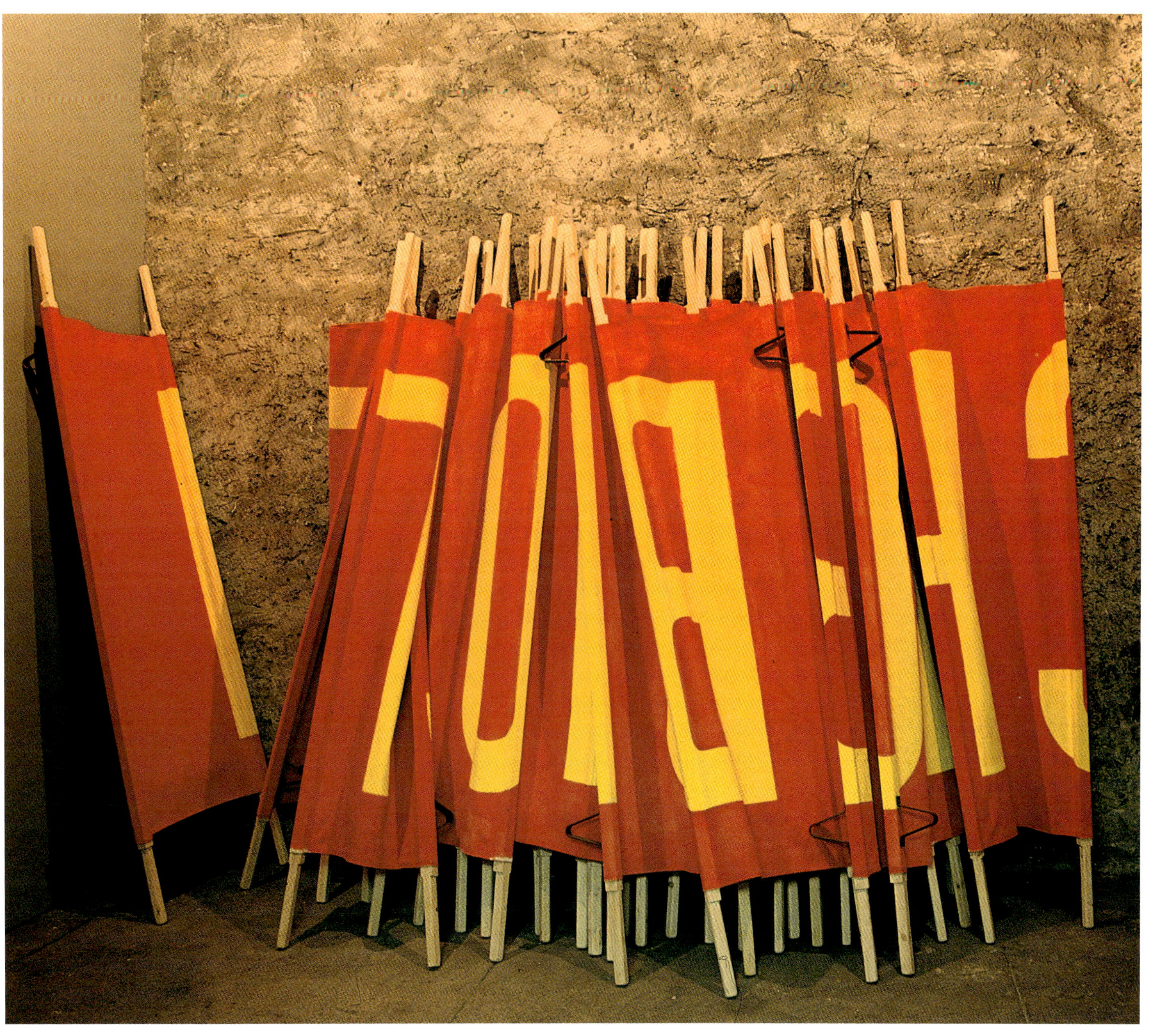

**Artist's Statement**

A banner with a political slogan on it (170 cm by 1,800 cm, red on yellow canvas) is cut up into twenty parts and, from these, twenty stretchers are made. The state of their presentation is temporary storage. In the 1950s, Czechoslovakia's streets were full of words painted on banners with political slogans. These were the cruelest years of communist totalitarianism. The 1950s are the period of my childhood. For me they are the most beautiful part of my life. Can one bear a grudge against one's childhood just because it took place against a background of lies?

## Rolf Julius

German, born 1939

**Music for a Garden,** 1996
Speakers, amplifier, CD
500 Sampsonia Way, *Garden*
(permanent audio installation)

Rolf Julius designed *Music for a Garden* to be heard within the *Garden* designed by Winifred Lutz. Three pairs of speakers, mounted high and low on the Mattress Factory's exterior walls, are aimed in various directions. From each speaker comes a distinct element of the music Julius has composed for the space.

**Red,** 1996 (long-term loan)
Speakers, amplifier, CD, red pigment, wire
500 Sampsonia Way, lower level

Two speakers, suspended from the ten-foot ceiling by thin wire, hang just inches from the ground. They are coated with a brilliant, powdery, orange-red pigment that vibrates with the pulsing sound emanating from the speakers.

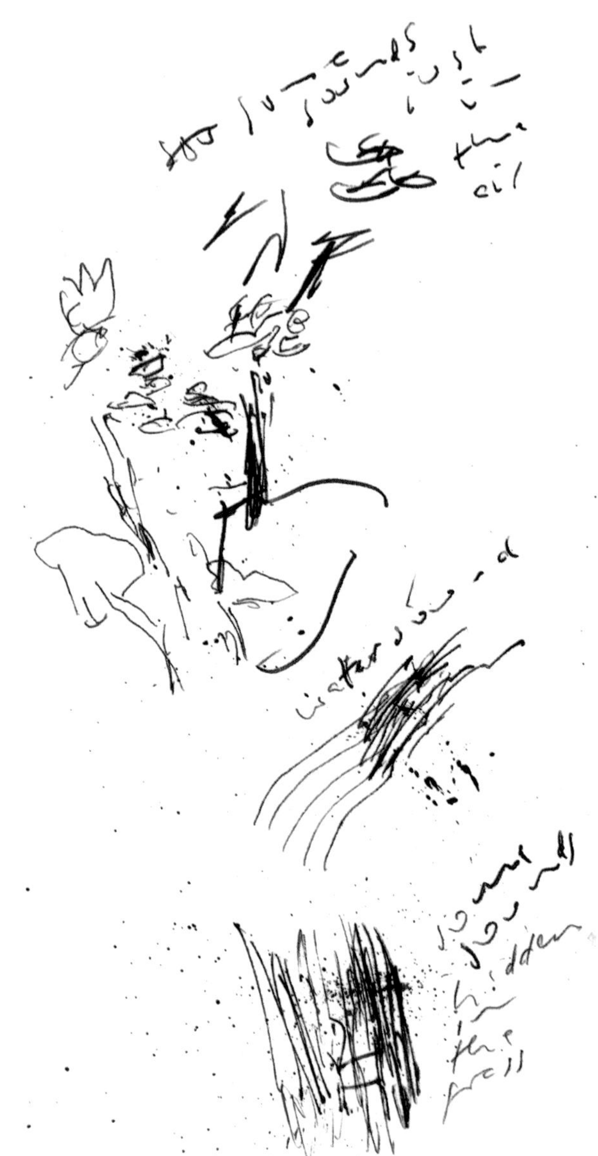

**Artist's Statement**
[My work] is as high as the building, and fills the entire lot adjacent to it. In this way, I have created rooms. As the visitor moves from one room to another—either vertically or horizontally—the experience of the work changes.

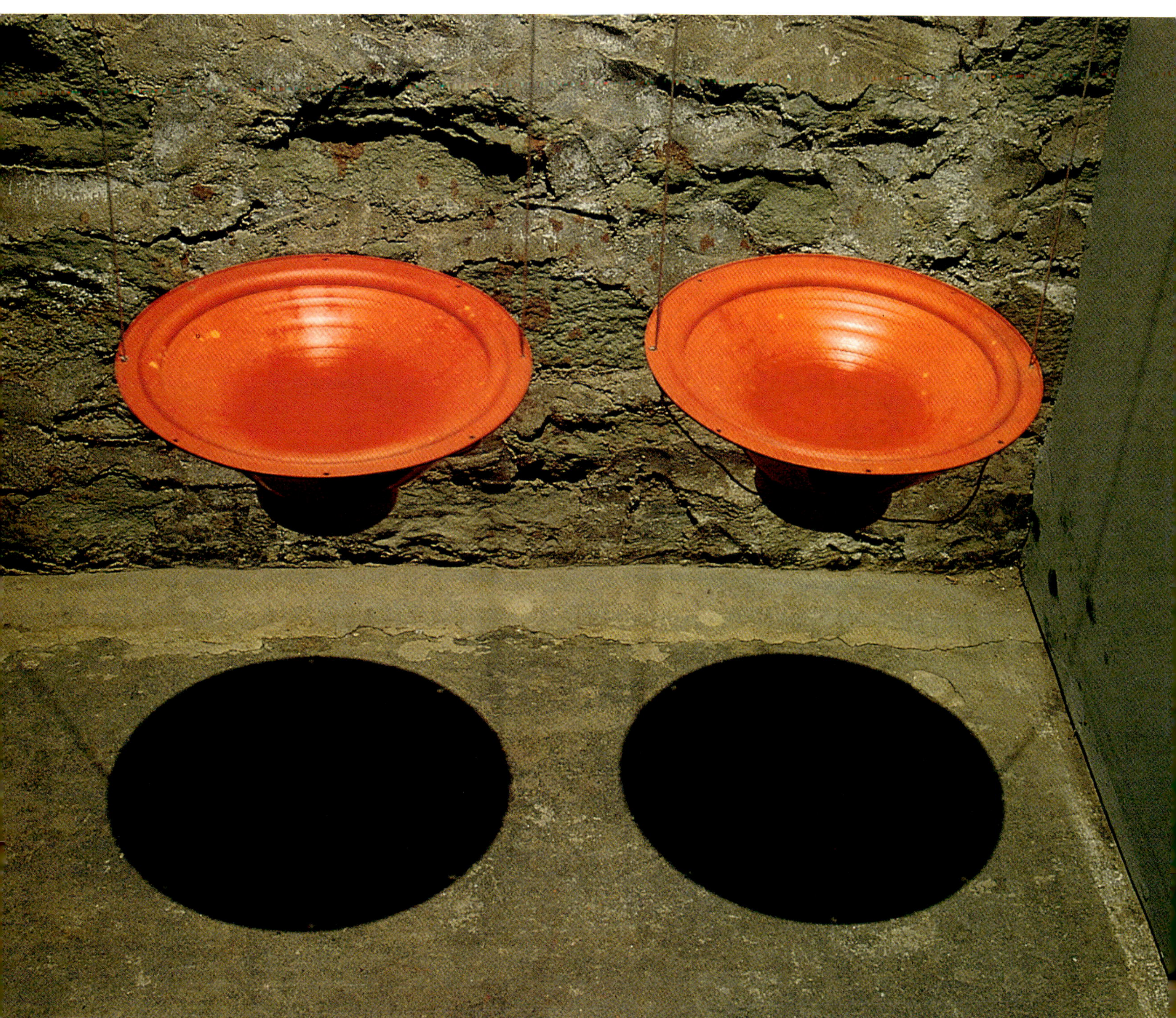

## John Latham

British, born 1921

**Long Glass,** 1996
Glass, books, steel, plastic tubing, wire
1414 Monterey Street, 1st floor

A glass wall divides the room into two halves. Books, wire, and tubing pass through the glass.

**Documentation,** 1996
Plaster, books, text
1414 Monterey Street, 2nd floor

Books encased in plaster are scattered about the floor in the first room.

Text on the wall of the first room reads, "on band Q, you, humankind, show up as a plague organism." In the second room, the text is, "on band S you show up as seed germ of the sun . . . given the way you are brought up to think though, you do not choose . . ."

Documentation in the second room explains some of Latham's theories, including Event structure.

**Long Painting,** 1996
Painted and rolled canvas
1414 Monterey Street, 3rd floor

A 72-foot painting sprayed with stripes is folded in half lengthwise and twisted tightly, passing through the walls into different rooms.

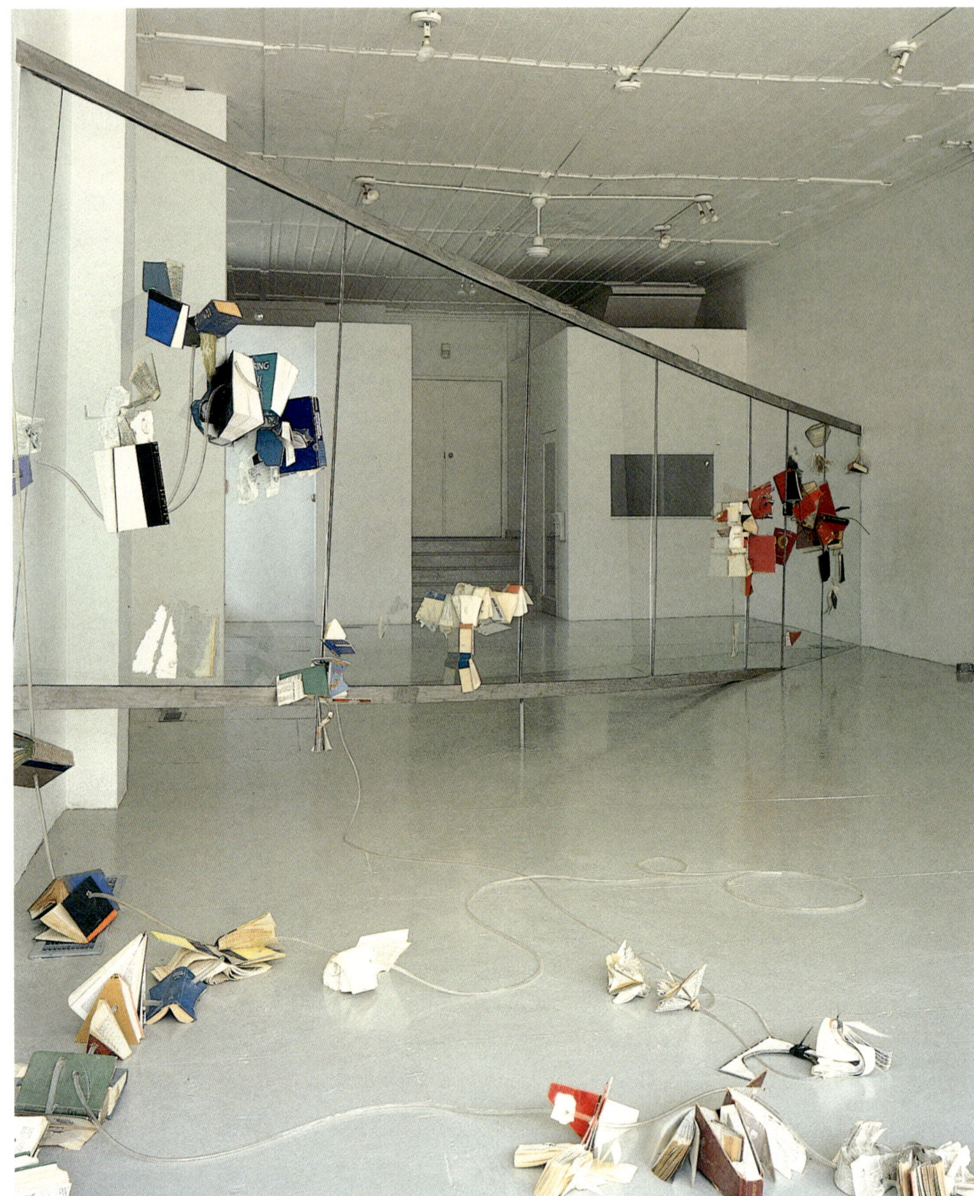

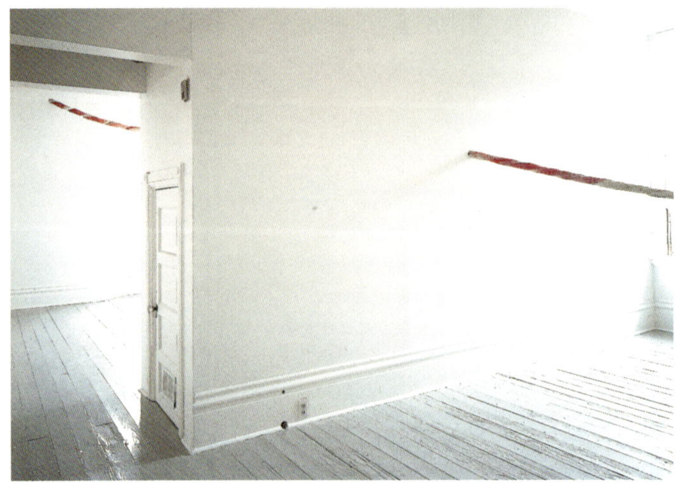

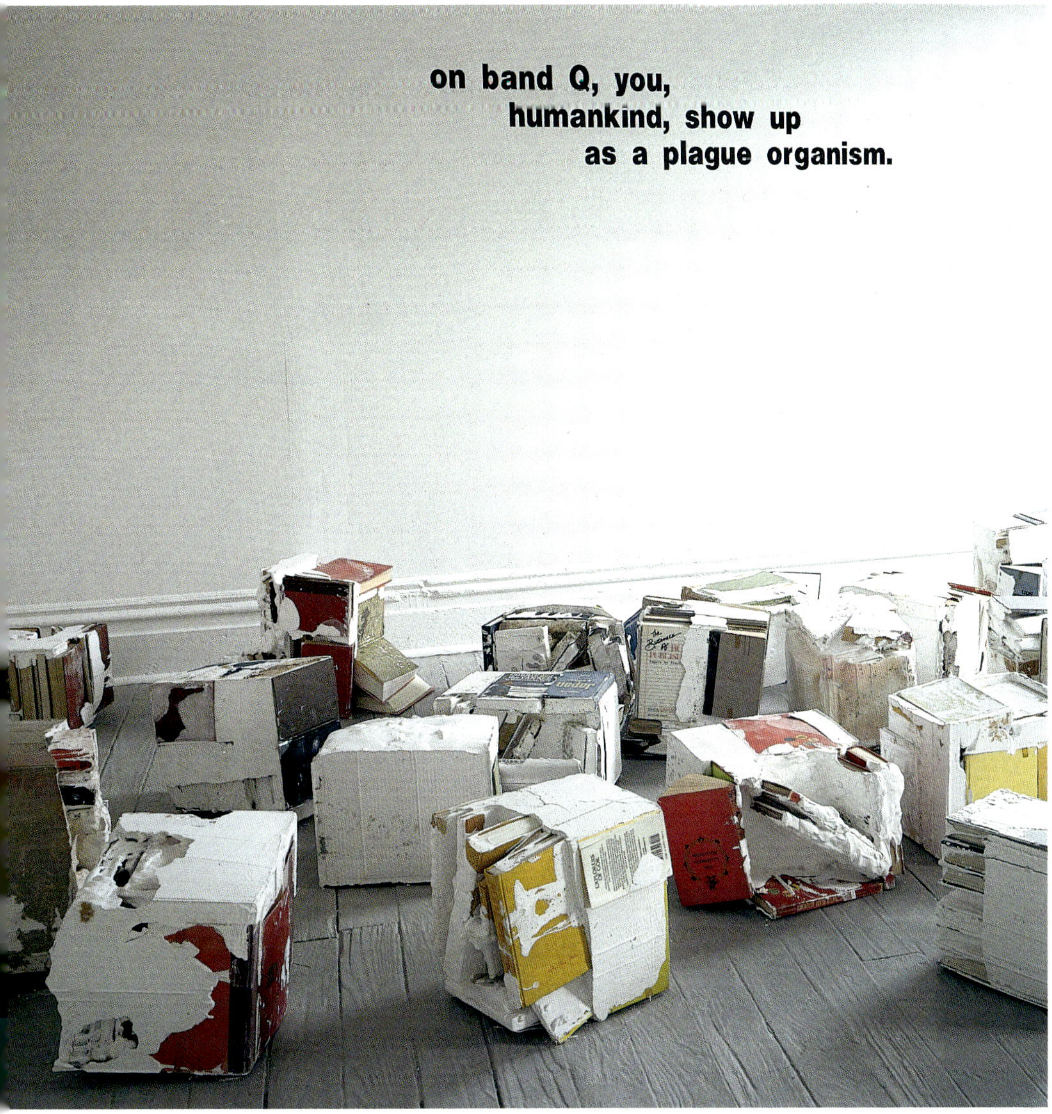

on band Q, you,
humankind, show up
as a plague organism.

**Skoob Tower,** performance on June 1, 1996
Glass, iron, books, fire
500 Sampsonia Way, *Garden*

Latham created a tower of old encyclopedias on a base of angle irons. He burned this tower of books—spelled backward, skoob—at the opening reception.

> "The book tower was a formal sculpture and intended in every way to be an extension of the tradition of sculpture. It was not in any degree a gesture of contempt for the books or literature. What it did intend was to put the proposition into mind that perhaps the cultural base was burnt out. Thus with the towers it seemed more logical to make a sculpture which disintegrated by fire—as the more dignified statement."
>
> **John Latham quoted in an essay by Marion Keiner in *John Latham: Art After Physics*, The Museum of Modern Art, Oxford, 1991.**

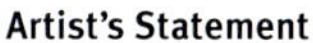

**Artist's Statement**

The new thing, the (T) concept and Event structure, is not like authenticated versions of art—it is exactly about the world one sees and touches but it is not figurative. So it foxes the Fox. (T) is a geometry of sources of action, maths—intelligible and exact, but it contradicts the cornerspeak of science. When you realise that the two super-theories of physics each carry a demonstrated flaw, and that (T) may sort these flaws out, you are okay to take the (T) claim seriously. It might even start at the beginning to sort out what has just about done for this planet. For one thing, in (T) the Universe shows up as a person. Half the world knows it but can't say how so.

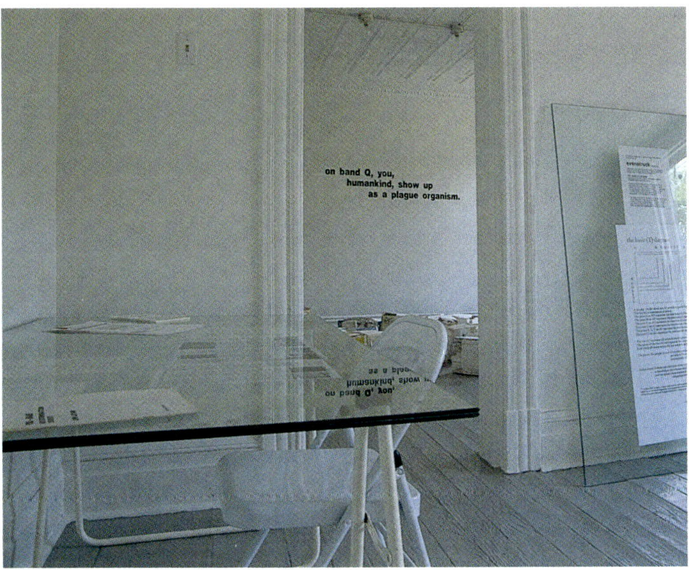


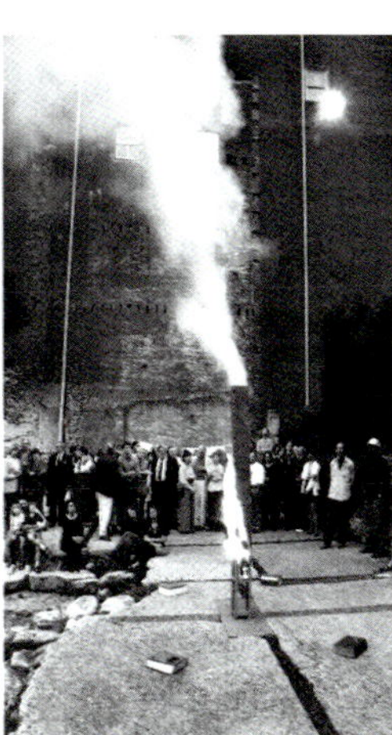

## Yayoi Kusama

Japanese, born 1929

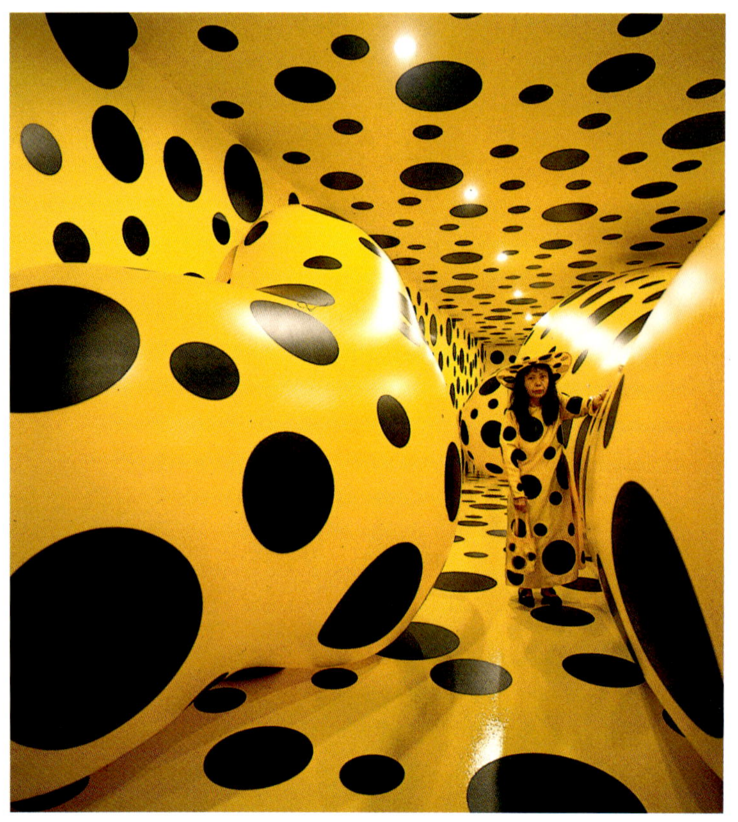

**Dots Obsession,** 1996
Paint, steel, adhesive dots, balloons
500 Sampsonia Way, 3rd floor
(Margery King, curator)

A room sixteen feet wide, fifty feet long, and ten feet high has been painted an intense yellow. Three sizes of black dots (eight inches to twenty inches in diameter) have been placed on the walls, the floor, and the ceiling. Three giant, organically shaped yellow balloons (one is thirty feet long by ten feet high) covered with the same black dots fill the space, physically and visually, crowding out visitors.

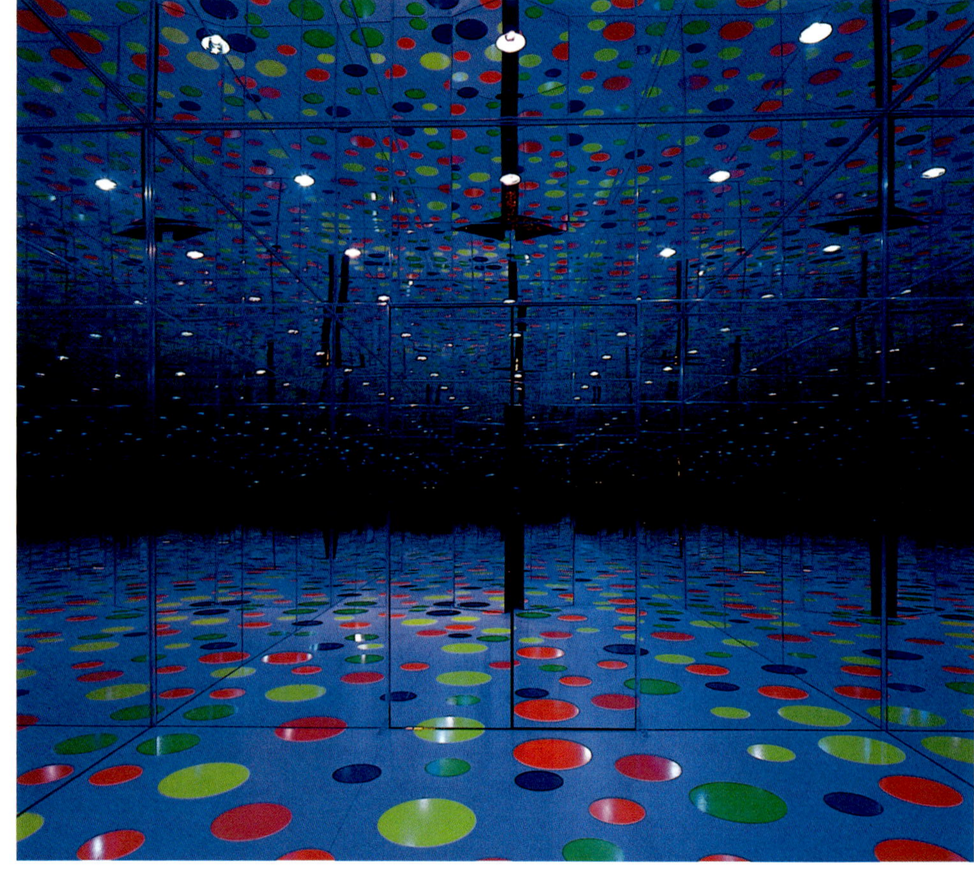

**Infinity Dots Mirrored Room,** 1996
Adhesive dots, black light, Formica, mirrors
500 Sampsonia Way, 3rd floor
(Margery King, curator)

The visitor approaches a black double door, which opens to a space with mirrored ceilings and walls. The white Formica floor is covered with three sizes of colored fluorescent dots and the room is lit by a black light. Reflected in mirrors on the ceiling and walls, the visitor becomes an integral part of the space.

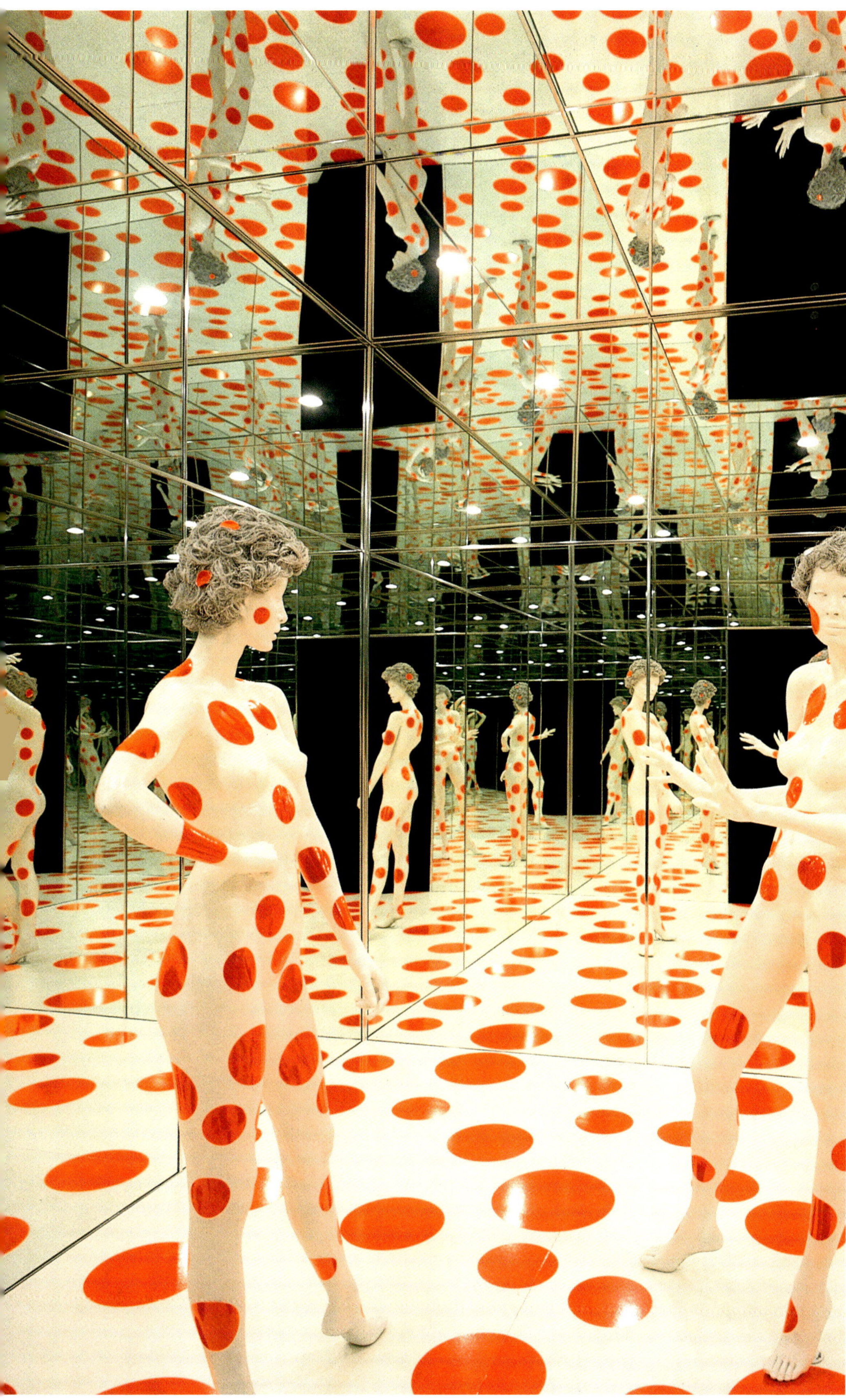

**Repetitive Vision,** 1996
Formica, adhesive dots,
mannequins, mirrors
500 Sampsonia Way, 3rd floor
(Margery King, curator)

The visitor enters the brightly lit space of *Repetitive Vision* through *Infinity Dots Mirrored Room.* The floor is covered in red dots. Three female mannequins, painted white, their bodies and hair covered with similar dots, are reflected, along with the visitor, in the mirrored walls and ceiling.

**Artist's Statement:**
A Passage to Another World

A mirror is a device which obliterates everything including myself and others in the light of another world or a gallant apparatus which creates nothingness.

My ominous recollection: one day, I was looking at a tablecloth covered in red flowers, which was spread out on the table. Then I looked up towards the ceiling. There, on the windows and even on the pillars, I would see the same red flowers. They were all over the place in the room, my body, and entire universe. I finally came to a self-obliteration and returned to be restored to the infinity of eternal time and the absoluteness of space. I was not having a vision. It was true reality. I was astounded. Unless I got out of here, the curse of those flowers will seize my life! I ran frantically up the stairs. As I looked down, the sight of each step falling apart made me stumble. I fell all the way down the stairs and sprained my leg.

Dismantling and accumulating, proliferating and separating, the sense of obliterating and the sounds from the invisible cosmos. What are all these things?

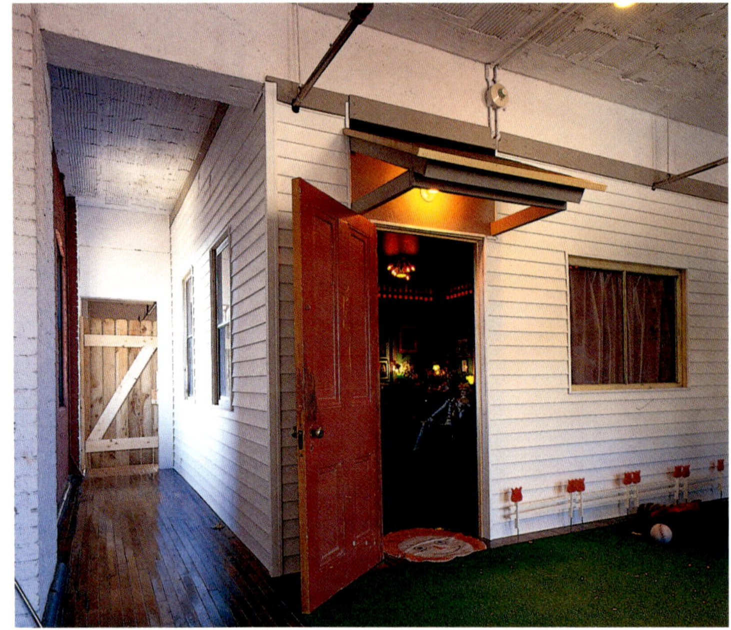

## Greer Lankton

American, 1958–1996

**It's all about ME, Not You,** 1996
Wood, vinyl siding, AstroTurf, paint, artwork
500 Sampsonia Way, 4th floor
(Margery King, curator)

The visitor enters the installation through a gate, which opens onto a narrow alley behind a "white trash" house. The house is covered with white siding and is outfitted with old windows and an AstroTurf patio littered with fall leaves. Ruby slippers, at the end of legs in striped stockings, emerge from underneath the house.

Inside is a recreation of the Chicago apartment in which Greer Lankton lived and worked. The walls are painted deep colors, and stars cover the ceiling. The room is inhabited by the dolls and figures Lankton made during the course of her life. Anorexic Raggedy Anns appear next to a bedridden morphine addict doll, over which a multitude of pill bottles are strewn. Throughout the room are very personal shrines Lankton created to Patti Smith, Candy Darling, and Jesus. Other shrines honor the artist herself.

Much of Lankton's work is clearly autobiographical, revealing her obsession with her own body. Born male, she became female at the age of 21. She died in November 1996, shortly after *It's all about ME, Not You* opened to the public.

**Artist's Statement**

I've been in therapy since 18 months old, started drugs at 12 was diagnosed as schizophrenic at 19, started hormones the week after I quit Thorazine got my dick inverted at 21, kicked Heroin 6 years ago. Have been Anorexic since 19 and plan to continue and you know what I say FUCK Recovery, FUCK PSYCHIATRY Fuck it all because I'm over it. Over the roof. I'm so sick I'm dead, so from now on I take no responsibility for my actions. Oh and I was fucked up the ass by my grandfather since age 5, been brutally raped twice and have had almost every major organ in my body fail at some point. Life support is no picnic for Rhoda so don't EVEN take me there. By the way I'm an artist and Andy Warhol was the dullest person I ever met in my life. But he's got a museum so what do I know. Hans Bellmer is my favorite artist.

Love Always,
Greer

Artificial Nature
Total Indulgence
Dolls engrossed in glamour and self abuse
The vanity
The junkie
The anorexic
The chronic mastabater
"Its all about ME"
Not You
Trapped in my own world in my
head in my tiny tiny
apartment

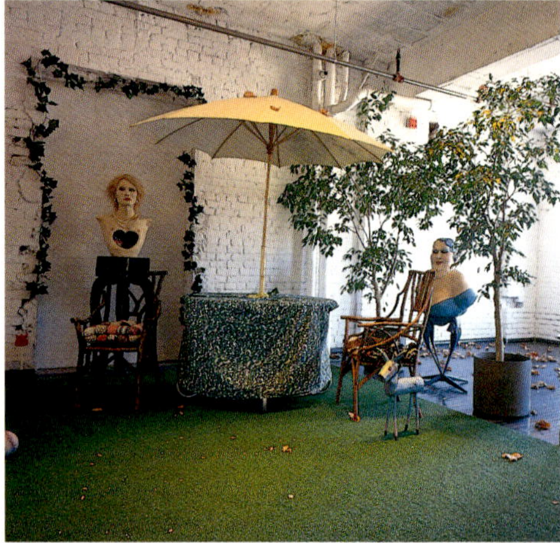

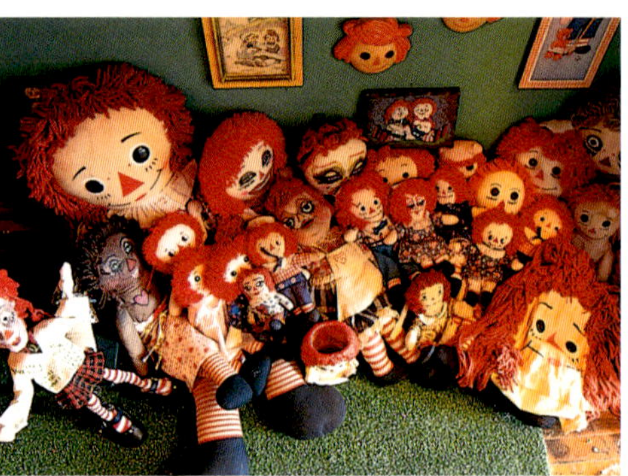

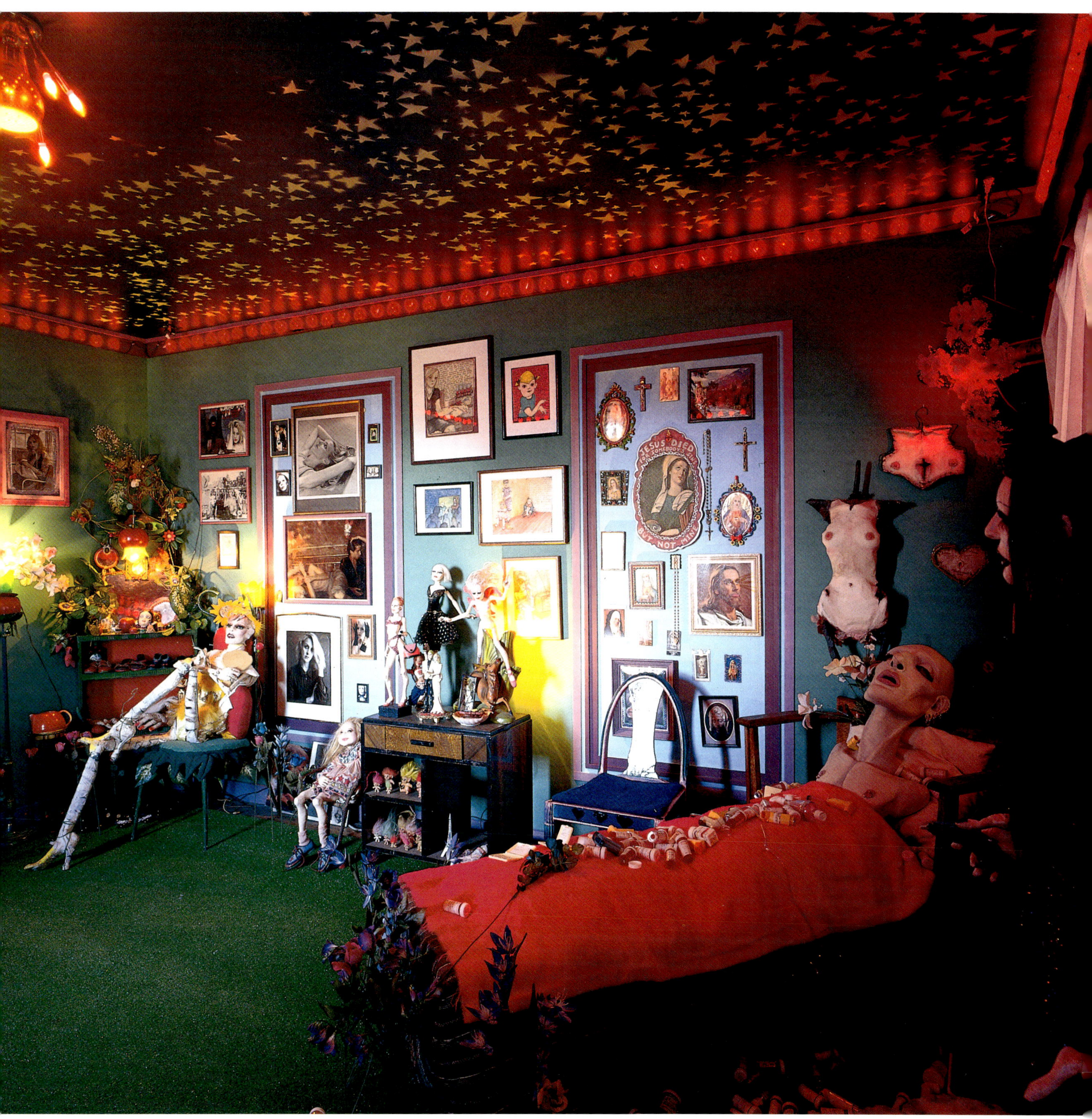
JESUS DIED
FOR SOMEBODY'S SINS
BUT NOT MINE

## Andre Walker

British, born 1965

**Untitled**, 1996
Steel, fabric, vinyl, paint
500 Sampsonia Way, 4th floor
(Margery King, curator)

False walls are constructed inside the gallery. The actual museum room is visible through the window at the far end of the constructed space. The fourteen-foot by fifty-foot floor is covered with polished steel on which the artist has written the following poem in light green paint.

An eleven-foot tall figure, visible only from the waist down, strides as if on a runway. The larger than life sized legs wear Walker's self-designed "Musketeer Pant," which reveal sandal-clad feet with toenails painted a deep shade of purple-brown. The walls and floor coverings coordinate with the fabric used to clothe the figure, as in a fashion show.

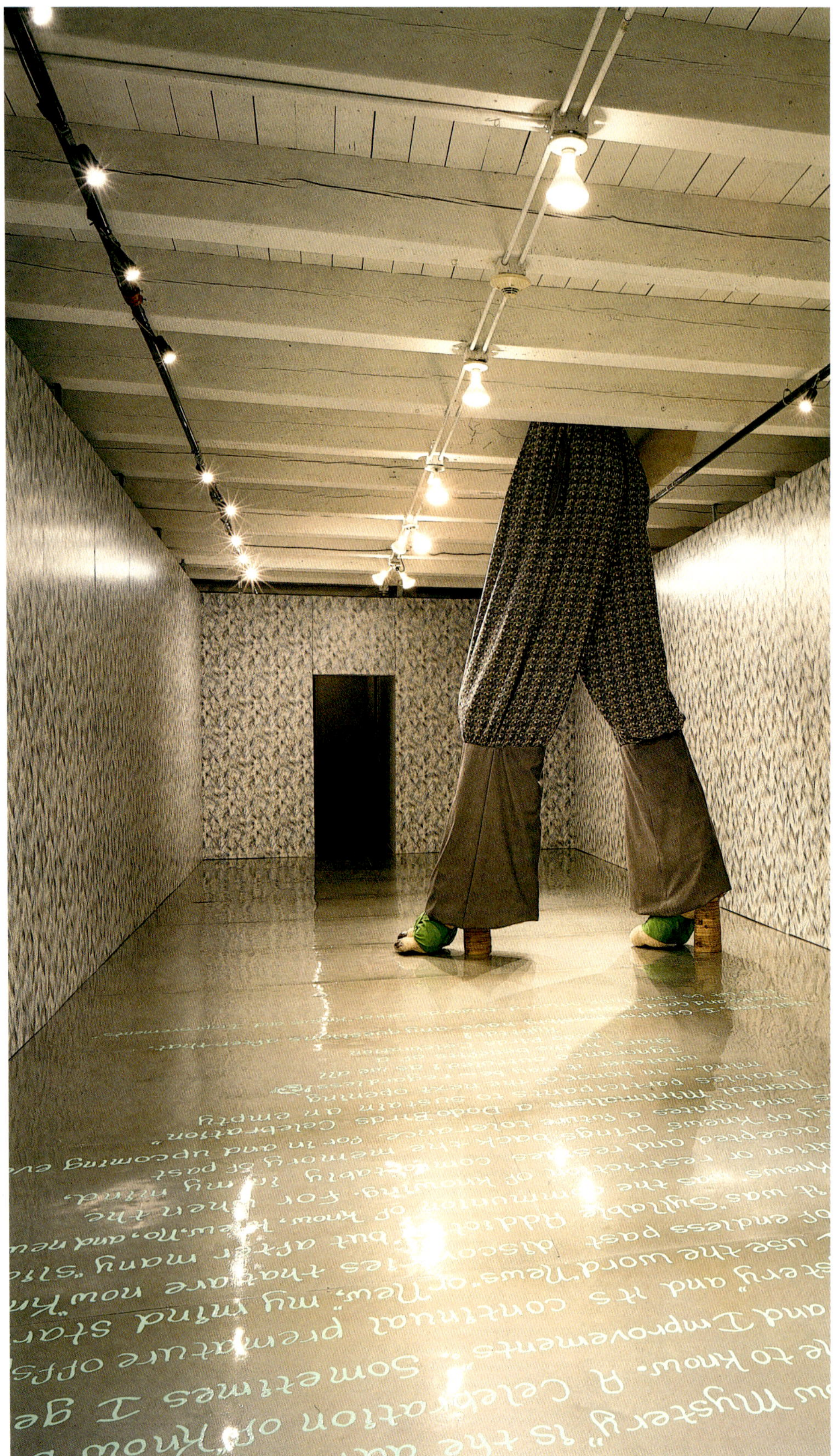

**Artist's Statement**

*Complexitease*. . . By Gene Tyrahns
It's all our different strong characters
that are looking to find
The strong character that we are not
Monologue—individual clarity of expression,
igniting fuel for dialogue . . .
Monologue—individual clarity of feeling, thought,
understanding . . . express . . . listen . . . express
Dialogue—plural exchange of individual clarities
of thought . . . possibly leading to a unified
exchange of ideas . . . thought . . .
Patience, Care, Optimism . . . shared, casually
leading up to shared clarity . . . these things
come to mind . . .
Ventures in exposure of "endless" . . .
endless events endless uncertainty
endless desire "rings" of true confessioning
internal glamour of clothes really don't
matter but where "internal glamour"
True Exaggerationing Surrounds . . . here
True Exaggerationsurrounding . . . events
is_______________endless
We all want to be smart freestyle internal pleasure
"folks"
"Knews" . . . Judge yourself until you find out its okay

Miniaturizing fears about unveiling the reason
I just wanted . . . let my true feelings
Won't even bother to say___________ "show"
"Syllable Addiction"
Move Meant . . . Go
Move Meant . . . Now
Move Meant . . . Right (Rhydtt!)
Move Meant . . . Out
Move Meant . . . Forward
Move Meant . . . We
Move Meant . . . Continue
Move Meant . . . Come on Already!
Move Meant . . . You
Move Meant . . . Move!
All Ready . . . Your all of Yours. . .
Pull it over to decide
Pull it over to decide

High Heal Positioning . . . "Who sculpted the Mono Lisa
Who painted the Michelangelo" Vincent Mc Doom
"Some Chew Us" . . . "Somechewus" because there's
nothing left to buy
Sumptuous—Rich and Costly suggesting lavish expenditure
. . . you know
"Knews" . . . You thought you were hot
and I thought so too
You thought you were hot
(And) I thought so too . . .
You thought you had to write it again
And I thought that's "Knews"
Pull it over and take it in
Pull it over and take it in . . .

Miniaturizing Categories for
"Tranquil Hospitalities"
Special Prays Is": Gene Trahns
Nurea Nockslead
Stina Shray
Repmee Barloads
Fouwhed Youlds
Federico Massotto
Shirley of London
"through"
Andre Walker

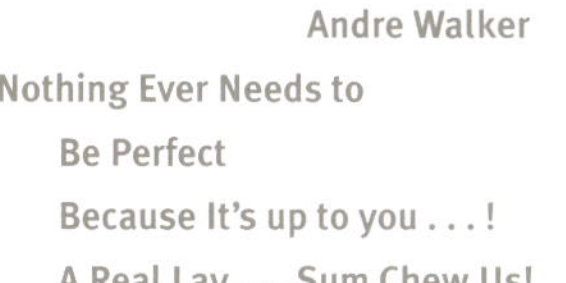

Nothing Ever Needs to
Be Perfect
Because It's up to you . . . !
A Real Lay . . . Sum Chew Us!

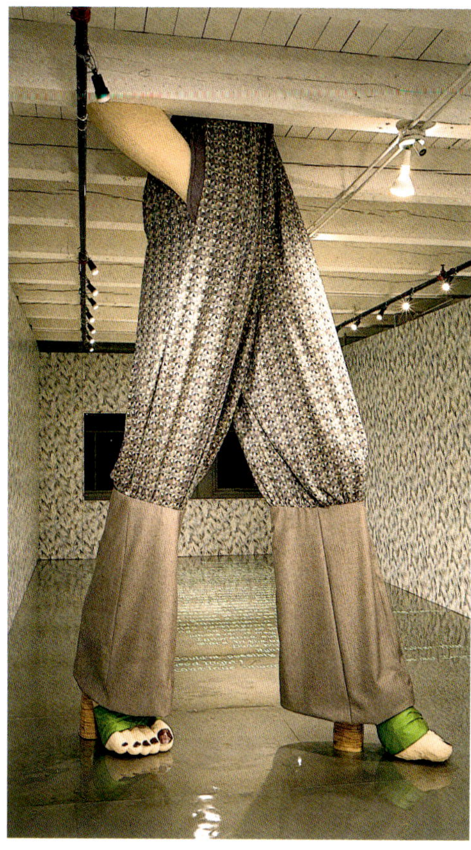

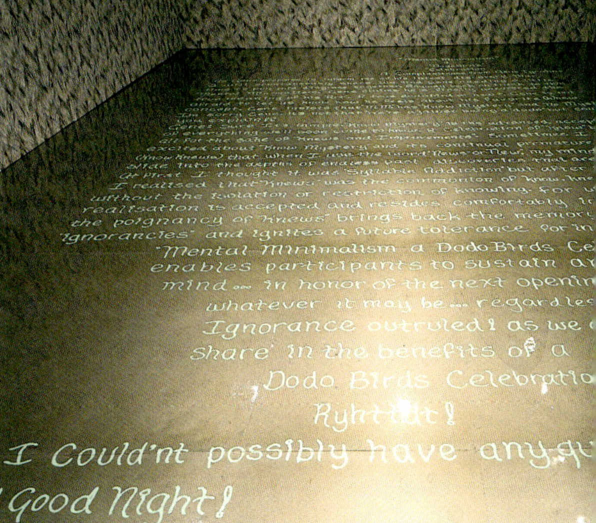

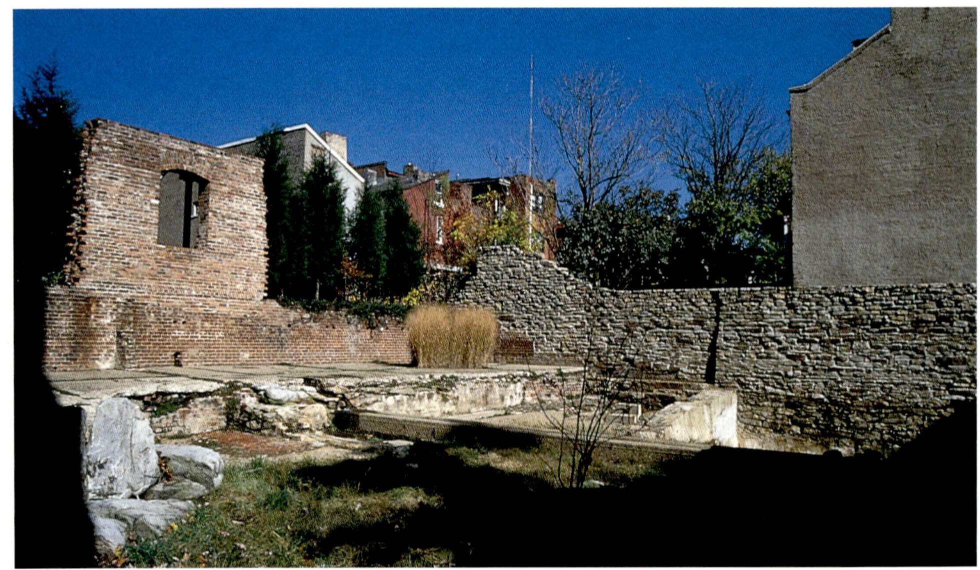

## Winifred Lutz

American, born 1942

**Garden**, dedicated in 1997, ongoing
Stones, concrete, brick, rebar, wood, plants
(permanent installation)

By the time Winifred Lutz began work on her permanent garden installation in 1993, she had already studied the site for five years. She used the information she had uncovered—both historical and physical—to design a garden that responded to and incorporated the history and attributes of the site, including the foundation of a paper factory that had burned to the ground many years ago.

The three-quarters of an acre adjacent to 500 Sampsonia Way is a living work. In the area known as the Private Prairie, an enclosure for a single chair is surrounded by tall grass. A trellis, made from huge wooden beams, acts as an entryway from the parking area. Water flowing through a concrete trough splashes and gurgles. Large stones, individually selected from a western Pennsylvania quarry, dot the landscape. Cast-cement apertures in the brick and stone walls frame specific views.

Twisted rebar railings descend ten feet below ground level to a cement basin filled with water. Water emerges from the brick retaining wall and flows back into the stone beneath the viewfinder in the boundary wall. It is diverted to fall into a basin in the basement stairwell, cooling the space and intensifying its privacy with a screen of sound.

Birds are attracted to the urban garden by indigenous wildflowers as well as newly planted trees of species which would have grown on that site long before buildings were erected there.

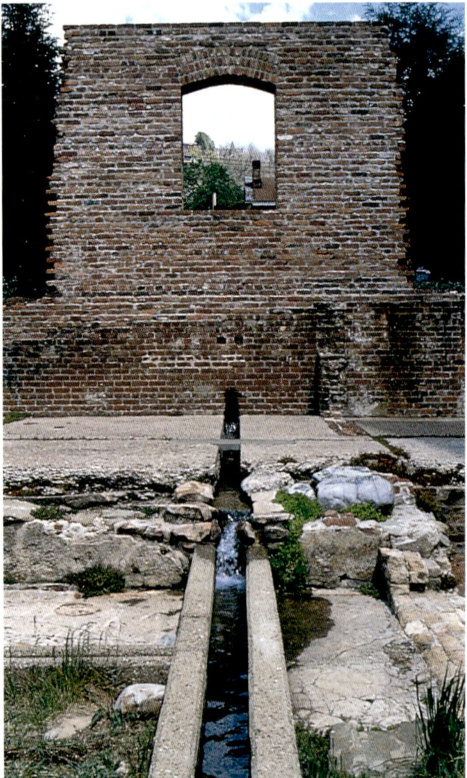

**Artist's Statement**
***(excerpted from an interview with the artist, May 14, 1997)***

Everything that I've done in the *Garden* has really been about uncovering its urban and natural history in terms of both the site and my own knowledge and experience. I've been to a number of very old cities where they've dug down through the layers of the history of the city. In standard archeological practice, they preserved that as a vignette of time within the framework of a contemporary city. I also used the strategy of looking at what is here and what I can do with it. Where are the edges of time, cultural influence, recent history, past history, and natural history?

The Private Prairie changes with the seasons, becoming a cyclical event. When you sit in the chair, the grass is so high that you can't be seen and you can't see out. Your experience is one of sitting in the middle of a vast sea of grass.

The water trough in the garden divides the natural history and the urban history of the space and connects the upper and lower levels. As you look to the lower level, the memory of the fields and glacial moraine are to your right and the excavation of the paper factory is to your left.

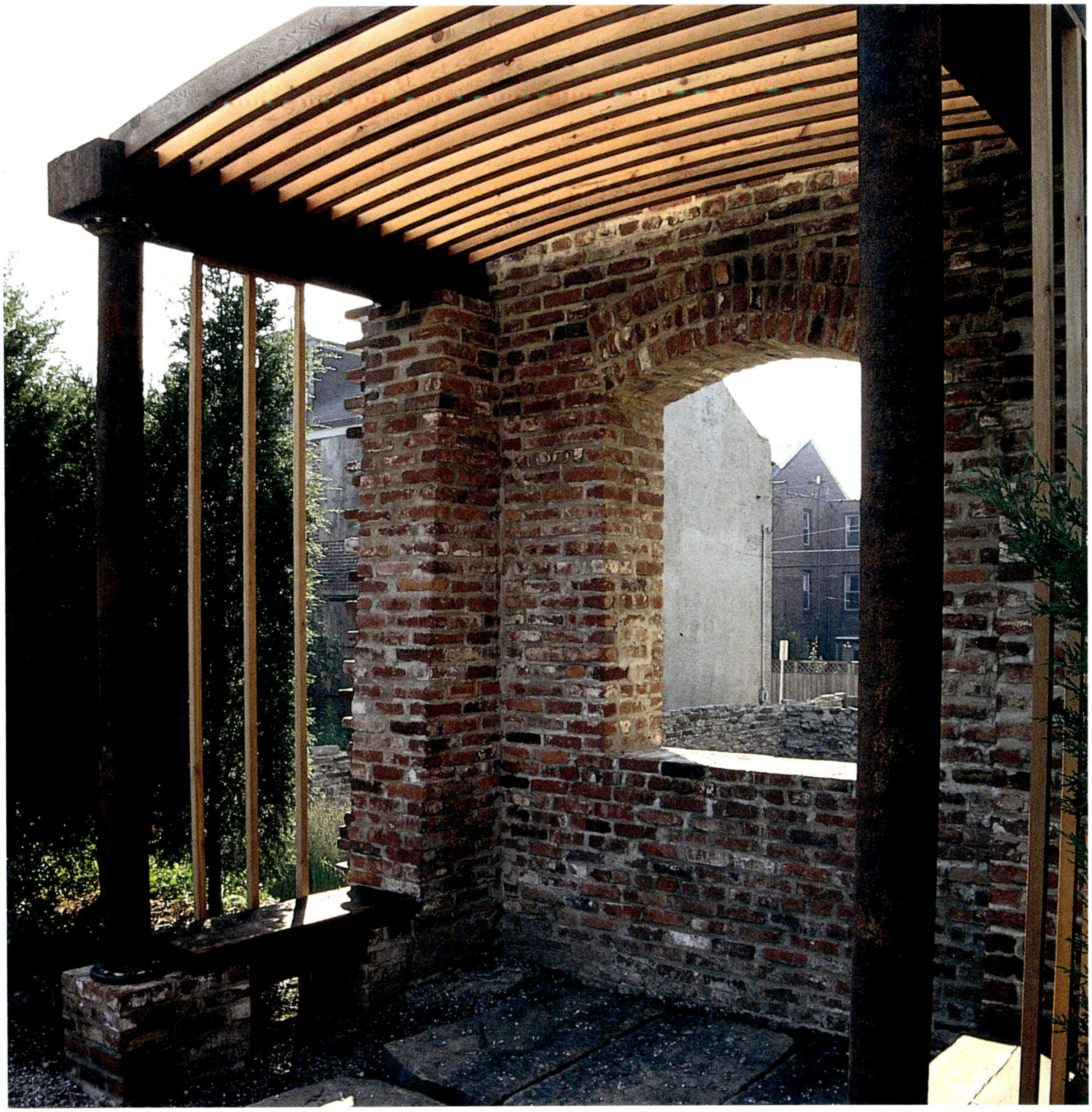

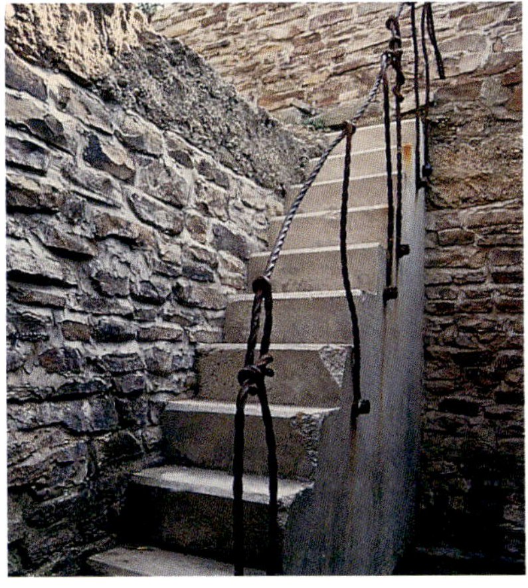

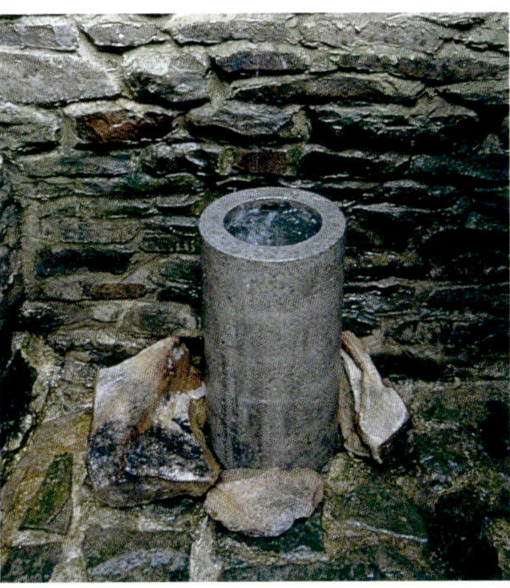

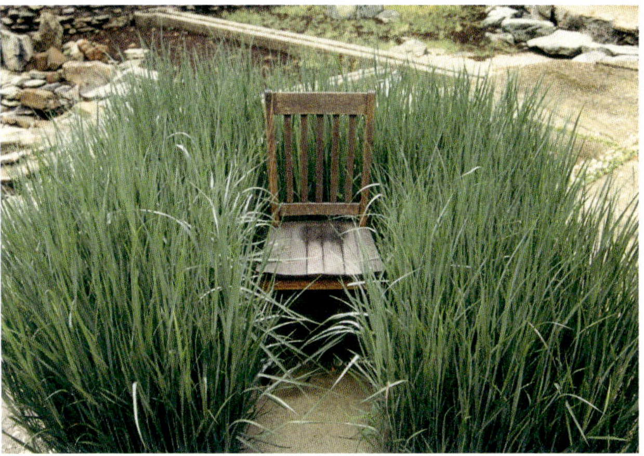

## William Anastasi

American, born 1933

**Printed Out,** October 4, 1997
Performance with computer and voice-recognition software

Sitting blindfolded, behind a rope that kept him from being disturbed, artist William Anastasi talked into a recording device connected to a computer. The computer translated his vocal statements into text, which was visible on the monitor and then printed out and posted on the wall. The random mistakes and misunderstandings that occurred in the translation created a new text, devoid of the artist's control and intent. For instance, the artist said, "Duchamp," and the computer printed out "the champ."

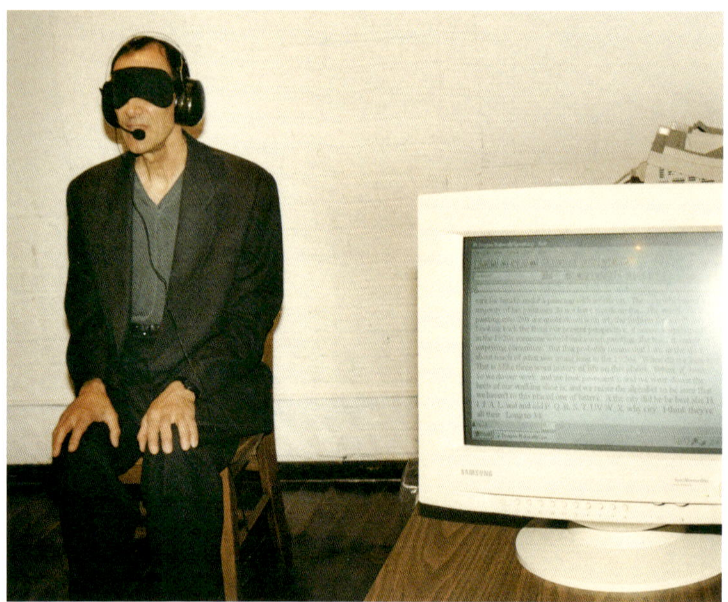

**Example of printout**

A the of the river on pest even Adams brings us by the river on past the refrigerant on past even Adams brings us by the river on past the refrigerator praises by come 0 is because of re-circulation back to health castle and and the river if the system to this isn't this is the program its bows Sonoma courts to a heavy recruited a isn't a up somebody else his voices thereof known a because here some time time because here's some time to time here's some time to time a by the is quite sensitive so if people talking the soap talking in the room and in love is so wonderful and in law and in love is is good of escort should this so wonderful in the rule of is a wonderful add-on coming right over there is to the finish killing Wimbledon was still goes with a he the designer in in a he the live in an emitted in the he you of the looms in a day room room in the didn't hit in the in the in of the in lieu of the looms in the in the in the only his a

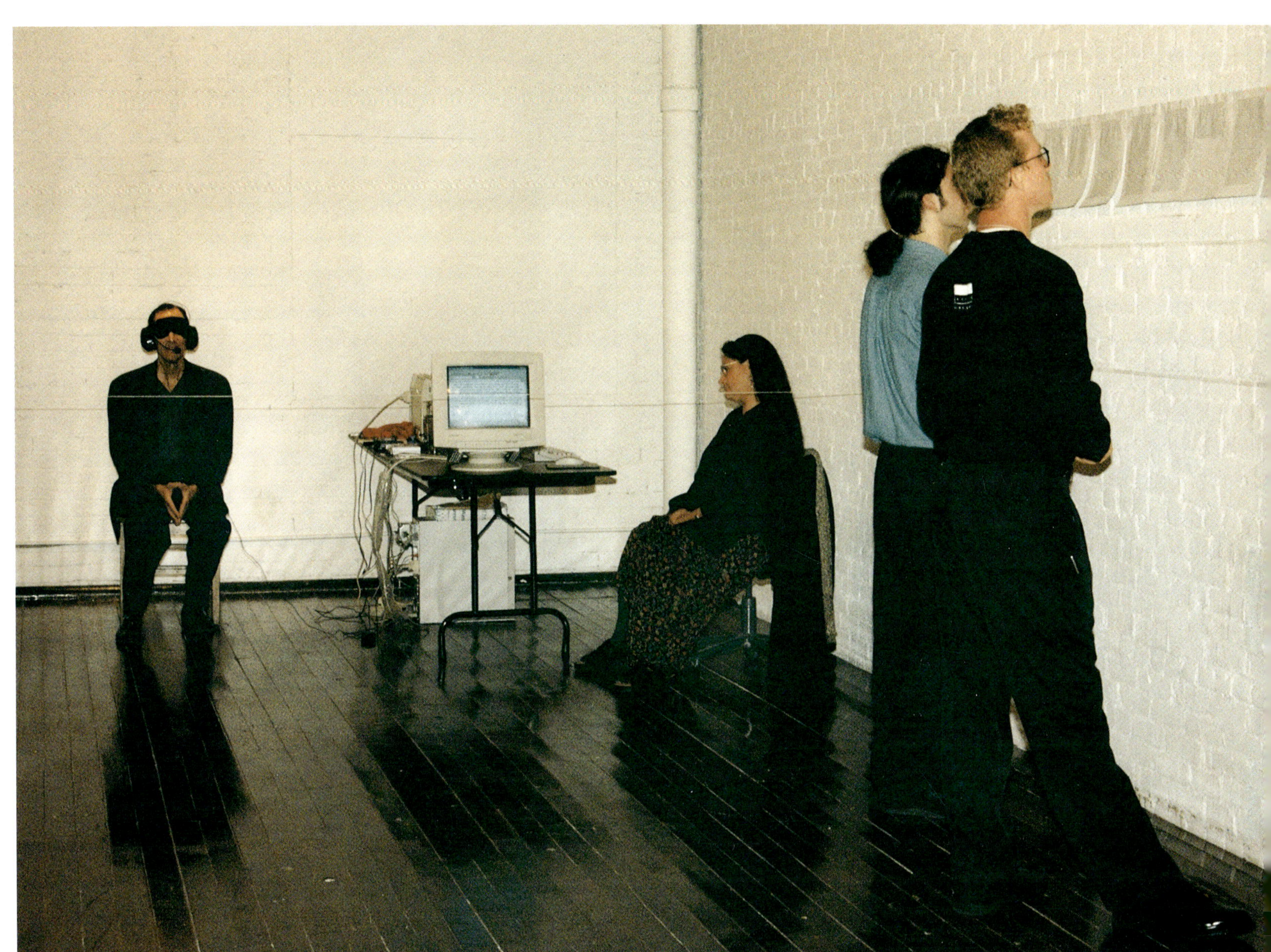

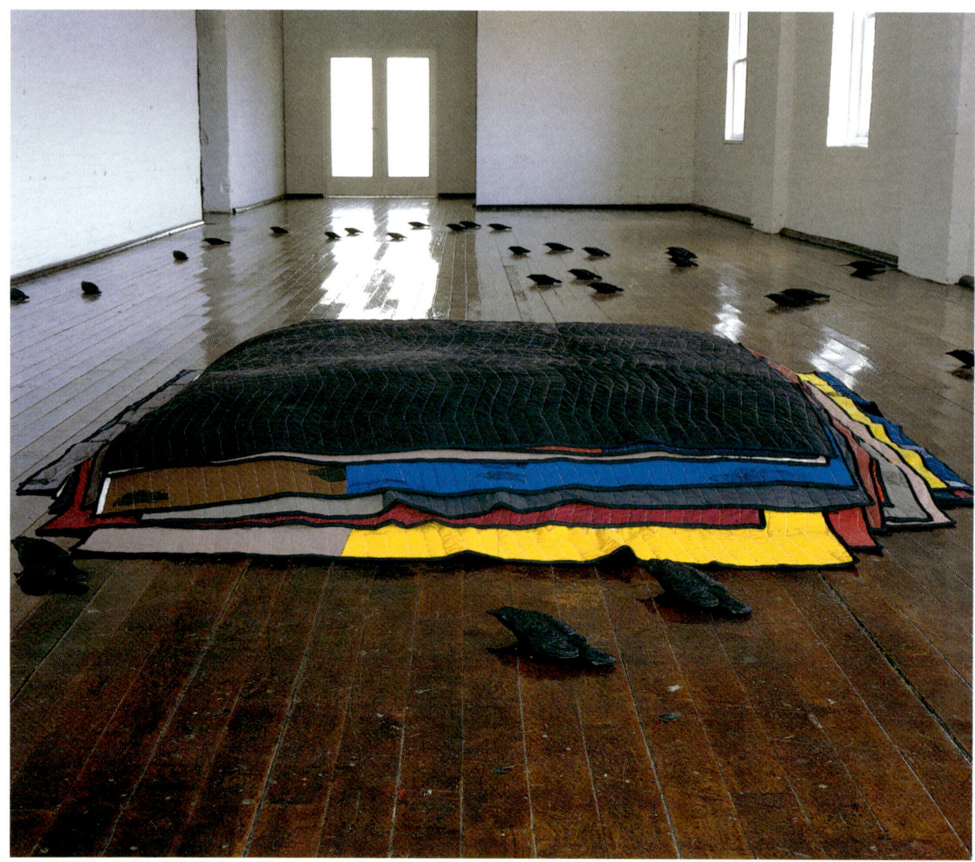

## Kiki Smith

American, born 1954

**Flight Mound,** 1998
Silk-screened fabric, cotton batting, silicon bronze
500 Sampsonia Way, 4th floor

Smith made drawings of specimens from The Carnegie Museum of Natural History's study collection of birds by scratching into Kodalith film. These drawings were transferred to silk screens, which were printed onto fabric in the colors of bird feathers. The printed fabric was then lined with cheap floral fabric, quilted and made into packing blankets.

Smith arranged the packing blankets in a single mound on the floor of the gallery. Forty cast-bronze blue jays are arranged on the floor, all facing in one direction. The title, *Flight Mound*, refers to Indian burial mounds in North America by which, some believe, birds navigate in their migrations.

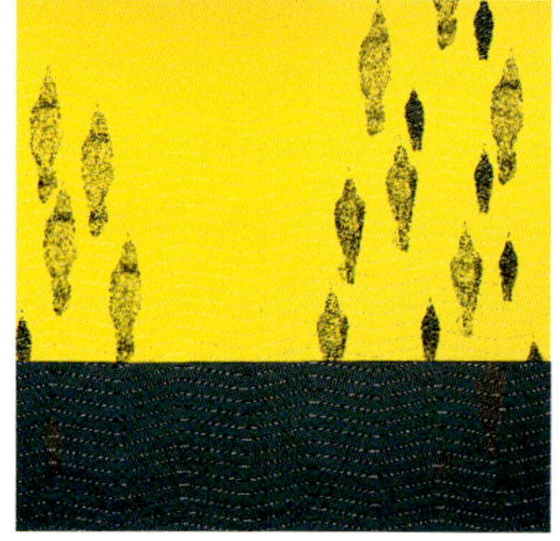

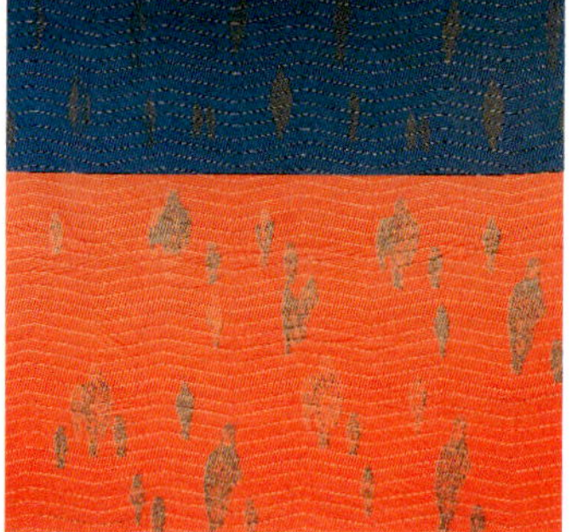

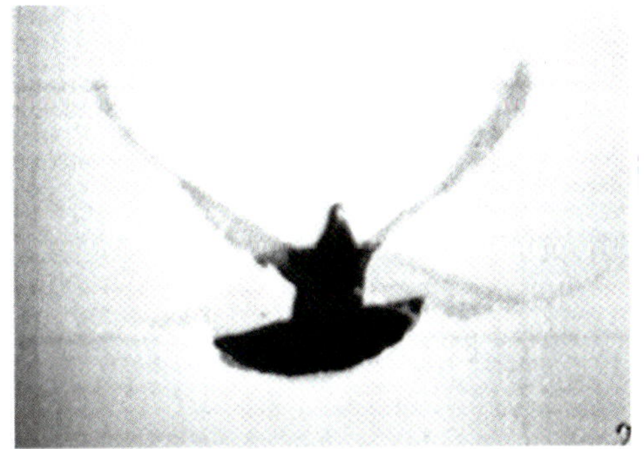

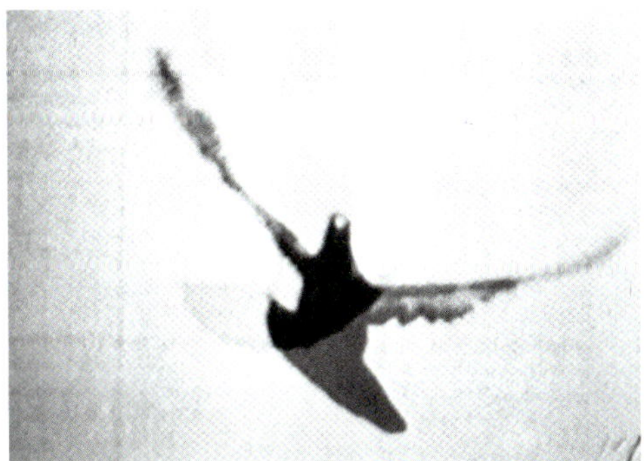

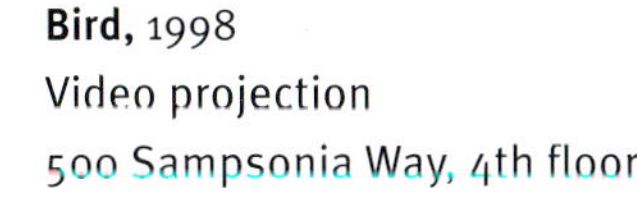

**Bird,** 1998
Video projection
500 Sampsonia Way, 4th floor

The adjacent darkened room houses a video reanimation of Eadweard Muybridge's 1885 photographic sequences of a bird in flight. The twelve consecutive photographs, transferred to video and projected larger than life, repeat continuously.

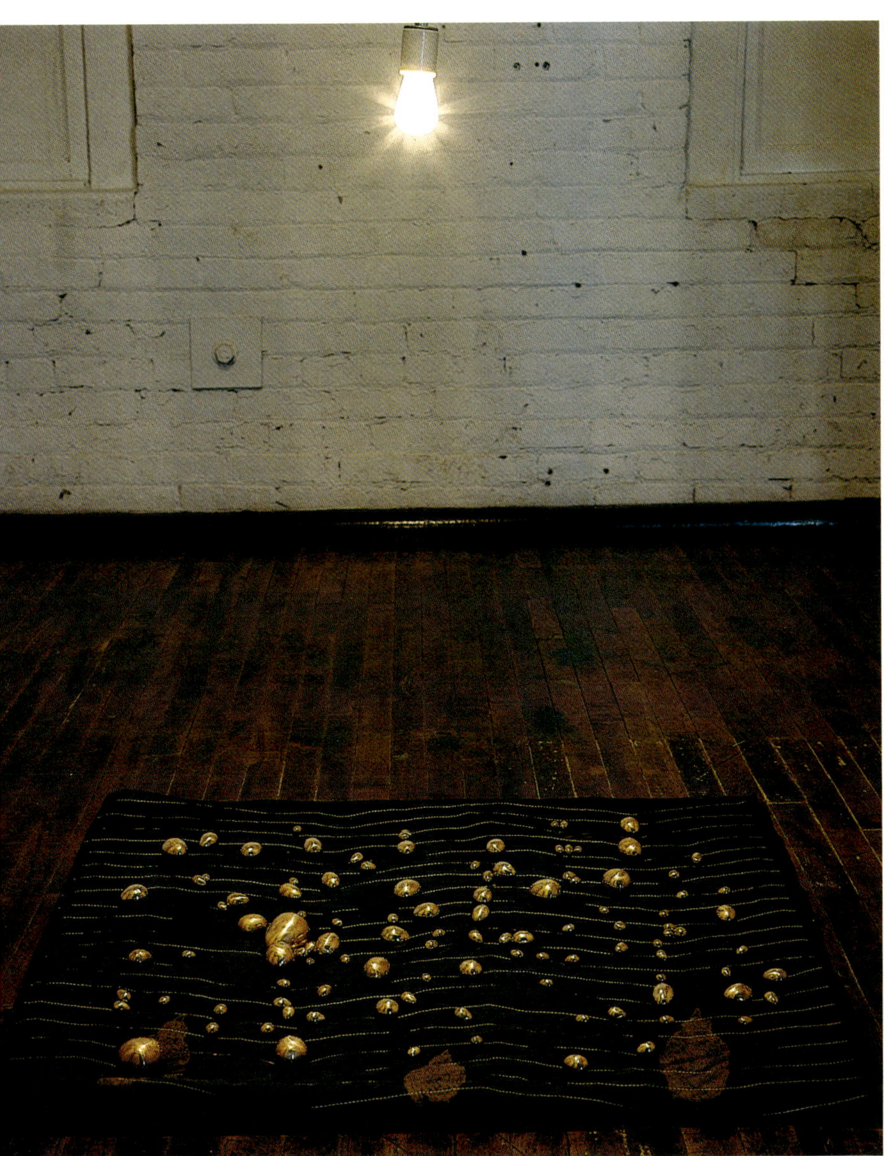

**Little Space,** 1998
Brass, screen-printing ink, fabric, cotton batting, thread, hanging light
500 Sampsonia Way, 4th floor

At the opposite end of the same room, resting on a single folded black packing blanket, are over a hundred brass eggs, ranging in size from a robin's egg to a duck's. A single low-wattage light bulb illuminates them.

## Rolf Julius

German, born 1939

**Black Listens to Red (Piano Concerto),** 1998
Ink-jet prints, sound equipment, glass, pigment
1414 Monterey Street, 3rd floor

In the first room, sixty-three ink-jet prints of red and black dots have been mounted on the far wall. Interspersed through the pattern of dots are sheets with text. They read: "Black listens/ Red/ piano/concerto."

In the next room, two glass sheets are positioned on the floor next to each other. Red and black powdered pigments have been poured onto the glass. These pigments move based on the vibrations created by the speakers underneath. The ink-jet prints in the adjoining room are records of the shapes made by these powdered pigments.

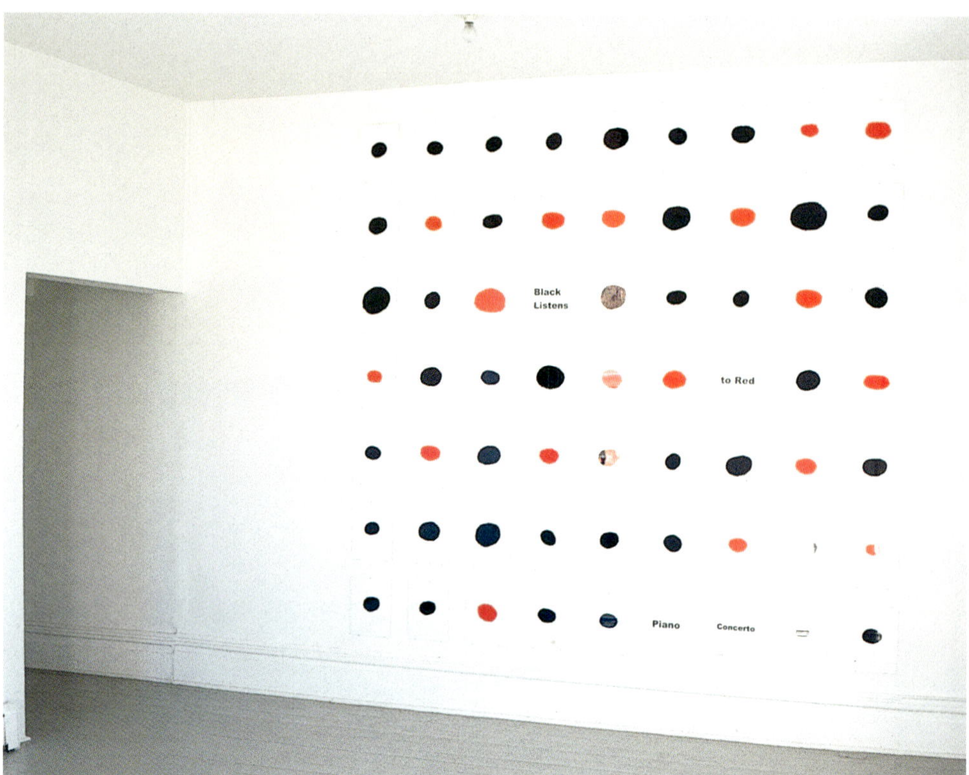


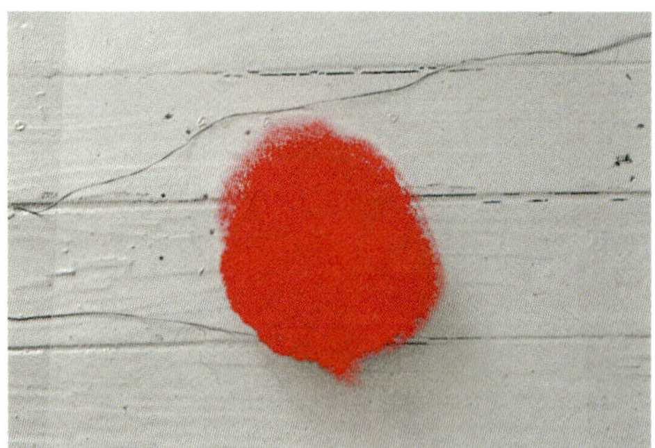

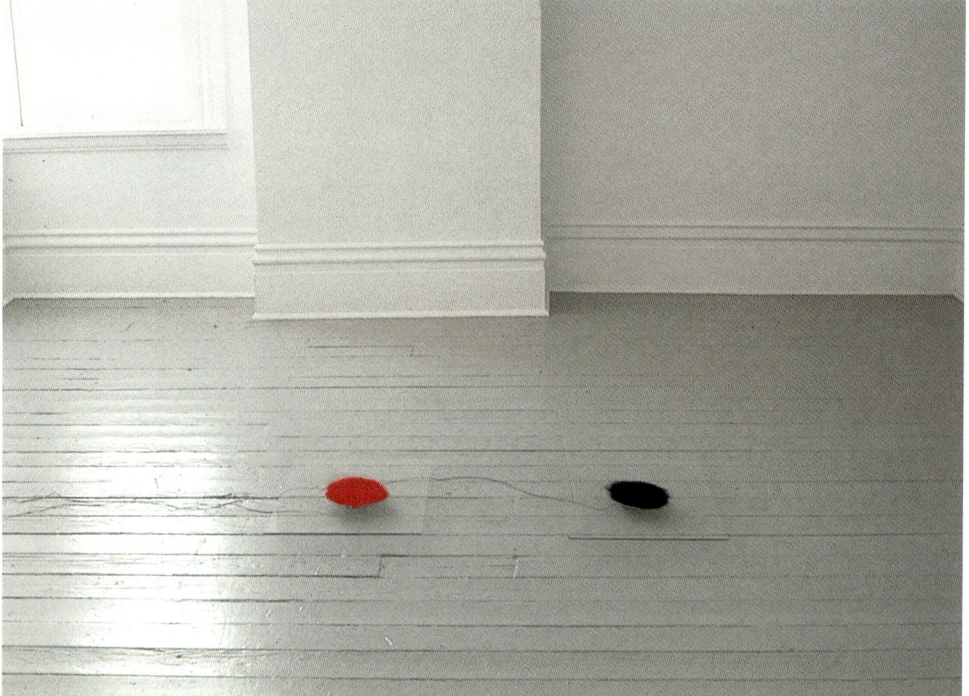

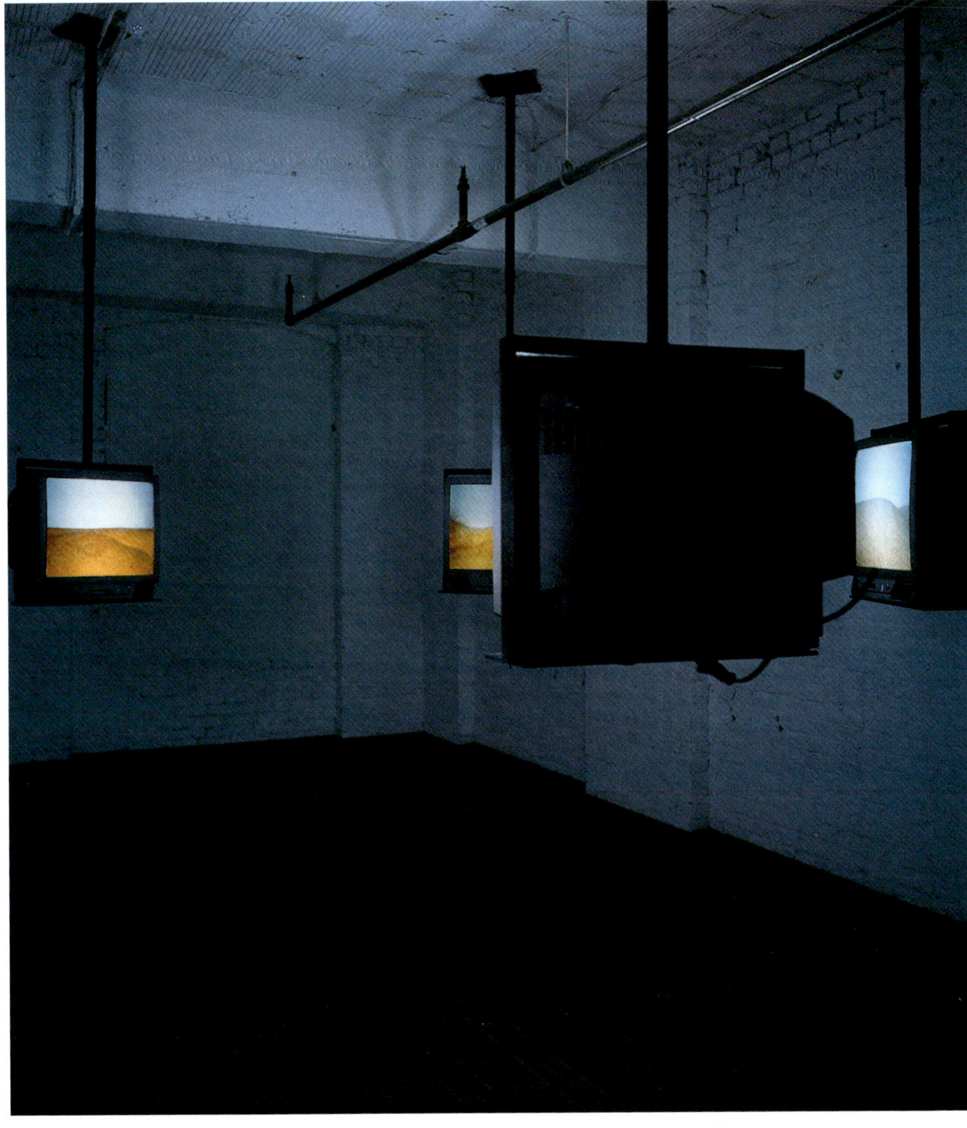

## David Blatherwick

Canadian, born 1960

**Multiple Horizon,** 1998
Videos, monitors, steel
500 Sampsonia Way, 4th floor

The installation is situated at the far end of a darkened space. Five video monitors face each other in a circle and display close-up images of different parts of the artist's body. Each of these images initially appears to be a landscape. A cycle of inhaling and exhaling begins in a pattern that travels around the circle of monitors, ceasing only for several seconds, when the figure in the video holds his breath.

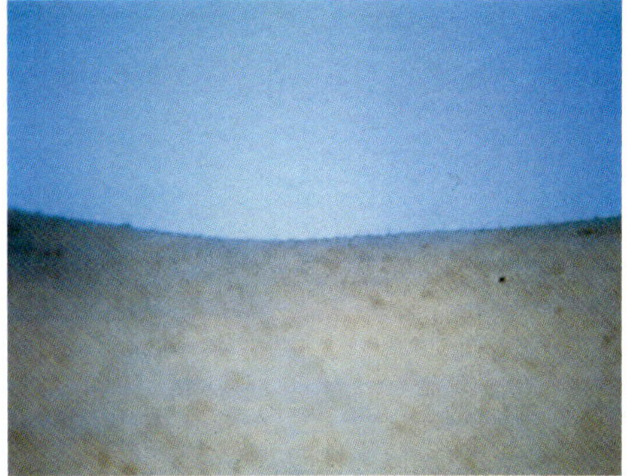

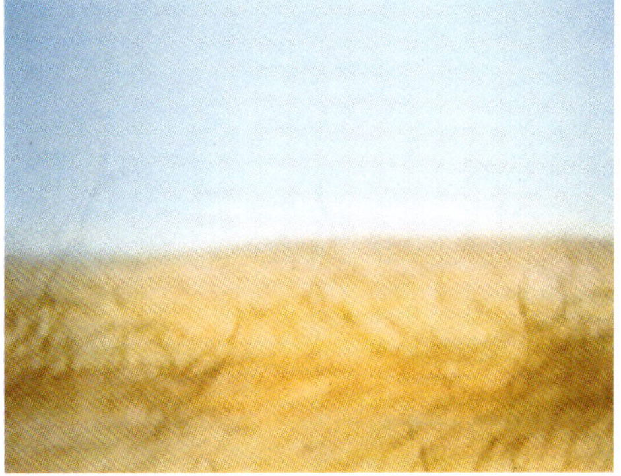

**Artist's Statement**

Primarily I wanted to deal with breathing as an act performed unconsciously that acts as a real exchange between zones perceived to be separate. As with other bodily functions viewed in detail, listening to someone, or yourself, can be a very beautiful and frightening experience. Another subject present here is the notion of the individual as the multiple. What if we could have separate breaths for each of the separate selves inside us? Rather than the psychological, I am more interested in looking at this in an almost musical way . . . as if our bodies could be seen / heard as a small ensemble playing a form of concrete music. Finally, I wanted to create confusion between body and landscape, to blur that aforementioned boundary, to make a reversal fleetingly possible. When looking at things, anything (even the piece of paper you are reading) can become a landscape, or better still a microcosmos.

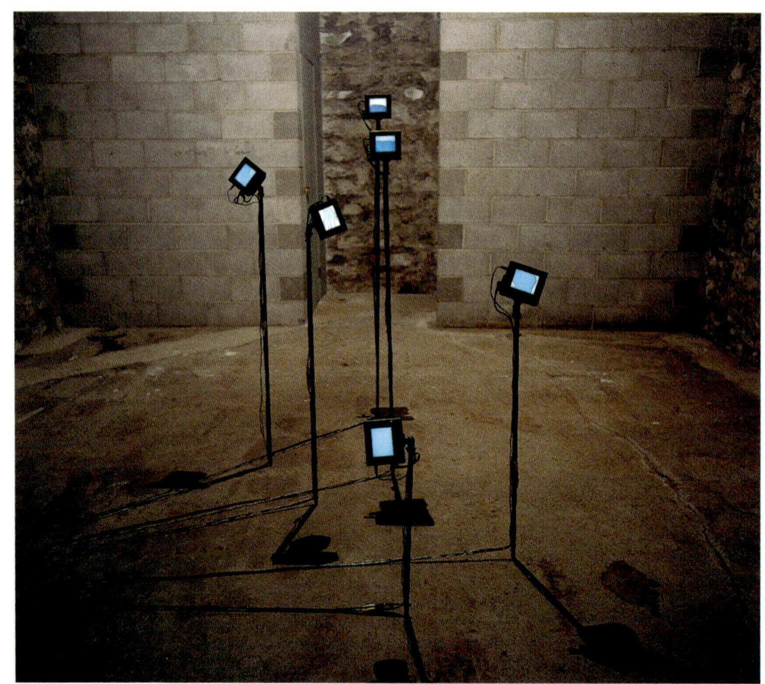

## Lynn Cazabon

American, born 1964

**Spot,** 1998
Audio, video, monitors, steel, clothing, table, curtain, spotlight
500 Sampsonia Way, lower level

The first room appears to be backstage. A dark red curtain hangs behind a table. On this table is a dark curly wig, a bustier, tight white jeans and black panties, which have been sewn together to create one piece. Next to this are red fingernails of various sizes and below the table are a pair of open-toed high heels of translucent plastic. Also on the table is a miniature television monitor, showing the artist dressed in the clothing on the table. In this room, a woman's voice narrates a verbal transcription of the initial scenes of a pornographic film.

The visitor walks through the curtain and is initially blinded by a spotlight. Small monitors carrying still images of body parts intermittently change to close-ups from the pornographic movie spoken of in the first room. The sound of breathing is faintly audible.

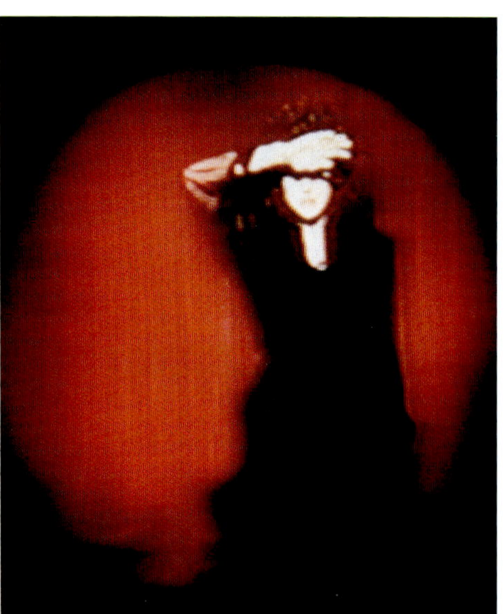

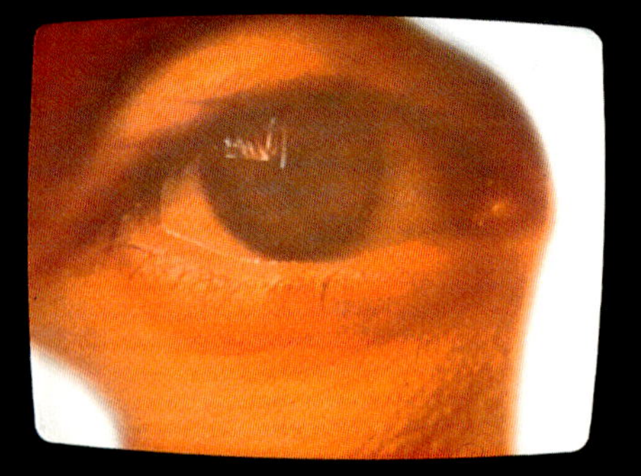

**Artist's Statement**

The title of the installation provides a kind of map for the piece itself. The word "spot" functions in multiple ways throughout the piece, on both literal and metaphoric levels. First, in descriptive terms, there is a theatrical spotlight that serves to illuminate one side of the red curtain. This spotlight literally and figuratively puts the viewer in the position of being "on the spot" (the context and central focus of the piece) as the viewer slips into the position of the "viewed" for a moment. This points to yet another meaning of the word—a position or location . . . the tension between participation and non-participation parallels a similar tension within gender itself—a binary set of oppositions within which individuals continually reposition themselves.

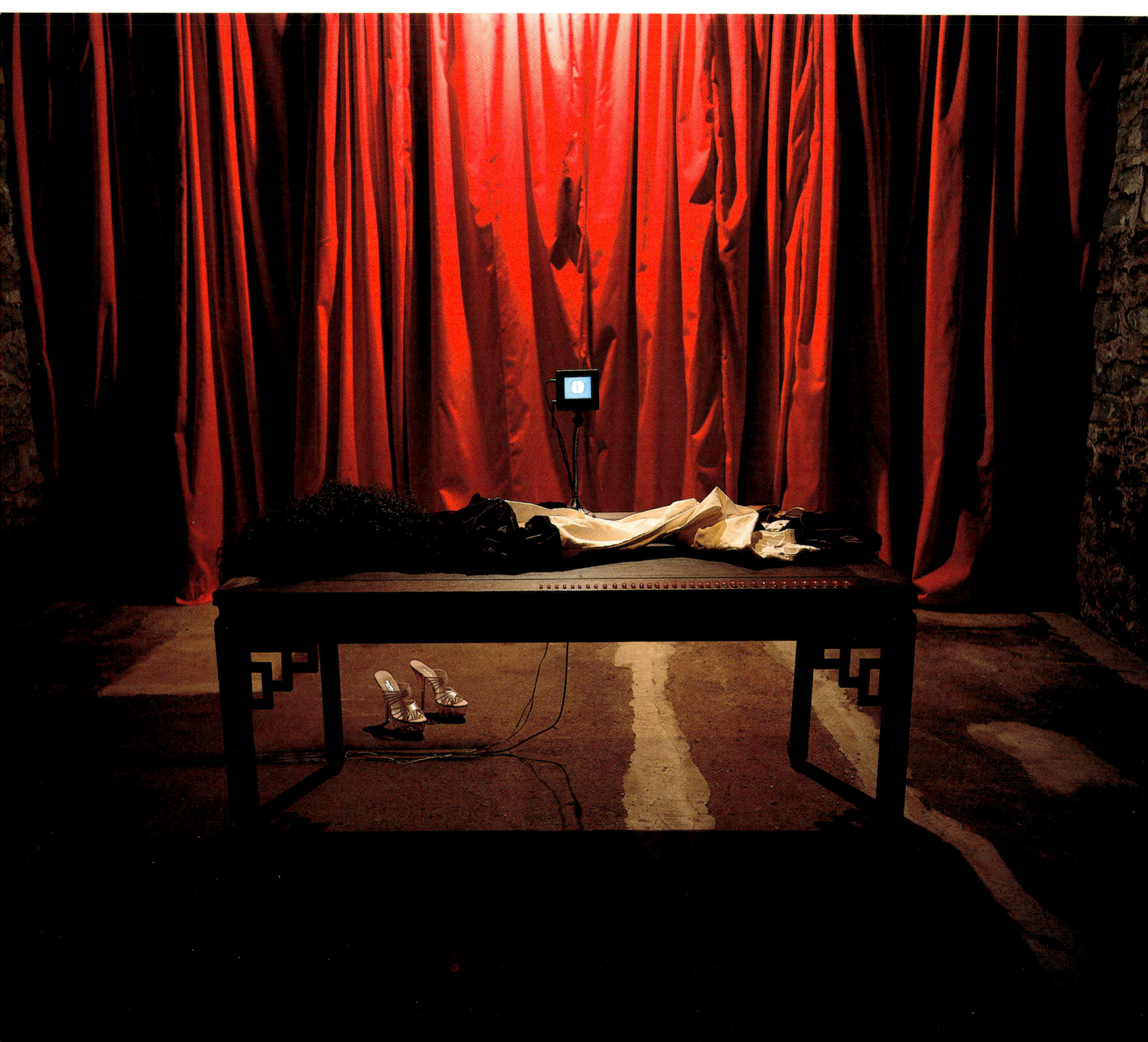

## Quisqueya Henriquez

Cuban, born 1966

**Locus,** 1998
Rubber, laminated color photographs
500 Sampsonia Way, 4th floor

On the walls of the exhibition space are photographs of sites, objects, and close-ups of body parts. The photos are framed by pieces of rubber in which circular openings have been cut. Red, rubber shapes with three arms are arranged on the floor. White circles cut into the rubber at the ends of these arms create points for three viewers to interact in relation to each other. These points direct the viewers' gaze to particular photographs on the walls.

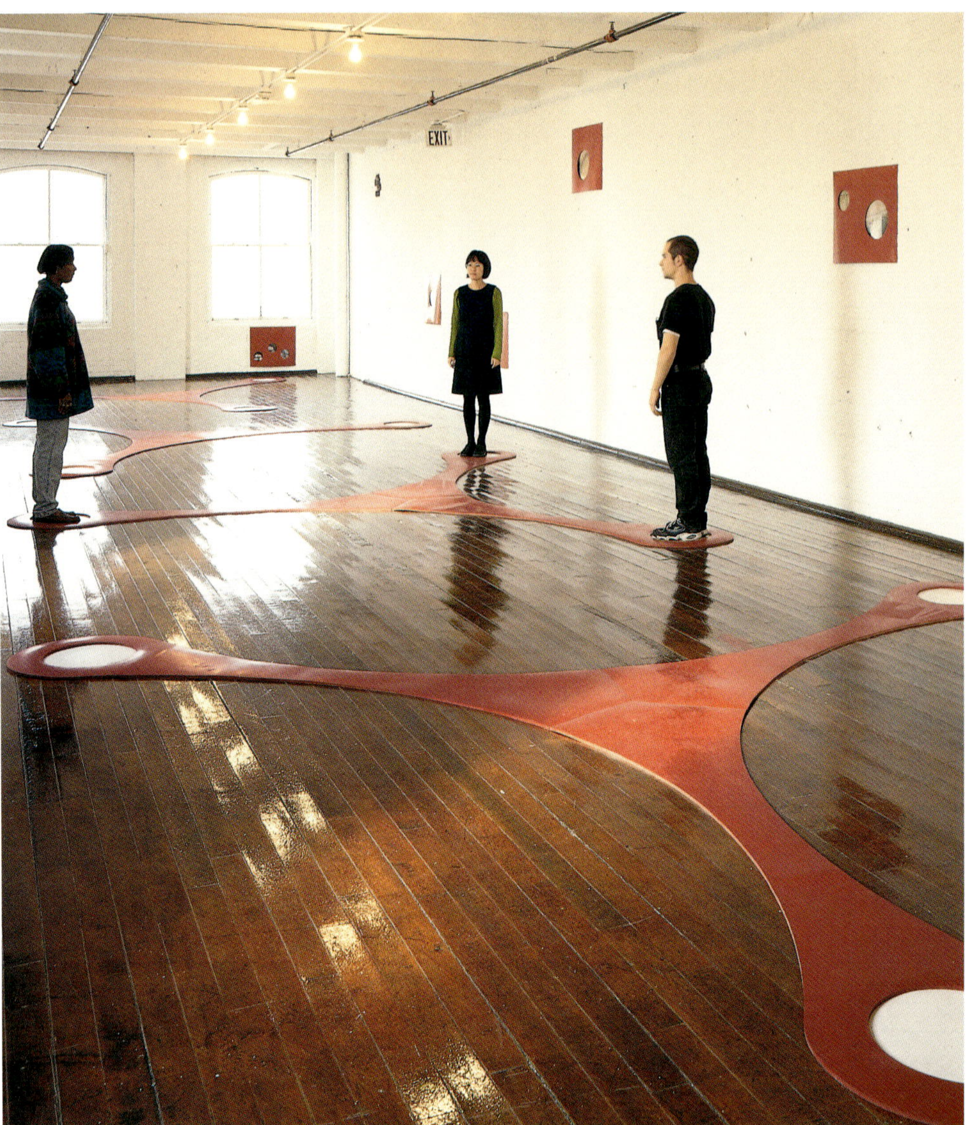


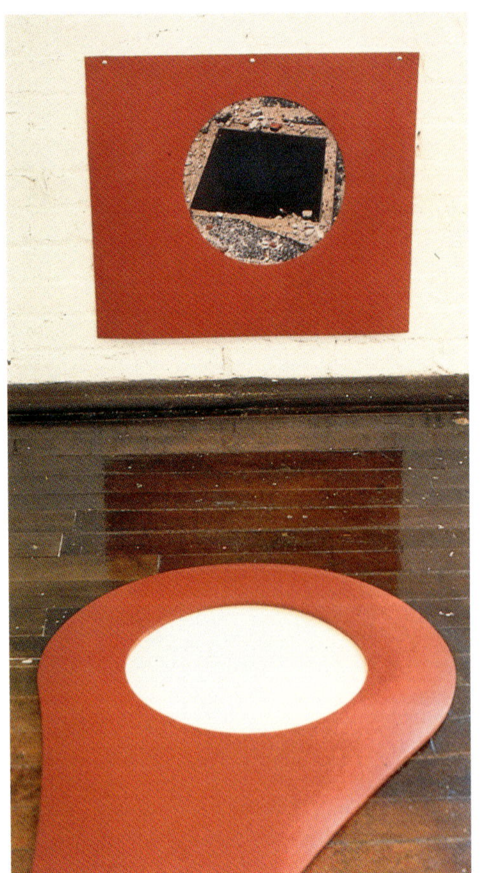

**Artist's Statement**

This installation was designed with triptych forms to address issues of human communication under ideal physical and psychological conditions. This triadic form is based on the geometric shapes of a circle and a triangle. More specifically, I have named the shape "Terminal." It is a shape in which perfect communication must take place between three individuals. As such, neither a one-dimensional nor a binary relationship is possible. The places photographed share common factors: they either do not exist, are places that have been destroyed, or are sites under construction. Time, as rendered in the images, includes a past and a future; the present is formless. I've identified the images of the human body, egg shapes, and fire as "agencies of mediation" because they do not relate to a specific time or place. These are ideas that emerge during nomadic times, within virtual societies composed of individuals unable to physically communicate with each other.

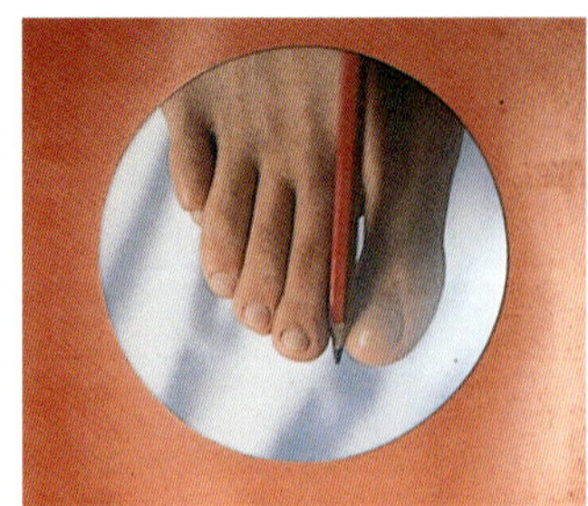

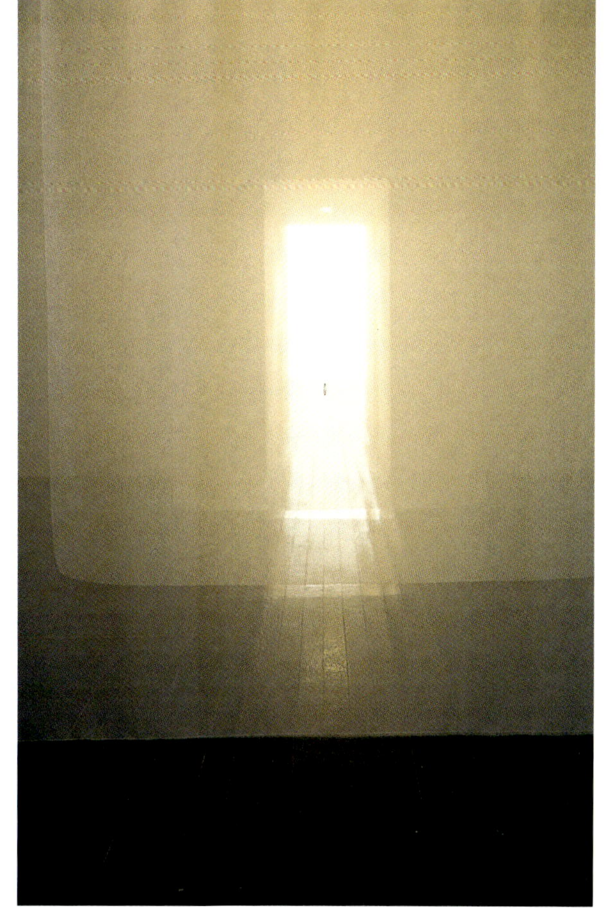

## Delanie Jenkins

American, born 1964

**Root Bound,** 1998
Cotton, chicken wire, fabric, plaster
500 Sampsonia Way, 3rd floor

The installation is divided into three distinct parts. In the first room, three sheer curtains of graduated size are suspended from the ceiling. Buttonholes are sewn into each curtain at navel height. Branching from the corridor on both sides are vaulted rooms lined with soft, thick cotton. In the last room, a plaster cast of the artist's navel has been embedded in the wall also at navel height.

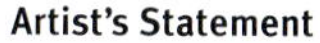

**Artist's Statement**

The belly button and the buttonhole. Locations of junction and disjunction. Points of connection rendered useless without an umbilical cord or button; their own presence a scar, a reminder of their lack and loss. A gap, a bridge, a landmark between two things. Between . . . that hovering state of suspension. Not quite committed, still somewhat attached. The past has just occurred and the future has not yet happened. Presence.

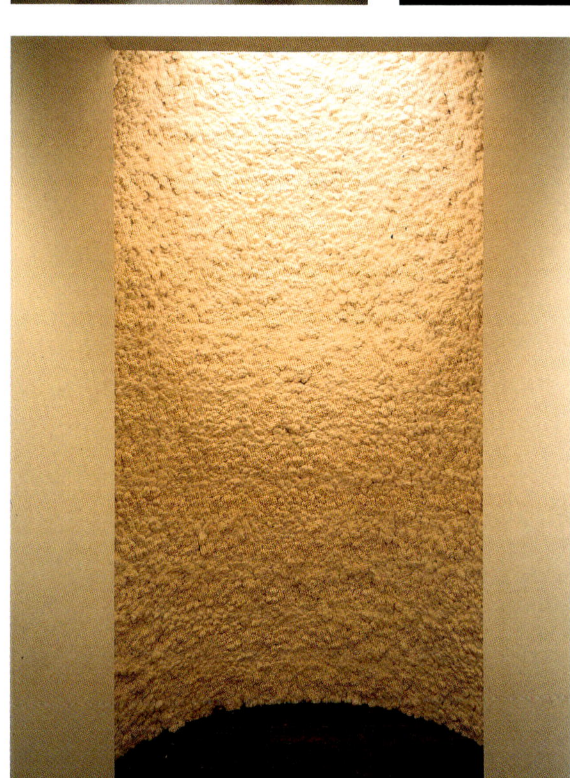

Chaos as a constant becomes weary and grounding is sought. The body is strong, the brain an endless loop of reminders and patterns, the heart contemplates life with no distractions. There are memories here in the movement of these curtain barriers, the way they fill the room with seemingly little substance. A skin, a veneer. A journey is in progress, a settling of sorts, by way of the long road. And there is reverence here, too, in the seduction of the illumination. Desire, expectation. A dream, a breeze, the warmth of a padded room leads back to the beginning . . . vulnerability, openness and muffled laughter.

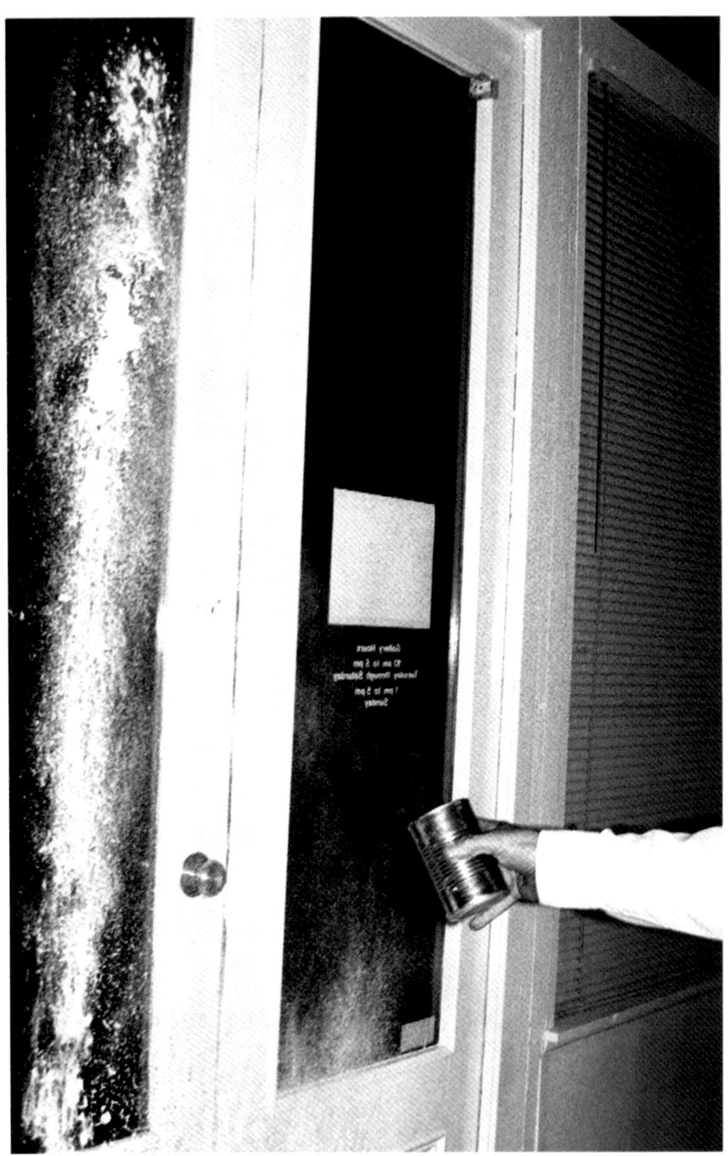

## Bob Karstadt

American

**Every Time a Bell Rings** or **The Seraphim Picture Show** or **The Infinity Flute Concerto in Salt Flat** or **The Transmutation Tree** or **Circus Alchemical** or **The Lead and Copper War** or **The Hummingbird Waltz** or **The Leviathan vs. the Hummingbird, Turtle, Fish and Corn in a No-Holds-Barred Tag Team Wrestling Extravaganza** or **The Good Ship Enoch**
Performance, December 5, 1998
1414 Monterey Street, 1st floor

Described by Karstadt as a "battle between agrarian and technological materials," this performance involved the audience in ritual manipulation and transformation of domestic objects and materials as a form of "symbolic communication."

The piece progressed through a series of actions by the artist and the audience, using materials such as lead, corn, honey, vinegar, salt, and constructions made of found objects.

The resulting experience is a "carnival of earth magic of alchemical activities" in which the artist uses materials to change people's perceptions and to create altered states of consciousness.

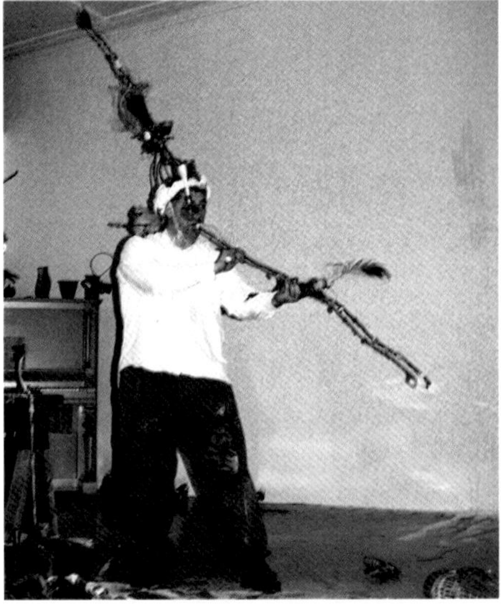

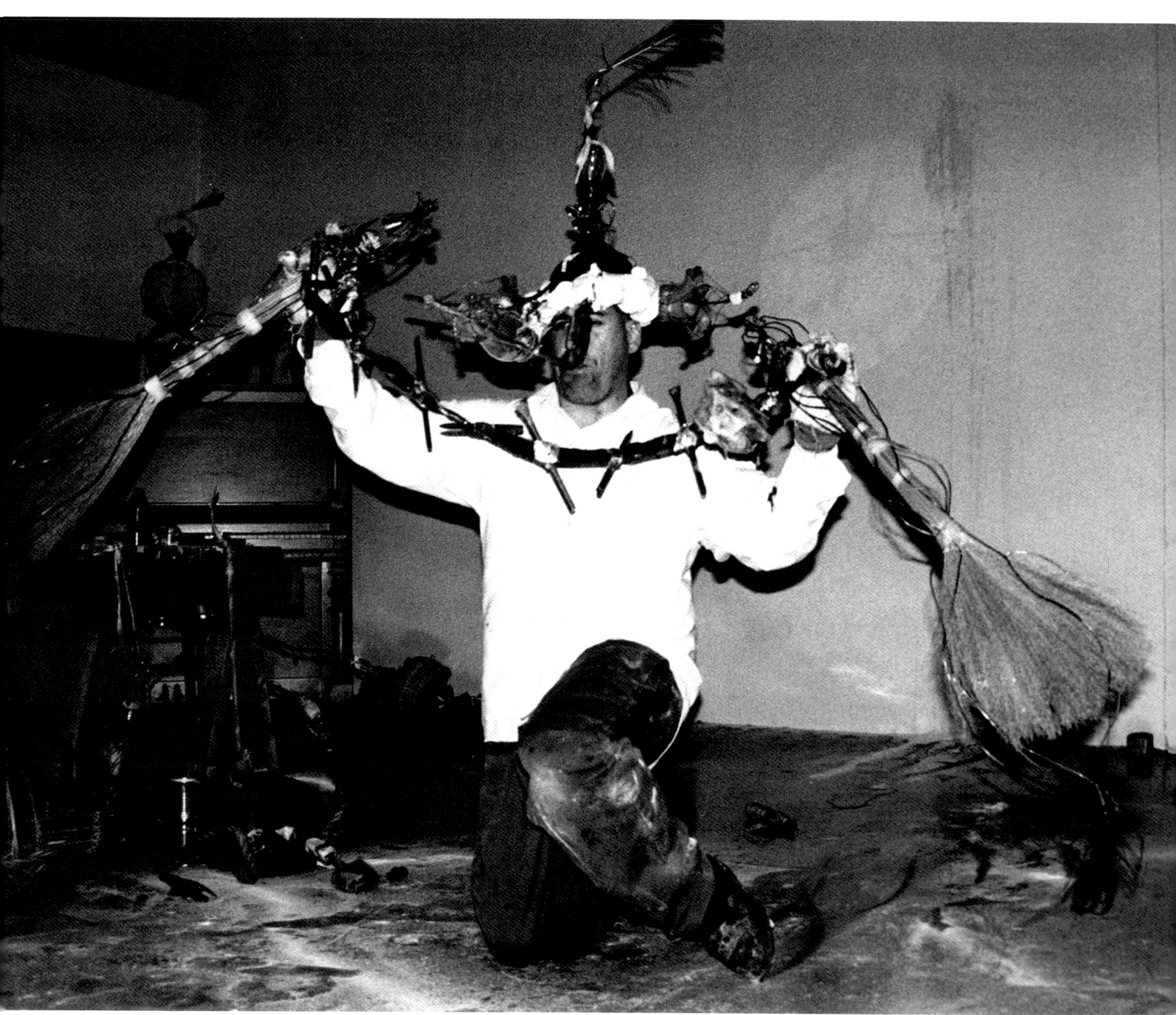

## James Giordani Montford

American, born 1952

**The Artist Dollars Project,** 1999
365 dollar bills, glass, mirrors, conference phone, students' dollars
1414 Monterey Street, 1st and 2nd floors

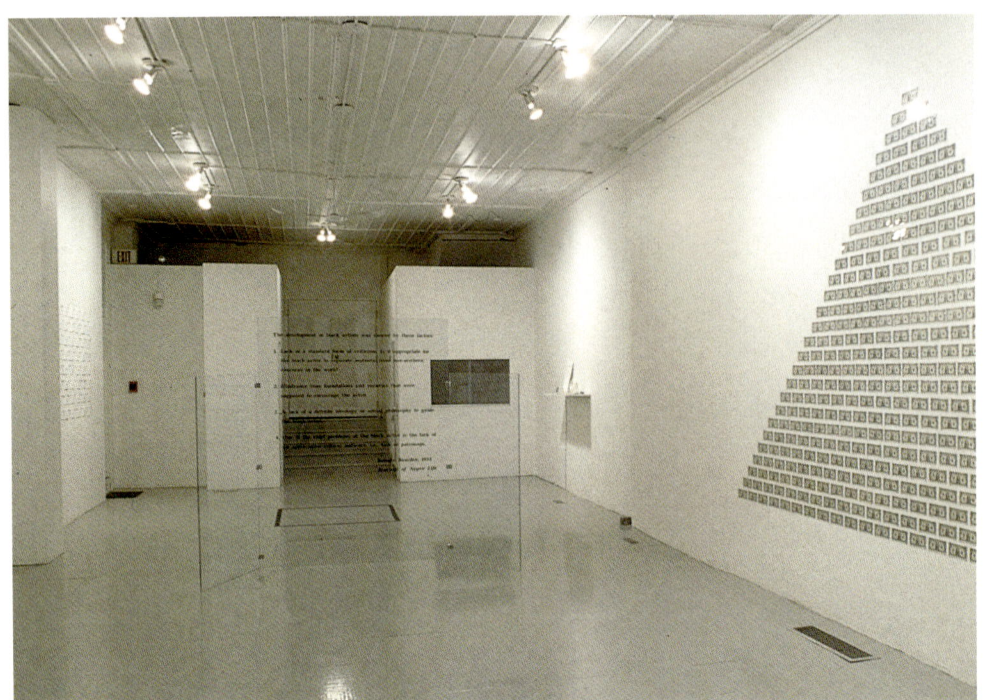

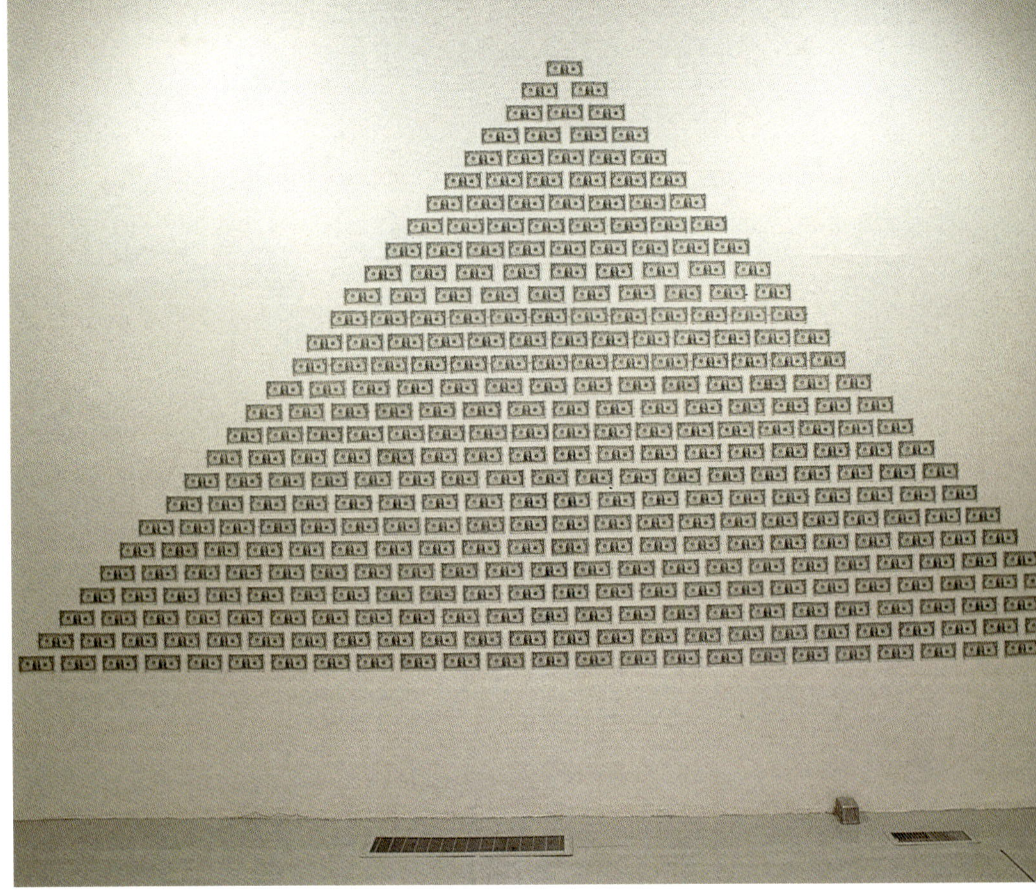

On October 10, 1998, the Mattress Factory received an envelope containing a one-dollar bill, mailed anonymously from Norwich, Connecticut. More mysterious bills continued to arrive each day. Each dollar bill had a different name written in its margin and was assigned a number between 1 and 365. The first bill received read, "2 of 365 Marlene Rogers." The bill of November 14 said, "1 of 365 Leonardo Drew," and so on. Mattress Factory staff soon determined that the names in the margins were of African American artists and artists of color. James Montford ultimately revealed himself as the anonymous sender and proposed his collaborative project to the Mattress Factory on October 22, 1998.

The 365 artist dollars are mounted on the wall in a pyramidal form under individual pieces of glass. On the opposing wall, slightly off-center, is another pyramid of dollar-sized mirrors, reflecting both the dollar pyramid and its viewers. A quote by the late artist Romare Bearden, outlining the factors that have hindered black artists, is printed on a glass divider at the center of the exhibition space. A conference phone is set up for students and visitors to talk to artists of color, such as Howardina Pindell and Thaddeus Mosley, at prearranged times.

On the second floor, an entire room is filled with students' submissions of dollar-bill-sized art works. each celebrating an artist of color. In an adjacent room, an archive created by staff, volunteers, and local students contains folders with information about the artists named on the dollar bills.

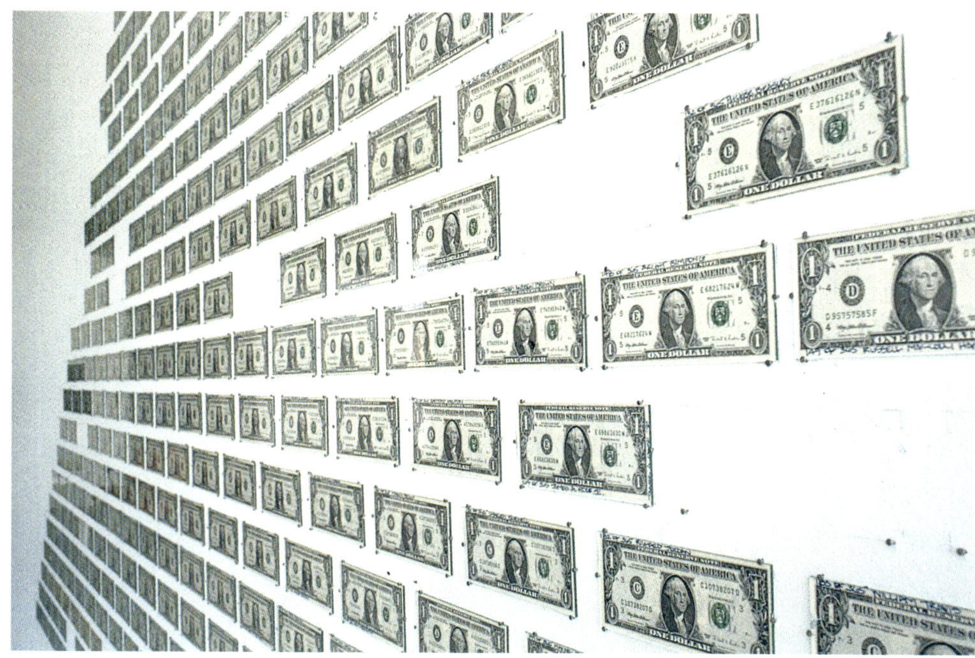


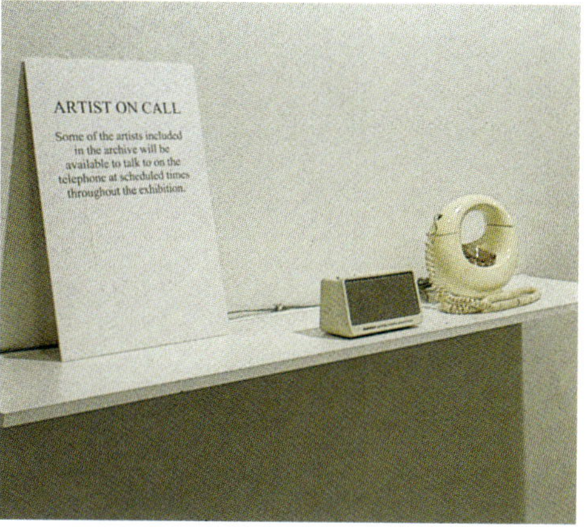


**Artist's Statement**

My studies and research for the work are involved with the sociopolitical concerns derived from an aesthetic, formalist, and educational perspective, infused with the arts, in the context of representing cultural history. This has been the focus of the work, which more specifically, is ongoing exploration and research to derive a cogent and meaningful process for the purpose of understanding the stereotyped image, its mythology, and ideology. Exploring these manifestations as they pertain to the demystification of the social/economic and cultural factors that continue to foster the existence of the African American Holocaust is essential to the work.

The Holocaust that I refer to here has not found its way into the common lexicon and, as such, is not viewed in its proper context. How many millions of Africans and African Americans have perished in the name of Christian slavery? There is no bitterness here, only the realization that my ancestors survived the horrors and indignation of Jim Crow. Therefore, my work is reflective of this process, and its investigation is designed to offer a discussion of what I have come to identify as the African American Holocaust. The work seeks to foster a transformative process for the viewer, one that might encourage sociopolitical change to occur. The direction of my work is further centered on universality and the pursuit of a humanistic ideology or model. While formalist issues are most important for the work to express its edginess, the work is founded in its melding of the formal with the contextual. It has been my recent experience that the representational direction of the work is often associated with advocacy. This is not the case. By producing the work I am not advocating its content but rather adding to the discussion through the chosen contextualization of the image.

The conceptualization of the work and its formal concerns are derived from postreductivist constructs and their related spatial dichotomies. Earlier work, although nonrepresentational in nature, had a metaphoric reference to cultural sources. There is an effective, ambiguous nature to the work that aptly lends itself to the focus of the discussion on subjugation while still being interested in resolving formal conceptual issues. I am acutely interested in and fascinated by the issues raised by the work in addressing the false "universal" societal constructs—racism, community, and environments, their intersection with myth, their pervasiveness, and society's unwillingness to unquestionably absorb them. I intend these works to be very fertile juxtapositions focusing on the deconstruction of stereotyped images as they relate to people of color, i.e. the Holocaust.

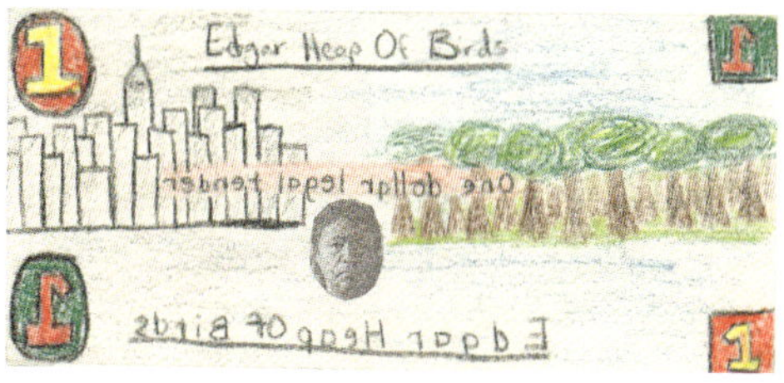


Westmont Hilltop Middle School
in honor of Edgar Heap of Birds

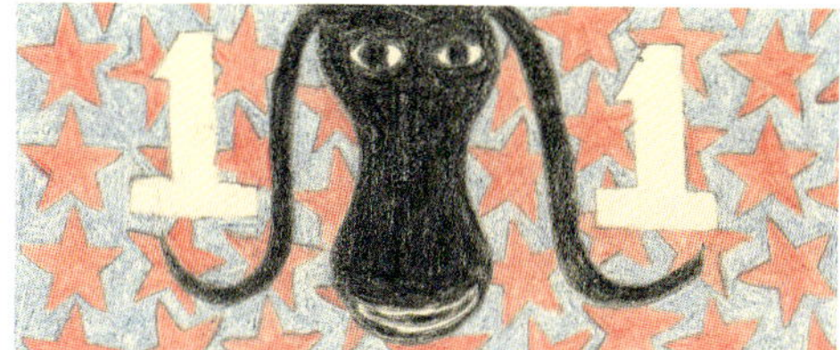

Trent Konade, Hayes High School
in honor of Amos Ferguson

## Gimhongsok

Korean, born 1964

**The Magic Sword of MMCCDXCVII,** 1999
Signboard, light box, wood, foam rubber, Dolby surround sound
500 Sampsonia Way, 3rd floor
(included in *Installations by Asian Artists in Residence*)

Two pillars, one round and covered in gray foam and the other square, wooden and stained a dark cherry color, appear at the center of the gallery. Voices, emitted from speakers inside the pillars' vents, seem to shift position within the space. The story related by these voices involves the relationship between two siblings who have been raised by two different fathers. At the far end of the room, signs have been mounted on the wall. Printed in various formats, a transcription of the spoken text winds from sign to sign across the wall. However, it is not printed in a logical progression. The artist aims to disorient the viewer through the irregularities in the story, the discordant color combinations in which the text is printed, and through the variable and indiscernible origins of sounds.

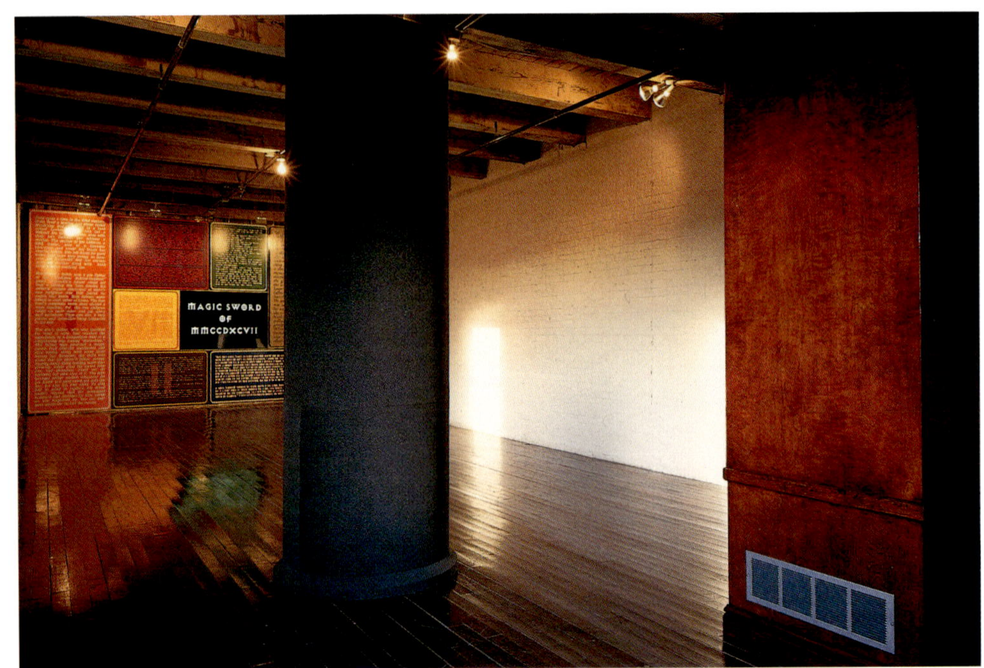


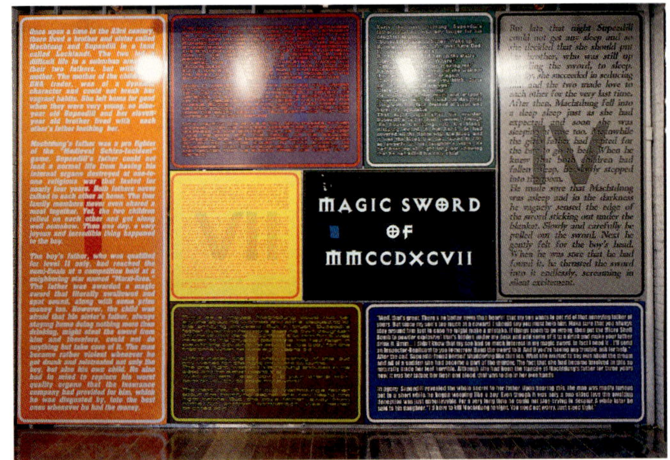


**Artist's Statement**

It is hard for me to concentrate recklessly on only one thing in a society where everything is divided (or pluralized) and specialized. I try to experience many fields by pretending to be someone in the field. And if that does not lead to a successful (or satisfactory) result of my intent, I can at least have self-contentment. I enjoy transforming myself into someone and it usually takes on a cultural boundary. The reason for the boundary is to minimize the jeopardy (or risk) of transformation that can happen outside a given boundary, and to regard it as a practice prior to other attempts that can happen outside the boundary. So far I have tried to be a fashion coordinator, furniture designer, cook, party organizer, display designer, exhibition coordinator, and scenario writer, and these attempts have enabled me to communicate with many fields. Transforming into someone is the only thing that fulfills my satisfaction and it also leads me to conclude that I am a multi-identified being and a schizo maniac who needs to have many uniforms and name cards. This time, I became a writer and wrote a story for little kids, but even though it's written by me—one who is Korean and lives in Korea—the story has a plot that cannot happen in Korea. Its setting and details are more like the ones of Hollywood blockbusters or German fables. The main character has the name "Machtung," which originates in German, rather than the typical Korean name "Chul-soo." By giving birth to a main character as "Machtung," I find myself in ecstasy over escaping and frequenting the world where I exist. I find this very interesting because it means that my identity is destroyed and exists no more, which tallies my intention of transformation. However, it is hard to eliminate the theory that says, "a statement that's extremely self-disputing can destroy and deny oneself."

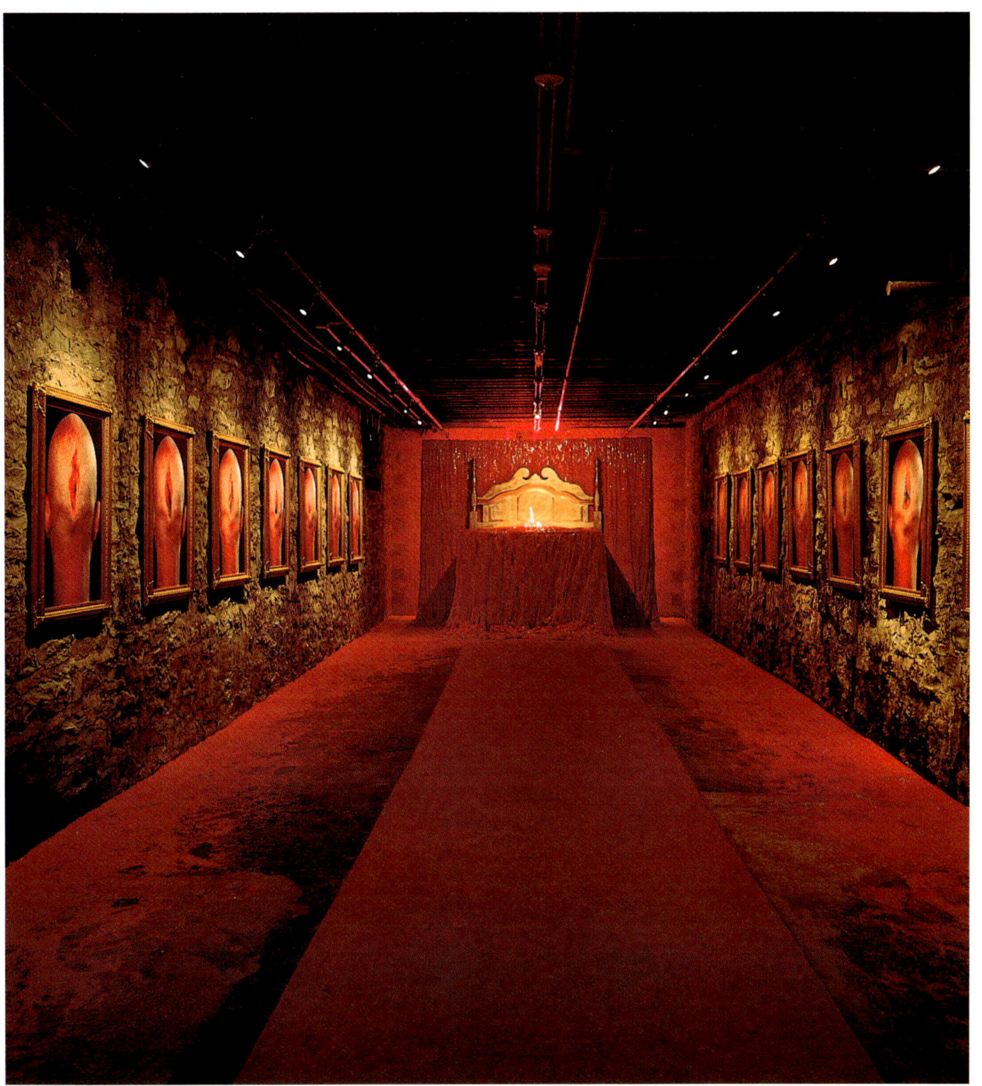

## Gu Dexin

Chinese, born 1962

**10-30-1999,** 1999
Ink-jet prints, plastic, sex instrument, wood
500 Sampsonia Way, lower level
(included in *Installations by Asian Artists in Residence*)

Lining the walls on both sides of the room are twenty gold-framed pictures of a shaved head, on which vaginas have been digitally superimposed. A long, red carpet lies in the center of the floor. Red resin pellets have been scattered on either side of it. An oversized bed covered with melted red plastic and an enormous golden headboard stands at the back of the space. A spotlight illuminates the top of the bed, on which a moving dildo has been positioned.

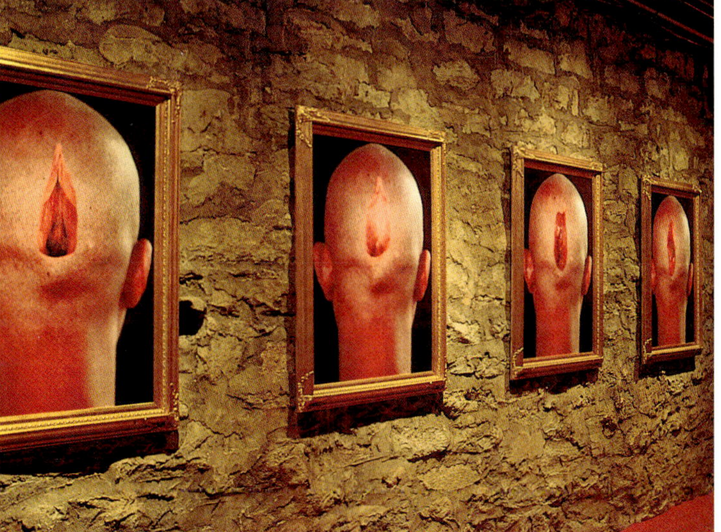

**Artist's Statement**

I have always been interested in people. Anyway, one is forced to find inspiration outside of art. There is nothing to discover in the realm of art itself.

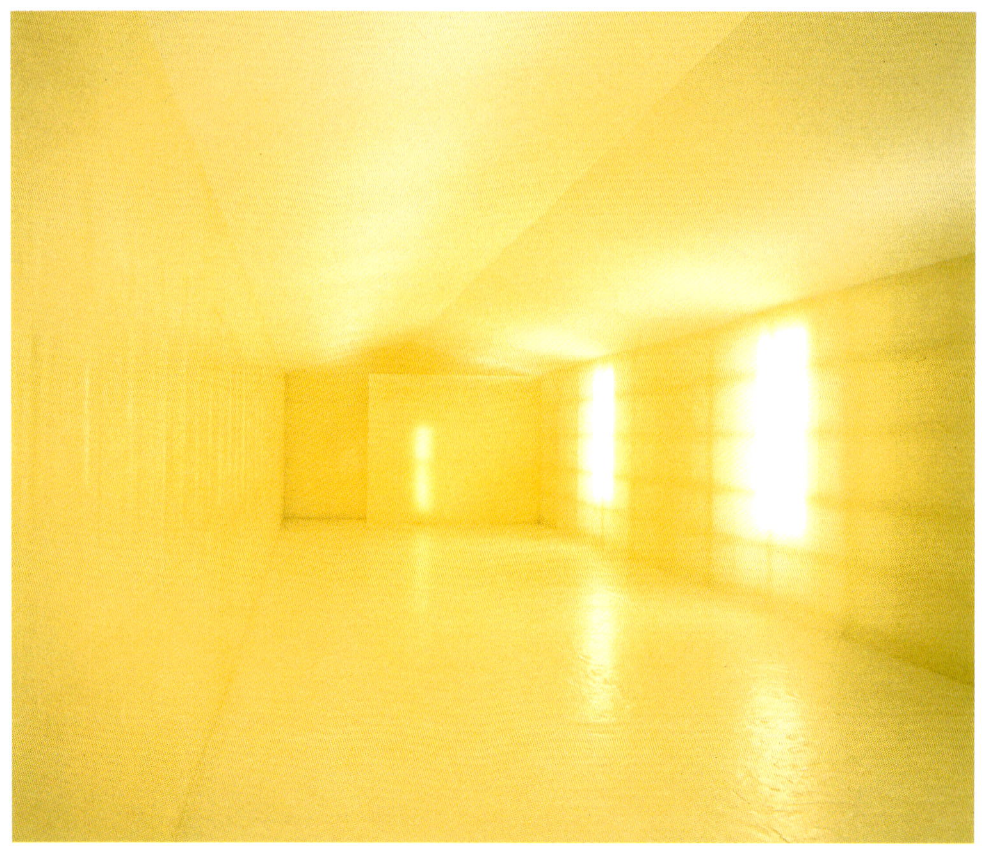

## Goro Hirata

Japanese, born 1965

**Mind Space,** 1999
Paraffin wax, cotton cloth
500 Sampsonia Way, 4th floor
(included in *Installations by Asian Artists in Residence*)

The artist melted fifteen thousand pounds of paraffin wax, then poured it into molds to make panels, which he used to line a room fifteen feet wide by fifty feet long. The floor was also covered with wax panels poured into molds in place. The color of the wax walls changed as the daylight varied.

**Artist's Statement**

Covering the floor and walls of the entire exhibition space with paraffin wax, I will produce a room of white light. Taking in light from the outside, the brightness of the room will change with time. As a lot of light will pour into the room from the rear window, I will produce an installation that will seem to make the back wall radiate with light.

The room of white light itself will not especially symbolize anything nor will it express a specific image. Instead I hope that the visitors who enter the room will, through their own spirituality, feel as though they are in a sacred space. With the effect of the change in lighting that is created by the passage of time, I hope that I will be able to reproduce a "spiritual space" that will in turn produce a psychological effect—and touch the souls of the visitors that enter this room made of light.

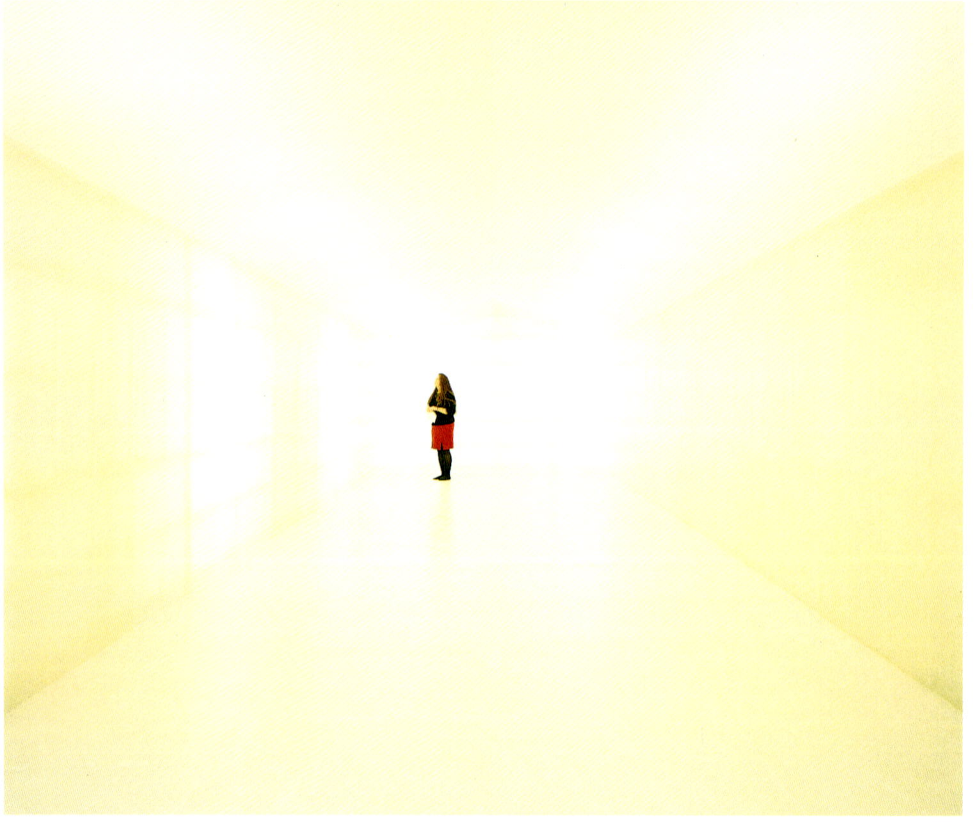

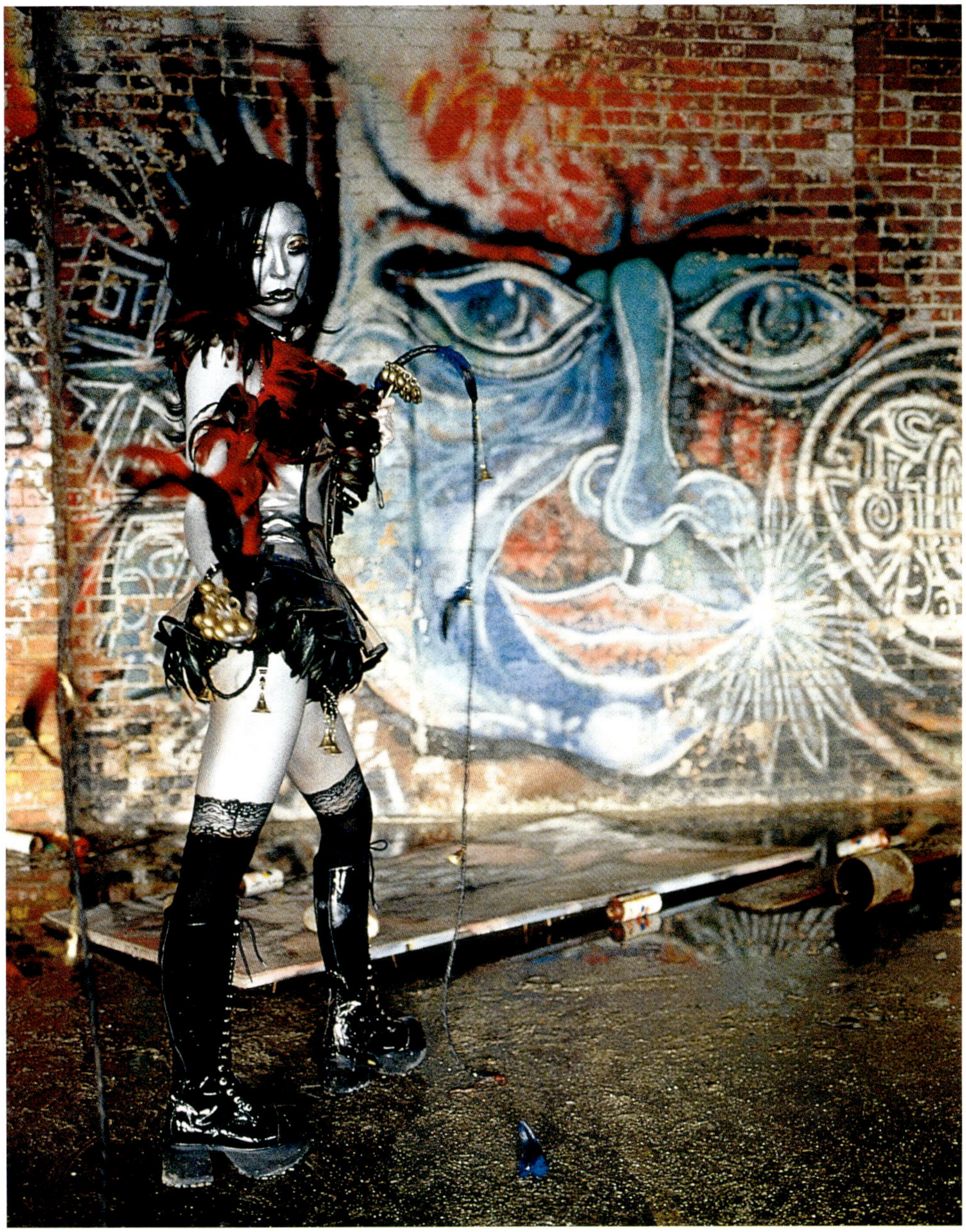

## ium

Korean, born 1971

**Tales from the Warehouse,** 1999
Video projection, 20 minutes
500 Sampsonia Way, 4th floor
(included in *Installations by Asian Artists in Residence*)

ium's video is set in the abandoned Armstrong Cork Building, where the interior walls are covered with graffiti. The bold spray-painted images and colors were the inspiration for the characters that ium created. The costumes and the make-up mimic the spray-painted images. The performance was based on the ideas of conflict, which she feels are the impetus for all graffiti art.

**Artist's Statement**

Pledge: I wish to remain
all my life an outsider
wish that the art world
remains a foreign place
wish that my work remains
alien to the world and I
wish the art world will
think of me as a stranger
Me and the art world, let us
remain mutually alien.

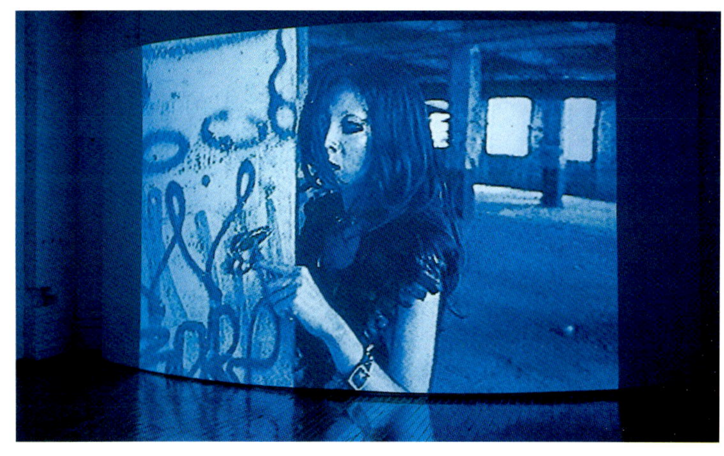

## Sora Kim

Korean, born 1965

**D-Gravitizer,** 1999
Steel, aluminum, plastic, AstroTurf, cans, signage
500 Sampsonia Way, 4th floor
(included in *Installations by Asian Artists in Residence*)

This installation was designed as a promotional display for *D-Gravitizer*—a drink which can free a maintenance person from gravity in order to clean high places. Kim used a computer program, combining the shape of the aluminum can and her deep sleep brain waves, to design the logo for the product and the stainless steel "Do-Nothing" shelving unit. Various signs in the space explain and promote the product. Cans of *D-Gravitizer* hang from the ceiling, and a large photograph of an orange-clad, airborne maintenance man provides a backdrop for the display. This image was also displayed on six billboards throughout the Pittsburgh area.

*D-Gravitizer* was displayed at INPEX, The Invention Convention, held from May 17–21, 2000 at the Monroeville ExpoMart near Pittsburgh.

*Process:*

1. *Research*
2. *Computer Graphics*
3. *Product Design*
4. *Product Manufacturing*
5. *Retail Display*
6. *Advertising*
7. *Sales*

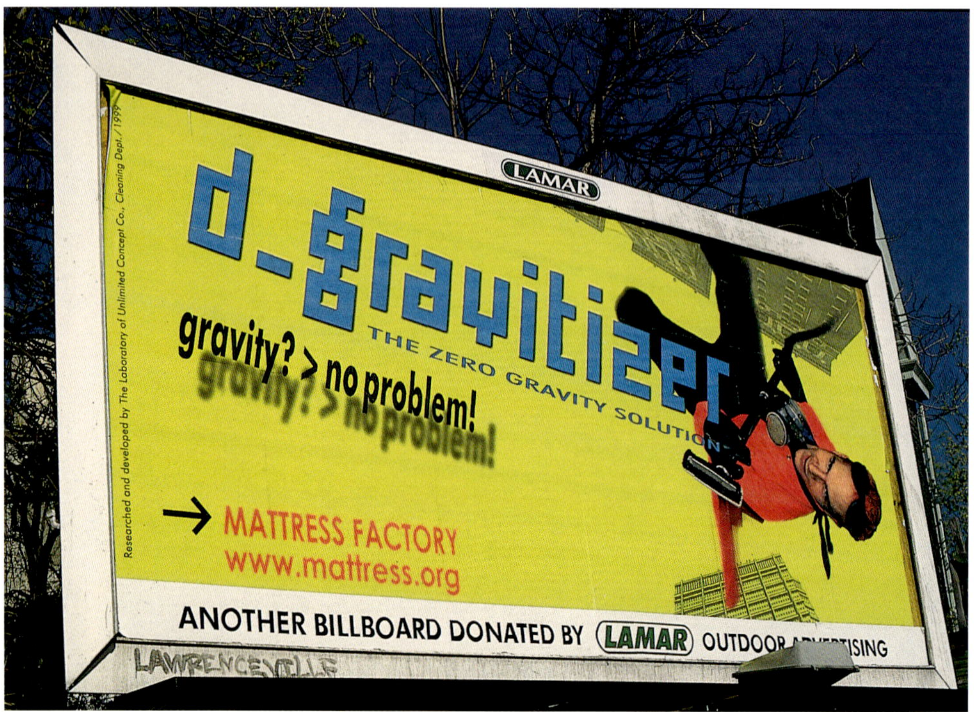


**Artist's Statement**

*D-Gravitizer* is a zero gravity solution which, when ingested, would allow one to float around space wherever one wished. It is strongly recommended for all types of tough labors in hard-to-reach areas such as ceilings, skyscrapers, etc., and for further applications. It has been extensively researched and developed by *The Laboratory of Unlimited Concept Co.*, and has now been made available at the Mattress Factory.

For the product and its promotion of the *D-Gravitizer* at the Mattress Factory, *The Laboratory of Unlimited Concept Co.*, has engaged a computer program to create a Multi-Dimensional Diagram that has been evolved from the relationship between the Aluminum Can (explicit source: the container of the product itself) and the Delta waves of the human brain while in deep sleep (implicit source: from the effect of the product).

Making a diagram for *D-Gravitizer* is to bring structure to the Nothing-to-Do Station; a station where the disassembled tiny particles of the consumer's body under the effect of the product visit every 0.0000000000000000001 second so as not to respond to the gravitational pull.

Re-constructed Nothing-to-Do-Station as a Generative Diagram, developed from conceptual sources of *D-Gravitizer*, has served as a design machine to materialize and visualize the functional design including the product's label, the retail space, and sales furniture.

*D-Gravitizer* is not only a product to be free from gravity, but also from all other ideas of being in absolute value.

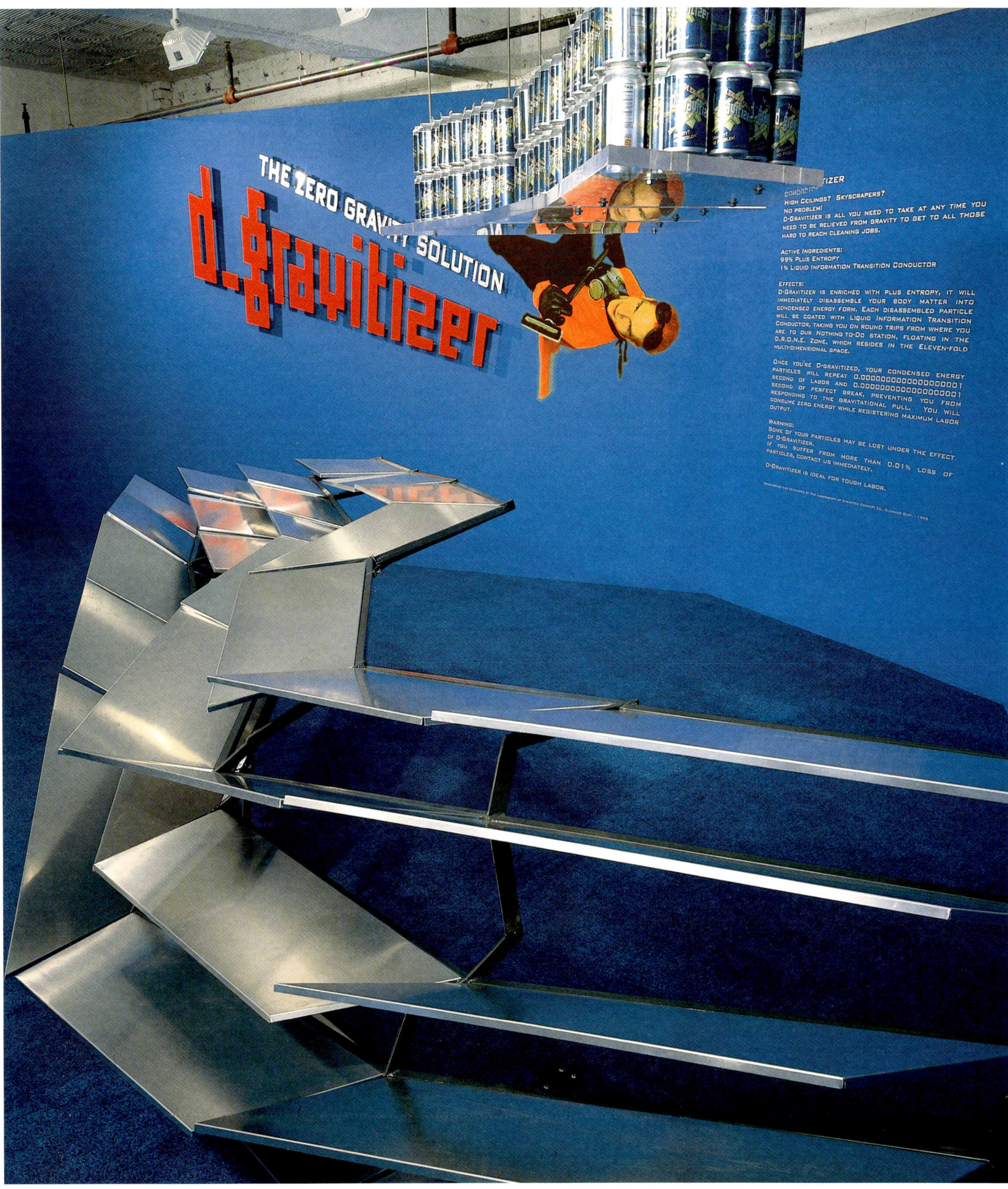
THE ZERO
SOLUTION
d.Gravitizer
High Ceilings? Skyscrapers?
No problem!
D-Gravitizer is all you need to take at any time you need to be relieved from gravity to get to all those hard to reach cleaning jobs.
Active Ingredients:
99% Plus Entropy
1% Liquid Information Transition Conductor
Effects:
D-Gravitizer is enriched with plus entropy, it will immediately disassemble your body matter into condensed energy form. Each disassembled particle will be coated with Liquid Information Transition Conductor, taking you on round trips from where you are to our Nothing-to-Do station, floating in the D.R.O.N.E. Zone, which resides in the Eleven-fold multi-dimensional space.
Once you're D-gravitized, your condensed energy particles will repeat 0.000000000000000000001 second of labor and 0.000000000000000000001 second of perfect break, preventing you from responding to the gravitational pull. You will consume zero energy while registering maximum labor output.
Warning:
Some of your particles may be lost under the effect of D-Gravitizer.
If you suffer from more than 0.01% loss of particles, contact us immediately.
D-Gravitizer is ideal for tough labor.

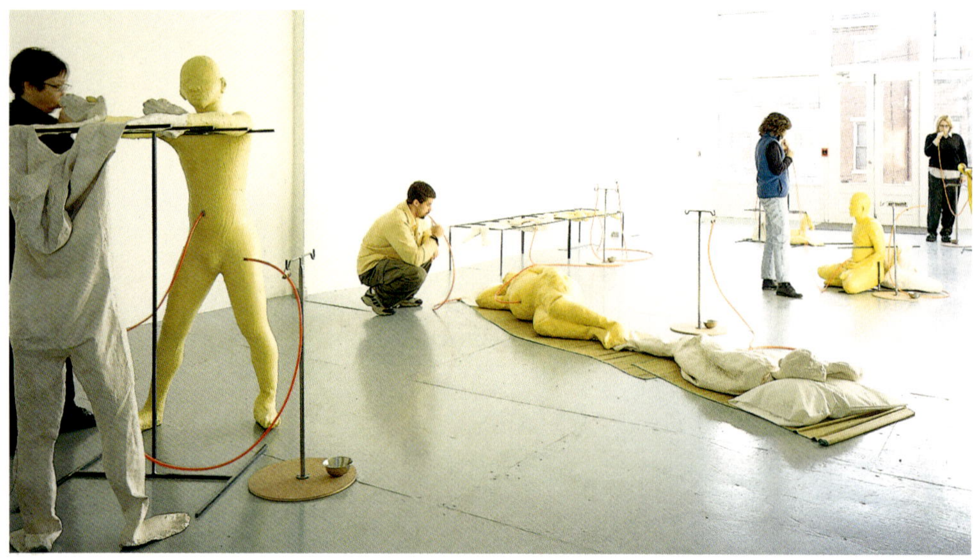

## Sutee Kunavichayanont

Thai, born 1965

**Siamese Breath (Twins),** 1999
Silicone, hoses, steel, filters, stainless steel bowls
1414 Monterey Street, 1st floor
(included in *Installations by Asian Artists in Residence*)

Six pairs of life-sized silicone "Siamese twins" one yellow, one white, are joined at different parts of the body. The artist intends these twins to symbolize the relationship between the West and Thailand. Visitors participate in the installation by blowing into the structures to inflate the silicone structures to full size. Each "twin" is self-contained—the air used for one does not pass through to the other. When the visitor stops blowing into the sculpture, it deflates, hanging limply on a steel structure.

**Artist's Statement**

For more than one hundred years, one of the most challenging tasks for the people of Siam, or Thailand, has been to balance indigenous values with modern western development. The integration of the old and new is both harmonious and completely conflicted at the same time.

Living with two different values reminds me of the Siamese Twins. In Siam, in the early nineteenth century, there were twins named Chang and Eng who were joined together at the waist. The Scottish trader, Robert Hunter, introduced Chang and Eng to the Western world. When he first saw them, he described them this way: "It was a creature that appeared to have two heads, four arms and four legs." Dr. Dan Bradley later recorded an addition, "all of which were moving in perfect harmony."

In 1826, Hunter brought the twins to America. They were on display in show business as the Siamese Double Boys, which soon became "The Siamese Twins." They later became naturalized American citizens, married two sisters, had children, and died in North Carolina.

*Siamese Breath (Twins)* in the Mattress Factory, Pittsburgh, is a new version of the Siamese Twins that is on display to viewers in America at the end of the twentieth century, 173 years after the arrival of Chang and Eng. But this time, they come as inflatable bodies colored yellow and white, representing Asian yellow skin and Western white skin. They are joined together at some parts of the bodies. They are expecting the breath from the visitors to fill their bodies.

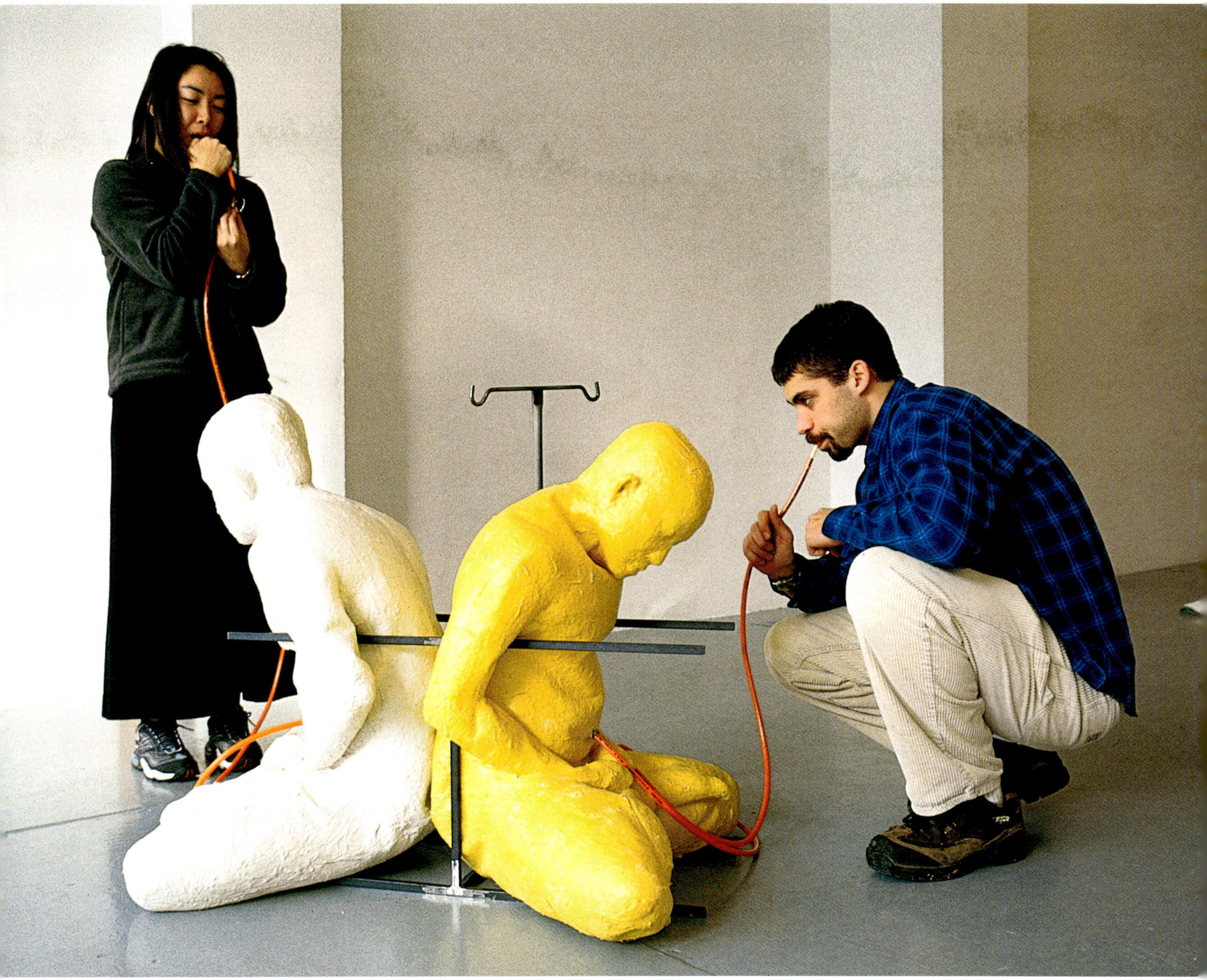

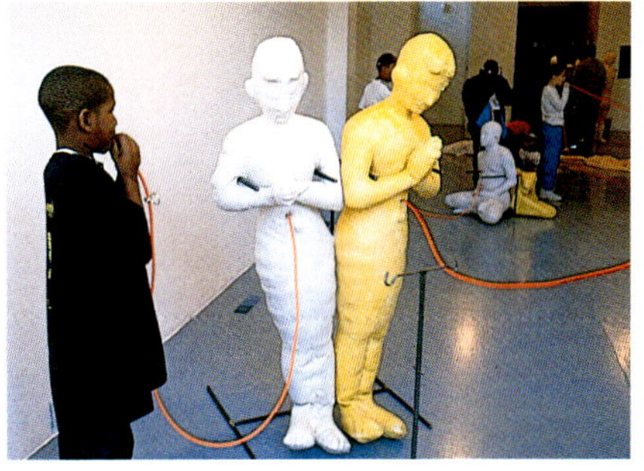

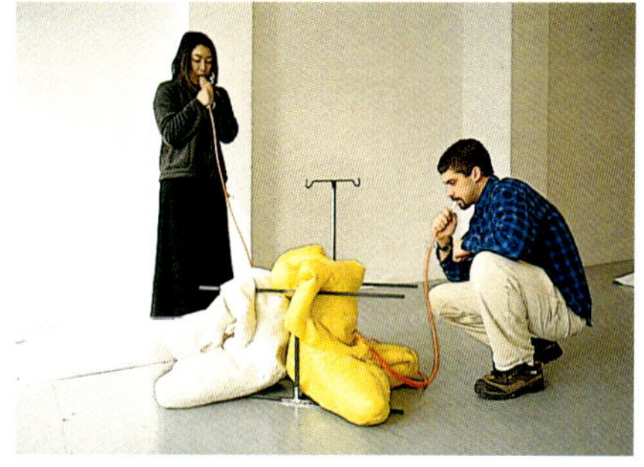

## Yoshihiro Suda

Japanese, born 1969

**Weeds,** 1999
Carved magnolia wood, paint
500 Sampsonia Way, 3rd floor
(included in *Installations by Asian Artists in Residence*)

On the floor near the wall, several small, green weeds and a few wilted, brown plants appear to have begun growing up between the cracks in the floorboards. These small plants are actually carved from magnolia wood and painted. They were placed by the artist in holes and cracks in the floor, which he then filled with dirt. The artist carved and hid a similar "botanical sculpture" outside in the *Garden.*

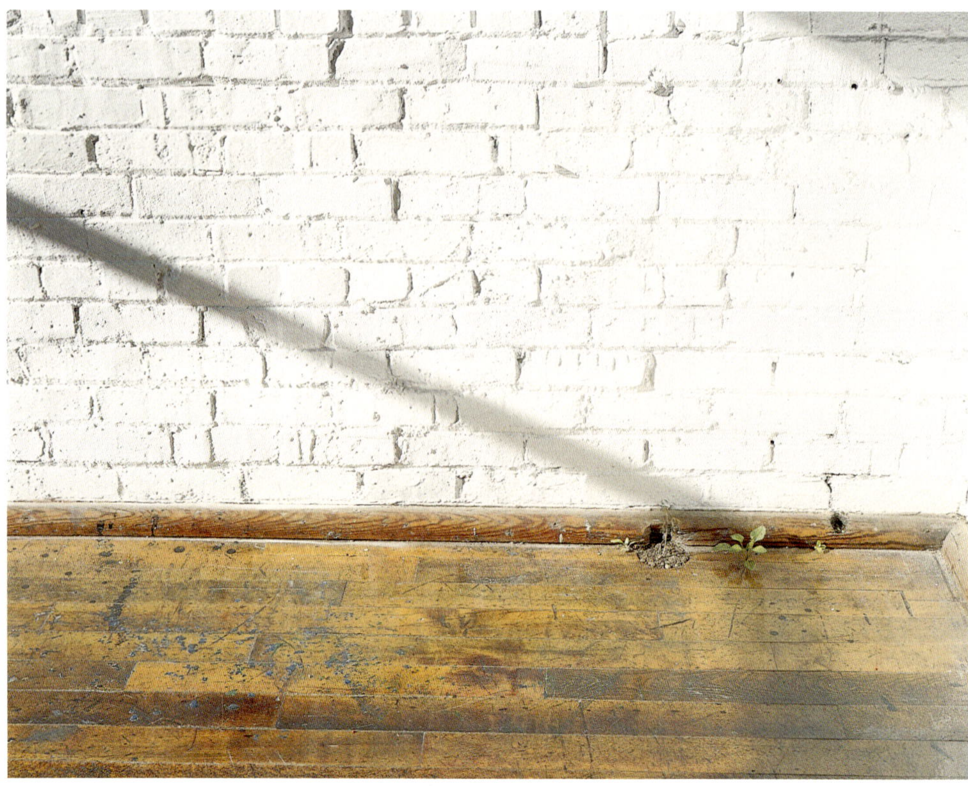

**Artist's Statement**
My installation work consists of wood-carved plant sculptures and the embodying space. What is important in the installation is to choose the most appropriate plant to a given space, in its meaning, formal quality, and surrounding situation. When the created space is visited by an audience, and he/she perceives something from it, the work will finally gain a significance.

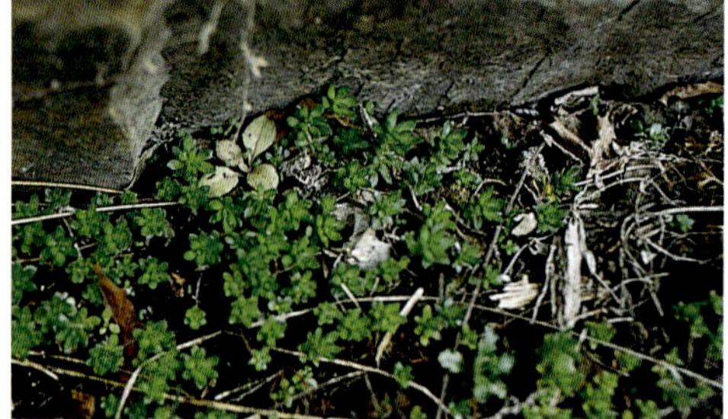

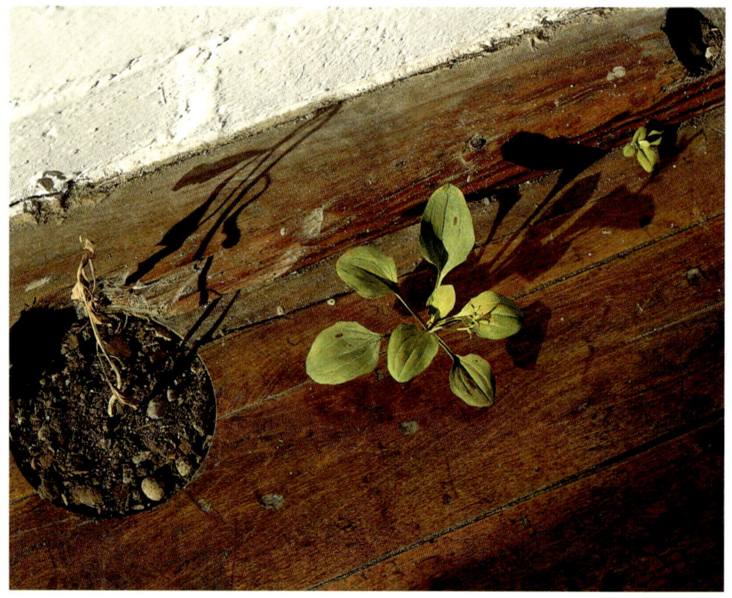

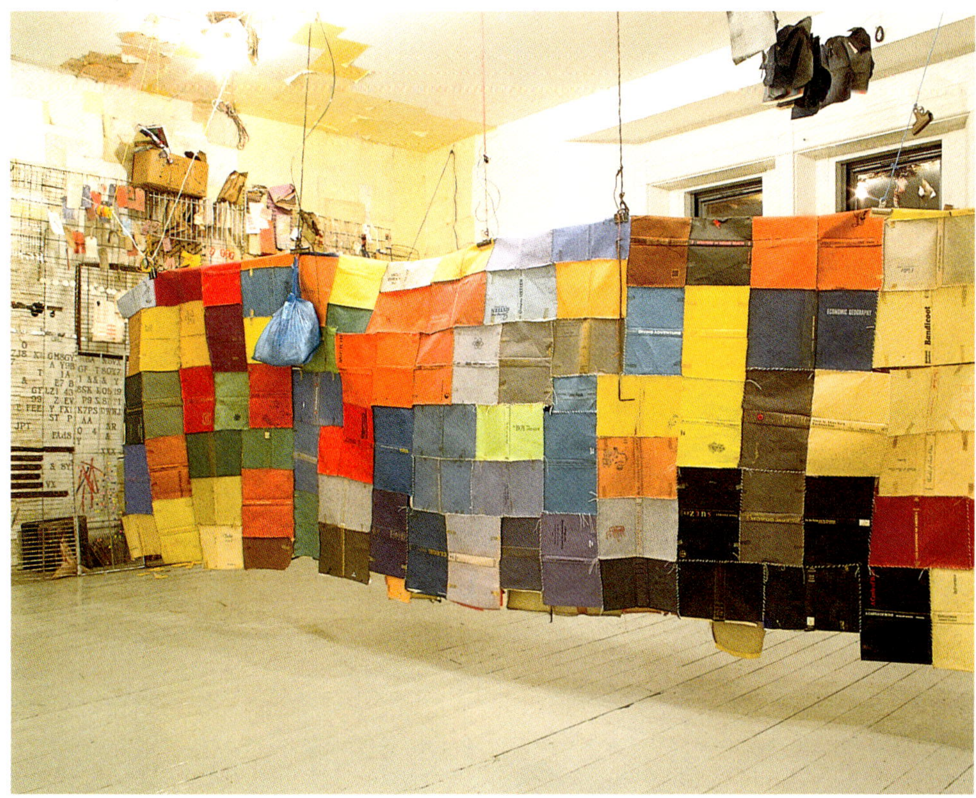

## Fumio Tachibana

Japanese, born 1968

**Untitled,** 1999
Found paper, metal, wood, plastic
1414 Monterey Street, 3rd floor
(included in *Installations by Asian Artists in Residence*)

Suspended from the ceiling, and extending diagonally across the center of the room, is a group of fabric book covers. They have been sewn together in a way that resembles a patchwork quilt. In the corner of the room is a stack of children's building blocks that display various letters. Behind the quilt of book covers are two windows. The view outside these windows is obscured by the books' insides, stacked vertically as if on a shelf. On top of the books are small houses made of cereal boxes. Collections of papers, small packets of stamps, and plastic and metal letters are hung on rusted metal grid work at the far end of the room. Library book due date stickers are affixed to the wall immediately beside the grid, and the wall and ceiling area above the rack is papered with ledger sheets.

**Artist's Statement**

The Hitomi kindergarten which I attended taught us calligraphy. We were given pieces of writing paper, a little larger than the standard size, and using writing brushes that were three centimeters (about one and one-quarter inch) in diameter, we wrote letters such as "ushi" (cow) and "tora" (tiger). We were encouraged to "write larger, write more boldly, write over the borders of the paper." I remember tightly holding the brush, which was literally a handful, soaking it in ink, and writing away using my full body. It was more like drawing over the whole page with black ink than writing. In fact, when I look over the piece of paper, which I still have in my possession, it is indistinguishable whether the black ink or the white spaces should be read "ushi."

Nowadays, I seem to regard letters as drawings. Like, for instance, when I look at newspaper headlines, not only do I see words printed in black ink, but my attention is drawn to the white blank spaces in the paper as well. If, for people in general, the black parts stand as letters, for me, the white blank spaces in the paper stand as "letters" too. That's why I collect pieces of paper. I'm not collecting trash. I'm collecting "letters."

And I am obsessed with trying out the "letters" I've gathered, arranging them horizontally, piling them up and into groups.

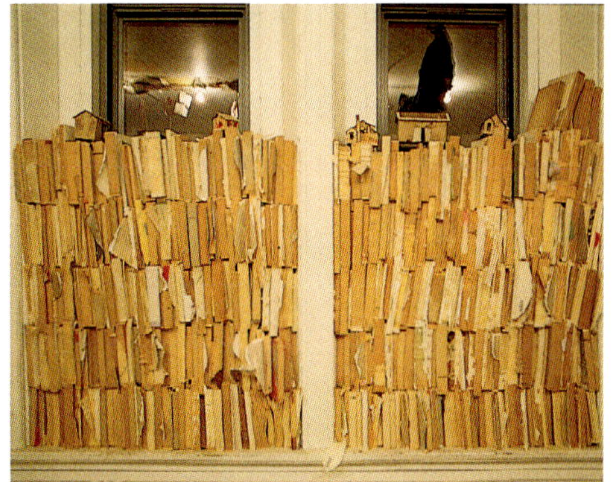

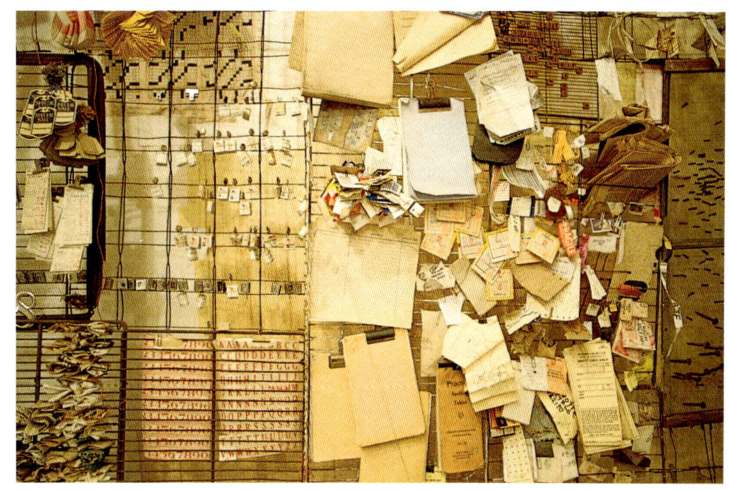

## Wang Youshen

Chinese, born 1964

**Dark Room,** 1999
Darkroom equipment and materials
1414 Monterey Street, 3rd floor
(included in *Installations by Asian Artists in Residence*)

Behind a red curtain is a hallway, in which a table stands. On the table are books containing negatives, magazines, and a light table. Beside the table is the entrance to a darkroom, which is filled with all the equipment and materials necessary for developing the negatives. Visitors may print their own photographs with the stipulation that they leave at least one behind as part of the exhibition. (More than 300 photographs were left by visitors during the course of the exhibition.) Photographs hang from lines on the walls, and others remain floating in the developing trays. Red light bulbs provide the only light in the room.

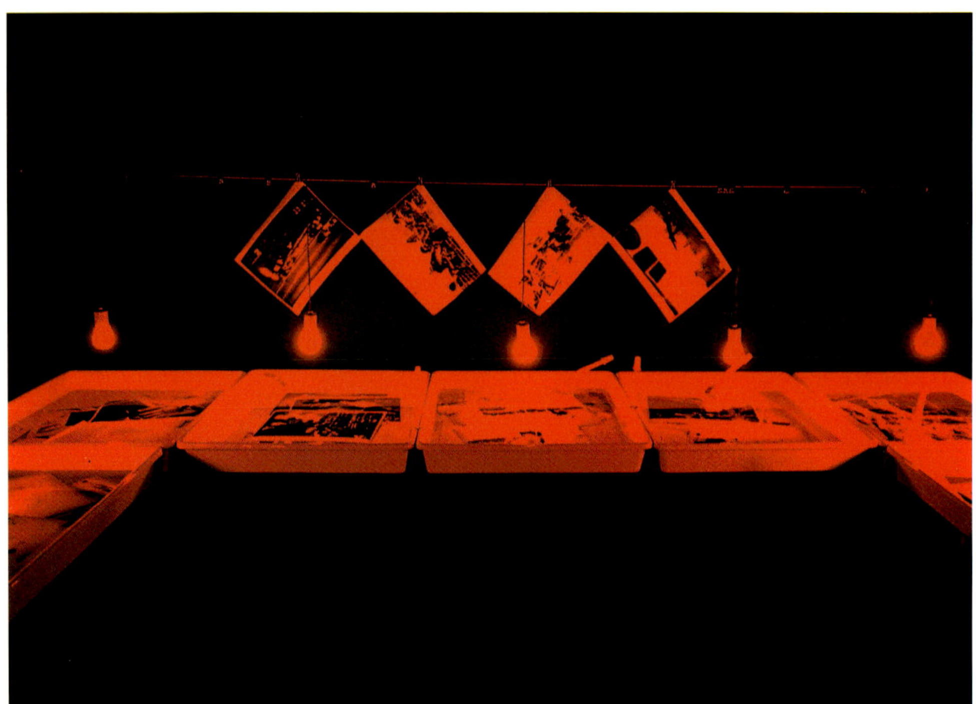

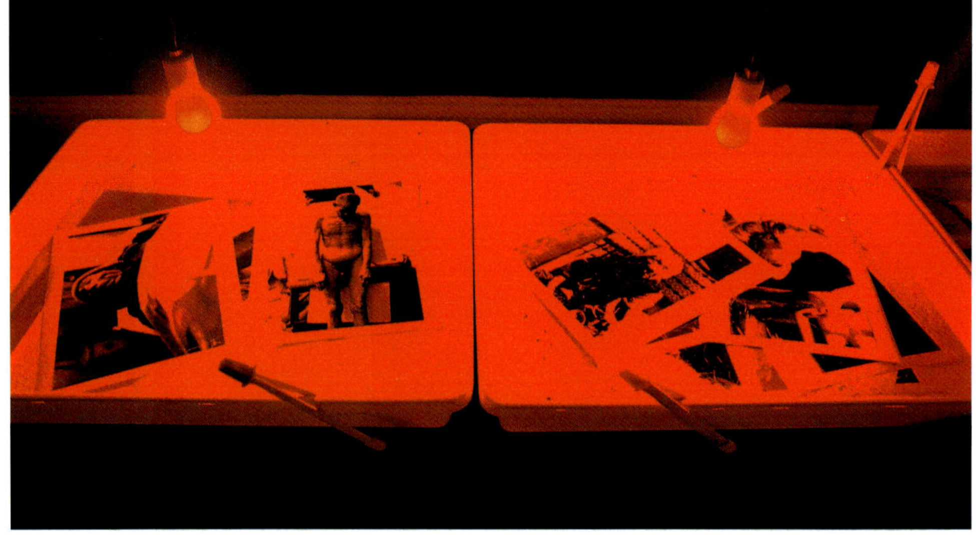

**Artist's Statement**
News
Job
Procedure

What, When, Where, Who, Why
Record, Edit, Produce, Consume, Feed Back

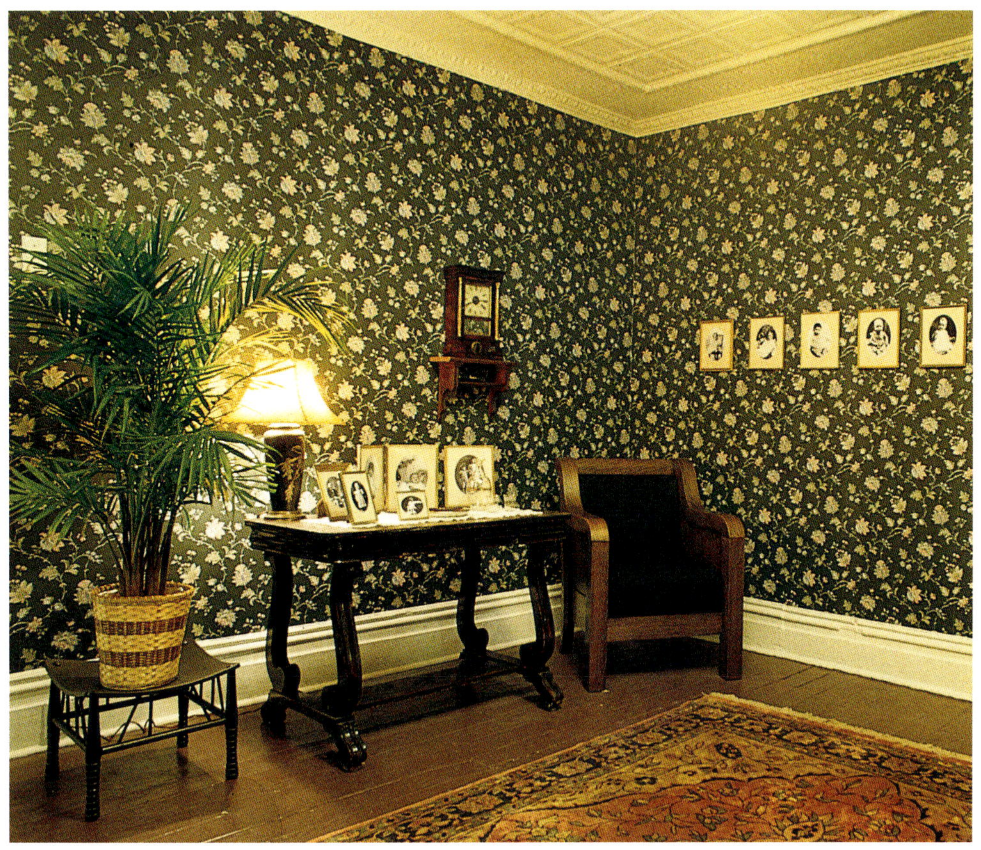

## Wu Mali

Taiwanese, born 1957

**Victorian Sweeties,** 1999
Framed ink-jet prints, furniture, wallpaper
1414 Monterey Street, 2nd floor
(included in *Installations by Asian Artists in Residence*)

A Victorian parlor and sitting room are recreated at 1414 Monterey Street, which was built during that era. Photographs of children and babies line the walls. A music stand holds a book which identifies each of the babies. Pictures of Adolph Hitler, Mahatma Gandhi, Marcel Duchamp, and Albert Einstein figure among these photographs. All the babies featured in the installation were born after the invention of the camera in the mid-1800s. All have already made their mark on history.

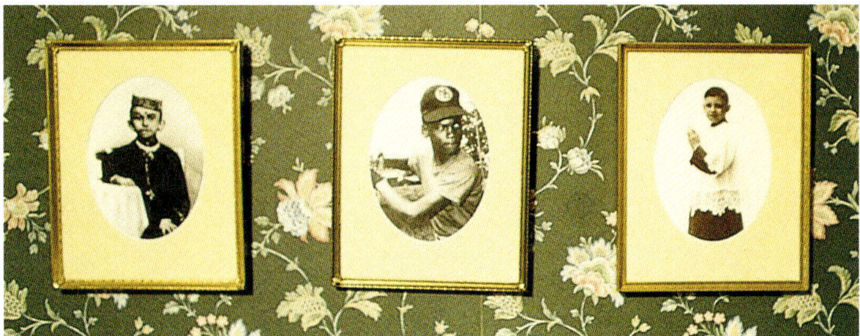

**Artist's Statement**

We were all once children: no matter who you are or what you are in this life.
And we all try hard in our lives to get back to this "condition."
This constant desire to return to the "child condition" is beyond time and history.
It has been our past. And it will always be our dream of the future.

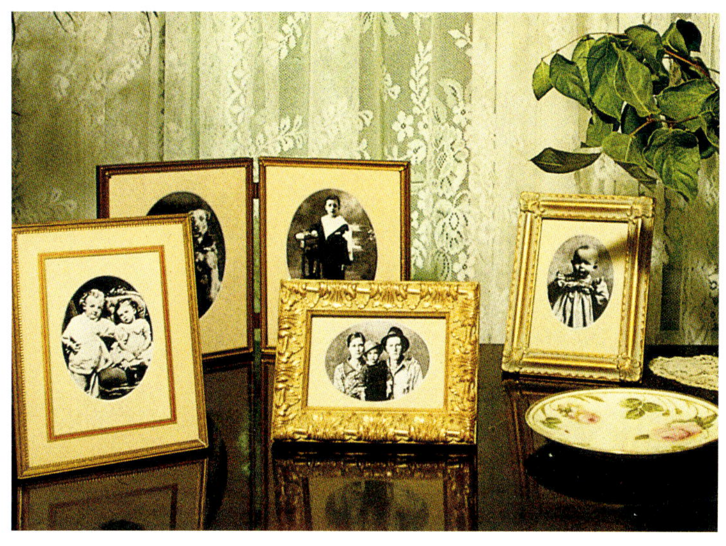

## Permanent Collection

The goal of the Mattress Factory's acquisition program is to commission new permanent works that represent a range of points of view and offer visitors an interesting and stimulating juxtaposition with temporary works. As installation art becomes more popular, museums around the world are increasingly devoting space and time to make this type of work accessible to audiences. However, few museums are able to exhibit installation art on a permanent basis. The Mattress Factory's collection of permanent installations is unique in the United States, because installations are always on view and never put in storage.

The Mattress Factory was, for a long time, the only museum in the United States to focus on collecting installation art. In most cases, it is the artist who is chosen and invited to create a new work for the collection. As with temporary exhibitions, the artist chooses a site and is provided with the materials and technical assistance needed to complete the work. Some works in the collection, such as those by Yayoi Kusama, are acquired from temporary exhibitions.

## William Anastasi

American, born 1933

**Trespass**, 1966–1991
Wall removal with stone
1414 Monterey Street, 2nd floor

This work is located in the second room of Allan Wexler's *Bed Sitting Rooms for an Artist in Residence*, on the wall between the old fireplace and the window. Anastasi picked up a stone from the sidewalk outside, and instead of drawing on the wall, he rubbed and scratched at the surface until some of the paint (and even some of the wall itself) came off. He calls this kind of drawing a "wall removal."

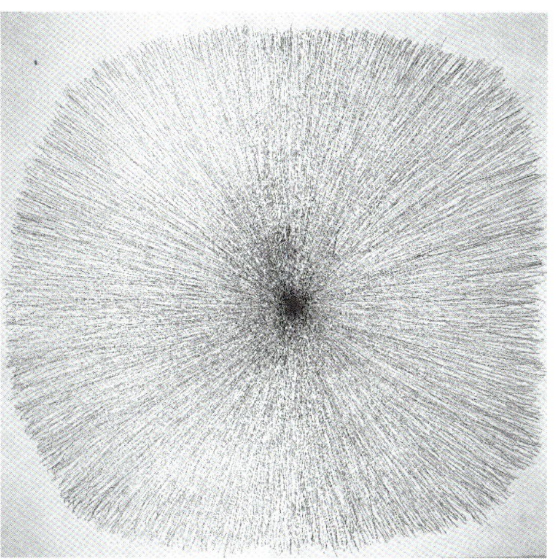

**Untitled (Calisthenic Series)**
Wall drawing after DaVinci's *Vitruvius Man*,
October 4, 1997, 16:02–16:48
Graphite on wall
1414 Monterey Street, 2nd floor

Anastasi has been creating timed drawings while blindfolded for close to forty years. The radius of this circular wall drawing is equal to the artist's reach and refers to the relationship of the human body to geometry, illustrated by Leonardo DaVinci's *Vitruvius Man*, whose height and arm span define the measure of a circle and a square.

## Monica M. Bock
## Mary Carlisle
## Cathy Lynn Gasser
## Melissa Goldstein
## Sandrine Sheon
## Catherine Smith

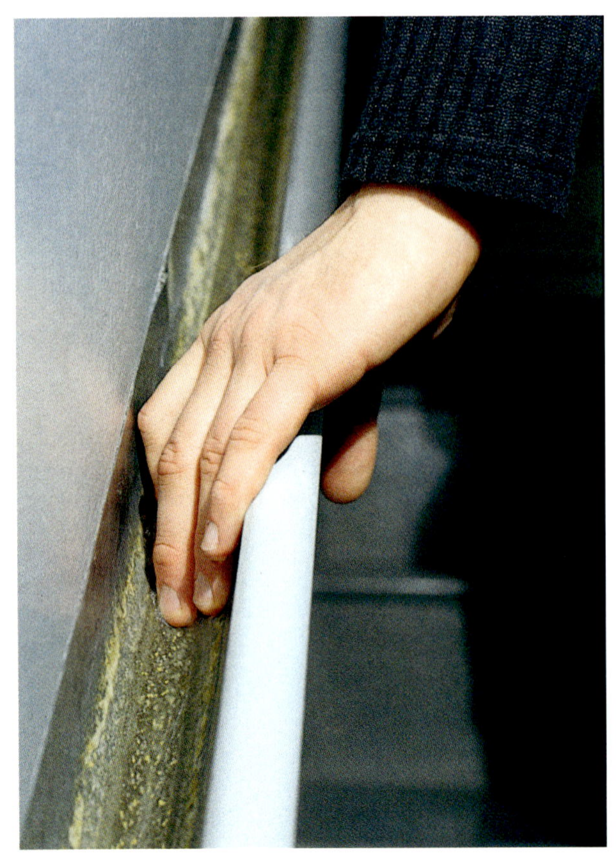

**Handrail,** 1993
Aluminum troughs, water
1414 Monterey Street, stairwell between
the 2nd and 3rd floors

As one walks up the stairway and casually lays a hand on the rail, one is surprised by the feel of water that flows down each side of the stairway. Visually, the gray aluminum blends discreetly with the gray painted wood of the railing. *Handrail* was retained from the alterations to the architecture of 1414 Monterey made in 1993 by six artists working in collaboration.

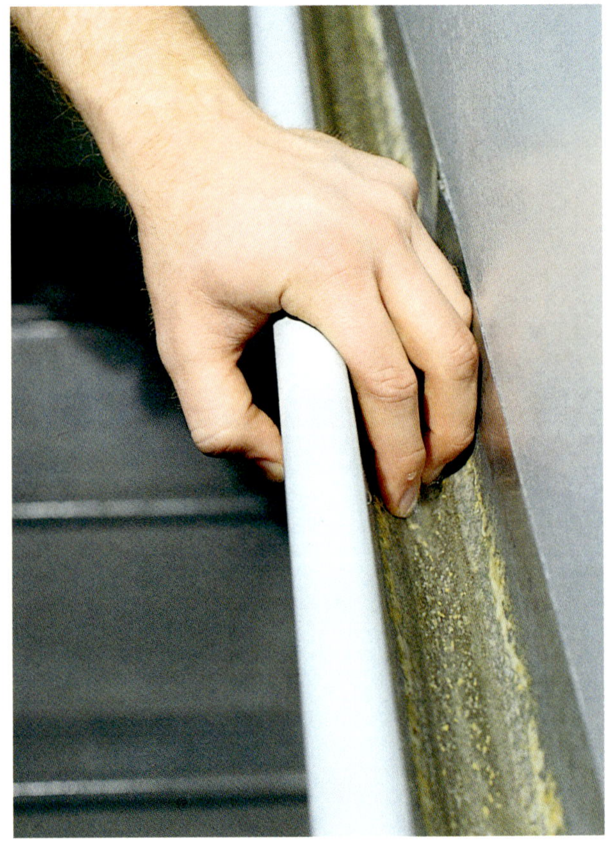

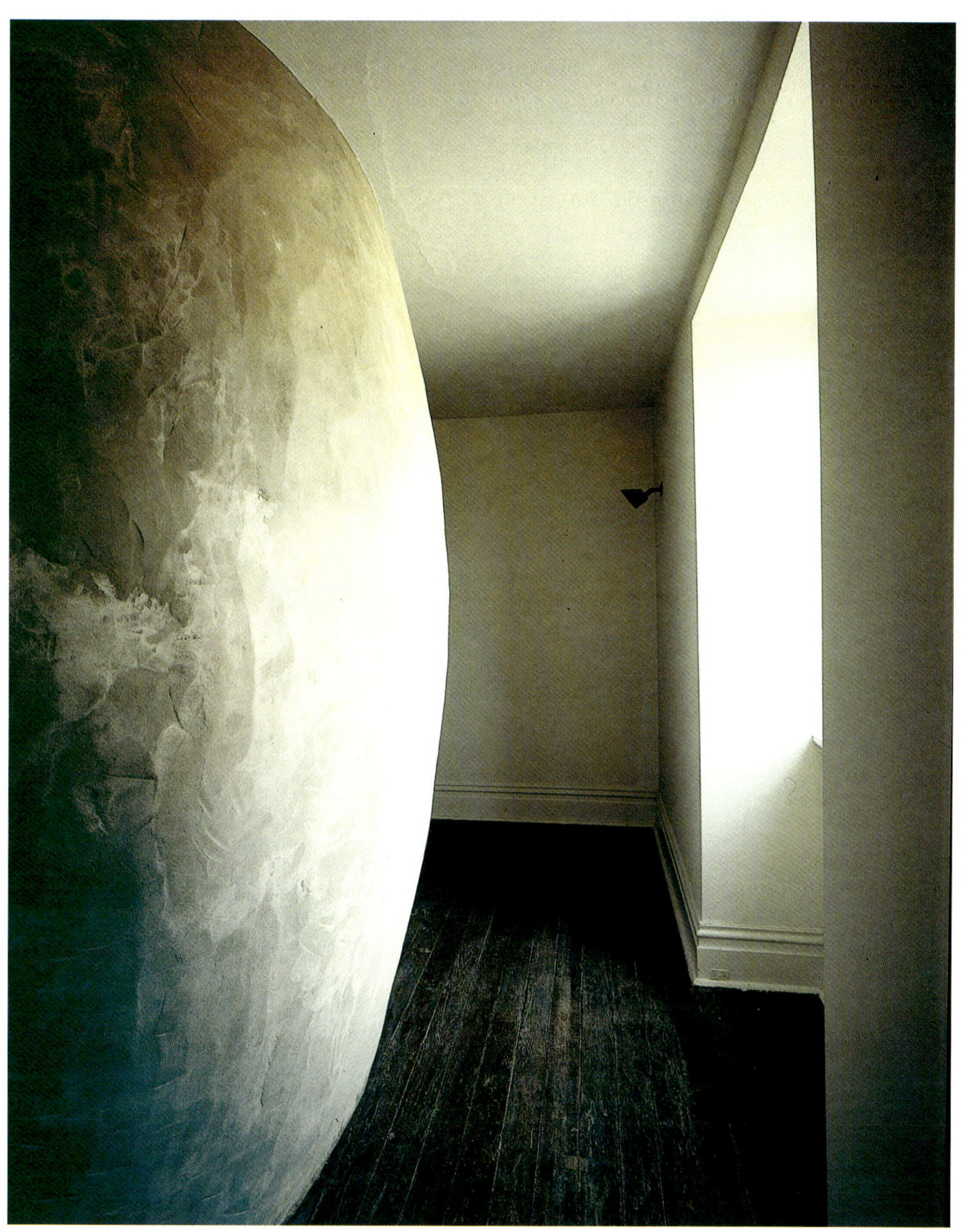

## Jene Highstein

American, born 1942

**Untitled**, 1986
Concrete over wood and wire armature
1414 Monterey Street, 3rd floor

To create his Mattress Factory work, Jene Highstein used six flexible bamboo poles that were longer than the ceiling was tall. After drawing a circle on the floor as a guide, he wedged the poles between the floor and the ceiling so that they bowed out in the center. He built a wooden frame, covered it with chicken wire, and used a trowel to spread concrete over it very smoothly. Most people have one of two opposite reactions to it: some people feel crowded, and stay in the corners of the room; others want to walk right up and touch it, even hug it.

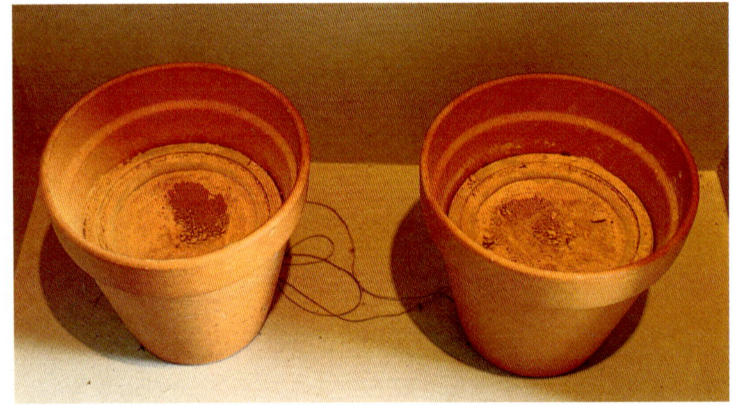

## Rolf Julius

German, born 1939

**Ash,** 1991
Terra-cotta flower pots, speakers, ash, recorded sound
1414 Monterey Street, 1st floor

Julius recorded ordinary sounds, such as birds, radiators, and crickets, and patched them together into a collage of sound. This "music" plays from speakers inside the flower pots. They are covered with an orange ash (from German coal-burning fireplaces) that seems to be dancing. It is as though the ash is making the sound "visible." It moves differently with every sound.

**Artist's Statement**

Clay pots with light brown ash inside,
and moving and sometimes jumping dark sounds
(some are quiet but these are difficult to understand).

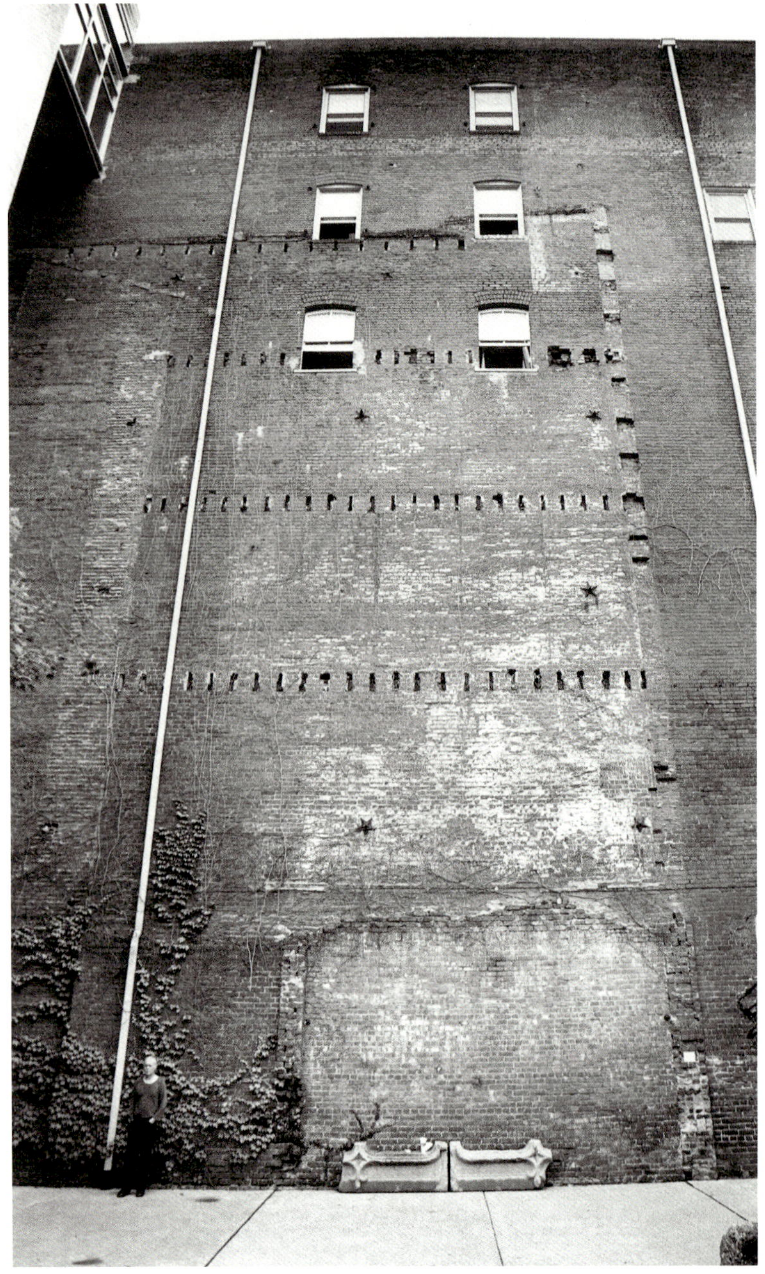

**Music for a Garden,** 1997
Audio recording, speakers
Mattress Factory *Garden*

Julius created this work as a site-specific sound piece that enhances the visitor's experience of space in the Mattress Factory *Garden*. A mix of natural and electronic sounds is broadcasted from speakers, which are placed high on the museum's wall facing the *Garden*. The speakers are angled in such a way that the visitor hears different sounds at different places. The sounds' pitches and volumes are modulated to sit at the edge of conscious awareness, subtly affecting one's experience of the site.

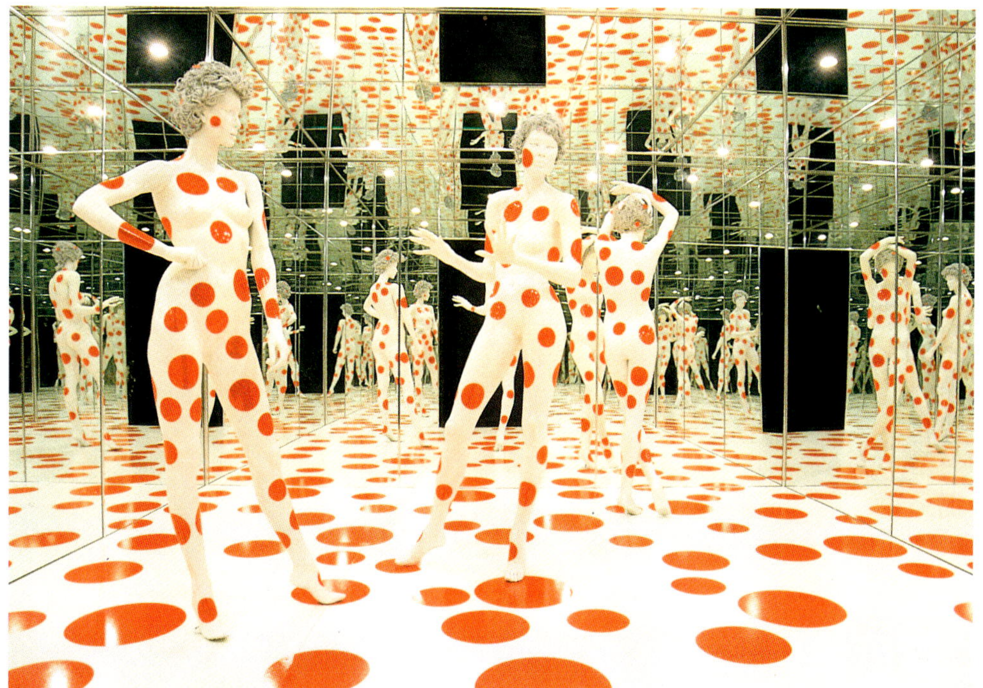

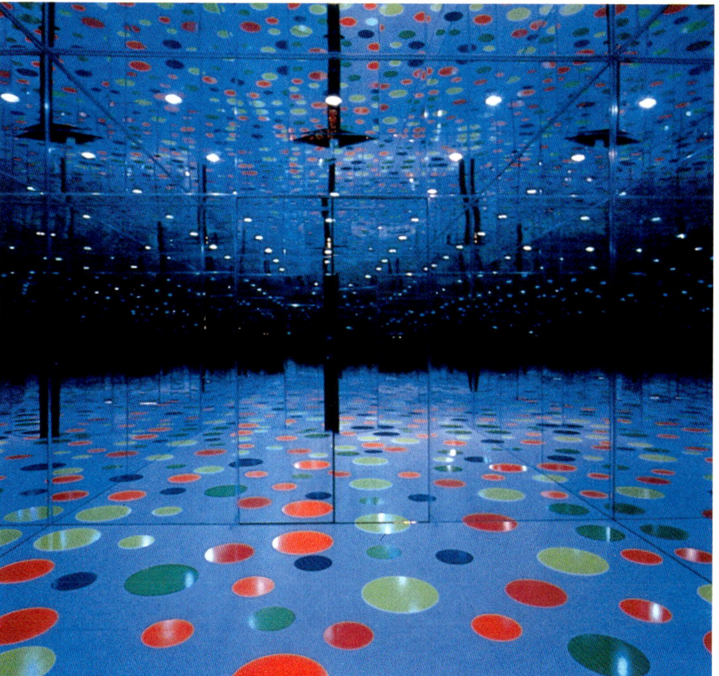

## Yayoi Kusama

Japanese, born 1929

**Infinity Dots Mirrored Room,** 1996
Adhesive dots, black light, Formica, mirrors
500 Sampsonia Way, 3rd floor

**Repetitive Vision,** 1996
Formica, adhesive dots, mannequins, mirrors
500 Sampsonia Way, 3rd floor

In 1996, the Mattress Factory invited Japanese artist Yayoi Kusama to come to Pittsburgh to create an installation piece as part of a temporary exhibition. In response to this invitation, Ms. Kusama developed plans for three installations, all of which were built. Working with Kusama and her assistants, the Mattress Factory contracted with carpenters and glaziers to create the installations *Infinity Dots Mirrored Room* and *Repetitive Vision,* along with *Dots Obsession,* according to her designs. These pieces have been such a success that the museum has kept *Infinity Dots Mirrored Room* and *Repetitive Vision* on continuous public view since they opened in October 1996. They are the only permanent, walk-in installations by Kusama on view in this country.

## Winifred Lutz

American, born 1942

**Garden,** dedicated in 1997, ongoing
Rock, brick, wood, iron, enamel on metal, plant materials

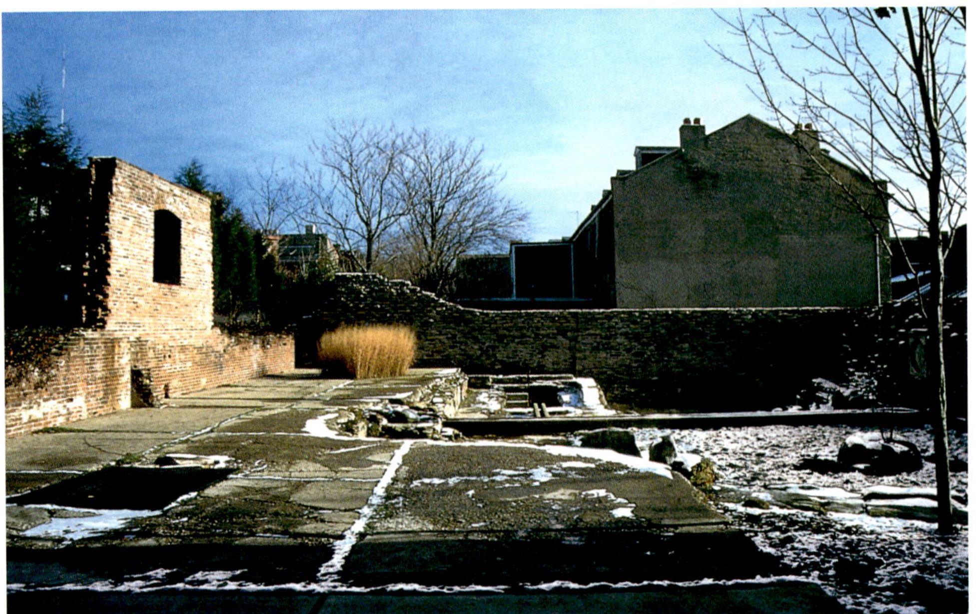

Winifred Lutz has created a permanent, site-specific installation in the two lots (one ninety feet by seventy feet and the other eighty feet by seventy feet) adjacent to the Mattress Factory's main facility at 500 Sampsonia Way. As a result of studying the site over several years, she planned a work that responded to and incorporated the particular natural and built attributes of the site. She began construction in the spring of 1993. She established public and private spaces with various physical elements: stones individually selected from a western Pennsylvania quarry, a tall grass enclosure surrounding a single chair, indigenous wild flowers, a wood pergola, a concrete trough filled with flowing water, and an amphitheater built from the remains of the Stewart Paper Factory, which burned down in 1963.

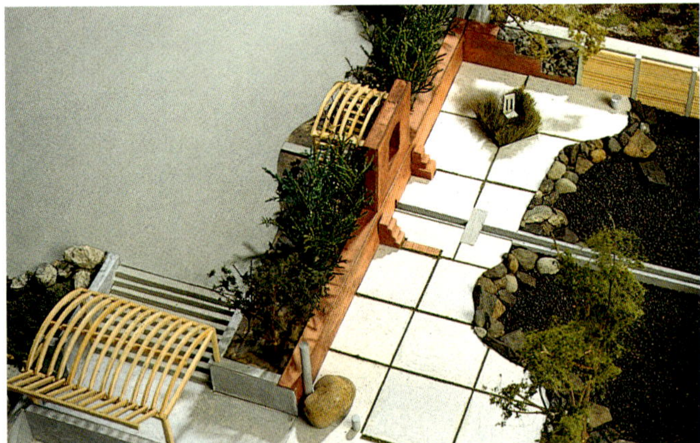

To focus the viewer's vision, Lutz has designed a series of apertures that frame specific vistas. Her goal is to create a sanctuary within an urban environment without isolating it from the community. In addition, she has addressed the natural environment of the site by conducting extensive research on the botanical and natural history of the area and using plants native to western Pennsylvania that provide food and habitat for birds.

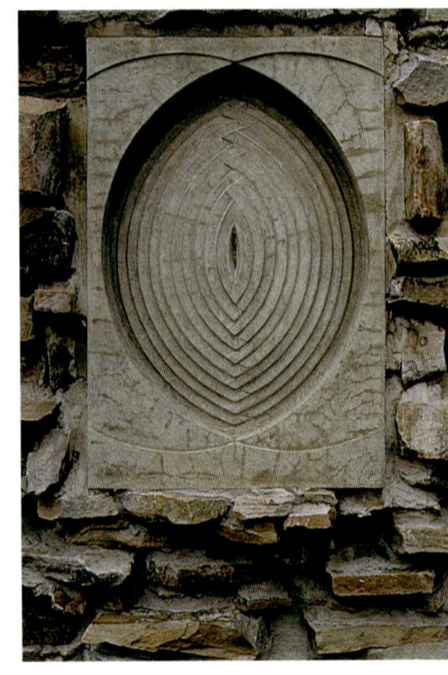

## James Turrell

American, born 1943

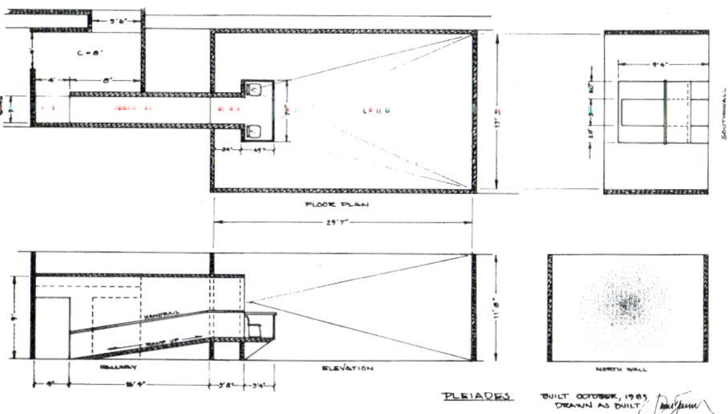


**Pleiades,** 1983
Drywall, paint, incandescent light
500 Sampsonia Way, 2nd floor

The viewer enters this piece through a maze-like corridor that blocks outside light from the room. Seated in a chair, the viewer must allow about fifteen minutes for his or her eyes to become adjusted to the extremely faint light in the room.

*Pleiades* is the first of Turrell's "Dark Pieces," which he developed to explore the experience of vision at night, especially in relation to his Roden Crater Project in Flagstaff, Arizona. In these works, Turrell is interested in creating a space in which the viewer experiences a blurring of the boundary between what is seen outside oneself and what is seen in the mind's eye.

**Artist's Statement**

*Pleiades* is a Dark Piece where the realm of night vision touches the realm of eyes-closed vision, where the space generated is substantially different than the physical confines and is not dependent upon it, where the seeing that comes from "out there" merges with the seeing that comes from "in here," where the seeing develops over and through dark adaptation but continues beyond it.

**Catso, Red,** 1967–1994
Drywall, paint, xenon projector
500 Sampsonia Way, 2nd floor

The artist has created what appears to be a red cube in the corner of the gallery by projecting a red square of light diagonally across the room. As viewers move closer, they see that the red light actually follows the contours of the walls.

**Artist's Statement**

As you look at a piece, or an experience, you can assemble the piece. As you move on it, you can reassemble it. And the fact is that you can go back in and assemble it again to its original state, and yet, having done that doesn't steal its magic. It's very important to me that you see it one way at first, and then it reveals itself as something else. Then you go back again and see it the initial way again.

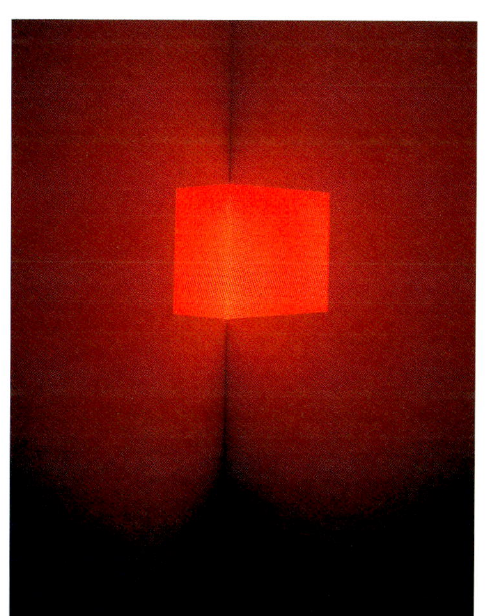

**Danaë,** 1983
Drywall, paint, ultraviolet and incandescent light
500 Sampsonia Way, 2nd floor

When the viewer enters *Danaë*, the glowing purple rectangle at the far end of the room appears to be a solid form. The artist has achieved this effect by painting the walls on the outside of the rectangular cut-out with a flat white paint and lighting this space with incandescent light, and painting the walls of the interior space with titanium white paint and lighting it with ultraviolet light.

**Artist's Statement**

*Danaë* is the first time I put light on the other side of the aperture. I have made pieces that took all their light from outside the space, like the one at the Whitney. In this one, I wanted to balance the light on the outside with light on the inside.

## Allan Wexler

American, born 1949

**Bed Sitting Rooms for an Artist in Residence,**
1988
Drywall, wood, paint, carpet
1414 Monterey Street, 2nd floor

When the Mattress Factory acquired 1414 Monterey Street, the museum commissioned architect Allan Wexler to create a living space for artists who work in residence. Wexler addressed the practical needs of artists by including a bedroom, bathroom, and small kitchen, but he also wanted to use the space in a creative way. He made many drawings, and envisioned the two rooms in a variety of different ways, finally deciding on the present configuration.

Creating rooms within the rooms, the interior space is defined by blue walls and gray carpet, while the walls and floors in the surrounding area are painted white. Cutouts, painted red, allow two bed/sofas and lighting fixtures to pass through the walls. The beds are on wheels to make them easy to roll through the walls. In just a few seconds, the space can be changed to accommodate:

- one occupant who wants a sitting area in one room and a single bed in the other,
- a couple who wants a sitting area in one room and a double bed in the other room,
- two people who each want privacy with a single bed and/or a sofa in each room,
- one person who wants an empty room for working and a bedroom.

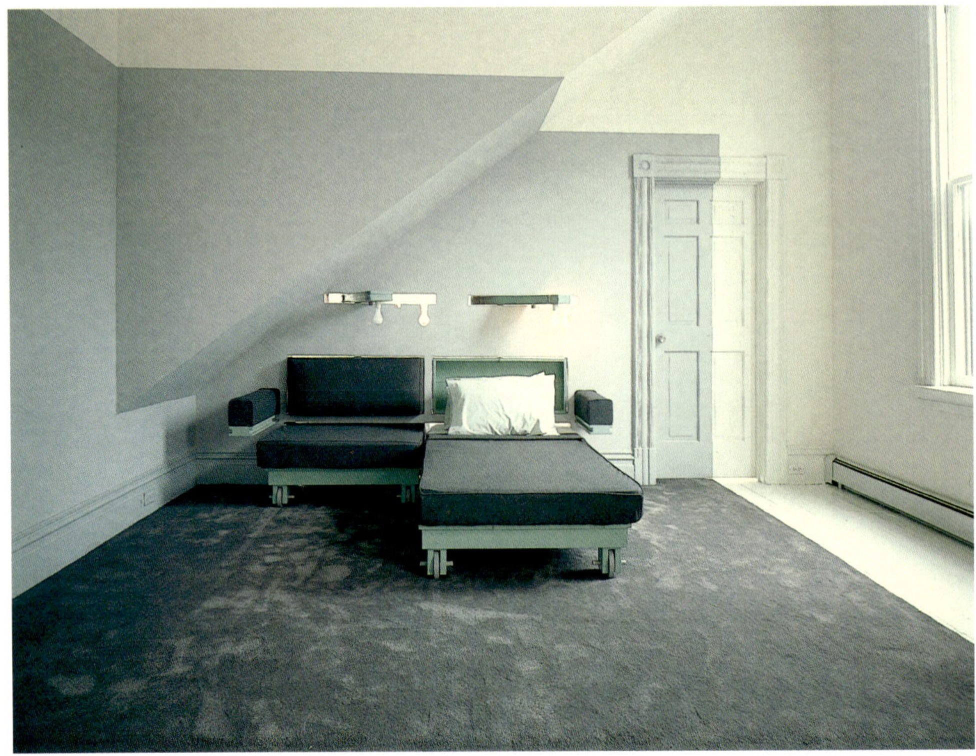

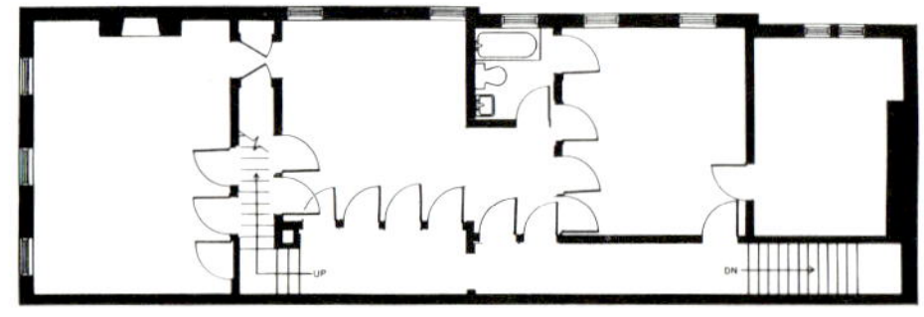


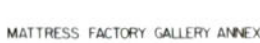


3. LIVING QUARTERS FOR ARTIST IN RESIDENCE PROGRAM
Public access into the artist's life
life becomes art. Wexler 86

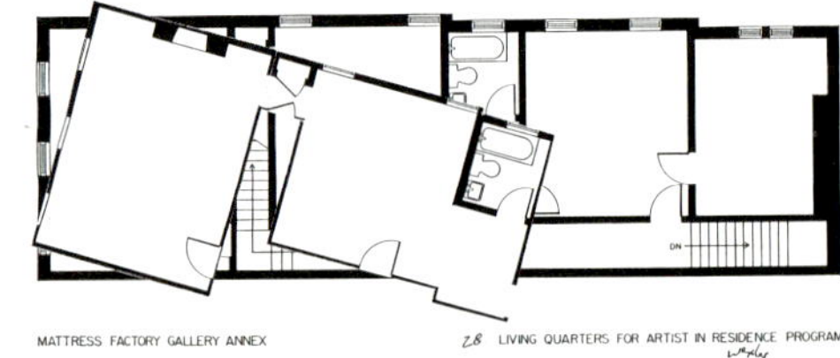


MATTRESS FACTORY GALLERY ANNEX

28 LIVING QUARTERS FOR ARTIST IN RESIDENCE PROGRAM
Wexler

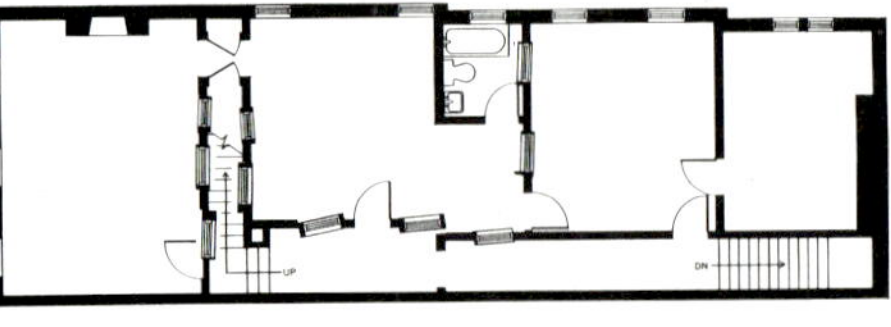


MATTRESS FACTORY GALLERY ANNEX

2. LIVING QUARTERS FOR ARTIST IN RESIDENCE PROGRAM
Windows into the artist residence
Wexler 86

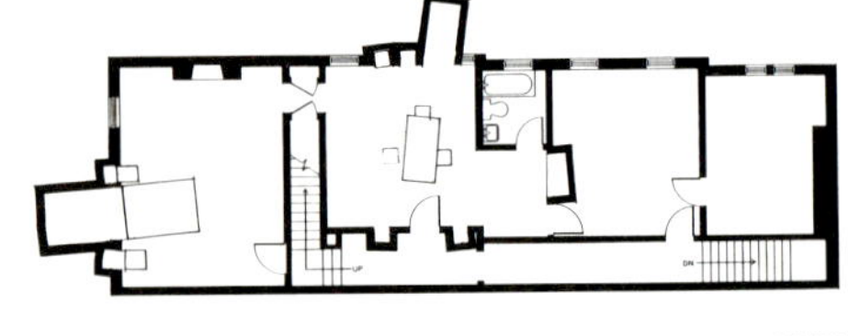


MATTRESS FACTORY GALLERY ANNEX

15 LIVING QUARTERS FOR ARTIST IN RESIDENCE PROGRAM
Furniture bulging the walls of the architecture revealing the artist's life behind. Wexler 86

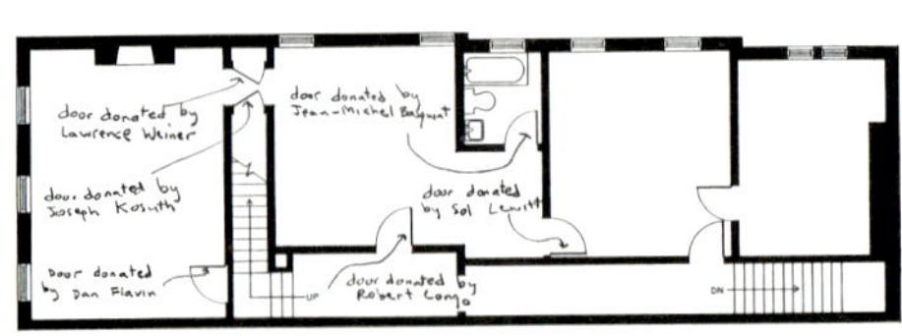


MATTRESS FACTORY GALLERY ANNEX

22. LIVING QUARTERS FOR ARTIST IN RESIDENCE PROGRAM
Architect acts as curator
Wexler 86

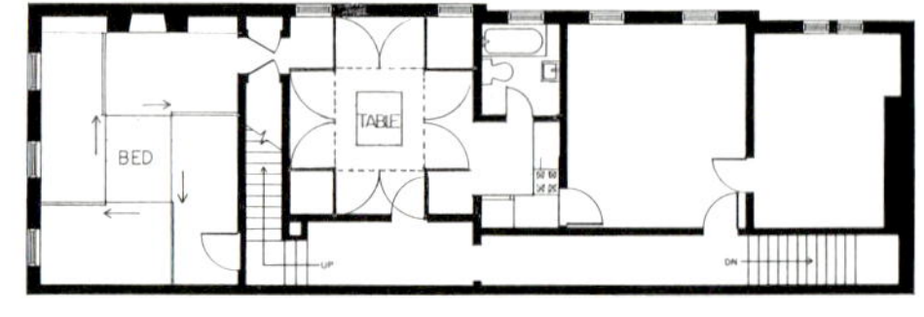


MATTRESS FACTORY GALLERY ANNEX

6. LIVING QUARTERS FOR ARTIST IN RESIDENCE PROGRAM
2 methods (hinging - sliding)
to isolate - to transform one
space into another space

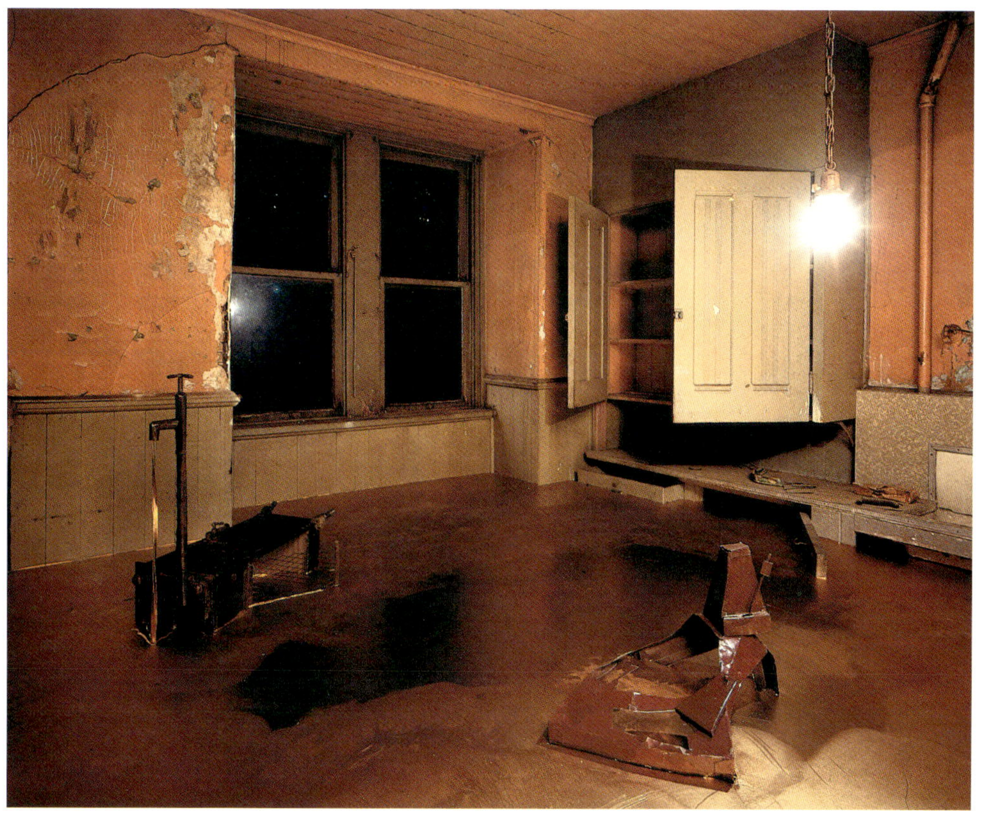

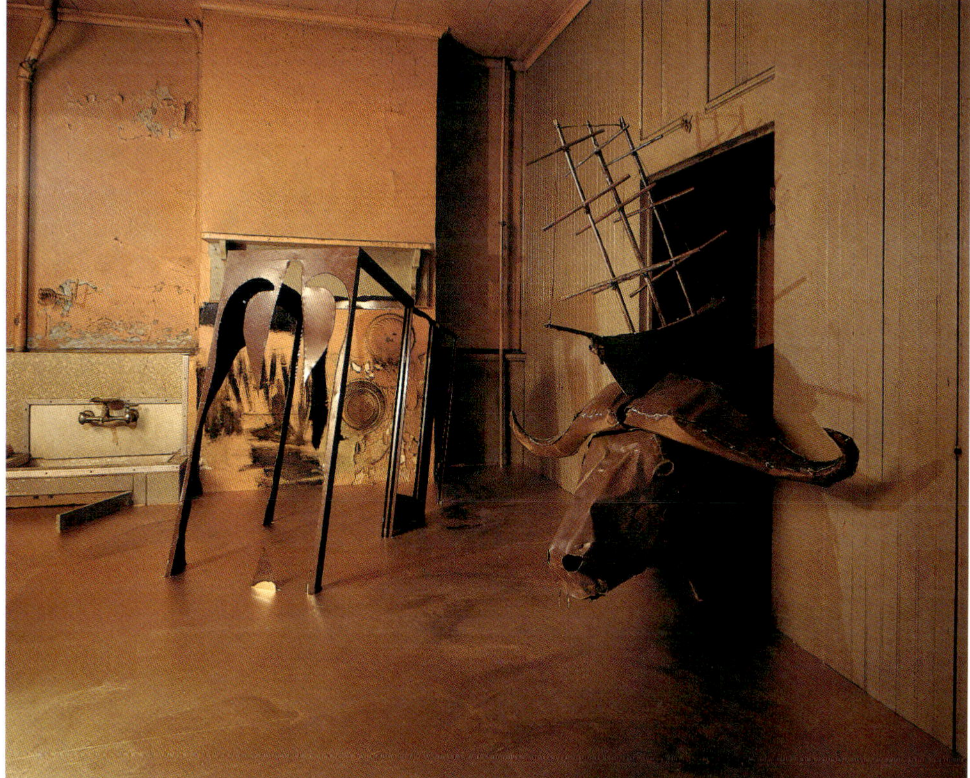

## Bill Woodrow

British, born 1948

**Ship of Fools: Discovery of Time,** 1986
Existing kitchen, metal cabinets, wood, paint
1414 Monterey Street, 3rd floor

Knowing that Bill Woodrow works with found objects, the museum's curator sent him photographs of the dilapidated third-floor kitchen in the recently acquired 1414 Monterey Street. Woodrow immediately wrote back, telling them that he loved the space and not to touch a thing. He came to Pittsburgh in the summer of 1986 and created *Ship of Fools: Discovery of Time*, which opened to the public in 1988. This work was Woodrow's first permanent installation and is integrated into the unrestored kitchen.

## The Limited Edition Project

In the mid-1980s, the Mattress Factory initiated The Limited Edition Project to provide artists with the opportunity to create editions of small works that are permanent and accessible to the public long after their temporary installations were dismantled. These prints or objects also serve as documentation of each artist's way of engaging the creative process.

Each situation is unique, and artists may choose to make prints, small objects, or both. Artists, assisted by museum staff, work with a variety of professional printmaking studios, foundries, and fabrication workshops to produce the editions. The Limited Edition Project enables artists who work in the medium of site-specific installation to make smaller, more intimate works.

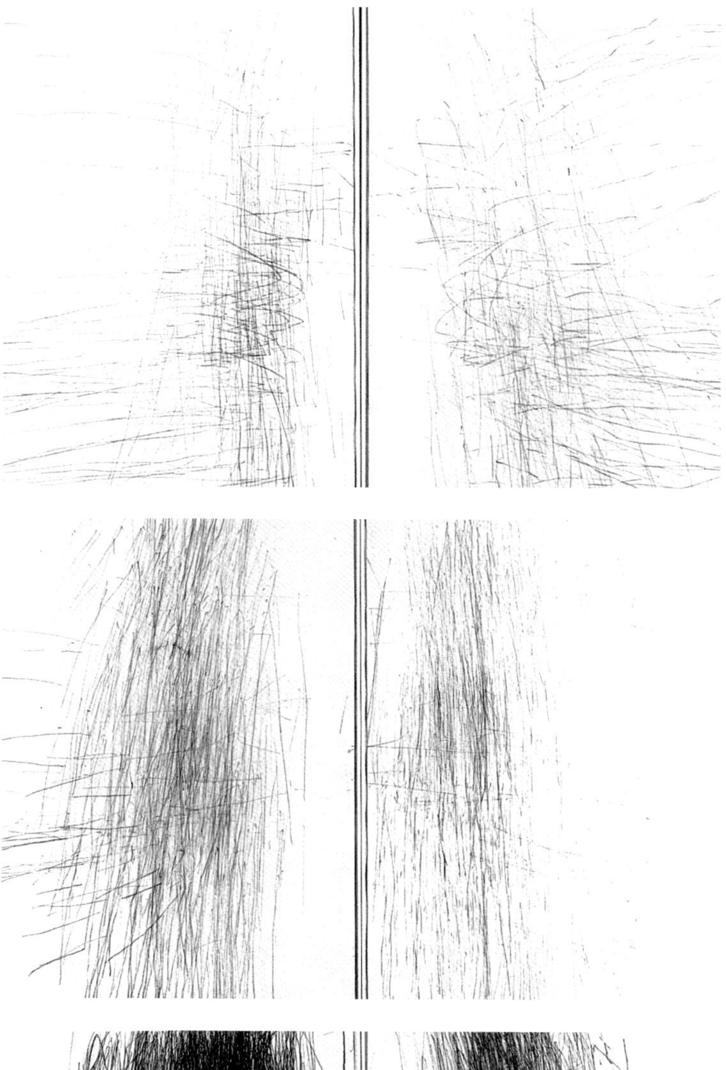

## William Anastasi

**sixteen minute blind drawing**
**thirty-two minute blind drawing**
**sixty-four minute blind drawing**
**one hundred twenty-eight minute blind drawing**, 1990–1991
Suite of four lithographs on rag paper
Each 40" x 60" in two sections of 40" x 30"
Edition size: 20

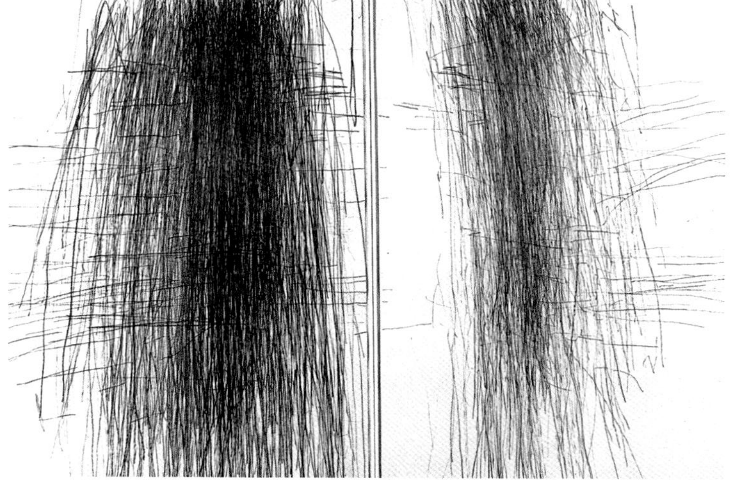

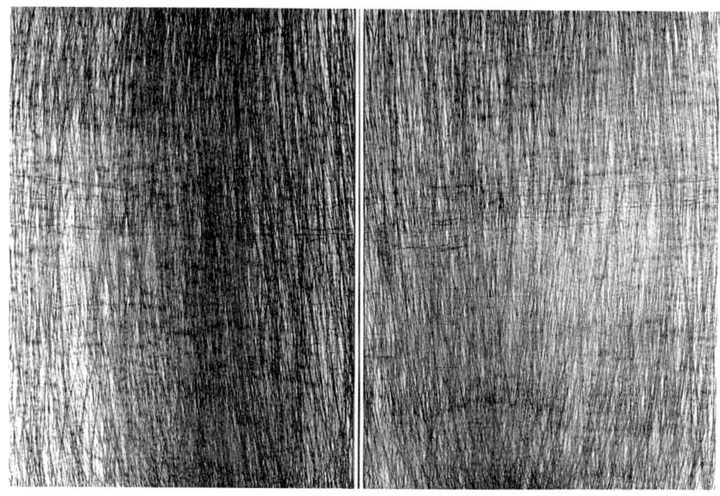

## Dove Bradshaw

**2√0,** 1999
Acetone in hand-blown glass
2 1/2"x 6" x 2 1/2"
Contained in metal box 9" x 9" x 6"
Edition size: 10

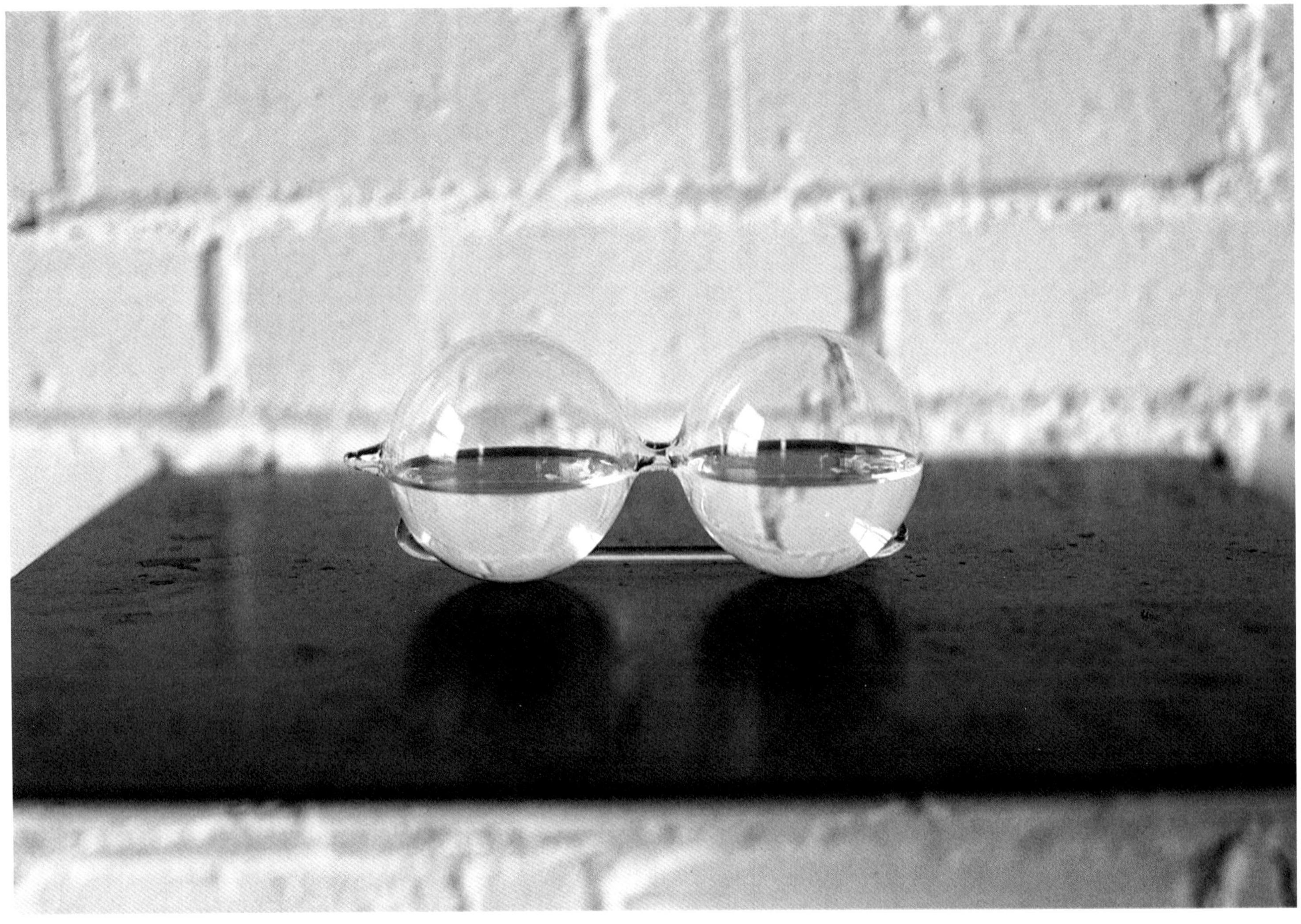

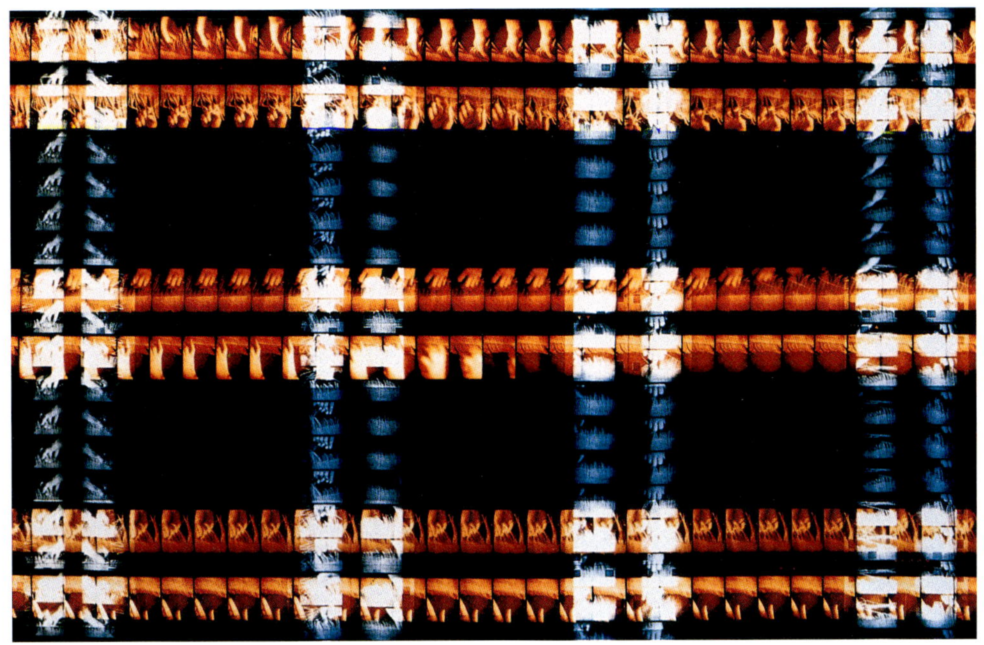

## Lynn Cazabon

**Rewind,** 2001
Lenticular image made up of 30 frames
from 8 millimeter movie film
8" x 10"
Edition size: 10

## Barbara Ess

**Untitled Billboard,** 1988
Offset lithograph printed in color from her pinhole camera photograph, in ten sections on billboard paper
Assembled size: 9' 7" x 21' 7"
Edition size: 16

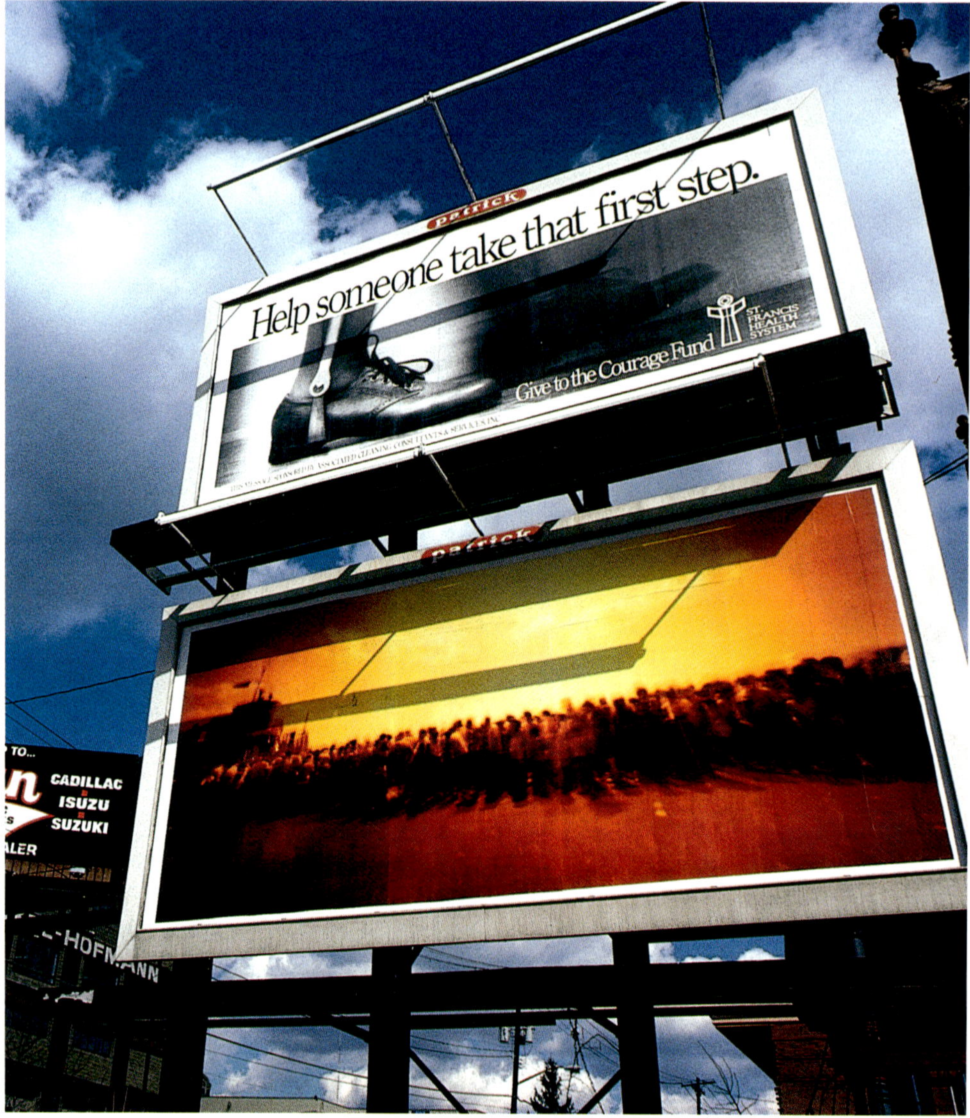

Jene Highstein

**Untitled,** 1988
Lithograph on rag paper
38" x 30"
Edition size: 100

## Rolf Julius

**Untitled,** 1988
Suite of three lithographs on rag paper
Each 13" x 10"
Edition size: 40

**Untitled,** 1994
Suite of two lithographs on rag paper
Each 9" x 11"
Edition size: 20

**Two Stones Singing,** 1997
Stones, speakers and audio tape
Variable sizes
Contained in a metal box 8" x 8 " x 5"
Edition size: 10

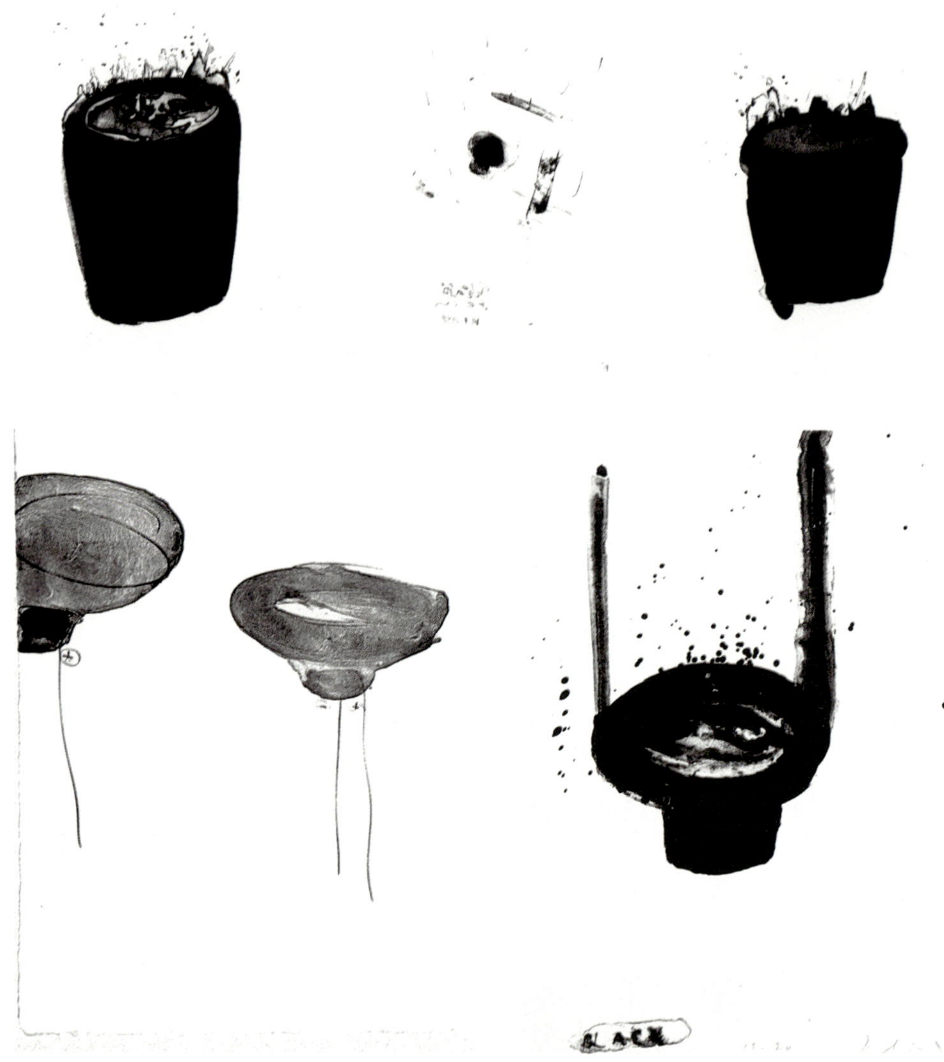

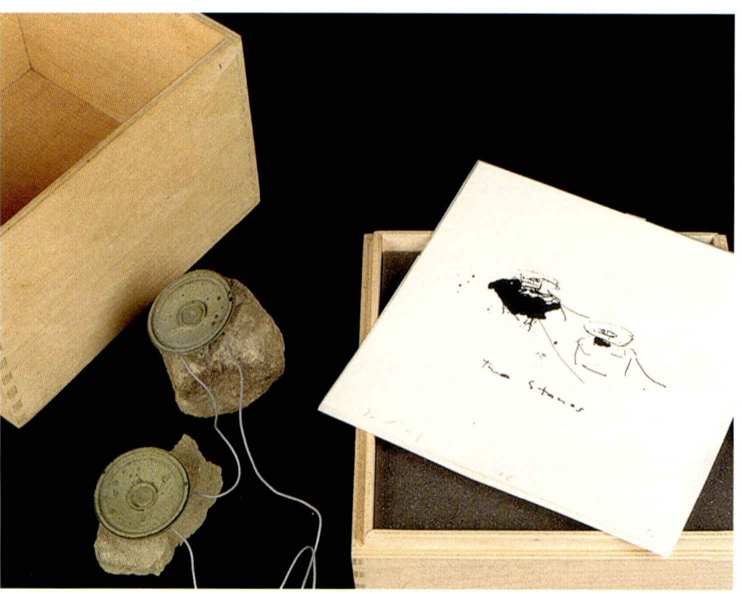

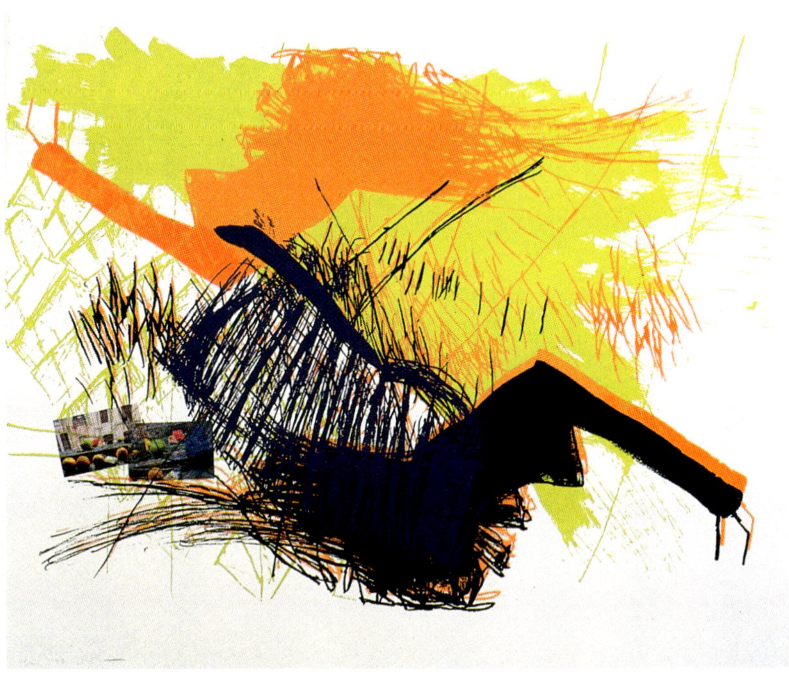

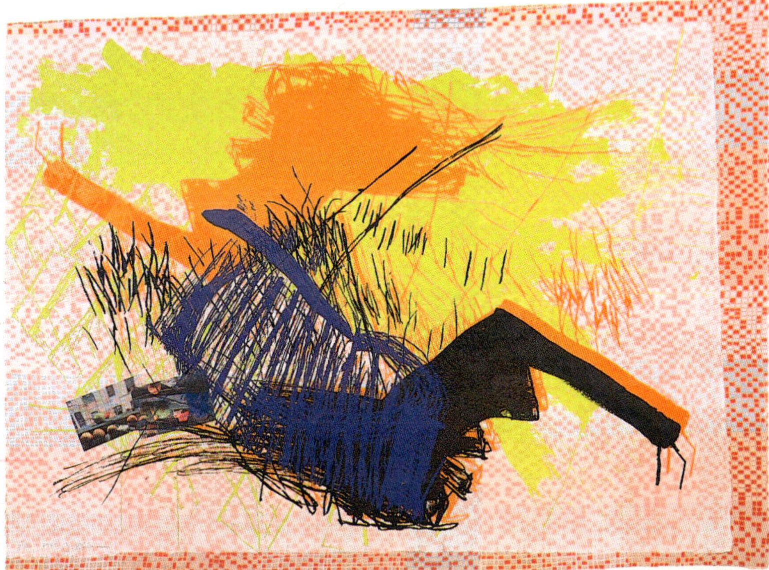

## Jessica Stockholder

**Untitled,** 1995
Serigraph on rag paper with two Iris prints on silk paper collaged to lower left corner
30" x 34"
Edition size: 20

**Untitled, State 2,** 1995
Serigraph on Japanese paper with two Iris prints on silk paper collaged to lower left corner, mounted on fabric and hand-painted steel
33" x 40"
Edition size: 20

## Bill Woodrow

**Untitled,** 1986
Suite of two lithographs on rag paper
Each 10 1/2" x 11"
Edition size: 100

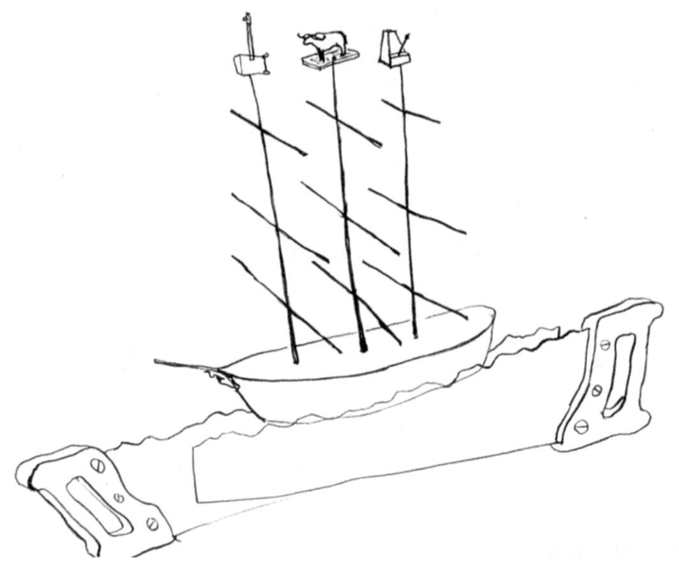

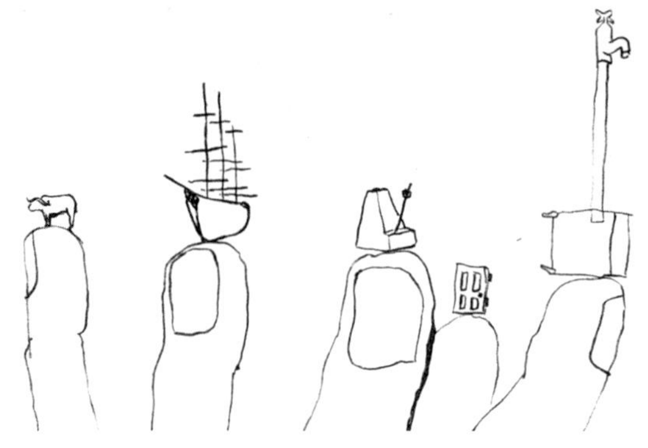

# Artists' Biographies

## Artists' Biographies

**Alumet (Astrid Tielemans and Aart Elshout)**
Dutch, Tielemans born 1953; Elshout born 1947
Live and work in Madaillan, France

### Selected Solo Exhibitions

1999 *Présences Partagées*, Skoyhuset, Copenhagen
1998 *Tekens van aanwezigheid*, Zoelmond, Netherlands
*Moving Slowly*, Monteton, France
1996 Chrysler Museum, Norfolk
1995 *Notes Between Heaven and Earth*, Mattress Factory, Pittsburgh
*ART FORUM*, Weilhelm am Teck, Germany
1993 Galerie Gerulata, Bratislava, Slovakia; Centre Culturel, Ringkobing, Denmark; Galerie Municipal, Bratislava, Slovakia
1992 Galerie Dedato, Amsterdam
1991 *Foire du Livre*, Frankfurt, Germany

### Selected Group Exhibitions

1996 *Installation dans la cour*, Musées Ingres, Montauban, France
1991 *Plein Champ*, Montpezat, France
1990 Musée Municipal, Schledam, Netherlands
1987 Bibliothèque Municipal, Grenoble

### Selected Bibliography

"Alumet." *Artension*, new series, no. 12 (1990).
"Alumet Collectif à l'Oeuvre 1976–1986." *Toulouse Culture*, no. 32 (1987).
Gaston, Marguerite. "Jeux d'Alumet." *Flash Hebdo Toulouse*, no. 594 (1990).
Miller, Donald. "Treasures Fill Tureen Exhibit." *Pittsburgh Post-Gazette*, 6 May 1995.
Regimbeau, Gerard. "Le Trio Alumet." *Artension*, no. 18 (1986).
Shearing, Graham. "Artist Shows How Man Deals with 'Heaven, Earth'." *Pittsburgh Tribune-Review*, 14 May 1995.

**William Anastasi**
American, born 1933
Lives and works in New York

### Selected Solo Exhibitions

1998 *I am a Jew*, The Philadelphia Museum of Judaica, Philadelphia
1997 *William Anastasi: Printed Out*, Mattress Factory, Pittsburgh
Untitled (*Calisthenic Series*), Mattress Factory, Pittsburgh
1996 Stalke Kunsthandel, Copenhagen
1995 *William Anastasi: A Retrospective (1960–95)*, Moore College of Art and Design, Philadelphia
1991 *Trespass*, Mattress Factory, Pittsburgh

### Selected Group Exhibitions

1999 *Merce Cunningham*, La Fundacio Antoni Tapies, Barcelona
1998 *Re: Duchamp/Contemporary Artists Respond to Marcel Duchamp's Influence*, Abraham Lubelsky Gallery, New York
1993 *Rolywholyover: A Circus*, Museum of Contemporary Art, Los Angeles; Georges Pompidou Center, Paris; The Solomon R. Guggenheim Museum, New York; The Philadelphia Museum of Art, Philadelphia; Art Tower Mito, Ibaraki, Japan
1991 *imitating nature in her manner of operation . . .*, Sandra Gering Gallery, New York

### Selected Bibliography

Anastasi, William. "Jarry, Joyce, Duchamp and Cage." In *Catalogue of the Venice Biennale*. Venice: 1993.
Anastasi, William and Michael Seidel. "Jarry in Joyce: A Conversation." *Joyce Studies Annual*. Austin, TX: University of Texas Press, 1995.
Cohen, Mark Daniel and Elizabeth Neuman. "William Anastasi: The Painting of the Word Jew at Sandra Gering." *Review*, 1 November 1997.
Kalina, Richard. "William Anastasi: Deadpan Conceptualist." *Art in America* (January 1990).
Kenton, Mary Jean. "Three New Installations." *New Art Examiner* (October 1989).
McDonough, Tom. "William Anastasi at Sandra Gering." *Art in America* (May 1998).
Miller, Donald. "Artists Give Space New Dimension." *Pittsburgh Post-Gazette*, 29 April 1989.
Ritchie, Matthew. "The Word Made Flesh." *Flash Art* (May/June 1994).
Rubenstein, Raphael. "William Anastasi at Sandra Gering." *Art in America* (April 1994).

**Robert Beckman**
American, born 1958
Lives and works in Pittsburgh

### Selected Solo Exhibitions

1995 *Ten on Eight*, Windows Gallery, New York
Clarion University of Pennsylvania Gallery, Clarion, PA
1994 *Examination*, Mattress Factory, Pittsburgh
1992 Bruce Gallery, Edinboro University of Pennsylvania, Edinboro, PA
1991 Blatant Image/Silver Eye Photo Gallery, Pittsburgh

### Selected Group Exhibitions

2000 *Pittsburgh Biennial*, Pittsburgh Center for the Arts, Pittsburgh
1999 *Group Print Exhibition*, Banana Factory, Bethlehem, PA
1998 *International Print Exhibition*, Musée Provincial Felicien Rops, Namur, France
1997 McDonough Museum of Art, Installation Gallery, Youngstown, OH
1992 *Associated Artists of Pittsburgh Annual*, The Carnegie Museum of Art, Pittsburgh

### Selected Bibliography

Miller, Donald. "Subtle Thinkers: Three Artists, Three Distinct Visions." *Pittsburgh Post-Gazette Weekend*, 21 October 1994.
Potter, Chris. "Site." *In Pittsburgh*, 17 November 1994.
Shearing, Graham. "Mattress Factory Exhibits Challenge the Imagination." *Pittsburgh Tribune-Review*, 30 October 1994.

**David Blatherwick**
Canadian, born 1960
Lives and works in Montreal

Selected Solo Exhibitions

1999 Pari Nadimi Gallery, Toronto
1998 *Multiple Horizon*, Mattress Factory, Pittsburgh
1997 *Peintures*, Plein Sud, Longueil, Quebec
1996 *The Breathing Room*, Articule, Montreal Corridor, Reykjavik, Iceland
1992 *The Mathematics of the Fake World*, Galerie Clark, Montreal

Selected Group Exhibitions

1998 David Beitzel Gallery, New York
1997 *Recent Acquisitions*, Musée du Quebec, Quebec
1996 *Beach Culture*, A.M. Gallery, New York
1995 *Lush*, Articule, Montreal
1992 *Tutti Qui*, Anderson Ranch Arts Center, Snowmass, CO

Selected Bibliography

Brennan, Lissa. "Parts Is Parts." *In Pittsburgh*, 14 October 1998.
Catchlove, Lucinda. "Heavy Petting." *HOUR* (Montreal), 4 April 1996.
Kozinska, D. "Art with an Unusual Visual Vocabulary." *Montreal Gazette*, 18 July 1998.
Metcalfe, C. "David Blatherwick." *Metropole* (Montreal), 15 January 1990.
St.-Gelais, T. "David Urban, Barry Allikas/David Blatherwick." *Parachute* (January 1998).
Thomas, Mary. "Bodies of Work." *Pittsburgh Post-Gazette*, 7 November 1998.

**Monica M. Bock**
American, born 1960
Lives and works in Willington, CT

Selected Solo Exhibitions

2001 Phillips Museum Dana Room Gallery, Franklin and Marshall College, Lancaster, PA
2000 *Don' t Forget the Lunches (count your losses)*, Real Art Ways (RAW), Hartford, CT; Chicago Cultural Center, Chicago
*Maternal Exposure*, ArtWorks! New Bedford, MA; University Gallery, University of Massachusetts, Lowell, MA
1999 *Afterbirths: 20 Days King and Queen*, Adams House Art Space, Cambridge, MA
1998 *Humours*, University of Connecticut Atrium Gallery, Storrs, CT
1997 *Eye for Eye*, Old State House, Hartford, CT

Selected Group Exhibitions

1998 *Consummations: Three Women*, Galleria Kameoka, Kameoka, Japan
1997 *Far from Home*, Cranbrook Art Museum, Cranbrook, MI
1996 *Hush*, N.A.M.E. Gallery, Chicago
1994 *Little Things*, Art in General, New York
1993 *A Collaboration*, Mattress Factory, Pittsburgh
1992 *Contentious and Precious*, Nexus Contemporary Art Center, Atlanta
1991–92 *Margin of Safety*, collaborative installation, Museum of Contemporary Art, Atlanta
1991 *Body Cover*, Betty Rymer Gallery, Chicago
1990 *Gigantic Women/Miniature Work*, S.A.I.C. Gallery 2, Chicago

Selected Bibliography

Charmelo, Julie. "Some Assembly Required." *New Art Examiner* (May 2000).
Collins, Sue. "Margin of Safety: A Collaborative Installation." *New Art Examiner* (February/March 1992).
Hixson, Kathryn. "Margin of Safety: A Collaborative Installation." *Art Magazine* (April 1992).
Miller, Donald. "Sharing the View." *Pittsburgh Post-Gazette Weekend*, 17 December 1993.
Rubinkowski, Leslie. "Flying in the Face of the Art Establishment." *Pittsburgh Post-Gazette Weekend*, 1 May 1994.
Zimmer, William. "Summer Exhibitions, Ghosts and Wee Folk." *New York Times*, 27 August 2000.

**Christian Boltanski**
French, born 1944
Lives and works in Paris

Selected Solo Exhibitions

1997 Anthony d'Offay Gallery, London
1995 *Menschlich*, Wien Kunsthalle, Vienna
1994 *Christian Boltanski: Menschlich*, Ludwig Forum, Aachen, Germany
1993 *Suisse Morts*, Center for Contemporary Arts, Glasgow
1991 *Archives of the Carnegie International 1896–1991* (in collaboration with the *Carnegie International*), Mattress Factory, Pittsburgh

Selected Group Exhibitions

1997 *Deep Storage*, Haus der Kunst, Munich
1996 Marian Goodman Gallery, New York
1995 *Weimarer Republik*, Kulturdirektion, Weimar, Germany
1994 *Hors limites*, Musée National d'Art Moderne, Georges Pompidou Center, Paris
1990 *A Group Show*, Marian Goodman Gallery, New York

Selected Bibliography

Dannatt, Adrian. "The Carnegie International." *Flash Art* (March 1992).
Donovan, Sandra Fischione. "Off-the-wall Art Exhibits Titillate the Senses, Stimulate the Mind." *New York Times Sunday Magazine*, 24 May 1992.
Eccher, Danilo, Christian Boltanski, Daniel Soutif, and Paolo Fabbri. *Christian Boltanski* (New York: Distributed Art Publishers, 1997).
Gerzova, Jana. "Mattress Factory." *Profil* (January/February 1996).

Gumpert, Lynn and Christian Boltanski. *Christian Boltanski*. New York: Abbeville Press, 1994.
Hymowitz, Carol. "This Museum has a Liking for Artists Who Trash the Place." *Wall Street Journal*, 17 October 1991.
Miller, Donald. "International Dominates Fall Art Season." *Pittsburgh Post-Gazette*, 6 September 1991.
Miller, Donald. "51st International True to Curator's Conception." *Pittsburgh Post-Gazette*, 19 October 1991.
Ritchie, Christina. "The Carnegie International." *Canadian Art* (spring 1992).
Schwalb, Harry. "Sleeper: No Overnight Sensation, the Mattress Factory is a Hit of a Museum." *Pittsburgh* (March 1992).
Semin, Didier, Christian Boltanski, Tamar Garb, Donald B. Kuspit, Melvin Bragg. *Christian Boltanski: Contemporary Artist*. London: Phaidon Press, 1997.
Stacho, L'ubo. "Mattress Factory Muzeum Ako Zivotny Styl." *Linia* (September 1998).
Yood, James. "Taking Stock." *New Art Examiner* (January 1992).

**Dove Bradshaw**
American
Lives and works in New York

Selected Solo Exhibitions
1999 *2√0*, *Negative Ions*, and *Indeterminacy*, Mattress Factory, Pittsburgh
1995 *Indeterminacy*, Sandra Gering Gallery, New York
1993 *Contingency*, Sandra Gering Gallery, New York
1991 *Plain Air*, P.S. 1 Contemporary Art Center, Long Island City, NY
1990 *Plain Air*, Mattress Factory, Pittsburgh

Selected Group Exhibitions
1993 *Works from the Permanent Collection*, Art Institute of Chicago, Chicago
1992 *Rolywholyover: A Circus*, Museum of Contemporary Art, Los Angeles; Georges Pompidou Center, Paris; The Solomon R. Guggenheim Museum, New York; The Philadelphia Museum of Art, Philadelphia; Art Tower Mito, Ibaraki, Japan
1991 *New York Diary: Almost 25 Different Things to See*, P.S. 1 Contemporary Art Center, Long Island City, NY
1990 *imitating nature in her manner of operation . . .*, Sandra Gering Gallery, New York

Selected Bibliography
*Dove Bradshaw—Work 1969–1993*. New York: Sandra Gering Gallery, 1993.
Homisak, Bill. "Installations Take Flight at 1414 Monterey." *Pittsburgh Tribune-Review*, 10 August 1990.
Lowry, Patricia. "Bombs Away—Pigeon Art." *Pittsburgh Post-Gazette*, 9 June 1990.
McEvilley, Thomas. "In the Form of a Thistle." *Artforum* (October 1992).
——. "plain air." *Artforum* (April 1990).
Miller, Donald. "Building Plans, Exhibits at Factory." *Pittsburgh Post-Gazette*, 22 June 1990.
Odom, Michael. "Group Show." *In Pittsburgh*, 1 August 1990.
Thomas, Mary. "At 2 sites, 4 artists play with senses and spaces." *Pittsburgh Post-Gazette*, 12 June 1999.
Winn, Alice. "Art Takes Flight." *Pittsburgh City Paper*, 16–23 June 1999.

**Valerie Brodar**
American, born 1962
Lives and works in Tempe, Arizona

Selected Exhibitions
1999 *Coincidence of Opposites*, Zico House, Beirut, Lebanon
1997 *The Gloves Are Off*, The Three Arts Club of Chicago, Chicago
1995 *All Flesh Is Proud of its Wounds*, Artemesia Gallery, Chicago
1993 *A Tiny Crown of Scars*, S.A.I.C. Warehouse, Chicago
1992 *19:2*, The Book Project, Chicago
*Territorial Imperative: A Dialogue with Fear*, Gallery 2, Chicago
1991 *Naming the Necessity*, The School of the Art Institute of Chicago, Chicago
1990 *X knows P*, Mattress Factory, Pittsburgh

Selected Bibliography
Khal, Helen. "Trompe L'oeil and Intellectual Dialogue at the Galleries." *Daily Star* (Lebanon), 13 March 1999.
McCracken, Dave. "Gallery Scenes." *Chicago Tribune*, 6 November 1992.
McLaughlin, Bonnie. "Fears of a Woman." *The Reader*, 30 October 1992.
Miller, Donald. "Factory Exhibit Explores Words, War." *Pittsburgh Post-Gazette*, 17 November 1990.
——. "People to Watch in 1991—Valerie Brodar at the Mattress Factory." *Pittsburgh Post-Gazette*, 3 January 1991.

**Diana Burgoyne**
Canadian, born 1957
Lives and works in Vancouver

Selected Exhibitions
1999 *Kitchen Drawer*, Richmond Art Gallery, Richmond, VA
1998 *The Gallery Project*, Vancouver
1994 *Chaos Never Dies*, Seattle
1992 *Gianzzo Live*, Berlin
1991 *Untitled*, Mattress Factory, Pittsburgh

Selected Performances
1999 *Talk/Cross Talk*, Ace Space, Winnipeg, Manitoba
1996 *Electronic Arts Festival*, Western Front, Vancouver
1995 *Music with a Peel*, Science World, Vancouver
1990 *Untitled*, Sound Disturbance, Cleveland
*Untitled*, SoNo Festival, Norwalk, CT

Selected Bibliography
Blackman, Susan. "The Mattress Factory: An Alternative Museum." *Carnegie Magazine* (November/December 1991).
Charpentier, Elie. "Patty Martori, Buzz Spector, Diana Burgoyne, Bogdan Perzynski: Four New Installations." *In Pittsburgh*, 6 November 1991.

**John Cage**
American, 1912–1992
For more information please see http://newalbion.com/artists/cagej

Selected Exhibitions
1991 *changing installation at the mattress factory* (in collaboration with the *Carnegie International*), Mattress Factory, Pittsburgh
*Rolywholyover: A Circus*, Museum of Contemporary Art, Los Angeles; Georges Pompidou Center, Paris; The Solomon R. Guggenheim Museum, New York; The Philadelphia Museum of Art, Philadelphia; Art Tower Mito, Ibaraki, Japan.
1989 *Dancers on a Plane*, Anthony d'Offay Gallery, London
1987 *Dokumenta 8*, Kassel, Germany
1986 Blum Helman Gallery, New York
Galerie Watari, Tokyo

Selected Bibliography
Bohn, Donald Chant. "A Kinder, Gentler Museum?" *New Art Examiner* (February/March 1992).
Cage, John. *I–VI (The Charles Eliot Norton Lectures)*. Cambridge, MA: Harvard University Press, 1990.
——. *Silence: Lectures and Writings of John Cage*. Middletown, CT: Wesleyan University Press, 1961.
——. *Writings '67–72*. Middletown, CT: Wesleyan University Press, 1973.
——. *A Year from Monday*. Middletown, CT: Wesleyan University Press, 1961.
Craig, John G., Jr. "Art Works Hard, Too." *Pittsburgh Post-Gazette*, 21 December 1991.
Dannatt, Adrian. "The Carnegie International." *Flash Art* (March 1992).
Hymowitz, Carol. "This Museum has a Liking for Artists Who Trash the Place." *Wall Street Journal*, 17 October 1991.
"John Cage's Installation at the Mattress Factory . . ." *Artspace* (December 1991).
Katz, Vincent. "John Cage: An Interview." *Print Collector's Newsletter* (January/February 1990).
Knight, Christopher. "Cage 'Circus' a Three-Ring Sensual Beast." *Los Angeles Times*, 17 September 1993.
Kostelanetz, Richard. *Conversing with John Cage*. New York: Limelight Editions, 1988.
——. *John Cage: Writer*. New York: Limelight Editions, 1993.
——, ed. *John Cage: An Anthology*. Cambridge, MA: Perseus Books, Da Capo Press, 1991.
McKenna, Kristine. "The Randomest Show On Earth." *Los Angeles Times/Calendar*, 5 September 1993.
Miller, Donald. "51st International True to Curator's Conception." *Pittsburgh Post-Gazette*, 19 October 1991.
——. "International Dominates Fall Art Season." *Pittsburgh Post-Gazette*, 6 September 1991.
——. "Worlds Together at the Carnegie International." Pittsburgh Post-Gazette Weekend, 18 October 1991.
Odom. Michael. "A Cage Without Bars." *In Pittsburgh*, 16 October 1991.
——. "John Cage: Rolywholyover A Circus." *Art Papers* (May/June 1994).
Perloff, Marjorie and Charles Junkerman, eds. *John Cage: Composed In America*. Chicago: University Of Chicago Press, 1994.
Retallack, Joan, ed. *Musicage: Cage Muses on Words Art Music*. Middletown, CT: Wesleyan University Press, 1996.
Revill, David. *The Roaring Silence*. New York: Arcade Publishing, 1992.
Schwalb, Harry. "Showtime." *Pittsburgh Magazine* (October 1991).
Shultis, Christopher. *Silencing the Sounded Self: John Cage and the American Experimental Tradition*. Boston: Northeastern University Press, 1998.
Stacho, L'ubo. "Mattress Factory Muzeum Ako Zivotny Styl." *Linia* (September 1998).
Yood, James. "Taking Stock." *New Art Examiner* (January 1992).

**Mary Carlisle**
American
Lives and works in Louisville, Kentucky

Selected Exhibitions
1993 *A Collaboration*, Mattress Factory, Pittsburgh
1992 *At the Drop of a Hat*, International Performance Studio, Chicago
1991 *Margin of Safety*, collaborative installation, The Museum of Contemporary Art, Chicago
1990 *Gigantic Women/Miniature Work*, S.A.I.C. Gallery 2, Chicago

Selected Bibliography
Collins, Sue. "Margin of Safety: A Collaborative Installation." *New Art Examiner* (February/March 1992).
Hixon, Kathryn. "Reviews: Chicago." *Arts Magazine* (April 1992).
Miller, Donald. "Sharing the View." *Pittsburgh Post-Gazette*, 17 December 1993.

**Ladislav Čarný**
Slovakian, born 1949
Lives and works in Bratislava

Selected Solo Exhibitions
1995 *Phase of Nigreda*, Mattress Factory, Pittsburgh
1991 Galerie mesta Bratislavy, Palais Palffy, Bratislava, Slovakia
Galeria Maszachaba, Krakow, Poland
1990 Kloster in Marianka, Marianka bei Bratislava, Slovakia
1985 Galerie na Karlovce, Prague, Czech Republic

Selected Group Exhibitions

1992 *The Laboratory*, centrum mesta Presov, Presov, Slovakia

1990 Cesko-Slovevenske Umenie, Paris
*Ecological Motive*, Kladno, Czech Republic

1988 Trienale Kresby, Wroclaw, Poland

Selected Bibliography

Gerzova, Jana. "Mattress Factory." *Profil* (January/February 1996).

Krainak, Paul. "Siting Slavs at the Factory." *New Art Examiner* (March 1996).

Markham, Pamela. "Artists from Eastern and Central Europe." *Arti* (May/June 1996).

Miller, Donald. "East Europeans in Show of Strength." *Pittsburgh Post-Gazette*, 28 October 1995.

Potter, Chris. "Site." *In Pittsburgh*, 25 January 1996.

Shearing, Graham. "Best Show of the Year Worth Czeching Out." *Pittsburgh Tribune-Review*, 26 November 1995.

Shearing, Graham. "Shows and artists make their marks on 1995." *Pittsburgh Tribune-Review*, 31 December 1995.

Stein, Judith. "Import/Export: Out of the East." *Art in America* (April 1998).

**Lynn Cazabon**

American, born 1964

Lives and works in Baltimore

Selected Solo Exhibitions

1999 *Rushes*, Bucknell Art Gallery, Bucknell University, Lewisburg, PA

1998 *Spot*, Mattress Factory, Pittsburgh

1997 *operation*, Lawndale Art and Performance Center, Houston

1996 *Auto-erotic*, Relay Sone Gallery, Kansas City Art Institute, Kansas City, MO

1995 *You and Me*, ARC Gallery/Raw Space, Chicago

Selected Group Exhibitions

1998 *Scope I*, Artists Space, New York

1997 *Lynn Cazabon, Gavin O' Grady*, Anderson Ranch Arts Center, Snowmass, CO

1996 *The Body*, Pyramid Arts Center, Rochester, NY

1995 *Open Forms*, Hudson Valley Institute for Art, Peekskill, NY

1993 *New Work: Martha Bush and Lynn Cazabon*, Diverse Works, Houston

Selected Bibliography

Brennan, Lissa. "Parts Is Parts." *In Pittsburgh*, 14 October 1998.

Cazabon, Lynn. "Photography." In *A Dictionary for Cultural and Critical Theory*. London: Blackwell Publishers, 1995.

Cazabon, Lynn. "The Representation of Feminine Sexuality in the Works of Paul Outerbridge, Jr." *History of Photography* (spring 1994).

Horodner, Stuart. "Plaid 6 (red paranoia)." *Surface* (summer, 1998).

Krainak, Paul. "Pittsburgh." *Art Papers* (July/August 1999).

*Rushes: Lynn Cazabon*. Lewisburg, PA: Bucknell Art Gallery, 1999.

Thomas, Mary. "Bodies of Work." *Pittsburgh Post-Gazette*, 7 November 1998.

**Stephen Davis**

American, born 1945

Lives and works in New York

Selected Solo Exhibitions

1990 *Plato's Inn—Zeus Suite*, Mattress Factory, Pittsburgh
*Jacob and His Twelve Sons*, Addison Gallery of American Art, Andover, MA

1986 *Stephen Davis: Paintings*, Washington Project for the Arts, Washington, D.C.

1985 Malinda Wyatt Gallery, New York

1983 The Banff Centre, Banff, Canada

Selected Group Exhibitions

1985 *Jake Berthot, Stephen Davis, Stephen Greene*, Malinda Wyatt Gallery, New York

1983 *Terminal Show*, Brooklyn, NY

Selected Bibliography

Decter, Joshua. *Stephen Davis: Jacob and His Twelve Sons*. Andover, MA: Addison Gallery of American Art, 1990.

Miller, Donald. "Factory Exhibits Explore Words, War." *Pittsburgh Post-Gazette*, 15 November 1990.

**Gu Dexin**

Chinese, born 1962

Lives and works in Beijing

Selected Exhibitions

1999 *10-30-1999*, Mattress Factory, Pittsburgh

1998 *16 June, 1997–13 June, 1998*, Taipei Biennial, Taiwan
*Tactile Art*, 1988, (a collaborative work produced by the New Analysis Group: Wang Luyan, Chen Shaoping, Gu Dexin, active 1988–1995), in *Inside Out: New Chinese Art*, Asia Society Galleries, New York; P.S. 1 Contemporary Art Center, Long Island City, NY; San Francisco Museum of Modern Art, San Francisco

Selected Bibliography

Fumio, Nanjo and Miki Akiko. *Site of Desire: 1998 Taipei Biennial*. Taiwan: Taipei Fine Art Museum, 1998.

Giannini, Claudia and Michael Olijnyk. "Conversation." *Art Journal* (fall 2000).

Madden, Dave. "Gee, Zero-G." *In Pittsburgh*, 27 October 1999.

Minglu, Gao, ed. *Inside Out: New Chinese Art*. Berkeley: University of California Press, 1998.

Thomas, Mary. "Exhibition of Asian artists exemplifies the paradox of spectacular restraint." *Pittsburgh Post-Gazette*, 15 April 2000.

**Milena Dopitová**
Czech, born 1963
Lives and works in Prague

Selected Solo Exhibitions

1996 *Urban Legends—Prague*, Staatliche Kunsthalle, Baden-Baden, Germany
1995 *Follow Me*, Mattress Factory, Pittsburgh
1994 *Milena Dopitová in Context*, The Institute for Contemporary Art, Boston
1993 *Second Exit*, Ludwig Forum, Aachen, Germany
*Aperto*, Venice Biennale, Venice
1992 Ninth Sydney Biennale, Sydney
Galerie MXM, Prague

Selected Group Exhibitions

1994 *You must remember this*, Ronald Feldman Gallery, New York
1993 *Post Security*, Gallery 5020, Salzburg
1992 Sirup, Munich
Musée d'Art Moderne de la Ville de Paris, Paris
1991 Galerie 68, Cologne
1990 Stalin's Monument, Prague
International Grand Concourse of Painting, Musée 2000, Luxembourg

Selected Bibliography

Gerzova, Jana. "Mattress Factory." *Profil* (January/February 1996).
Krainak, Paul. "Siting Slavs at the Factory." *New Art Examiner* (March 1996).
Markham, Pamela. "Mattress Factory: Artists from Eastern and Central Europe." *Arti* (May/June 1996).
*Milena Dopitová: Urbane Legenden Program*. Baden-Baden: Staatliche Kunsthalle, 1996.
Miller, Donald. "East Europeans in Show of Strength." *Pittsburgh Post-Gazette*, 28 October 1995.
Shearing, Graham. "Best Show of Year Worth Czeching Out." *Pittsburgh Tribune-Review*, 26 November 1995.
Stacho, L'ubo. "Mattress Factory Muzeum Ako Zivotny Styl." *Linia* (September 1998).
Stein, Judith. "Import/Export: Out of the East." *Art in America* (April 1998).
Winn, Alice. "Installations at the Mattress Factory." *Artwords* 1, no. 2.

**Tracey Emin**
British, born 1963
Lives and works in London

Selected Solo Exhibitions

1998–99 *Every Part of Me's Bleeding*, Lehmann Maupin Gallery, New York
1997 *I Need Art Like I Need God*, South London Gallery, London
1996 *Solo Exhibition*, Habitat, London
1994 *Performance: Exploration of the Soul—A Journey Across America*, Mattress Factory, Pittsburgh
*Gramercy International Art Fair*, Jay Jopling/White Cube, New York
1993 *My Major Retrospective*, Jay Jopling/White Cube, New York
1990 *The Calling of St. Anthony*, London

Selected Group Exhibitions

1998 *The Colony Room 50th Anniversary Art Exhibition*, A22 Projects, London
*Live and Let Die*, Apex Art C.P., New York
1997 *Absolute Secret*, Royal College of Art, London
*Summer Love*, Fotouhi Cramer Gallery, New York
1996 *Sad*, Gasworks, London
*Co-operators*, Southampton City Art Gallery, Southampton, England
1995 *Whistling Women*, Chelsea Room, Royal Festival Hall, London
1994 *Brilliant: New Art from London*, Contemporary Arts Museum, Houston
*Karaoke and Football*, Portikus, Frankfurt
*Other Men's Flowers*, London Portfolio, London
1993 *The Shop* (with Sarah Lucas), London
1992 *A Woman's Perspective*, Bookworks, London

Selected Bibliography

Archer, Michael. *Text zur Kunst: a monograph on Tracey Emin*. Germany, 1994.
Collings, Matthew, et al. *Blimey!: From Bohemia to Britpop: The London Artworld from Francis Bacon to Damien Hirst*. London: 21 Publications, 1998.
Daly, Pauline and Brendon Quick. "Crazy Tracey/Sensible Lucas." *Purple Prose* (June 1993).
Emin, Tracey. "On Holiday with my Dad." *Frieze* (January 1994).
Norman, Geraldine. "In Bed with My Art." *The Independent* (London), 15 May 1994.
*Other Men's Flowers*. London: Paragon Press, 1994.

**Daniel Fischer**
Slovakian, born 1950
Lives and works in Bratislava

Selected Solo Exhibitions

1996 *Synagogue, The Art of Aura*, Center for Contemporary Art, Trnava, Slovakia
1995 *Memento*, Mattress Factory, Pittsburgh
1993 Maison de la Culture, Namur, Belgium
1991 Abbaye des Cordiliers, Chateauroux, France
Galerie Mitte, Vienna
1990 Galerie J. Streita, Sovenic, Slovakia

Selected Group Exhibitions

1996 *The Epikuros Garden*, Slovak National Gallery, Bratislava, Slovakia
1993 *Venice Biennale*, Slovak Republic Pavilion, Venice
1992 *Hills and Mills*, Arti et Amicitiae, Amsterdam
*Group A–R. Slovakian Avant-Garde from Bratislava*, Museum Ulm, Ulm, Germany
1991 *Slowakian Art*, Krems, Austria
1990 *Art against Totalitarianism*, Hrad, Bratislava, Slovakia
*Defense*, Musée du Luxemborg, Paris

Selected Bibliography

Gerzova, Jana. *Daniel Fischer: Venice Bienale XLV*. Správa kultúrnych zariadení, Bratislava: 1993.
———. "Mattress Factory." *Profil* (January/February 1996).
Krainak, Paul. "Siting Slavs at the Factory." *New Art Examiner* (March 1996).
Markham, Pamela. "Artists from Eastern and Central Europe." *Arti* (May/June 1996).

Miller, Donald. "East Europeans in Show of Strength." *Pittsburgh Post-Gazette*, 28 October 1995.
——. "Picture of the World: *Carnegie International* was Better than Reviews." *Pittsburgh Post-Gazette Weekend*, 29 December 1995.
Potter, Chris. "Site." *In Pittsburgh*, 25 January 1996.
Stein, Judith. "Import/Export: Out of the East." *Art in America* (April 1998).

**Cathy Lynn Gasser**
American, born 1960
Lives and works in Kansas

### Selected Exhibitions

1998 *Untitled*, Rockford Art Museum, Rockford, IL
1996 *hush*, N.A.M.E. Gallery, Chicago
1995 *Glow*, Salina Art Center, Salina, KS
*Idle Accord*, University of Kansas Gallery, Lawrence, KS
*A-I-R Exhibition*, The Children's Museum, Seattle
1994 *Infra Site*, collaborative installation, Greene Street, New York
1993 *A Collaboration*, Mattress Factory, Pittsburgh
On the Edge, University of Florida Gallery, Tallahassee
1991 *Margin of Safety*, collaborative installation, The Museum of Contemporary Art, Chicago
*Gigantic Women/Miniature Work*, S.A.I.C. Gallery 2, Chicago

### Selected Bibliography

Collins, Sue. "Margin of Safety: A Collaborative Installation." *New Art Examiner* (February/March 1992).
England, Dan. "Glow." *Salina (Kansas) Journal*. 5 May 1995.
Hixon, Kathryn. "Reviews: Chicago." *Arts Magazine* (April 1992).
Marger, Mary Anne. "Women's Tenacity." *St. Petersburg Times*, 5 February 1993.
Miller, Donald. "Sharing the View." *Pittsburgh Post-Gazette*, 17 December 1993.
Williams, Monte. "Who Are Those Women Embedded in the Sidewalk?" *New York Times*, 20 August 1995.

**Gimhongsok (Hongsuk Kim)**
Korean, born 1964
Lives and works in Seoul

### Selected Solo Exhibitions and Performances

1999 *The Magic Sword of MMCCDXCVII*, Mattress Factory, Pittsburgh
1998 *I'm gonna be number one*, Keum San Gallery, Seoul
*Egg-Hokey-Pokey*, performance at the Seoul Metropolitan Museum, Seoul
*Vertical Sleep, Narcotic Piggy*, performance at the Ritz Carlton, Seoul

### Selected Group Exhibitions

1999 *Phobia*, Ilmin Museum of Art, Seoul
1998 *Food, Clothing and Shelter*, Seoul Municipal Fine Arts Museum
Ssamzie Art Project, Seoul
1997 *Ein Gesprach im Beriech des Ein und Ausgangs*, Dong-Ah Gallery, Seoul
1996 *Rinke Klasse 96*, Kunstakademie, Dresden
*Small Sculpture Triennial*, Walker Hill Art Center, Seoul
1995 *Marathon*, Kunstakademie, Dusseldorf

### Selected Bibliography

Giannini, Claudia and Michael Olijnyk. "Conversation." *Art Journal*, (fall 2000).
Gimhongsok. *I'm gonna be number one*. Seoul: Gimhongsok, 1999.
Madden, Dave. "Gee, Zero-G." *In Pittsburgh*, 27 October 1999.
Shearing, Graham. "Far East on the North Side." *Ticket*, 29 October 1999.

**Paul Glabicki**
American, born 1951
Lives and works in Pittsburgh

### Selected Solo Exhibitions and Film Screenings

1997 *Artist's Films from the 1960s and 1970s: Films of Paul Glabicki*, Carnegie Museum of Art Film Gallery, Pittsburgh
1993 Film and Computer Animation, Kino im Augarten, Graz, Austria
1992 *Paul Glabicki Video and Art Installation*, ITOKI Gallery, Hiroshima, Japan
1990 *This Is/Just That*, Mattress Factory, Pittsburgh

### Selected Group Exhibitions and Film Screenings

1998 *Cine Calculado: Revision de Los Origenes y Pioneros de La Animacion por Ordenador*, Fundacio Antoni Tapies, Barcelona
*Experimental Animation*, Kyoto College of Art, Kyoto, Japan
1993 *Cinematograph-Filmverleih*, Innsbruck, Austria
1990 The New School for Social Research, New York
Bombay International Film Festival, Bombay, India

### Selected Bibliography:

Grissemann, Stefan. "Das Possenspiel der Geometrie." *Die Presse* (Vienna), 17 June 1993.
Homisak, Bill. "Installations Take Flight at 1414 Monterey." *Pittsburgh Tribune-Review*, 10 August 1990.
Lowry, Patricia. "Filmmaker's Work an Intriguing Journey." *Pittsburgh Press*, 10 May 1990.
Mattress Factory. "Paul Glabicki, The Diagram Trilogy and Early Works." In *Mattress Factory: Installation and Performance 1982–1989*. Pittsburgh: Mattress Factory, 1990.
Miller, Donald. "Abstract Computer Difficult to Critique." *Pittsburgh Post-Gazette*, 4 January 1992.
——. "Building Plans, New Exhibits at Factory." *Pittsburgh Post-Gazette*, 22 June 1990.
——. "Drawing Inspiration From His Computer." Pittsburgh Post-Gazette, 13 December 1991.

Odom, Michael. "Group Show." *In Pittsburgh*, 1 August 1990.
Nulf, Karen. "The Animated Films of Paul Glabicki." In *Idea*. Tokyo: Seibundo Shinkosha, 1990.
Thomas, Mary. "Mattress Factory Exhibition Focuses on Process of Art Works." *Pittsburgh Post-Gazette*, 3 January 1998.

**Melissa Goldstein**
American, born 1961
Lives and works in New York

### Selected Exhibitions

1994 *Infra Site*, collaborative installation, Greene Street, New York
1993 *A Collaboration*, Mattress Factory, Pittsburgh
*Women, Fire, and Iron*, Wilensky Arts, Minneapolis, MN
1992 *A Constellation of Cups*, Kirkland Arts Center, Kirkland, WA
*Inheritance*, Los Angeles Center on Exhibitions (L.A.C.E.), Los Angeles
1991 *Margin of Safety*, collaborative installation, The Museum of Contemporary Art, Chicago
*Gigantic Women/Miniature Work*, S.A.I.C. Gallery 2, Chicago

### Selected Bibliography

Collins, Sue. "Margin of Safety: A Collaborative Installation." *New Art Examiner* (February/March 1992).
Hixon, Kathryn. "Reviews: Chicago." *Arts Magazine* (April 1992).
Marger, Mary Anne. "Women's Tenacity." *St. Petersburg Times*, 5 February 1993.
Miller, Donald. "Sharing the View." *Pittsburgh Post-Gazette*, 17 December 1993.
Williams, Monte. "Who Are Those Women Embedded in the Sidewalk?" *New York Times*, 20 August 1995.

**Ann Hamilton**
American, born 1956
Lives and works in Columbus, Ohio

### Selected Solo Exhibitions

1999 *Venice Biennale*, United States Pavilion, Venice
1996 Wexner Center for the Arts, Ohio State University, Columbus, OH
1995 *lumen*, Institute for Contemporary Art, Philadelphia
1994 *Projects 48: seam*, The Museum of Modern Art, New York
1993 *a round*, The Power Plant, Toronto
1991 *offering*, Mattress Factory, Pittsburgh (in collaboration with the *Carnegie International*)
*Works*, Hirshhorn Museum and Sculpture Garden, Washington, D.C.
*parallel lines*, 21st International Sao Paulo Bienal, Sao Paulo, Brazil
1990 *between taxonomy and communion*, San Diego Museum of Contemporary Art, La Jolla, CA

### Selected Group Exhibitions:

1999 *Avoiding Objects*, Apex Art Curatorial Program, New York
*The Carnegie International 99:00*, Pittsburgh
1997 *Artists Projects*, P.S. 1 Contemporary Art Center, Long Island City, NY
1995 *About Place: Recent Art of the Americas*, The Art Institute of Chicago, Chicago
1993 *readymade identities*, The Museum of Modern Art, New York
1992 *Dirt and Domesticity: Constructions of the Feminine*, Whitney Museum of American Art, New York
1991 *indigo blue*, The Spoleto Festival, Charleston, SC

### Selected Bibliography

Bohn, Donald Chant. "A Kinder, Gentler Museum?" *New Art Examiner* (February/March 1992).
Cooke, Lynne, Bruce Ferguson, Dave Hickey, and Marina Warner. *Ann Hamilton: mneme*. Liverpool, England: Tate Gallery Liverpool, 1994.
———. *Ann Hamilton, tropos*. New York: Dia Center for Arts, 1995.
Craig, John G., Jr. "Art Works Hard, Too." *Pittsburgh Post-Gazette*, 21 December 1991.
Donovan, Sandra Fischione. "Breaking all the Rules." *New York Times Sunday Magazine*, 24 May 1992.
Faust, Gretchen. "Ann Hamilton, Louver." *Flash Art* (March/April, 1992).
Hirsch, Faye. "Ann Hamilton." *Sculpture* (July/August 1993).
———. "Art at the Limit: Ann Hamilton's Recent Installations." *Sculpture* (July/August 1993).
Kimmelman, Michael. "At Carnegie 1991, Sincerity Edges Out Irony." *New York Times*, 27 October 1991.
King, Elaine A., "*Carnegie International* 1991, Mattress Factory, Pittsburgh." *Sculpture* (May/June, 1995).
Lowry, Patricia. "House Offerings." *Pittsburgh Press*, 29 October 1991.
Madoff, Steven Henry. "Codes and Whispers." *Time*, 12 July 1999.
Miller, Donald. "51st International True to Curator's Conception." *Pittsburgh Post-Gazette*, 19 October 1991.
Plagens, Peter. "A Visionary Hits Venice." *Newsweek*, 12 July 1999.
Rogers, Sarah. *The Body and the Object, Ann Hamilton 1984–1996*. Columbus, OH: Wexner Center for the Arts, 1996.
Schwalb, Harry. "Sleeper: No Overnight Sensation, the Mattress Factory is a Hit of a Museum." *Pittsburgh* (March 1992).
Simon, Joan. "Ann Hamilton: Inscribing Place." *Art in America* (June 1999).
Thomas, Mary. "Mattress Factory Exhibition Focuses on Process of Art Works." *Pittsburgh Post-Gazette*, 3 January 1998.
Yood, James. "Taking Stock, the 51st Carnegie International." *New Art Examiner* (January 1992).

**Quesqueya Henriquez**
Cuban, born 1966
Lives and works in Santo Domingo

Selected Solo Exhibitions
1996 *Locus*, Mattress Factory, Pittsburgh
*Consuelo Castaneda-Quisqueya Henriquez Collaboration*, Morris-Healy Gallery, New York
1995 *Real—More Real*, Museum of Contemporary Art, Miami
1994 Intar Gallery, New York
1992 Ninart Centro de Cultura, Mexico City

Selected Group Exhibitions
1996 *Sculpture*, Cohen-Berkowitz Gallery, Kansas City, MO
1995 *Human Nature*, The New Museum of Contemporary Art, New York
1994 *Vanguardia Errante: La Generacion de los 80s*, Centro de arte Euroamericano, Caracas, Venezuela
1993 *Arte Cubana*, Museo Cubano de Arte y Cultura, Miami
1990 *Arte Contemporaneo Cubano, Cinco Pintoras*, Galeria Arte y Promocion, Mexico City

Selected Bibliography
Brennan, Lissa. "Parts is Parts." *In Pittsburgh*, 14 October 1998.
Clearwater, Bonnie. *Defining the Nineties: Consensus-making in New York*. Los Angeles: Museum of Contemporary Art, 1996.
——. *Real—More Real: Teresita Fernandez, Quisqueya Henriquez*. Miami: The Joan Lehman Museum of Contemporary Art, 1995.
Knight, Christopher. "Independent Spirit Lives on in 'Majas'." *Los Angeles Times*, 16 July 1994.
Kohen, Helen. "A Woman's View." *Miami Herald*, 28 November 1993.
Krainak, Paul. "Pittsburgh." *Art Papers* (July/August 1999).
Thomas, Mary. "Bodies of Work." *Pittsburgh Post-Gazette*, 7 November 1998.

**Jene Highstein**
American, born 1942
Lives and works in New York

Selected Exhibitions and Performances
1999 *Primarily Structural*, P.S. 1 Contemporary Art Center, Long Island City, NY
1998 *Stairway to Heaven: Jene Highstein Sculpture and Drawing*, Anders Tornberg Gallery, Lund, Sweden
1997 *New Theatrical Trends* performance of *Flatland* at Belgrade International Theatre Festival, Belgrade
1996 *Art Space Seoul/Hakkojae*, Seoul
1991 The Philips Collection, Washington, D.C.
1986 *American Abstract Artists 1936–1986*, Bronx Museum of the Arts, New York
Untitled, Mattress Factory, Pittsburgh
1985 *Buttresses*, Mattress Factory, Pittsburgh

Selected Bibliography
Castle, Ted. "Jene Highstein at the Mattress Factory." *Art in America* (September 1985).
Donovan, Sandra Fischione. "Off-the-wall Art Exhibits Titillate the Senses, Stimulate the Mind." *New York Times Sunday Magazine*, 24 May 1992.
Heartney, Eleanor. "Jene Highstein, Wave Hill." *ARTnews* (January 1990).
Klausner, Betty. *Jene Highstein: Gallery Landscape*. Santa Barbara, CA: Santa Barbara Contemporary Arts Forum, 1991.
Kuspit, Donald. "Jene Highstein at Stark Gallery." *Artforum International* (April 1998).
Margolies, Jane. "Inside Pittsburgh." *House Beautiful* (January 1993).
Southeastern Center for Contemporary Art. *Jene Highstein*. Winston-Salem, NC: Southeastern Center for Contemporary Art, 1996.
Zimmer, William. "Matters of Scale and Nostalgia, Too." *New York Times*, 8 March 1998.

**Goro Hirata**
Japanese, born 1965
Lives and works in Tokyo

Selected Solo Exhibitions
1999 *Mind Space*, Mattress Factory, Pittsburgh
1996 *Appearance of the Garden #13*, Index Gallery, Osaka
1995 *Striped House*, Museum of Art, Tokyo
*Mind Space*, Gallery Nikko, Tokyo
1992 Gallery Art Soko, Tokyo

Selected Group Exhibitions
1993 *Snow House*, Onnetou Lake, Hokkaido
*Mangrove Ship—Green Ship Project*, Okinawa
1992 *Mind Space*, Kamagaya, China
1991 *Bolted Gate*, Akita
*Secret Passage*, Yudo Lake, Hokkaido
1990 *Mind Space*, Tokyo National University of Arts and Music, Tokyo

Selected Bibliography
Giannini, Claudia and Michael Olijnyk. "Conversation." *Art Journal*, (fall 2000).
Kee, Joan. "Transiency and Time: A Mattress Factory Residency." *ART AsiaPacific* 28 (2000).
Kurabayashi, Yasushi. *Mind Space—To See the Sky*. Translated by Yoko Takei. Tokyo: Gallery Alpha M, 1998.
Madden, Dave. "Gee, Zero-G." *In Pittsburgh*, 27 October 1999.
Shearing, Graham. "Far East on the North Side." *Ticket*, 29 October 1999.
Shimizu, Toshio. *Sur Everyday Life*. Shanghai: Shanghai Art Museum, 1998.

**Damien Hirst**
British, born 1965
Lives and works in London and Berlin

Selected Solo Exhibitions
2000 Gagosian Gallery, New York
1995 *No Sense of Absolute Corruption*, Gagosian Gallery, New York

1994 *Bad Environment for White Monochrome Paintings*, Mattress Factory, Pittsburgh
*Making Beautiful Drawings*, Bruno Brunnet, Berlin
1992 *Unfair*, Jay Jopling, Cologne
1991 *In and Out of Love*, Woodstock Street, London

Selected Group Exhibitions
1999 *Sensation: Young British Artists from the Saatchi Collection*, Brooklyn Museum of Art, Brooklyn, NY
1996 *The Experimenters*, Lombard-Freid Fine Arts, New York
*a/drift: Scenes from the Penetrable Culture*, The Center for Curatorial Studies Museum, Bard College, Annondale-on-Hudson, New York
1993 *The Nightshade Family*, Museum Fridericianum, Kassel
*Aperto*, Venice Biennale, Venice
1992 *Young British Artists*, Saatchi Collection, London
*Strange Developments*, Anthony d'Offay Gallery, London
*Turner Prize Exhibition*, Tate Gallery of British Art, London
1991 *Broken English*, Serpentine Gallery, London

Selected Bibliography
"Between Mona Lisa and the Coca Cola Can, an interview with Damien Hirst." *Flash Art* (October 1994).
Burn, Gordon. "Damien Hirst." *Parkett* (June 1994).
Burton, Jane. "Shark Tactics." *ARTnews* (November 1998).
Carrier, David. "Pittsburgh." *Sculpture* (July/August 1995).
Collings, Matthew, et. al. *Blimey!: From Bohemia to Britpop: The London Artworld from Francis Bacon to Damien Hirst*. London: 21 Publications, 1998.
Dannatt, Adrian. "Artist Interview, New York: Damien Hirst." *Art Newspaper* (October 2000).
Frankel, David. "Interview with Damien Hirst." *Bookforum* (winter 1997).
Hirst, Damien. *I Want to Spend the Rest of My Life Everywhere, with Everyone, One to One, Always, Forever, Now*. New York and London: The Monacelli Press, 1997.
Kastner, Jeffrey. "Damien Hirst: Gagosian Gallery, New York." *Art Monthly* (December 2000/January 2001).
Miller, Donald. "Moving Art: the Spirit and the Fly." *Pittsburgh Post-Gazette*, 16 April 1994.
Restany, Pierre. "Back into the Pop Era: Pierre Restany Interviews Damien Hirst." *Domus* (July/August 1998).
Rubinkowski, Leslie. "Flying in the Face of the Art Establishment." *Pittsburgh Post-Gazette*, 1 May 1994.
Shearing, Graham. "Damien Hirst's Masterpiece: Maggots and More." *Pittsburgh Tribune-Review*, 10 April 1994.
——. "In Retrospect." *Pittsburgh Tribune-Review*, 19 December 1997.
Thomas, Mary. "Mattress Factory Exhibition Focuses on Process of Art Works." *Pittsburgh Post-Gazette*, 3 January 1998.

**Jaroslav Hulbój**
Polish, born 1969
Lives and works in Poland

Selected Exhibitions and Performances
1995 *Reconstruction for Lazarus's Situation*, Mattress Factory, Pittsburgh
1994 *Stone/Body*, Skoki, Poland
*Gast-Staette*, Frankfurt
1993 *Ideas without Ideology*, Center for Contemporary Art, Warsaw
1992 *5362 m³*, Place of Art, Mosina, Poland
*Places no Places*, Center of Polish Sculpture, Orrorisko, Poland
*Istropolitana*, Bratislava, Slovakia

Selected Bibliography
Gerzova, Jana. "Mattress Factory." *Profil* (January/February 1996).
Krainak, Paul. "Siting Slavs at the Factory." *New Art Examiner* (March 1996).
Markham, Pamela. "Mattress Factory: Artists from Eastern and Central Europe." *Arti* (May/June 1996).
Miller, Donald. "East Europeans in Show of Strength." *Pittsburgh Post-Gazette*, 28 October 1995.
——. "Picture of the World: Carnegie International was Better than Reviews." *Pittsburgh Post-Gazette Weekend*, 29 December 1995.
Shearing, Graham. "Best Show of Year Worth Czeching Out." *Pittsburgh Tribune-Review*, 26 November 1995.
Stein, Judith E. "Import/Export: Out of the East." *Art in America* (April 1998).
Winn, Alice. "Installations at the Mattress Factory." *Artwords* 1, no. 2.

**David Ireland**
American, born 1930
Lives and works in San Francisco

Selected Solo Exhibitions
1999–2000 *Reflections*, Jack Shainman Gallery, New York
1995–96 *Untitled*, Jay Gorney Modern Art, New York
1993 Untitled Installation, Mattress Factory, Pittsburgh
1992 *David Ireland: ego/id*, Ruth Bloom Gallery, Los Angeles
1991 *You Can't Make Art By Making Art*, Helmhaus, Zurich
1990 *David Ireland: Works*, Hirshhorn Museum and Sculpture Garden, Washington, D.C.

Selected Group Exhibitions
1992 *Ann Hamilton/David Ireland*, Walker Art Center, Minneapolis, MN, and Portland, OR
1988 Collaboration with architect Mark Mack, Headland Center for the Arts, Ft. Barry, Marin, CA
1985 *David Ireland and Robert Wilhite: The Jade Garden/Artists' Apartment*, The Washington Project for the Arts, Washington, D.C.

Selected Bibliography
Miller, Donald. "Meeting Venus." *Pittsburgh Post-Gazette*, 15 March 1993.
Raczka, Robert. "David Ireland." *New Art Examiner* (September 1993).
Stacho, L'ubo. "Mattress Factory Muzeum Ako Zivotny Styl." *Linia* (September 1998).

**Tomoaki Ishihara**
Japanese, born 1958
Lives and works in Osaka

Selected Solo Exhibitions
1998 *Tomoaki Ishihara: A Constellation of Work from 1983 to 1998*, Tochigi Prefectural Museum of Fine Arts, Tochigi, Japan
1996 Kirin Plaza Osaka, Osaka
1995 Gallery Kuranuki, Osaka
1994 Gallery Kuranuki, Osaka
1993 Gallery Ootemon, Fukuoka
1992 Hosomi Gallery, Tokyo
1991 *Untitled Installations*, Mattress Factory, Pittsburgh
Shinanobashi Gallery, Osaka
1990 Gallery View, Osaka

Selected Group Exhibitions
1997 *Surface Exposed: Photography in Art of the 90s*, Museum of Contemporary Art, Tokyo
1995 *(Un)Framing*, Hara Museum of Contemporary Art, Tokyo
1993 *The Return of the Cadavre Exquis*, The Drawing Center, New York
1992 *Centrifugal Sculpture*, The National Museum of Art, Osaka
1991 *Animated Imagination*, Tokyo Metropolitan Museum of Photography, Tokyo
*Compound of the Maniera*, Machida City Museum of Graphic Arts, Tokyo
1990 *Tomoaki Ishihara, Hotaro Koyama, Yasumasa Morimura*, So Gallery, Tokyo
1988 *Venice Biennale*, Venice

Selected Bibliography
Cooke, Lynne. "Contemporary Japanese Art." *Burlington Magazine* (June 1991).
King, Elaine. "Kuniyasu, Matsumura, Ishihara." *Arts Magazine* (November 1991).
Miller, Donald. "Japanese Artists Turn Factory into a Gentle Place." *Pittsburgh Post-Gazette*, 22 March 1991.
Odom, Michael. "Three Japanese Artists." *In Pittsburgh*, 3 April 1991.
*Tomoaki Ishihara: A Constellation of Work from 1983 to 1998*. Tochigi, Japan: Tochigi Prefectural Museum of Fine Arts, 1998.

**ium (Yoomi Rhee)**
Korean, born 1971
Lives and works in Seoul

Selected Solo Exhibitions
1999 *Tales from the Warehouse*, Mattress Factory, Pittsburgh
1997 *The 2nd Imagination 'Highway,'* Gallery Jo, Seoul
1996 *The 1st collection 'Living Sculpture,'* Gallery Siuter, Seoul
1995 *The First Imagination 'Red Blouse'* Gallery Boda, Seoul

Selected Group Exhibitions and Performances
1998 *Body Drawing*, Mun-Yae Theater, Seoul
*Paranoia and Schizophrenia*, Art Center, Seoul
1997 Performance with Electric Violinist Yujin Park, MBC Broadcasting System Studio, Seoul
*Joyful Brooch*, Craft House, Seoul
1996 *City and Vision*, Seoul Art Museum, Seoul
*Lipsinc and Adrip*, Gallery Sadi, Seoul

Selected Bibliography
Giannini, Claudia and Michael Olijnyk. "Conversation." *Art Journal* (fall 2000).
ium. *ium: 1995–1998*. Seoul: IL Publishing Company, 1998.
Raczka, Robert. "Installations by Asian Artists in Residence." *Sculpture* (March 2000).
Shearing, Graham. "Carnegie International to Dominate Season." *Pittsburgh Tribune-Review*, 12 September 1999.
——. "Far East on the North Side." *Ticket*, 29 October 1999.
——. "A Little Bit of Asia." *Pittsburgh Tribune-Review*, 12 December 1999.
Thomas, Mary. "Installing Pittsburgh." *Pittsburgh Post-Gazette*, 29 October 1999.
——. "Still Life in Motion." *Pittsburgh Post-Gazette*, 14 September 1999.
Zhuang, Huang, ed. *New Asian Art Show 1995*. Tokyo: Committee of International Contemporary Art, 1995.

**Delanie Jenkins**
American, born 1964
Lives and works in Pittsburgh

Selected Solo Exhibitions
2001 Paul Mesaros Gallery, West Virginia University, Morgantown, WV
1999 *Between Fear and Fascination*, Beck Art Gallery, Alma College, Alma, MI
1998 *Root Bound*, Mattress Factory, Pittsburgh
1996 *Veil*, Automatic Art Gallery, Chicago
1995 *Greene Street Windows*, SOHO 20, New York
*trace elements*, A.R.C. Gallery-Raw Space, Chicago; Museum of Contemporary Art, Boulder, CO
1994 *Mapping Memory: Recollections of the Self*, Artemisia Gallery, Chicago
1993 *Conversations Over Tea: Negotiating Language*, Edge Gallery, Denver

Selected Group Exhibitions
2000 *Pittsburgh Biennial*, Pittsburgh Center for the Arts, Pittsburgh
1998 *Sofa Not Included 2*, gallery: untitled, Dallas
1997 *Interiors*, Pittsburgh Center for the Arts, Pittsburgh
1996 *Missing Me*, University of Iowa, Iowa City
1994 *Look Ma, No Hands*, Edge Gallery, Denver
1993 *Women and Madness*, Congress Street Gallery, Tucson
1992 *Self Portrait: A Feminist Manifesto*, Art Community Revival, Dallas

#### Selected Bibliography

Brennan, Lissa. "Parts is Parts." *In Pittsburgh*, 14 October 1998.

Kotani, Akiko and Bernard Freydberg. "The Road Less Traveled." *Sculpture* (September/October 2000).

Krainak, Paul. *Art Papers* (July/August 1999).

May, Mike. "Visual Arts: Delanie Jenkins, Navel Gazing." *Pittsburgh Magazine* (September 1999).

Pierce, Debra and Tina McNearney. *Women and Madness*. Tucson: Congress Street Gallery, 1993.

Stamets, Bill. "Mapping Memory." *New Art Examiner* (October 1994).

Thomas, Mary. "Bodies of Work." *Pittsburgh Post-Gazette*, 7 November 1998.


### Kim Jones

American, born 1944
Lives and works in New York

#### Selected Installations and Performances

1999 *A Cripple in the Right Way May Beat A Racer in the Wrong One*, John Weber Gallery, New York
*Monumental Drawings*, Exit Art/The First World, New York

1998 *Current Undercurrent: Working in Brooklyn*, Brooklyn Museum of Art, Brooklyn, NY

1995 *Temporarily Possessed*, The New Museum, New York

1994 *Mapping*, The Museum of Modern Art, New York

1991 *Spero*, Franklin Furnace, New York

1990 Untitled Installation/*Mudman Performance*, Mattress Factory, Pittsburgh
*Out of Site*, P.S. 1 Contemporary Art Center, Long Island City, NY


#### Selected Bibliography

Adams, Brook. "Kim Jones at Lorence Monk." *Art in America* (June 1990).

Glueck, Grace. "You Won't Be Happy Till I'm in a Box." *New York Times*, 2 January 1998.

Levin, Kim. "Kim Jones." *Village Voice*, 13 March 1991.

McEvilley, Thomas. "Art and Otherness: Crisis in Cultural Identity." In *Documentext*. New York: McPherson and Company, 1992.

Miller, Donald. "Factory Exhibits Explore Words, War." *Pittsburgh Post-Gazette*, 17 November 1990.

Princenthal, Nancy. "Kim Jones at John Webber." *Art in America* (October 1999).

Raynor, Vivien. "From Twigs, Leaves and Mud: A Show of Landscape." *New York Times*, 14 July 1991.


### Rolf Julius

German, born 1939
Lives and works in Berlin

#### Selected Exhibitions and Installations

2001 *Visual/Sound*, Mattress Factory, Pittsburgh

1999 *the xx. century—one century of art in Germany*, National Gallery, Berlin

1998 *Music for An Almost Empty Room*, National Gallery in Hamburg Train Station, Hamburg
*Black Listens to Red* (Piano Concerto), Mattress Factory, Pittsburgh

1996 *Red*, *Iron Flowers* and *Music for a Garden*, Mattress Factory, Pittsburgh

1995 Kunst Halle Krems, Austria

1993 *Rolf Julius*, 360 Gallery, Tokyo

1991 *Ash*, Mattress Factory, Pittsburgh
*John Cage and the Modern*, Neue Pinakothek, Munich


#### Selected Bibliography

Bischoff, Ulrich, ed. *Kunst als Grenzueberschreitung—John Cage und die Moderne*. Munich: Neue Pinakothek, 1991.

Krueper, Jochen and Hans Deecke. *Rolf Julius: 6 Raeume (Zellen)*. Essen: Ausstellungsgesellschaft fuer zeitgenoessische Kunst, 1994.

Kunstverein Bremerhaven. *Rolf Julius: small music*. Bremerhaven: Kunstverein Bremerhaven, 1991.

Shearing, Graham. "Mattress Factory Garden Sprouts Art Form." *Pittsburgh Tribune-Review*, 30 August 1996.

Stadtgalerie Saarbruecken/Heidelberger Kunstverein. *Rolf Julius: eine deutsch-englische Monographie*. Saarbruecken, Germany: Stadtgalerie Saarbruecken, 1996.

Thomas, Mary. "At 2 Sites, 4 Artists Play with Senses and Space." *Pittsburgh Post-Gazette*, 12 June 1999.


### Bob Karstadt

American
Lives and works in Pittsburgh

#### Selected Installations/Performances

1998 *Every Time a Bell Rings or The Seraphim Picture Show . . .*, Mattress Factory, Pittsburgh

1996 *Illumination*, Centre Gallery, Pittsburgh
*The Humming Bird Symphony*, CB's 313 Performance Space, New York
*The Archangel Inn*, Raising Aliquippa Art Event, Aliquippa, PA

1994 *Raphael (A Healing Machine)* or *The Humming Bird Waltz*, Mattress Factory, Pittsburgh

1992 *Turnip Ascension*, The Knitting Factory, New York
*Lemon Ascension*, CB's 313 Performance Space, New York
*Little Worm Wood Don't You Do What Your Big Worm Done*, Corcoran Art Gallery, Washington, D.C.

1990 *Guff Apparatus*, The Alternative Gallery, Pittsburgh


#### Selected Bibliography

Goldblooms, Charles. "In the Summer Weeds." *In Pittsburgh* (May 1993).

Kenton, Mary Jean. "Studio Talk." *New Art Examiner* (summer 1994).

Miller, Donald. "Subtle Thinkers: Three Artists, Three Distinct Visions." *Post-Gazette Weekend*, 21 October 1994.

Potter, Chris. "Physical Poetry." *In Pittsburgh*, 8 October 1993.

——. "Site." *In Pittsburgh*, 17 November, 1994.

Shearing, Graham. "Heroes and Angels Hits." *Pittsburgh Tribune-Review*, 15 April 1994.
——. "Mattress Factory Exhibits Challenge the Imagination." *Pittsburgh Tribune-Review*, 3 October 1994.
Thomas, Mary. "Fine Arts: Language of Objects." *Pittsburgh Post-Gazette Magazine*, 4 December 1998.

**Shelagh Keeley**
Canadian, born 1954
Lives and works in New York

**Selected Solo Exhibitions**
1998 *Art Book*, Amsterdam
1997 Galerie Annette de Keyser, Antwerp
1996 John Gibson Gallery, New York
1995 Galerie Aline Vidal, Paris
1990 *Flesh of the Body*, Mattress Factory, Pittsburgh

**Selected Group Exhibitions**
1997 *Add Bodies/Corps Etrangers*, National Gallery of Canada, Ottawa
1995 *20 Jaar*, Gallery de Gryse, Tielt, Belgium
1992 *Studio*, Galeria, Budapest
1992 *From the Intimacy of the Page*, The Power Plant, Toronto
1991 *Encounters with Diversity*, P.S. 1 Contemporary Art Center, Long Island City, NY

**Selected Bibliography**
Centre d'Art contemporain d'Herblay. *Shelagh Keeley: Space for Breathing*. Paris: Les Cahiers des Regards, 1994.
Homisak, Bill. "Installations Take Flight at 1414 Monterey." *Pittsburgh Tribune-Review*, 10 August 1990.
Gaillot, Michael. *Shelagh Keeley: Wall Drawings*. Saint-Fons: Centre d'Art Plastiques, 1997.
Keeley, Shelagh. *Shelagh Keeley: Boudoir*. New York: Exit Art, 1994.
——. *A Space for Breathing*. New York: Granary Books, 1992.
Miller, Donald. "Building Plans, New Exhibits at Factory." *Pittsburgh Post-Gazette*, 22 June 1990.
Odom, Michael. "Group Show." *In Pittsburgh*, 1 August 1990.
Sherrin, Bob. "Inner Passages." In *In Side Up: Helen Chadwick and Shelagh Keeley.* Alberta, Canada: The Walter Phillips Gallery, 1991.

**Mary Jean Kenton**
American, born 1946
Lives and works in Grindstone, PA

**Selected Exhibitions**
1999 *Botanica*, Tweed Museum of Art, University of Minnesota, Duluth, MN; traveling exhibition *Tiny Works, Little Licks*, Project, Wichita, KS
1998 Portions of *The Free Rectangles* and *Geometry of Color*, Mattress Factory, Pittsburgh
1992 *The Free Rectangles*, Mattress Factory, Pittsburgh
1990 *Mary Jean Kenton: A Survey, 1973–1990*, Allegheny College Gallery, Meadeville, PA
1989 *The Geometry of Color*, Laughlin House Property, Fayette County, PA

**Selected Bibliography**
Dlugos, Kathleen. "Mary Jean Kenton: Mattress Factory." *New Art Examiner* (December 1998/January 1999).
Jowitt, Deborah. "Slipknots." *Village Voice*, 29 March 1994.
Kenton, Mary Jean. "Engineers' Notebooks: The Geometry of Color." *Leonardo* 25, no. 1 (1992).
Lowry, Patricia. "'Geometry of Color' putting nature into art exhibit." *Pittsburgh Press*, 4 December 1989.
Odom, Michael. "Mary Jean Kenton and David Nyzio." *In Pittsburgh*, 3 September 1992.
Pilecki, Michelle. "Mattress Factory Installations—Algae and Irony." *Pittsburgh City Paper*, 22 July 1992.
Raczka, Robert. "Mary Jean Kenton's Freedom (with limits)." *The Penn State Journal of Contemporary Criticism* 3.
Shearing, Graham. "An Ongoing Process." *Pittsburgh Tribune Review*, 28 May 1998.
Tweed Museum of Art. *Botanica*. Exhibition Catalogue. Duluth, MN: Tweed Museum of Art, 1999.
Wagstaff, Sheena. "Earth Colors." *Pittsburgh Magazine* (August 1992).

**Sora Kim**
Korean, born 1965
Lives and works in Seoul

**Selected Exhibitions**
1999 *D-Gravitizer*, Mattress Factory, Pittsburgh
1998 *Mrs. Brown Project*, Public Art Project, New York *Very Up & Very Down*, Project for Taipei, Taiwan, R.O.C.
1997 *Very Special Yellow Mission*, Omi, New York
1996 Founds Unlimited Concept Company and manages Cleaning Department

**Selected Bibliography**
Fumio, Nanjo and Miki Akiko. *Site of Desire: 1998 Taipei Biennial*. Taiwan: Taipei Fine Art Museum, 1998.
Giannini, Claudia and Michael Olijnyk. "Conversation." *Art Journal* (fall 2000).
Kee, Joan. "Transiency and Time: A Mattress Factory Residency." *ART AsiaPacific* 28 (2000).
Madden, Dave. "Gee, Zero-G." *In Pittsburgh*, 27 October 1999.
Raczka, Robert. "Installations by Asian Artists in Residence." *Sculpture* (March 2000).
Shearing, Graham. "A Little Bit of Asia." *Pittsburgh Tribune-Review*, 12 December 1999.
Thomas, Clarke. "Contemporary Art's New Dimension." *Pittsburgh Post-Gazette*, 1 September 1999.
Thomas, Mary. "Installing Pittsburgh." *Pittsburgh Post Gazette*, 29 October 1999.

**John Kirchner**
American, born 1955
Lives and works in Woodville, PA

Selected Exhibitions
1995 Foster Gallery, New York
District of Columbia Arts Center, Washington, D.C.
1993 Wohlfarth Galleries, Washington, D.C.
1992 *Faith and Aphasia*, Mattress Factory, Pittsburgh
1991 Bistborno Gallery, Malmo, Sweden
1990 Charles Lucien Gallery, New York
1989 Rastovski Gallery, New York

Selected Group Exhibitions
1994 Allegheny College Gallery, Meadeville, PA
1993 Foster Gallery, New York
1991 De Andino Fine Arts, Washington, D.C.
1989 *Personae*, Islip Art Museum, Islip, NY
Gallerie Bebert, Rotterdam, Netherlands

Selected Bibliography

Adams, Brooks. "Shock of the Mundane." *Vogue* (March 1990).
Harrison, Helena. "Likeness: A Subjective Concept." *New York Times*, 1 October 1989.
Rastovski, Lorie. "John Kirchner." *Contemporary Artists, Tokyo-Japan* (April 1993).
Tonetti, Linda. "John Kirchner." *New Art Examiner* (May 1993).


**Monica Kulicka**
Polish, born 1963
Lives and works in New York

Selected Solo Exhibitions
1995 *Reconstructions*, Mattress Factory, Pittsburgh
1992 Hudson D. Walker Gallery, Provincetown, MA
1990 Art Research Center, Kansas City, MO
1989 Dzialan Gallery, Warsaw, Poland

Selected Group Exhibitions
1994 *Who Has Enlarged This Whole?* 53 West 9th Street, New York
1991 Kansas City Art Coalition, Kansas City, MO
1990 *Sculpture in Process*, Art Gallery, University of Nebraska at Omaha
*Four Artists In and Out*, Boulder Art Center, Boulder, CO

Selected Bibliography

Gerzova, Jana. "Mattress Factory." *Profil* (January/February 1996).
Lindsay, David. "Mad House: Art That Imitates an Eccentric Life." *New York Press*, 8 June 1994.
Markham, Pamela. "Artists from Eastern and Central Europe." *Arti* (May/June 1996).
Miller, Donald. "East Europeans in Show of Strength." *Pittsburgh Post-Gazette*, 28 October 1995.
Shearing, Graham. "Artist Shows How Man Deals with Heaven, Earth." *Pittsburgh Tribune-Review*, 14 May 1995.


**Sutee Kunavichayanont**
Thai, born 1965
Lives and works in Bangkok

Selected Solo Exhibitions
1999 *Siamese Breath (Twins)*, Mattress Factory, Pittsburgh
*Burden of Joy*, Bangkok University Art Gallery, Bangkok
1998 *Rain Drops—Pig's Shit Running*, TADU Contemporary Art, Bangkok
1997 *The Myth of the Asian Tiger*, Galerie Gauche, École Nationale Superieure des Beaux-Arts, Paris
1995 *The White Elephants of Siam*, The Art Gallery of the Faculty of Painting, Sculpture and Graphic Arts, Silpakorn University, Bangkok
1993 *Time and Mind*, Tin Sheds Gallery, New South Wales, Australia
*Flowing Tide*, Allen Street Gallery, New South Wales, Australia
1991 *From the Outside Looking In*, New England Regional Art Museum, Armidale, Australia

Selected Group Exhibitions
1999 *Jardins Secrets, Art dans la Ville*, Saint-Etienne, France
*No Guarantee*, Sydney College of the Arts, Sydney
*TRACE: The Liverpool Biennial of Contemporary Art*, Liverpool, England
1998 *Report from the Forest 1998*, National Gallery, Bangkok
1997 *Contemporary Fine Arts Exhibition*, Hanoi Fine Arts Institute, Hanoi
1996 *Golden Jubilee Art Exhibition: 50 Years of Thai Art*, Queen Sirikit National Convention Center, Bangkok
1991 *The 6th International Print Biennale*, Varna, Bulgaria
1990 *International Exhibition of Graphic Art*, Freshen, Germany
*The 5th Busan Biennial*, Busan, Korea

Selected Bibliography

Forman, Kerry. "Sutee's Thought Makes a Pretty Picture." *Armidale Express* (Australia), 20 November 1991
Giannini, Claudia and Michael Olijnyk. "Conversation." *Art Journal* (fall 2000).
Kee, Joan. "Transiency and Time: A Mattress Factory Residency." *ART AsiaPacific* 28 (2000).
Marazzi, William. "Anxiety and Frustration." *Living* (September 1998).
Pettifor, Steven. "Sutee Kunavichayanont." *ART AsiaPacific* 22 (1999).


**Takamasa Kuniyasu**
Japanese, born 1957
Lives and works in Sapporo

Selected Solo Exhibitions
1997 *Season in Spiral*, Seventh and Penn Avenues, Pittsburgh
1992 Gallery Natsuka, Tokyo
1991 *Return to Self*, Mattress Factory, Pittsburgh
Hillside Gallery, Tokyo
Het Apollohuis, Eidhoven, Netherlands
Museum of Contemporary Art, Sapporo

### Selected Group Exhibitions

2000 Hakone Open-Air Museum, Hakone, Japan
1993 *Cultural Landscape Akersvika*, Lillehammer Olympic Culture Program, Lillehammer, Norway
1992 *Five Artists*, Kaneko Art Gallery, Tokyo
1991 *Fifth Asian Art Biennial*, Shilpakala Academy, Dhaka, Bangledesh
1990 *A Primal Spirit: Ten Contemporary Japanese Sculptors*, Hara Museum ARC, Japan. (Traveled to Los Angeles County Museum of Art; Museum of Contemporary Art, Chicago; Modern Art Museum of Fort Worth; and National Museum of Canada, Ottawa)
*The Fourth Australian Sculpture Triennial*, National Gallery of Victoria, Melbourne

### Selected Bibliography


Cooke, Lynne. "Contemporary Japanese Art." *Burlington Magazine* (June 1991).
Green, Charles. "National Gallery of Victoria, Melbourne; Installation." *Artforum International* (February 1991).
King, Elaine. "Kuniyasu, Matsumura, Ishihara." *Arts Magazine* (November 1991).
Koplos, Janet. "Material Meditations." *Art in America* (March 1991).
Kuniyasu, Takamasa. *The Best Selections of Contemporary Ceramics in Japan: Takamasa Kuniyasu*. Kyoto: Kyoto Shoin Co., Ltd., 1992.
Miller, Donald. "Japanese Artists Turn Factory into a Gentle Place." *Pittsburgh Post-Gazette*, 22 March 1991.
Odom, Michael. "Three Japanese Artists." *In Pittsburgh*, 3 April 1991.


### Yayoi Kusama

Japanese, born 1929
Lives and works in Tokyo

### Selected Exhibitions

2000 *Yayoi Kusama*, Serpentine Gallery, London
1998 *Love Forever: Yayoi Kusama, 1958–1968*, Los Angeles County Museum of Art, Los Angeles
1996 *Dots Obsession*, *Infinity Dots Mirrored Room*, and *Repetitive Vision*, Mattress Factory, Pittsburgh
1994 *Japanese Art After 1945: Scream Against the Sky*, Yokohama Museum of Art, Japan; The Solomon R. Guggenheim Museum, New York; San Francisco Museum of Modern Art, San Francisco.
*Cross and Square Grids*, Museum of Modern Art, Saitama, Japan
1993 *Venice Biennale*, Japanese Pavilion, Venice
1992 *Adam and Eve*, Museum of Modern Art, Saitama, Japan
1991 *Monochrome on Monochrome*, Tokyo Metropolitan Museum of Art, Tokyo
1990 *Multiplying Image*, Hyogo Prefectural Museum of Modern Art, Kobe
*Artists Gone to America*, Nagano Prefectural Shinano Art Museum, Kobe

### Selected Bibliography


Hoptman, Laura, Akira Tatehata, Udo Kultermann. *Yayoi Kusama*. London: Phaidon Press, 2000.
King, Elaine A. "Reviews." *Sculpture* (February 1997).
Kotani, Akiko and Bernard Freydberg. "Crossover in the Arts." *Fiberarts Magazine* (summer 1997).
Kusama, Yayoi. *Angels on Cape Cod*. Tokyo: Jiritsu Shobo, 1990.
———. *The Foxgloves of Central Park*. Tokyo: Jiritsu Shobo, 1991.
———. *Lost in Swampland*. Tokyo: Jiritsu Shobo, 1992.
———. *New York Story*. Tokyo: Jiritsu Shobo, 1993.
———. *The Psychological Hospital of Ants*. Tokyo: Jiritsu Shobo, 1994.
Kultermann, Udo. "The Art of Yayoi Kusama Unveils a Female Worldview." *Sculpture* (January 1997).
Munroe, Alexandra. *Japanese Art After 1945: Scream Against the Sky*. New York: Harry N. Abrams, 1994.
News Brief. "Installation Show." *Asian Art News* (November/December 1996).
Posa, Cristina. "Of Mind and Body." *Pittsburgh City Paper*, 12 June 1997.
Raczka, Robert. "Yayoi Kusama." *New Art Examiner* (March 1997).
Segal, Stephen H. "High Tech, Low Tech and No Tech." *Pitt News*, 18 June 1997.
Shearing, Graham. "Retro-hip at the Mattress Factory." *Pittsburgh Tribune-Review*, 27 October 1996.
———. "Small Museum Nears Goals." *Pittsburgh Tribune-Review*, 2 May 1997.
Solomon, Andrew. "Dot Dot Dot." *Artforum* (February 1997).
Stacho, L'ubo. "Mattress Factory Muzeum Ako Zivotny Styl." *Linia* (September 1998).
Thomas, Mary. "Off the Beaten Path." *Pittsburgh Post-Gazette*, 12 June 1997.
———. "Mattress Factory Trio's Installation Dynamic." *Pittsburgh Post-Gazette*, 19 July 1997.
———. "Connect the Dots." *Pittsburgh Post-Gazette Weekend*, 18 October 1996.
Zelevansky, Lynn, Laura Hoptman, Akira Tatehata, and Alexander Munroe. *Love Forever: Yayoi Kusama, 1958–1968*. Los Angeles: Los Angeles County Museum of Art, 1998.


### Greer Lankton

American, 1958–1996

### Selected Solo Exhibitions

1996 *It's All About ME, Not You*, Mattress Factory, Pittsburgh
1985 Civilian Warfare, New York
1984 Civilian Warfare, New York

### Selected Group Exhibitions

1995 *Venice Biennale*, Venice
1995 *Biennial Exhibition*, Whitney Museum of American Art, New York
1993 *Real Sex*, Salzburger Kunstverein, Austria
1991 *From Desire . . . A Queer Diary*, St. Lawrence University, Canton, NY
1984 *Limbo*, P.S. 1 Contemporary Art Center, Long Island City, NY
1985 *City Dolls and Other Effigies*, New Math Gallery, New York
1981 *New York/New Wave*, P.S. 1, Contemporary Art Center, Long Island City, NY

Selected Bibliography

Bourdon, David. "Sitting Pretty." *Vogue* (November 1985).

Crawford, Lynn. "My Life to Live." *Metrotimes*, 9 September 1998.

Goldin, Nan. "A Rebel Whose Dolls Embodied Her Demons." *New York Times*, 22 December 1996.

Granger, Helen. "It's All About Me Not You, Greer Lankton at the Mattress Factory." *Artwords* (December 1996).

Indiana, Gary. "Greer Lankton at Civilian Warfare." *Art in America* (November 1994).

"Installation Show." *Asian Art News* (November/December 1996).

King, Elaine A. "Reviews." *Sculpture* (February 1997).

Miller, Donald. "Installation Artist in Show on North Side." *Pittsburgh Post-Gazette*, 21 November 1996.

Posa, Cristina. "Of Mind and Body." *Pittsburgh City Paper*, 12 June 1997.

Potter, Chris. "Site." *In Pittsburgh*, 12 December 1996.

Shearing, Graham. "Retro-hip at the Mattress Factory." *Pittsburgh Tribune-Review*, 27 October 1996.

Thomas, Mary. "Artist's Power Lingers Even After Death." *Pittsburgh Post-Gazette*, 30 November 1996.

——. "Connect the Dots." *Pittsburgh Post-Gazette Weekend*, 18 October 1996.

——. "Mattress Factory Trio's Installation Dynamic." *Pittsburgh Post-Gazette*, 19 July 1997.


**John Latham**

British, born 1921

Lives and works in London

Selected Solo Exhibitions

1996 *Long Glass*, *Documentation*, and *Long Painting*, Mattress Factory, Pittsburgh

1992 *OHO*, Lisson Gallery, London

1991 *John Latham: Art After Physics*, Staatsgalerie, Stuttgart and Museum of Modern Art, Oxford

1990 Josh Baer Gallery, New York

Selected Group Exhibitions

1995 *Postscript*, Lisson Gallery, London

1994 *Punishment and Decoration*, Hohenthal und Bergen, Köln

1991 *The Discerning Eye*, Mall Galleries, London

1990 *Um 1968: konkrete utopien in kunst und gesellschaft*, Stadtische Kunsthalle, Duesseldorf and Museum for Gestaltung, Zurich


Selected Bibliography

Conzen-Meairs, Ina, Marion Keiner and Rolf Sachsse. *Art after Physics*. Stuttgart, Germany: Staatsgalerie, 1991.

Freeser, Sigrid. "John Latham, Kunst nach der Physik." *Kunstforum* (May/April 1991).

Heartney, Eleanor. "John Latham at Josh Baer." *Art in America* (February 1988).

Kenton, Mary Jean. "John Latham at the Mattress Factory." *Sculpture* (November 1996).

Latham, John. "John Latham: Statement." *Art Monthly* (November 1992).

Potter, Chris. "Site." *In Pittsburgh*, 4 July 1996.

Raczka, Robert. "John Latham." *New Art Examiner* (November 1996).

Sauro, Maria. "John Latham, Mattress Factory (Pittsburgh)." *Vanidad* (July/August 1996).

Shearing, Graham. "Confident Artist Reaches Toward the Complex." *Pittsburgh Tribune-Review*, 9 June 1996.

Thomas, Mary. "Books and Glass Slice Through Space." *Pittsburgh Post-Gazette*, 6 July 1996.

Trott, Lloyd. "John Latham: artist and activist." *Socialist Campaign News* (February 1995).

Walker, John. *John Latham—The Incidental Person—his Art and Ideas*. London: Middlesex University Press, 1995.

Winn, Alice. "Installations at the Mattress Factory." *Artwords* 1, no. 2.


**Otis Laubert**

Slovakian, born 1946

Lives and works in Bratislava

Selected Solo Exhibitions

1995 *Gastronomic Tapestry*, 1987, Mattress Factory, Pittsburgh
*Deer*, 1994, Mattress Factory, Pittsburgh
*Bicycle*, 1992, Mattress Factory, Pittsburgh
*Stars*, Mattress Factory, Pittsburgh
*Fire Making Darkness*, Mattress Factory, Pittsburgh
*Knowing They are Losing their Heads,* Mattress Factory, Pittsburgh
*Stairs*, 1987, Mattress Factory, Pittsburgh
*Connections*, Mattress Factory, Pittsburgh

1992 Knoll Gallery, Vienna
Slovak National Gallery, Bratislava, Slovakia

1991 Meijernik Gallery, Amsterdam

1990 Gallery Na Palisadach, Bratislava, Slovakia

Selected Group Exhibitions

1992 *Hills and Mills*, Arti et Amicitiae, Amsterdam
*Minisalon*, New Hall, Prague

1991 *Metropolis*, Martin Gropius Bau, Berlin

1990 *Czechoslovak Art: 1960–1990*, Coupole Haussman, Paris
*Art Against Totalitarianism*, Hrad, Bratislava, Slovakia


Selected Bibliography

Bartosova, Zuzana. *Otis Laubert—Probes*. Bratislava: Slovak National Gallery, 1992.

Gerzova, Jana. "Mattress Factory." *Profil* (January/February 1996).

Krainak, Paul. "Siting Slavs at the Factory." *New Art Examiner* (March 1996).

Markham, Pamela. "Mattress Factory: Artists from Eastern and Central Europe." *Arti* (May/June 1996).

Miller, Donald. "East Europeans in Show of Strength." *Pittsburgh Post-Gazette*, 28 October 1995.

Stein, Judith. "Import/Export: Out of the East." *Art in America* (April 1998).

Winn, Alice. "Brave New World." *Pittsburgh City Paper*, 29 November 1995.

**Peter Lodato**
American, born 1946
Lives and works in Santa Monica

Selected Solo Exhibitions

1993 *Open Triangle 1*, *Open Triangle 2*, Mattress Factory, Pittsburgh
1991 *Silver Tower*, Public Art Project, Brunswig Square, Los Angeles
1990 *Wrathful Means Project No. 2*, Sharon Truax Fine Art, Venice, CA
1989 *Painting, Drawing and Sculpture*, Hunsaker-Schlesinger Gallery, Los Angeles

Selected Group Exhibitions

1992 *Survey of California Art, 1960–90*, Aspen Center for the Visual Arts, Aspen, CO
1991 *Salerno Incontrid-Arte*, Rassegne della Ressegne Amalfi Arte, Salerno, Italy
1988 *Vessels*, Sharon Truax Fine Art, Los Angeles
*Sculpture De Camera* (Chamber Sculptures), Fisher Gallery, University of Southern California, Los Angeles

Selected Bibliography

Armstrong, Richard. "California." *Flash Art* (March/April 1980).
Baker, Kenneth. "Peter Lodato, La Jolla Museum of Contemporary Art." *Artforum* (November 1985).
Clothier, Peter. "Los Angeles." *ARTnews* (February 1990).
Colpitt, Frances. "Peter Lodato at Burnett Miller Gallery in Los Angeles." *Art in America* (September 1985).
Johnstone, Mark. "Exploration and Installation." *Artweek*, 24 October 1981.

**Winifred Lutz**
American, born 1942
Lives and works in Philadelphia

Selected Site-Integrated Installations

1999 *The Best of the Season*, Aldrich Museum of Contemporary Art, Ridgefield, CT
1997 Institute of Contemporary Art, University of Pennsylvania, Philadelphia
Levy Gallery, Moore College of Art, Philadelphia
1992–97 *Garden*, Mattress Factory, Pittsburgh
1992–96 *A Reclamation Garden*, Abington Art Center, Abington, PA
1992 *Floor to Ceiling Surface to Edge/Vista*, Cranbrook Academy Museum of Art, Bloomfield Hills, MI
1991 *Mending Room*, Institute of Contemporary Art, University of Pennsylvania, Philadelphia
1990 *AGO/ANON*, Grand Lobby Installation, The Brooklyn Museum, Brooklyn, NY

Selected Exhibitions

2000 *Works in Paper*, Gallery Joe, Philadelphia
1999 *Stillness*, The Gallery of the Dieu Donne Papermill, New York
1996 *A Century of Women Landscape Architects and Gardeners in Pittsburgh*, The Heinz Architectural Center of the Carnegie Museum of Art, Pittsburgh
*Prison Sentences*, Eastern State Penitentiary, Philadelphia
1995 *Crossing Over/Changing Places*, Villa Croce Museum of Contemporary, Genoa, Italy
1992 Marilyn Pearl Gallery, New York

Selected Bibliography

Beardsley, John. "Sculpting the Land." *Sculpture* (April 1996).
Burnham, Laura. *The Reclamation Garden 1993–1995*. Abington, PA: The Abington Art Center, 1996.
Campbell, Lawrence. "Winifred Lutz at Marilyn Pearl and The Brooklyn Museum." *Art in America* (April 1991).
Csaszar, Tom. "The Sculpture of Winifred Lutz: Perception's Nature." *Sculpture* (March 1998).
Giannini, Claudia and Winifred Lutz. *The Garden by Winifred Lutz*. Pittsburgh: Mattress Factory, 1997.
Griswold, Mac. "Brooding Forest as Artist's Medium." *New York Times*, 21 November 1997.
Lutz, Winifred. "In/On/Of Paper." In *Surface as a Function of Distance*. Detroit: Detroit Institute of Arts, 1988.
*Place of Nature/Nature of Place*. Philadelphia: Moore College of Art, 1997.
Posa, Cristina. "Victory Garden." *Pittsburgh City Paper*, 12 June 1997.
Sauer, Georgia. "Artist Decides How Mattress' Garden Grows." *Pittsburgh Post-Gazette*, 1 June 1997.
Segal, Stephen H. "High Tech, Low Tech and No Tech." *Pitt News*, 18 June 1997.
Siedel, Miriam. "Report from Philadelphia: Art Behind Bars." *Art in America* (November 1995).
Steinberg, Ellen. "Winifred Lutz, ICA, University of PA." *New Art Examiner* (June 1997).
Tascarella, Patty. "Sowing the Seeds." *Pittsburgh Business Times*, 20 August 1999.
*Threshold/Interface/Transition ÷ (When)*. Philadelphia: Institute of Contemporary Art, University of Pennsylvania, 1997.

**Patty Martori**
American, born 1956
Lives and works in New York

Selected Solo Exhibitions

1998 *Works on paper and cigarette tableaux*, D'Amelio Terraz Gallery, New York
1992 Galerie Marc Jancou, Zurich
1991 *Love House*, Mattress Factory, Pittsburgh
1990 Pat Hearn Gallery, New York

### Selected Group Exhibitions

1998 *Pop Surrealism*, The Aldrich Museum of Contemporary Art, Ridgefield, CT
1996–97 D'Amelio Terras Gallery, New York
1996 *Everything That's Interesting is New*, Athens School of Fine Arts, Athens
1995 *Pat Hearn: Selected Survey*, Pat Hearn Gallery, New York
1993 *Dirty Ornament*, Rotunda Gallery, Brooklyn
1990 *Statut de la Sculpture*, Musée St. Pierre, Lyon, France

### Selected Bibliography


Blackman, Susan. "The Mattress Factory: An Alternative Museum." *Carnegie Magazine* (November/December 1991).
Charpentier, Elie. "Patty Martori, Buzz Spector, Diana Burgoyne, Bogdan Perzynski: Four New Installations." *In Pittsburgh*, 6 November 1991.
Humphrey, David. "Review." *Art Issues* (February 1990).
Miller, Donald. "Art." *Pittsburgh Post-Gazette*, 12 October 1991.
Schaffner, Ingrid. "Review." *Artforum* (summer 1998).
——. *Pop Surrealism*. Ridgefield, CT: Aldrich Museum of Contemporary Art, 1998.
Spector, Nancy. "At Home With Patty Martori." *Artscribe* (March 1991).
Stals, Jose. "The Köln Show." *Flash Art* (October 1990).


## Yoji Matsumura

Japanese, born 1950
Lives and works in Tokyo

### Selected Solo Exhibitions

1998 *Body Conscious 1998*, E and Y, Tokyo
1997 *Body Conscious*, Galerie Den + Floor 2, Tokyo
1996 *United States of Mind*, City Gallery of Contemporary Art, Raleigh, NC
1995 *Installation*, Honen-In Temple, Kyoto
1993 *Dear 1993*, Galerie Den + Floor 2, Tokyo
*BUGS-II*, Takashimaya Contemporary Art Space, Tokyo
1992 *BUGS*, Soh Gallery, Tokyo
*Circular Celebration*, Gallery Art Soko, Tokyo
1991 *Celebration*, Mattress Factory, Pittsburgh

### Selected Group Exhibitions

1995 *Gallery Artists*, Galerie Den + Floor 2, Tokyo
1993–95 *Miniature Size Exhibition*, Soh Gallery, Tokyo
1991 *Gallery Artists*, Soh Gallery, Tokyo
1989 *Moments Sonores*, Tochigi Museum, Tochigi, Japan

### Selected Bibliography


Cooke, Lynne. "Contemporary Japanese Art." *Burlington Magazine* (June 1991).
King, Elaine. "Kunitasu, Matsumura, Ishihara." *Arts Magazine* (November 1991).
Miller, Donald. "Japanese Artists Turn Factory into a Gentle Place." *Pittsburgh Post-Gazette*, 22 March 1991.
Odom, Michael. "Three Japanese Artists." *In Pittsburgh*, 3 April 1991.


## Matthew McCaslin

American, born 1957
Lives and works in New York

### Selected Solo Exhibitions

1999 Feigen Contemporary, New York
1998 *New Work*, Sandra Gering Gallery, New York
1997 Postmasters Gallery, New York
1993 Daniel Newburg Gallery, New York
1992 *(projects 33)*, The Museum of Modern Art, New York
1991 Anthony Reynolds Gallery, London
Le Consortium, Dijon, France
1990 *16 On Center*, Mattress Factory, Pittsburgh

### Selected Group Exhibitions

1996 *21c. Sculpture*, John Gibson Gallery, New York
1996 *The Bare Wall! . . .*, Michael Klein, New York
1995 *Vulto*, Sandra Gering Gallery, New York
1993 *Prospect 93*, Schirn Museum, Frankfurt
1992 *Translation*, Centre for Contemporary Art, Ujazdowski Castle, Warsaw
1991 *The Museum of Natural History*, Galerie Barbara Faber, Amsterdam
1990 *Work In Progress? Work?* The Andrea Rosen Gallery, New York

### Selected Bibliography


Avigkos, Jan. "Matthew McCaslin." *Artforum* (May 1991).
Bitterli, Konrad, Gretchen Faust, Robert Hobbs, Matthew McCaslin. *Matthew McCaslin: Works-Sites*. St. Gallen: Kunstverein St. Gallen Kunstmuseum, 1998.
Cantz, Reihe, Matthew McCaslin, Felix Gonzalez-Torres. *Matthew McCaslin: Exhibitions*. New York: Distributed Art Publishers, 1994.
Cotter, Holland. "A Builder's Eye—Matthew McCaslin." *New York Times*, 15 May 1992.
Decter, Joshua. "Installations From On High: Matthew McCaslin." *Flash Art* (May 1991).
Harris, Susan. "Matthew McCaslin at Feigen Contemporary." *Art in America* (May 2000).
Homisak, Bill. "Installations Take Flight at 1414 Monterey." *Pittsburgh Tribune-Review*, 10 August 1990.
Levin, Kim. "Matthew McCaslin." *Village Voice* (1992).
Miller, Donald. "Building Plans, New Exhibits at Factory." *Pittsburgh Post-Gazette*, 22 June 1990.
Odom, Michael. "Group Show, Mattress Factory." *In Pittsburgh*, 1 August 1990.
Smith, Roberta. "Matthew McCaslin." *New York Times*, 16 July 1990.

**Peter Meluzin**
Slovakian, born 1947
Lives and works in Bratislava

Selected Exhibitions
1999 *Wall of Laments*, Synagogue, Trnava
1997 *Behind the Limits*, Dresden
1996 *Slovak Sculptors*, Orousko, Slovakia
1995 *Wordburger Column*, Mattress Factory, Pittsburgh
1993 *Power Station T*, Poprad, Slovakia
*Space '93*, Piestany, Slovakia
1992 *Between Object and Installation*, Museum am Oswall, Dortmund, Germany
*Interplays '92*, Bratislava, Slovakia

Selected Bibliography
Gerzova, Jana. "Mattress Factory." *Profil* (January/February 1996).
Matustik, Radisklav. *1. Poschodie*. Bratislava: 1993.
Markham, Pamela. "Mattress Factory: Artists from Eastern and Central Europe." *Arti* (May/June 1996).
Miller, Donald. "East Europeans in Show of Strength." *Pittsburgh Post-Gazette*, 28 October 1995.
Stein, Judith. "Import/Export: Out of the East." *Art in America* (April 1998).
Winn, Alice. "Brave New World." *Pittsburgh City Paper*, 29 November 1995.
——. "Installations at the Mattress Factory." *Artwords* 1, no. 2.

**Tatsuo Miyajima**
Japanese, born 1957
Lives and works in Nagoya

Selected Solo Exhibitions
2000 *Tatsuo Miyajima: Counter Pieces*, Galerie der Stadt, Stuttgart, Germany
1999 Buchmann Galerie, Koln, Germany
1998 Luhring Augustine Gallery, New York
1997 Hayward Gallery, London
1996 Modern Art Museum of Fort Worth, Texas
1995 *Tatsuo Miyajima: Running Time*, Queen's House, Greenwich, England
1993 Kunsthalle, Zurich
1992 Gallery Takagi, Nagoya, Japan
1994 *Over the Border*, Mattress Factory (in collaboration with the *Carnegie International*), Pittsburgh
Anthony d'Offay Gallery, London

Selected Group Exhibitions
1998 *au courant*, The Center for Curatorial Studies Museum, New York
1997 *Land Marks*, John Weber Gallery, New York
1995 *Art in Japan Today: 1985–1995*, Museum of Contemporary Art, Tokyo
*Japanese Art After 1945: Scream Against the Sky*, Yokohama Museum of Art, Japan; The Solomon R. Guggenheim Museum, New York; San Francisco Museum of Modern Art, San Francisco
1993 *Oita Contemporary Art Exhibition*, Oita, Japan
1992 *Performing Objects*, The Institute of Contemporary Art, Boston
1991 *A Cabinet of Signs: Contemporary Art from Post-Modern Art*, Tate Gallery of British Art, London
1990 *The 8th Biennale of Sydney: The Readymade Boomerang*, Sydney
*Rhetorical Image*, The New Museum of Contemporary Art, New York

Selected Bibliography
Dannatt, Adrian. "The Carnegie International." *Flash Art* (March 1992).
Lufty, Carol. "Luhring Augustine Gallery, New York." *ARTnews* (April 1995).
Meinhardt, Johannes. "Tatsuo Miyajima: Counter Pieces, Galerie der Stadt, Stuttgart." *Kunstforum International* (July/September 2000).
Miller, Donald. "51st International True to Curator's Conception." *Pittsburgh Post-Gazette*, 19 October 1991.
——. "International Dominates Fall Art Season." *Pittsburgh Post-Gazette*, 6 September 1991.
Munroe, Alexandra. *Japanese Art After 1945: Scream Against the Sky*. New York: Harry N. Abrams, 1994.
Odom, Michael. "Tatsuo Miyajima." *Artforum International* (April 1997).
Robinson, Joel. "Tokyo: Tatsuo Miyajima." *Art Papers* (September/October 2000).
Schwalb, Harry. "Sleeper: No Overnight Sensation, the Mattress Factory is a Hit of a Museum." *Pittsburgh* (March 1992).

**James Giordani Montford**
American, born 1952
Lives and works in Providence, RI

Selected Solo Exhibitions
2000 *More Forbidden Fruit*, RISD Museum of Art, Providence, RI
Lyman Allyn Art Museum, Connecticut College, New London, CT
1999 *The Artist Dollars Project*, Mattress Factory, Pittsburgh
*The Artist Dollars Project II*, Chrysler Museum of Art, Norfolk, VA
1998 Slater Museum, Norwich, CT
1997 AS220 Gallery, Providence, RI
1996 *Throwaway Words: Red, White and Blue*, ARC Gallery, Chicago, IL
1994 *Artist Dollars*, The Taft Museum, Cincinnati, OH
1991 *Hate Words*, Real Art Ways (RAW), Hartford, CT
1990 *Praying Shoes/Preying Shoes*, Museum of the National Center of Afro-American Artists, Boston

Selected Group Exhibitions
1995 *Open to the Public*, Artspace Gallery, New Haven, CT
1994 *Don't Ask, Don't Tell*, Hampden Gallery, University of Massachusetts, Amherst, MA
1993 *A Wealth of Grays: Uncommon Perspectives from Connecticut Artists*, Silvermine Guild Arts Center, New Canaan, CT
*Personal Perspectives on Racial Identity*, Hera Gallery, Wakefield, RI
1991 *Maps in Contemporary Art*, DeCordova Museum, Lincoln, MA
1990 *In Your Face*, The Kitchen Center for Video, New York

Selected Bibliography
Carter, Alice. “Doling for Dollars.” *Ticket*, 18 March 1999.
Cembalist, Robin. “Sexist, Racist, or Otherwise Offensive.” *ARTnews* (April 1994).
Kemper, Steve. “Enough Rope: James Montford and His Angry Art.” *Hartford Courant Sunday Magazine*, 5 February 1995.
Perrott, Jeff. “Review: Mobius-Palladia.” *ArtsMEDIA* (October 1996).
Schwendenwien, Jude. “Art and Language.” *Art New England* (November 1991).
Segal, Stephen. “Problems of Patronage.” *In Pittsburgh*, 17 February 1999.
Thomas, Mary. “Passing the Buck.” *Pittsburgh Post-Gazette Weekend*, 19 February 1999.

**David Nyzio**
American, born 1958
Lives and works in New York

Selected Solo Exhibitions
1995 Asbaek Gallery, Copenhagen
1994 Postmasters Gallery, New York
1992 *Observation Platform*, Mattress Factory, Pittsburgh
Juriaan van Kranandonk, den Haag, Netherlands
1991 Postmasters Gallery, New York

Selected Group Exhibitions
1999 *David Nyzio and Ken Feingold*, Postmasters Gallery, New York
1996 *Shit*, Baron/Boisanté Gallery, New York
*Invented Realities*, The Contemporary Museum, Honolulu
*The Perfect World*, University at Buffalo Art Gallery, University at Buffalo, The State University of New York, Buffalo, NY
1995 *Veered Science*, Huntington Beach Art Center, Huntington Beach, CA
1994 *The Natural World*, A/C Project Room, New York
1993 *Two Generations*, Attelboro Museum, Attelboro, MA
1992 *Allocations 1992*, Floriade den Haag, Netherlands
1990 *Stendhal Syndrome: The Cure*, Andrea Rosen Gallery, New York
*Working in Brooklyn/Installations*, The Brooklyn Museum, New York
*The (Un)Making of Nature*, Whitney Museum of American Art Downtown, New York
*About Nature: A Romantic Impulse*, Barbara Toll Gallery, New York

Selected Bibliography
Avgikos, Jan. “Green Piece.” *Artforum* (April 1991).
Balken, Deborah. “David Nyzio.” *Art in America* (March 1995).
Ball, Edward. “The Greening of Art.” *Village Voice*, 31 July 1990.
Cone, Michele. “Baroque Nature.” *Arts* (March 1991).
Cottingham, Laura. “David Nyzio.” *Flash Art* (May/June 1990).
Faust, Gretchen. “David Nyzio.” *Arts* (February 1992).
Heartney, Eleanor. “Eco-Logic.” *Sculpture* (March/April 1990).
Lebowitz, Cathy. “David Nyzio and Ken Feingold at Postmasters.” *Art in America* (September 1999).
Mahoney, Robert. “David Nyzio.” *Arts* (January 1990).
Odom, Michael. “Mary Jean Kenton and David Nyzio: Installations at The Mattress Factory.” *In Pittsburgh*, 3 September 1992.
Pilecki, Michelle. “Mattress Factory Installations—Algae and Irony.” *Pittsburgh City Paper*, 22 July 1992.

**Roman Ondák**
Slovakian, born 1966
Lives and works in Bratislava

Selected Solo Exhibitions
1999 *Project Room*, Ludwig Museum, Budapest
1998 *Discrepancies*, V. Spala Gallery, Prague
*I' ve Definitely Been Here Before*, Gallery of the City of Prague
1996 Gallery Ruce, Prague
1995 *Taste of Thinking*, Mattress Factory, Pittsburgh
*Thrill of Mind*, ARTEST-BINZ, Zurich
*Roman Ondák: Objects and Drawings*, Museum of Art, Zilina, Slovakia

Selected Group Exhibitions
1999 *After the Wall*, Moderna Museet, Stockholm
*Rondo*, Ludwig Museum, Budapest
*Aspects-Positions 1949–1999*, Museum Moderner Kunst, Vienna
1998 *Zimmer frei*, Unikum, Klagenfurt, Germany
*Made in SK*, Galerie Knoll, Vienna
1996 *Conjunction*, Schallautzerstrasse 4, Vienna
*D-signed in SK*, Knoll Gallery, Budapest
1996 *Manifesta I*, Natural History Museum, Rotterdam, Netherlands
1994 *From the Art Dictionary*, Obecni dum, Prague
1993 *Germinations 7*, Kunstforeningen, Copenhagen
1992 *Germinations 7*, Le Magasin, Grenoble, France

Selected Bibliography
Gerzova, Jana. “Mattress Factory.” *Profil* (January/February 1996).
Krainak, Paul. “Siting Slavs at the Factory.” *New Art Examiner* (March 1996).
Liska, P. “Die Kunst Bleibt Frei: Kinst und Politik in Bratislava.” *Neue Bildende Kunst*, no. 2 (1995).
Markham, Pamela. “Mattress Factory: Artists from Eastern and Central Europe.” *Arti* (May/June 1996).
Miller, Donald. “East Europeans in Show of Strength.” *Pittsburgh Post-Gazette*, 28 October 1995.
Potter, Chris. “Site.” *In Pittsburgh*, 25 January 1996.
Rusnáková, Katarina. *Roman Ondák*. (Zilina, Slovakia: Museum of Art in Zilina, 1995).
Shearing, Graham. “Best Show of the Year Worth Czeching Out.” *Pittsburgh Tribune-Review*, 26 November 1995.
Stein, Judith. “Import/Export: Out of the East.” *Art in America* (April 1998).

**Bogdan Perzynski**
Polish, born 1954
Lives and works in Texas

Selected Solo Exhibitions
1992 *Diverse Works*, Houston
1991 *All at the Same Time*, Mattress Factory, Pittsburgh

1990 Shoshana Wayne Gallery, Santa Monica, CA
*Pieklo i Niebo* (Hell and Heaven), Galeria Wschodnia, Lodz, Poland

**Selected Group Exhibitions**

1993 *Faculty Show*, Archer Huntington Gallery, Austin
1992 *69 Beds*, Performance at Jefferson Plaza, Washington, D.C.
1991 *How to Use Small Areas in a Dozen Different Ways to Bring a Room to Life*, Mexic-Arte Museum, Austin
1990 *Lazy Pictures*, Mexic-Arte Museum, Austin
*Faculty Show*, Archer Huntington Gallery, Austin

**Selected Bibliography**

Appleton, Steven. "The Slow Unfolding of Pleasure, Bogdan Perzynski at Shoshana Wayne Gallery." *Artweek*, 15 February 1990.
Blackman, Susan. "The Mattress Factory: An Alternative Museum." *Carnegie Magazine* (November/December 1991).
Charpentier, Elle. "Patty Martori, Buzz Spector, Diana Burgoyne, Bogdan Perzynski: Four New Installations." *In Pittsburgh*, 6 November 1991.
Donovan, Sandra Fischione. "Off-the-wall Art Exhibits Titillate the Senses, Stimulate the Mind." *New York Times Sunday Magazine*, 24 May 1992.
Kandel, Susan. "Review." *Arts Magazine* (April 1990).
Miller, Donald. "Art." *Pittsburgh Post-Gazette*, 12 October 1991.
Peter, Frank. "Ilya Kabakov; Bogdan Perzynski." *Art Issues* (May 1990).

**Sandrine Sheon**
American, born 1964
Lives in Oakland, CA

**Selected Exhibitions**

1993 *A Collaboration*, Mattress Factory, Pittsburgh
1992 *Sentimental Art Show*, Beret International, Chicago
1991 *Margin of Safety*, collaborative installation, The Museum of Contemporary Art, Chicago
*Celeron, A Historical Fiction*, Celeron Street, Pittsburgh
*Body Cover*, Betty Rymer Gallery, Chicago
1990 *Cast Iron*, Betty Rymer Gallery, Chicago

**Selected Bibliography**

Collins, Sue. "Margin of Safety: A Collaborative Installation." *New Art Examiner* (February/March 1992).
Hixon, Kathryn. "Reviews: Chicago." *Arts Magazine* (April 1992).
Miller, Donald. "Sharing the View." *Pittsburgh Post-Gazette*, 17 December 1993.

**Catherine Smith**
American, born 1950
Lives and works in Fenton, Michigan

**Selected Solo Exhibitions**

1999 *Images of Resistance: Women in Pants, Photographs from the 1850s to the 1930s*, Residential College, University of Michigan, Ann Arbor, MI
*Witnesses and Warriors: The Flint Sit-Down Strike of 1936–1937*, GFAC, Flint, MI
1997 Kettering University, Flint, MI
*Laying Your Cards on the Table*, Flint Institute of Art, Flint, MI
1996 University of Illinois, Chicago
*The Study of Rain*, Raw Space, ARC Gallery, Chicago
1992 *Food for Thought*, MCC Fine Arts Gallery, Flint, MI

**Selected Group Exhibitions**

1997 *Far From Home*, Cranbrook Museum of Art, Bloomfield Hills, MI
1996 *Hush*, N.A.M.E. Gallery, Chicago, IL
1995 *Michigan Outdoor Sculpture Five*, Southfield, MI
*Order and Disorder*, SPACES, Cleveland
1993 *A Collaboration*, Mattress Factory, Pittsburgh
1992 *Abortion a priori*, ABCnoRIO, New York
1991 *Margin of Safety*, Museum of Contemporary Art, Chicago
1990 *Gigantic Women/Miniature Work*, S.A.I.C. Gallery 2, Chicago

**Selected Bibliography**

Collins, Sue. "Margin of Safety: A Collaborative Installation." *New Art Examiner* (February/March 1992).
Hixon, Kathryn. "Reviews: Chicago." *Arts Magazine* (April 1992).
Miller, Donald. "Sharing the View." *Pittsburgh Post-Gazette*, 17 December 1993.
Price, Mark. "Review: Order and Disorder." *Art Papers* (September/October 1995).
Utter, Douglas Max. "Out of Order and Disorder." *Cleveland Free Times*, 24 May 1995.
Williams, Monte. "Who Are Those Women Embedded in the Sidewalk?" *New York Times*, 20 August 1995.

**Kiki Smith**
American, born 1954
Lives and works in New York

**Selected Solo Exhibitions**

1999 *Kiki Smith: Creation*, Dioezesanmuseum, Freising, Germany
1998 *Bird, Flight Mound,* and *Little Space*, Mattress Factory, Pittsburgh
*Directions—Kiki Smith: Night*, Hirshhorn Museum and Sculpture Garden, Washington, D.C.
1995 *New Sculpture*, Pace Wildenstein, New York
1994–95 *Kiki Smith*, The Power Plant, Toronto
1993 Anthony d'Offay Gallery, London

### Selected Group Exhibitions

1999 *Skulptur—Figur—Weiblich*, Kunstsammlungen Chemnitz, Chemnitz, Germany
1996 *Young Americans: New American Art and the Saatchi Collection, Part 2*, Saatchi Gallery, London
1995 *Feminimasculin: Le sex de l' art*, Georges Pompidou Center, Paris
1993 *Biennial Exhibition*, Whitney Museum of American Art, New York
1992 *Strange Behavior*, Anthony d'Offay Gallery, London
1991 *Burning in Hell*, The Franklin Furnace, New York

### Selected Bibliography


Bonami, Francesco. "Kiki Smith: Diary of Fluids and Fears." *Flash Art* (January/February 1993).

Close, Chuck. "Interview with Kiki Smith." *Bomb* (Fall 1994).

Greenstein, M. A. "A Conversation with Kiki Smith." *Artweek*, 7 January 1993.

"Kiki Smith." *Artforum* (September 1997).

"Kiki Smith On-Site at The Israel Museum." *Flash Art* (June 1994).

Knight, Christopher. "Body Language: Kiki Smith." *Los Angeles Times*, 7 July 1991.

Matthiesson, Sophie. "Quirky Quilts at the Mattress Factory." *The Art Newspaper* (October 1997).

Smith, Kiki. "When the Spiritual Turns Physical." *Newsday*, 8 October 1999.

Tallman, Susan. "Kiki Smith, Anatomy Lessons." *Art in America* (April 1992).

University Art Museum. *Kiki Smith: Sojourn in Santa Barbara.* (Santa Barbara: University of California, 1995).


## Buzz Spector

American, born 1948
Lives and works in Illinois

### Selected Solo Exhibitions

1999 *Authors and Thinkers*, University of Iowa Museum of Art, Iowa City
Zolla-Lieberman Gallery, Chicago
1998 Cristinerose Gallery, New York
Marsha Mateyka Gallery, Washington, D.C.
1997 Kerlin Gallery, Dublin
1995 *Unpacking my Library*, Cleveland Center for Contemporary Art, Cleveland
Roy Boyd Gallery, Chicago
1994 Bellevue Art Museum, Bellevue, WA
1993 Roy Boyd Gallery, Chicago
1992 fiction/nonfiction, New York
Laurence Miller Gallery, New York
1991 *Cold Fashioned Room*, Mattress Factory, Pittsburgh
1990 Roy Boyd Gallery, Santa Monica, CA
Newport Harbor Art Museum, Newport Beach, CA

### Selected Group Exhibitions

1999 *Bookish*, Chicago Cultural Center
1998 *Chicago Hip*, Rocket Gallery, London
*Testo e Contesto: il libro-ambiente*, Accademia d'Ungheria, Palazzo Falconieri, Rome
1997 *About Face*, Transamerica Pyramid Lobby Gallery, San Francisco
1996 *Art in Chicago: 1945 1995*, Museum of Contemporary Art, Chicago
*Pasted Papers: Collage in the 20th Century*, Louis Stern Gallery, Los Angeles
*Portraits*, Angles Gallery, Santa Monica, CA
1991 *Wunderkammer*, Rena Bransten Gallery, Santa Monica, CA
*Transtextualism*, Mark Moore Gallery, Santa Monica, CA
*Serial*, Angles Gallery, Santa Monica, CA
1993 *Beyond the Written Word*, San Jose Institute of Contemporary Art, San Jose, CA
*Like a Body Without a Shadow*, Marsha Mateyka Gallery, Washington, D.C.
1992 *Library*, Granary Books Gallery, New York
*The Object is Bound*, Stephen Wirtz Gallery, San Francisco
1990 *Artists' Books*, Lorence Monk Gallery, New York
*The Lick of the Eye*, Shoshana Wayne Gallery, Santa Monica, CA
1990 *Transgressions*, Corcoran Gallery of Art, Washington, D.C.

### Selected Bibliography


Buening, Alice P. "Alternative Space Offers Conceptual Outlet." In *Artist's and Graphic Designer's Market*. Cincinnati, Ohio: F&W Publications for Writer's Digest Books, 1997.

Charpentier, Elie. "Patty Martori, Buzz Spector, Diana Burgoyne, Bogdan Perzynski: Four New Installations." *In Pittsburgh*, 6 November 1991.

Donovan, Sandra Fischione. "Off-the-wall Art Exhibits Titillate the Senses, Stimulate the Mind." *New York Times Sunday Magazine*, 24 May 1992.

Drucker, Johanna. "Static Object, Dynamic Form." *Sculpture* (November 1996).

Feldman, Edmund Burke. *Buzz Spector: Large Drawings and Objects*. Little Rock, AR: Arkansas Arts Center, 1996.

Gardner, Colin. "Buzz Spector." *Artforum* (summer 1990).

Heartney, Eleanor. "The Treacherous Library: Recent Book Art." *Sculpture* (September/October 1991).

Hubert, Renée and Judd Hubert. *The Cutting Edge of Reading: Artists' Books*. New York: Granary Books, 1999.

Hyde, James. "Buzz Spector." *Journal of Contemporary Art* (fall 1992).

Hymowitz, Carol. "This Museum has a Liking for Artists Who Trash the Place." *Wall Street Journal*, 17 October 1991.

Miller, Donald. "Art." *Pittsburgh Post-Gazette*, 12 October 1991.

Plagel, David. "Buzz Spector." *Bomb* (summer 1993).

Relyea, Lane. "Buzz Spector." *Artforum* (May 1992).

Ryan, Dinah. "Buzz Spector: Authors." *Art Papers* (November/December 1998).

Schwalb, Harry. "Sleeper: No Overnight Sensation, the Mattress Factory is a Hit of a Museum." *Pittsburgh* (March 1992).

——. "The Mattress Factory: 'Flexibility, Innovation and Risk.'" *ARTnews* (September 1997).

Spector, Buzz. *The Book Maker's Desire*. Santa Monica: Umbrella Editions, 1995.

Upshaw, Reagan. "Buzz Spector at fiction/nonfiction and Laurence Miller." *Art in America* (March 1993).

Vine, Richard. "Where the Wild Things Were." *Art in America* (May 1997).
Yood, James. "Buzz Spector at Roy Boyd Gallery." *Artforum* (April 1996).

**L'ubo Stacho**
Slovakian, born 1953
Lives and works in Bratislava

Selected Solo Exhibitions
1995 *Message from Saint Veronica*, Mattress Factory, Pittsburgh
*First Communion*, Mattress Factory, Pittsburgh
1993 Galeria Foto-Medium-Art, Wroclaw, Poland
1991 Maira de Villennes-sur-Seine, France
1990 MKS Prepostska, Bratislava, Slovakia

Selected Group Exhibitions
1993 *Slovakian Art Today*, Galerie Rottloff, Karlsruhe
1992 *Primavera Fotografica*, Barcelona
1991 *The Wall*, Colorado Photographic Arts Center, Denver
1990 *Contemporary Czech Photography*, Museum Ludwig, Cologne, Germany

Selected Bibliography
Gerzova, Jana. "Mattress Factory." *Profil* (January/February 1996).
Krainak, Paul. "Siting Slavs at the Factory." *New Art Examiner* (March 1996).
*L' ubo Stacho*. Slovakia: Soros Center for Contemporary Arts, 1995.
Markham, Pamela. "Mattress Factory: Artists from Eastern and Central Europe." *Arti* (May/June 1996).
Miller, Donald. "East Europeans in Show of Strength." *Pittsburgh Post-Gazette*, 28 October 1995.
Potter, Chris. "Site." *In Pittsburgh*, 25 January 1996.
Shearing, Graham. "Best Show of the Year Worth Czeching Out." *Pittsburgh Tribune-Review*, 26 November 1995.
Stein, Judith. "Import/Export: Out of the East." *Art in America* (April 1998).
Winn, Alice. "Brave New World." *Pittsburgh City Paper*, 29 November 1995.

**Yoshihiro Suda**
Japanese, born 1969
Lives and works in Tokyo

Selected Solo Exhibitions
2000 Galerie Rene Blouin, Montreal
D'Amelio Terras, New York
1999 *Weeds*, Mattress Factory, Pittsburgh
Gallery Koyanagi, Tokyo
1998 Caisse des Depots et Consignations, Paris
1997 Galerie Wohnmaschine, Berlin
1996 *Tokyo Installation 3*, Gallery K, Tokyo
1995 *Tokyo Installation 2*, Gallery K, Tokyo
1994 *Tokyo Installation*, Daiwa Parking Area, Tokyo
1993 *Ginza Weed Theory*, Ginza 1st to 4th blocks, Tokyo

Selected Group Exhibitions
2000 Gallery TAF, Kyoto
1998 *The Site of Desire*, Taipei Biennale, Taipei
*Everyday*, Sydney Biennale, Sydney
*Between Unknown Straits—Art Now in Japan and Korea*, Megro Museum of Art, Tokyo; The National Museum of Art, Osaka; The Korean Culture and Arts Foundation, Art Center, Seoul
*Little Creatures*, Galerie Micheal Zink, Regensbeurg, Germany
1997 *Art and Economy*, Gallery 360, Tokyo
*Spaces Between*, D'Amelio Terras, New York
*The Secret Garden*, Mitaka City Arts Foundation, Mitaka, Japan
1996 *Chiba Art Now*, Sakura City Art Museum, Sakura, Japan

Selected Bibliography
Giannini, Claudia and Michael Olijnyk. "Conversation." *Art Journal* (fall 2000).
Hanru, Hou. "The 1998 Taipei Biennale." *Flash Art* (October 1998).
Itoi, Kei. "Tokyo's Studio Shokudo." *Sculpture* (November 1997).
Japan Art and Culture Association. *Art Now in Japan and Korea*. Osaka: Japan Art and Culture Association, 1998.
Johnson, Ken. "Luca Pancrazzi and Yoshihiro Suda." *New York Times*, 24 October 1997.
Kee, Joan. "Transiency and Time: A Mattress Factory Residency." *ART AsiaPacific* 28 (2000).
Miki, Akiko. *Every Day*. Sydney: Sydney Biennale, 1998.
Nagoya, Satoru. "At the Galleries: Yoshihiro Suda." *Flash Art* (summer 1999).
Renaud, Olivier. *Beaux Arts* (October 1998).

**Fumio Tachibana**
Japanese, born 1968
Lives and works in Tokyo

Selected Solo Exhibitions
1999 *Untitled*, Mattress Factory, Pittsburgh
1998 *Fumio Tachibana 1998*, Obscure Gallery, Tokyo
*Kami-Gami*, Gallery 360, Tokyo
1995 *Made in the U.S.A.*, Sagacho Exhibition Space, Tokyo

Selected Group Exhibitions
1997 *Selections Winter '97*, The Drawing Center, New York
1996 *17th Brno International Graphic Design Biennal*, Brno, Czech Republic

Selected Bibliography and Publications
Giannini, Claudia and Michael Olijnyk. "Conversation." *Art Journal* (fall 2000).
Jones, Diana Nelson. "Finding Art in Scraps and Strips." *Pittsburgh Post-Gazette*, 2 September 1999.
Kee, Joan. "Transiency and Time: A Mattress Factory Residency." *ART AsiaPacific* 28 (2000).
Raczka, Robert. "Installations by Asian Artists in Residence." *Sculpture* (March 2000).
Shearing, Graham. "A Little Bit of Asia." *Pittsburgh Tribune-Review*, 12 December 1999.
Tachibana, Fumio. *Kami-Gami*. Tokyo: Burner Bros., 1998.
——. "Paper and Letters." *Idea 271* (November 1998).
Thomas, Mary. "Installing Pittsburgh." *Pittsburgh Post-Gazette*, 29 October 1999.

**Kate Temple**
American, born 1966
Lives and works in New York and Vermont

Selected Solo Exhibitions

1995 *Kate Temple: Prints*, Sweetwater Art Center, Sewickley, PA
1994 *Elemental Correspondence: Mineral Cycle* (October 22), *Plant Cycle* (December 5), *Animal Cycle* (January 16), Mattress Factory, Pittsburgh
1991 *Plainchant*, Carson Street Gallery, Pittsburgh

Selected Group Exhibitions

1999 *A.I.R. Biennial Exhibition*, A.I.R. Gallery, New York
1995 *In a Bind—Contemporary Book Artists*, Sharon Arts Center, Petersborough, NH
1994 *Contemporary Prints*, Frick Art Museum, Pittsburgh
1992 *Poetic Connections*, Castle Gallery, College of New Rochelle, New Rochelle, NY
1991 *Violence/Visual Pleasure*, Birmingham Lofts, Pittsburgh

Selected Bibliography

Kenton, Mary Jean. "Around Pittsburgh." *New Art Examiner* (September 1994).
Miller, Donald. "Subtle Thinkers: Three Artists, Three Distinct Visions." *Post-Gazette Weekend*, 21 October 1994.
Potter, Chris. "Site." *In Pittsburgh*, 17 November 1994.
Shearing, Graham. "Mattress Factory Exhibits Challenge the Imagination." *Pittsburgh Tribune-Review*, 30 October 1994.
Wachunas, Tom. "Alchemy." *New Art Examiner* (September 1994).
Whitney, D. Quincy. "Books as Art Form." *Boston Sunday Globe* (August 1995).

**Dezider Tóth**
Slovakian, born 1947
Lives and works in Bratislava

Selected Exhibitions

1995 *Last Aid*, Mattress Factory, Pittsburgh
*Reservation*, Mattress Factory, Pittsburgh
1994 *Ex (Retrospective)*, State Gallery, Bratislava, Slovakia
*Naturally*, Ernst Museum, Budapest
1993 *Landscape*, Istarska Sabornica, Porec, Croatia
1992 *Between Object and Installation*, Dortmund, Germany
*Challenge*, Expo '92, Seville, Spain
*Group A–R*, Bratislava, Slovakia
1991 *The Defiant Ones*, Heilbronn, Oldenburg, Germany
*Interpretations-Reinterpretations*, Bratislava, Slovakia
*The Art of Action*, Prague
1990 *Art against Totalitarianism*, Hrad, Bratislava, Slovakia

Selected Bibliography

Gerzova, Jana. "Mattress Factory." *Profil* (January/February 1996).
Krainak, Paul. "Siting Slavs at the Factory." *New Art Examiner* (March 1996).
Markham, Pamela. "Mattress Factory: Artists from Eastern and Central Europe." *Arti* (May/June 1996).
Miller, Donald. "East Europeans in Show of Strength." *Pittsburgh Post-Gazette*, 28 October 1995.
Potter, Chris. "Site." *In Pittsburgh*, 25 January 1996.
Shearing, Graham. "Best Show of the Year Worth Czeching Out." *Pittsburgh Tribune-Review*, 26 November 1995.
Stacho, L'ubo. "Mattress Factory Muzeum Ako Zivonty Styl." *Linia* (September 1998).
Stein, Judith. "Import/Export: Out of the East." *Art in America* (April 1998).
Winn, Alice. "Installations at the Mattress Factory." *Artwords* 1, no. 2.

**Michael Tracy**
American, born 1943
Lives and works in Mexico

Selected Solo Exhibitions

1994 *Chapel in the Mexican War Streets,* Mattress Factory, Pittsburgh
1993 *Cempazuchitl y Flores de Sangre*, Moody Gallery, Houston
1992 *Smoking Mirror*, Blue Star Art Space, San Antonio
1991 *Michael Tracy*, Daniel Weinberg Gallery, Santa Monica, CA
1990 *Mirror of Justice/House of Gold*, ARTSPACE, San Francisco
*The River Pierce Sacrifice II, 13.4.90*, Rio Grande near San Ygnacio, Texas

Selected Group Exhibitions

1991 *Maler/Bildhauer—Painter/Sculptor*, Raab Gallery, Berlin
*The Bleeding Heart*, The Institute of Contemporary Art, Boston
1989 *Escultures Diversos*, La Quinonera, Mexico City
1986 *Memento Mori*, Centro Cultural/Arte Contemporaneo, Mexico City
1984 *Content, A Contemporary Focus, 1974–1984*, Hirshhorn Museum and Sculpture Garden, Washington, D.C.

Selected Bibliography

Christophel, Joan and Edward Leffingwell, *The River Pierce: Sacrifice II, 13.4.90*. Houston: Rice University Press, 1992.
Foster, Ann T. "Baptism by Blood: Michael Tracy's Sacramental Art." *Image: A Journal of the Arts and Religion* (summer 1994).
Leffingwell, Edward. "Michael Tracy at the Mattress Factory." *Art in America* (November 1995).
——. "Michael Tracy's Rites of Passage." *Aperture* (summer 2000).

Leffingwell, Edward and Thomas McEvilley. *Terminal Privileges*. Long Island City: P.S. 1, The Institute for Art and Urban Resources, Inc., 1987.

May, Mike. "Exorcising Your Art Muscles." *Pittsburgh* (October 1994).

Miller, Donald. "Moving Art: Spirit and the Fly," *Pittsburgh Post-Gazette*, 16 April 1994.

Murphy, Jay. "Chapel in the Mexican War Streets." *Poliester* (winter 1995).

Muse, Vance. "Madman in Mexico." *Harper's Bazaar* (March 1994).

Potter, Chris. "Site." *In Pittsburgh*, 29 September 1994.

Shearing, Graham. "Michael Tracy: Goin' to the Chapel." *Pittsburgh Tribune-Review*, 15 May 1994.

Slaven, Michael. "Michael Tracy at the Mattress Factory." *New Art Examiner* (December 1994).

Snook, Debbi. "Pittsburgh Visit Can Refresh You." *Plain Dealer*, 1 April 1995.

**James Turrell**

American, born 1943

Lives and works in Flagstaff, Arizona

**Selected Exhibitions and Architectural Installations**

2000 Museum of Fine Arts, Houston
Fondation Electricite de France: Espace Electra, Paris, France
2000 Necklace Kawanishi Town Meditation House, Niigata, Japan
Live Oaks Friends Meeting House, Houston

1999 Museum of Contemporary Art, Miami

1997 *Where Does the Light in Our Dreams Come From?* The Museum of Modern Art, Saitama, Japan, Nagoya City Art Museum, Nagoya; Setagaya Museum, Tokyo.
*Milk Run/Grade A* (1996), Stroom Hobk, Den Haag, Netherlands

1996 Castello di Rivoli, Torino
Michael Hue-Williams Fine Art, London

1995 Art Tower Mito, Mito, Japan

1994 *Catso, Red* (1967) and *Soft Cell* (1992), Mattress Factory, Pittsburgh

1993 Hayward Gallery, Kilkenny, Ireland

1992 Wiener Secession, Vienna
Lenbachhaus, Munich
*The Irish Sky Garden*, Liss Ard Foundation, Skibbereen, Ireland

1991 Kunstmuseum Bern, Bern, Switzerland

1990 Museum of Modern Art, New York

**Selected Bibliography**

Adcock, Craig. *James Turrell: The Art of Light and Space*. Berkeley: University of California Press, 1990.

Adcock, Craig, Mario Diacono, E. C. Krupp and James Turrell. *Mapping Spaces: A Topological Survey of the Work by James Turrell*. New York: Peter Blum Edition, 1987.

Brown, Julia, ed. *James Turrell: Occluded Front*. Los Angeles: The Lapis Press and The Museum of Contemporary Art, 1985.

Diehl, Carol. "James Turrell at Barbara Gladstone." *ARTnews* (May 1994).

Donovan, Sandra Fischione. "Off-the-wall Art Exhibits Titillate the Senses, Stimulate the Mind." *New York Times Sunday Magazine*, 24 May 1992.

Hymowitz, Carol. "This Museum has a Liking for Artists Who Trash the Place." *Wall Street Journal*, 17 October 1991.

Jones, Diana Nelson. "Darkness Brings Eyes to Light," *Pittsburgh Post-Gazette*, 17 June 1999.

King, Elaine A. "Installation Haven." *Sculpture* (November/December 1989).

Lindner, Vicki. "Interview with James Turrell." *Omni Magazine* (winter 1995).

Marmer, Nancy. "James Turrell: The Art of Deception." *Art in America* (May 1981).

Osaka, Eriko, ed. *James Turrell*. Ibaraki, Japan: Contemporary Art Center, Art Tower Mito, 1995.

Russell, John. "An Earthwork Looks to the Sky." *New York Times*, 5 January 1986.

Segal, Stephen H. "High Tech, Low Tech and No Tech." *Pitt News*, 18 June 1997.

Snook, Debbi. "Pittsburgh Visit Can Refresh You." *Plain Dealer*, 1 April 1995.

Stevens, Mark. "Turrell's Celestial Vault." *Newsweek*, 10 February 1986.

Tanaka, Yukito, et al. *Where Does the Light in Our Dreams Come From?* Saitama: James Turrell Exhibition Committee, Setagaya Art Museum, The Museum of Modern Art, Nagoya City Art Museum, 1997.

Turrell, James. *Air Mass: James Turrell*. London: The South Bank Centre, 1993.

**Andre Walker**

British, born 1965

Lives and works in Paris

**Selected Solo Exhibitions**

1996 Untitled Installation, Mattress Factory, Pittsburgh

**Selected Bibliography**

Alford, Lucinda. "Gross Dressing." *The Observer Life*, 21 November 1993.

Als, Hilton. "The Style of Andre Walker." *Artforum* (October 1995).

Hastreiter, Kim. "Vision by Design: Interview with Andre Walker." *Paper* (September 1996).

King, Elaine A. "Reviews." *Sculpture* (February 1997).

Kotani, Akiko and Bernard Freydberg. "Crossover in the Arts." *Fiberarts Magazine* (summer 1997).

News Brief. "Installation Show." *Asian Art News* (November/December 1996).

Posa, Cristina. "Of Mind and Body." *Pittsburgh City Paper*, 12 June 1997.

Sauer, Georgia. "Art, after a Fashion." *Pittsburgh Post-Gazette*, 28 October 1996.

Shearing, Graham. "Retro-hip at the Mattress Factory." *Pittsburgh Tribune-Review*, 27 October 1996.

Thomas, Mary. "Mattress Factory Trio's Installation Dynamic." *Pittsburgh Post-Gazette*, 19 July 1997.

———. "Connect the Dots." *Pittsburgh Post-Gazette Weekend*, 18 October 1996.

Walker, Andre. "She's Stineesha, the Supreme, Ultimate, Supermodel." *Interview Magazine* 23, no. 5.

**Wang Youshen**
Chinese, born 1964
Lives and works in Beijing

Selected Solo Exhibitions

1999 *Dark Room*, Mattress Factory, Pittsburgh
1993 *Newspaper Advertisements*, Badaling Great Wall, Beijing
1990 Hong Kong Art Center
1988 Central Academy of Fine Arts Gallery, Beijing

Selected Group Exhibitions

1994 *'94 International Contemporary Art Show in Beijing, China/Korea/Japan*, The Art Museum of Capital Normal University of Beijing, Beijing
1993 *Venice Biennale*, Venice
*Mao Goes Pop*, Hong Kong Arts Centre, Hong Kong
1992 *China New Wave*, Australia
*K-18*, Outside Europe Modern Art, Kassel, Germany
1990 *1st Spring Festival of International New Art*, Art Gallery of New South Wales, Sydney
*The Wheel*, Beijing
1989 *China Avant-garde*, China Art Gallery, Beijing
*China Avant-garde-Now*, Tokyo Gallery, Tokyo

Selected Bibliography

Giannini, Claudia and Michael Olijnyk. "Conversation." *Art Journal* (fall 2000).
Raczka, Robert. "Installations by Asian Artists in Residence." *Sculpture* (March 2000).
Shearing, Graham. "Far East on the North Side." *Ticket*, 29 October 1999.
——. "A Little Bit of Asia." *Pittsburgh Tribune-Review*, 12 December 1999.
Thomas, Mary. "Installing Pittsburgh." *Pittsburgh Post-Gazette*, 29 October 1999.
Zhuang, Huang, ed. *New Asian Art Show 1995*. Tokyo: Committee of International Contemporary Art, 1995.

**Allan Wexler**
American, born 1949
Lives and works in New York

Selected Solo Exhibitions

1999 *Allan Wexler* (retrospective exhibition), City Gallery of Chastain and Atlanta College of Art, Atlanta; Contemporary Arts Center, Cincinnati
1994 *Allan Wexler: Buckets, Sinks, Gutter*, Ronald Feldman Fine Arts, Inc., New York
*The Small Buildings, Furniture, and Utensils of Allan Wexler*, Hochschule der Kunste, Berlin
1993 *Allan Wexler—Structures for Reflection*, Karl Ernst Osthaus Museum, Hagen, Germany
1992 *New Work*, Ronald Feldman Fine Arts, Inc. New York
1991 *Table/Building/Landscape*, The Forum Gallery, St. Louis
*Allan Wexler*, San Diego Museum of Contemporary Art, La Jolla, CA
1990 *Allan Wexler: Furniture Prototypes for Production*, Horace Richter Gallery, Old Jaffa, Israel
1988 *Bed Sitting Rooms for an Artist in Residence* (permanent installation), Mattress Factory, Pittsburgh

Selected Group Exhibitions

1995 *Universe of Meaning*, Brattleboro Museum and Art Center, Brattleboro, VT
1994 *Function/Dysfunction*, Gwenda Jay Gallery, Chicago
1993 *Summer '93*, Ronald Feldman Fine Arts, Inc., New York
*Fall from Fashion*, The Aldrich Museum of Contemporary Art, Ridgefield, CT
1992 *Trivial Machines*, Karl Ernst Osthaus Museum, Hagen, Germany
*Arts at Friends*, S. Bitter-Larkin, New York
1991 *Everything Matters*, Lorraine Kessler Gallery, Poughkeepsie, NY
*Discarded*, Rockland Center for the Arts, West Nyack, NY
1989 *Sukkah with Furniture Built from its Walls*, Israel Museum, Jerusalem
*The Jewish Experience in the Art of the 20th Century*, Barbican Art Gallery, Barbican Center, London
1987 *Pure Room for the Memory Theater*, Neuberger Museum, Purchase College, State University of New York, Purchase, NY
1984 *Metamanhattan*, Whitney Museum of American Art Downtown, New York

Selected Bibliography

"Art World: Jailhouse Commissions." *Art in America* (May 1995).
Cembalest, Robin. "Reviews." *ARTnews* (April 1992).
Cochran, Rebecca Dimling. "Custom Built: A Twenty-Year Survey of Work by Allan Wexler." *Sculpture* (September 1999).
Feaster, Felecia. " Allan Wexler: City Gallery at Chastain and Atlanta College of Art Gallery." *ARTnews* (September 1999).
Heartney, Eleanor. "Review of Exhibitions." *Art in America* (June 1992).
——. "Allan Wexler." *Artforum* (summer 1990).
Phillips, Patricia. "Sitting Up: Critical Chairs." *Sculpture* (summer 1993).
Schulz, Bernd. "A Wanderer Between Architecture, Design and Art." *Domus* (November 1999).
Seward, Keith. "Allan Wexler." *Artforum* (February 1995).
Siersma, Betsy. *Allan Wexler: Dining Rooms and Furniture for the Typical House*. Amherst, MA: University of Massachusetts Gallery, 1989.

**Alison Wilding**
British, born 1948
Lives and works in London

Selected Solo Exhibitions

1998 *Désormais*, Skipton Castle, North Yorkshire, England
1995 *Alison Wilding: Echo*, Angel Row Gallery, Nottingham, England
*Alison Wilding: Sculptures and Etchings*, Karsten Schubert Ltd., London

1994 *Ambit*, Mattress Factory, Pittsburgh
1993 *Alison Wilding: Exposure*, Tate Gallery of British Art, St. Ives, Cornwall
*Recent Sculptures*, Karsten Schubert Ltd, London
1992 *Recent Sculptures*, Asher Faure Gallery, Los Angeles
1991 *Alison Wilding: Immersion, Sculpture from Ten Years*, Tate Gallery of British Art, Liverpool
1990 Karsten Schubert Ltd., London

**Selected Group Exhibitions**

1995 *Natural Settings*, Chelsea Physic Garden, London
*Decadence*, Trondhjems Kunstforening, Norway
*Here and Now*, Serpentine Gallery, London
*British Art of the '80s and '90s: The Weltkunst Collection*, Irish Museum of Modern Art, Dublin
1994 Luis Adelantado, Valencia, Spain
*A Group Show: Keith Coventry, Peter Davis, Anya Gallaccio, Zebedee Jones, Bridget Riley and Alison Wilding*, Karsten Schubert Ltd., London
1993 *Then and Now: Twenty-Three Years at the Serpentine Gallery*, Serpentine Gallery, London
*Made Strange: New British Sculpture*, Museum Ludwig, Budapest
*In Site—New British Sculpture*, The National Museum of Contemporary Art, Oslo
1992 *Whitechapel Open '92*, Whitechapel Art Gallery, London
*Fifth Anniversary Exhibition*, Karsten Schubert Ltd., London
*Turner Prize Exhibition*, Tate Gallery of British Art, London
1991 *Pulsio: Louise Bourgeois, Pepe Espaliu, Alison Wilding*, Fundacio La Caixa, Barcelona
*The Lick of the Eye*, Shoshana Wayne Gallery, Santa Monica, CA
1990 *Now for the Future: Purchases for the Arts Council Collection Since 1984*, Hayward Gallery, London

**Selected Bibliography**


Allthorpe-Guyton, Marjorie. "Immersion and Exposure." *Artscribe* (September 1991).
Deslandes, Gerald. "Wilding Things." *Interview Magazine* (June 1991).
Jones, Amelia. "Alison Wilding at Asher-Faure." *Artforum* (May 1992).
Lee, David. "Alison Wilding." *Art Review Magazine* (1994).
McDonald, John. "Turner Takes the Flak." *Contemporary Art Magazine* (winter 1992).
Pomery, Victoria, ed. *Alison Wilding: Echo*. London: Angel Row Gallery and Karsten Schubert Contemporary Art, Ltd., 1995.
Potts, Alex. "Edinburgh and Skipton Castle: Carl Andre and Alison Wilding." *The Burlington Magazine* (December 1998).
Stoddart, Hugh. "Alison Wilding." *Art Monthly Magazine* (March 1995).
Tromp, Ian. "Making Visible: On Alison Wilding." *Sculpture* (January/February 2000).
Yarrington, Alison. "I Figure I'm a Woman." *Women's Art Magazine* (November 1992).


**Bill Woodrow**
British, born 1948
Lives and works in London

**Selected Solo Exhibitions**

2000 *Regardless of History*, Fourth Plinth, Trafalgar Square, London
1999 *Fool's Gold*, Tate Gallery of British Art, London; Institut Mathildenhoehe, Darmstadt, Germany
1996 Tate Gallery of British Art, London
1995 *About This Axis, Drawings 1990–1995*, Camden Arts Centre, London
1994 *Drawings*, Galerie Sabine Wachters, Brussels
*Chapter and Verse*, Musée Ianchelevici, La Louviere, Belgium
1993 *New Drawings*, Quint Krichman Projects, La Jolla, CA
1992 Galerie Sabine Wachters, Brussels
1991 *21st International Sao Paulo Bienal*, Sao Paulo, Brazil
Galleria Locus Solus, Genoa, Italy
1990 Galerie Fahnemann, Berlin
1986 *Ship of Fools: Discovery of Time*, Mattress Factory, Pittsburgh
1985 Kunsthalle Basel, Basel, Switzerland
1983 Museum of Modern Art, Oxford, England

**Selected Group Exhibitions**

1996 *Un Siecle de Sculpture Anglaise*, Jeu de Paume, Paris
1995 *From Picasso to Woodrow: Recently Acquired Prints and Portfolios*, Tate Gallery of British Art, London
*Contemporary British Art in Print*, Scottish National Gallery Of Modern Art, Edinburgh
1994 *Dessins et Sculptures*, FRAC de Picardie, Amiens, France
*Back to Basics: A Major Retrospective*, Flowers East, London
*International Print Triennial '94*, Krakow, Poland
1993 *Autoportraits Contemporain/Here's Looking at Me*, Espace Lyonnais d'Art Contemporain, Lyon, France
*Images from the Coalfields*, Angela Flowers Gallery, London
*Out of Sight Out of Mind*, Lisson Gallery, London
*No More Heroes Anymore: Contemporary Art from the Imperial War Museum*, Royal Scottish Academy, Edinburgh
1992 *The New Patrons*, Christies, London
*Artistes pour Amnesty International*, Hôtel des Arts, Paris
*A Marked Difference*, Arti et Amicitiae, Amsterdam
*The Cutting Edge*, Barbican Art Gallery, London
1991 Metropolis, Berlin
*Metamemphis 1991*, Galerie Tanit Koeln, Köln, Germany
*Dessin D' Une Collection, Extrait 7*, FRAC Picardie, Amiens, France
1990 *For a Wider World*, Ukranian Museum of Fine Art, Kiev, USSR
1981 *Objects and Sculpture*, Arnolfini, Bristol/I.C.A., London

Selected Bibliography

Conti, Viani. "Bill Woodrow: Locus Solus, Genova." *Flash Art* (February/March 1992).
Cooke, Lynne. "Das Narrenschiff." *Parkett* (March 1987).
Cueff, Alain. "Bill Woodrow." *Artistes* (June 1983).
Donovan, Sandra Fischione. "Off-the-wall Art Exhibits Titillate the Senses, Stimulate the Mind." *New York Times Sunday Magazine*, 24 May 1992.
Forsha, Lynda. *Natural Produce, An Armed Response; Sculpture by Bill Woodrow*. La Jolla, California: La Jolla Museum of Contemporary Art, 1985.
Francis, Mark. "Bill Woodrow: Material Truths." *Artforum* (January 1984).
Januszczak, Waldemar. "Bill Woodrow." *Guardian* (London), 14 January 1982.
Lambrecht, Luk. "Richard Deacon, Bill Woodrow, Sabine Wachters." *Flash Art* (May/June 1994).
Lawson, Thomas. "Reviews: Edinburgh, Bill Woodrow, New 57 Gallery." *Artforum* (December 1981).
Roberts, John. "Bill Woodrow: Musée des Beaux-Arts, Calais." *Artscribe* (January 1999).
Thomas, Mary. "Mattress Factory Exhibition Focuses on Process of Art Works." *Pittsburgh Post-Gazette*, 3 January 1998.

**Wu Mali**

Taiwanese, born 1957
Lives and works in Taipei

Selected Solo Exhibitions

1999 *Victorian Sweeties*, Mattress Factory, Pittsburgh
1998 *Treasure Island*, IT Park Gallery, Taipei
*A Parking Lot Is Not a Parking Lot*, BaDe Parking Lot, Taipei
1996 Taipei Fine Arts Motel, a conceptual action in Taipei
1995 *Scriptura*, Galleria Giorgio Persano, Turin, Italy
1994 *Fake*, Taipei Fine Arts Museum, Taipei
1993 *Gnawing Texts, Reaming Words*, IT Park Gallery, Taipei
1992 *Eagle Aesthetics*, Contemporary Art Gallery, Taichung, Taiwan

Selected Group Exhibitions

1998 *Inside Out—New Chinese Art*, P.S. 1 Contemporary Art Center, Long Island City, NY; San Francisco Museum of Modern Art, San Francisco
1995 *Venice Biennale*, Venice
*6. Trienniale Kleinplastik*, Stuttgart, Germany
1994 *Promenade in Asia*, Shiseido Gallery, Tokyo
*Balanceakte*, ifa Gallery, Stuttgart, Germany
1993 *Taiwan Art 1945–1993*, Taipei Fine Arts Museum, Taipei
1991 *Women and Contemporary Art*, Dimention Art Center, Taipei

Selected Bibliography

Fumio, Nanjo and Miki Akiko. *Site of Desire: 1998 Taipei Biennial*. Taipei: Taipei Fine Art Museum, 1998.
Giannini, Claudia and Michael Olijnyk. "Conversation." *Art Journal* (fall 2000).
Kee, Joan. "Transiency and Time: A Mattress Factory Residency." *ART AsiaPacific* 28 (2000).
Lien, Fu Chia-wen. "Wu Mali: Gnawing Texts, Reaming Words." *ARTnews* (November 1995).
Madden, Dave. "Gee, Zero-G." *In Pittsburgh,* 27 October, 1999.
Minglu, Gao. ed. *Inside Out: New Chinese Art*. Berkeley: University of California Press, 1998.
Raczka, Robert. "Installations by Asian Artists in Residence." *Sculpture* (March 2000).
Shearing, Graham. "A Little Bit of Asia." *Pittsburgh Tribune-Review*, 12 December 1999.
Thomas, Mary. "Installing Pittsburgh." *Pittsburgh Post-Gazette*, 29 October 1999.

## Mattress Factory History

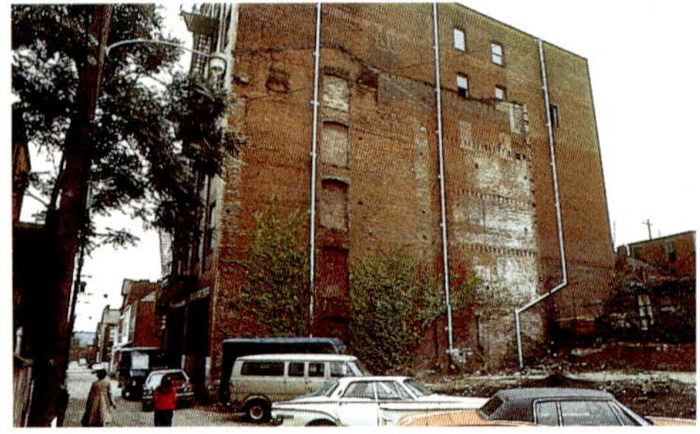

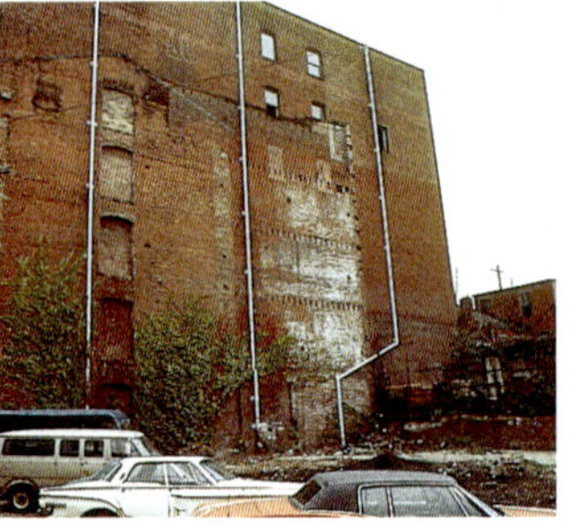

**1974**

Barbara Luderowski buys 500 Sampsonia Way, formerly a Stearns & Foster mattress warehouse built at the turn of the century. Components include:
Vegetarian Cooperative Restaurant
Polish Laboratory Theater
Dance Studio
Children's Theater
Gallery Exhibitions
Artists' Studio and Living Space

**1977**

The Mattress Factory, Ltd. becomes a legal non-profit corporation with a Board of Directors.

**1978**

Michael Olijnyk joins the staff.

**1979**

*Fabrications*, group exhibition of six fiber artists, September 8–October 8
*Lies Brothers*, films by George, Lenny and Michael Lies, September 11
The Iron Clad Agreement presents the play *Thomas A. Edison* by Scott Cummings, September 21–22
*By Kids*, films by kids from the Pennsylvania School for the Deaf, the Falk Lab School, and North Hills School, September 25
Jay Maisel, photography lecture, September 28
*Isadora, American Legend*, a solo exhibition by Ann Beigel, November 30–December 9
Pittsburgh Madrigal Singers, concert, December 14

**1980**

New Wave Music Concert, including Target with Karl Mullen, January 5
*Company One & Company Two*, short sketches by the Mattress Factory Children's Theater Workshop, January 20
*The Photographs of Beaumont Newhall*, September 6–30.
*A Night in Pittsburgh*, solo exhibition by Stephen Pellegrino, September 12–20
Duane Michaels photography lecture and workshop, September 26–28

**1981**

Mattress Factory Theater and Lobby are refurbished.
Baroque Music, performance by Jean Thomas, William Goff and Aimee Beggs, March 13
*Fiber*, an exhibition by students from Carnegie Mellon University, March 6–20
Dennis Miller, comedy performance, April 10–11
*Four Performances Avant-Garde*, three plays by Noumenon productions and one play by David Gene Fowler, April 18–21
*Images and Objects*, exhibition by four graduate students from Carnegie Mellon University, April 3–19
*Mirror Works*, a solo exhibition by Ron Desmett, May 1–31.
Harvey Stein, photography lecture, June 26
James Rosenberg, playwright's workshop, June 22–August 7
Judy Dater, photography lecture, July 31
Bill Owens, photography lecture, August 28
Gemini Gee Band, jazz concert, October 4
*Willy's Pool Room*, a film by Tony Buba, October 23
Exhibition of large, rubber stamp prints by Cees de Rooij, December 1–31

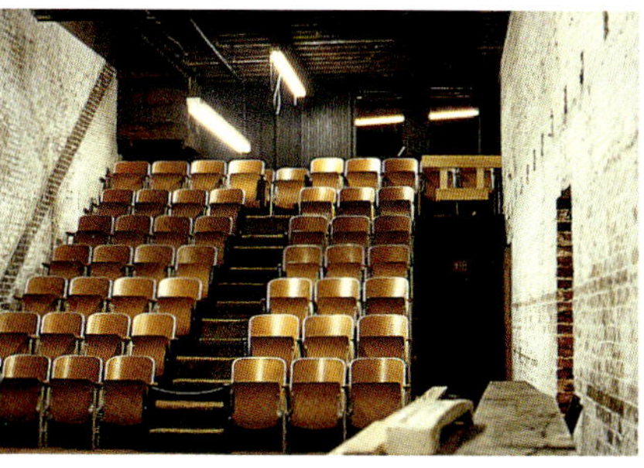

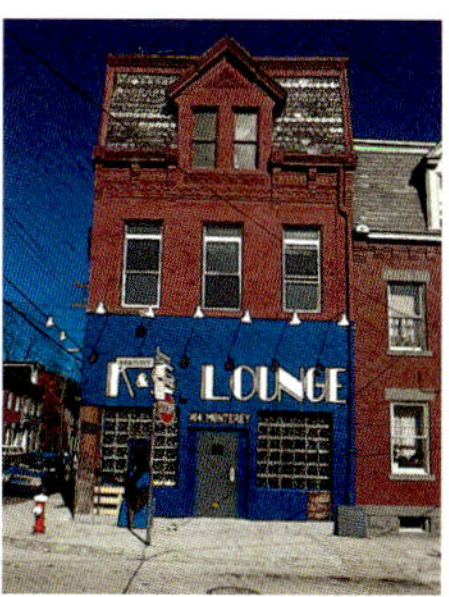


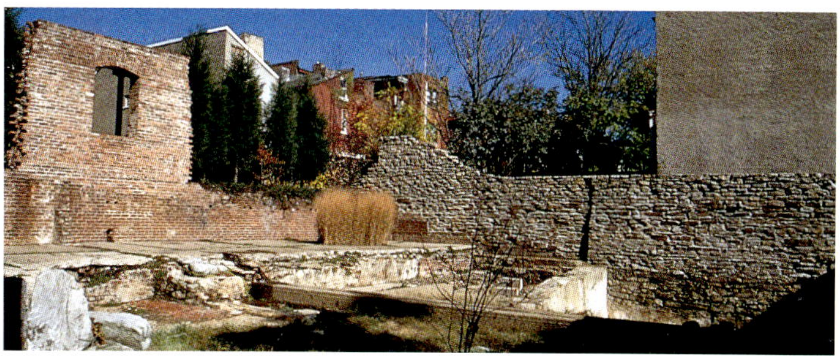

500 Sampsonia, 1970s

Co-op restaurant on the first floor of 500 Sampsonia Way, c. 1977

Theater housed in 500 Sampsonia Way

1414 Monterey acquired by the Mattress Factory in 1986

Winifred Lutz's *Garden* adjacent to 500 Sampsonia Way

**1982**

Mattress Factory focuses on creating new installations

First exhibition of installations, May 8–June 5, includes:

Athena Tacha, *Rain Forest Diptych*

Michael Olijnyk, Untitled Installation

Diane Samuels, *44 Installations at the Mattress Factory*

**1983**

James Turrell creates and exhibits *Danaë* and *Pleiades*, the first works in the Permanent Collection.

**1986**

Mattress Factory acquires a building at 1414 Monterey Street and three buildings on North Taylor Avenue.

Limited Edition Project begins: Bill Woodrow creates two lithographs.

**1988**

1414 Monterey Street opens as a satellite exhibition facility.

**1990**

Renovations made to 500 Sampsonia Way to meet code requirements for a public use building.

**1991**

*Mattress Factory: Installation and Performance 1982–1989*, the museum's first retrospective catalogue, is published.

Mattress Factory collaborates with the *Carnegie International*.

**1993**

Winifred Lutz begins excavation of vacant lot adjacent to 500 Sampsonia Way in preparation for her outdoor work, *Garden*.

**1994**

Mattress Factory invited to participate in the Garden Square North community development project.

**1995**

The Mattress Factory's Web site goes on-line.

**1996**

Art in Context Forum: Art and the Community, March 17

Art in Context Forum: Politics, Religion and Art, March 24

**1997**

Art in Context Forum: Gender and Identity, April 20

Winifred Lutz's *Garden* dedicated at the First Annual Garden Party, June 13–14

20th Anniversary Art Auction, October 4

*Process: Fragments and Documentation from the Mattress Factory Archives*, exhibition at 1414 Monterey Street, November 19–March 22, 1998

**1998**

Art in Context Forum: Natural History, May 17

# Mattress Factory Facilities

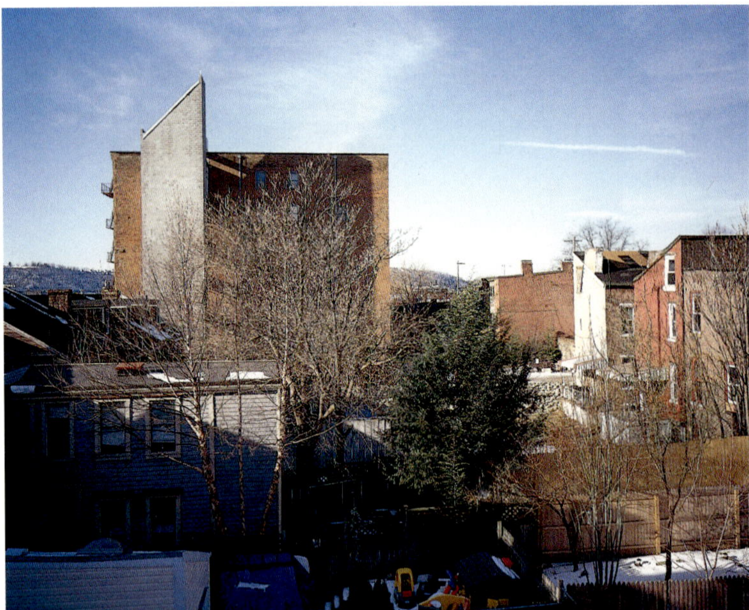

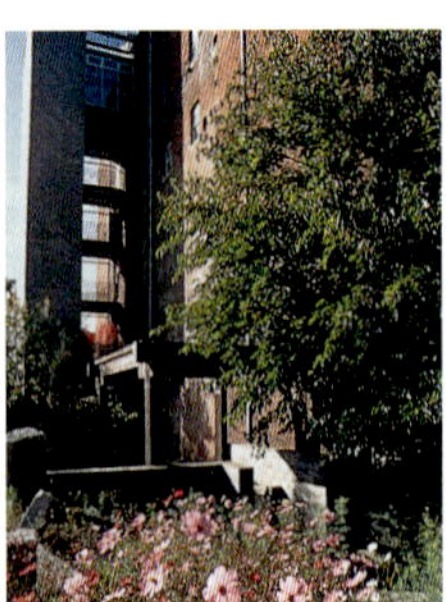

500 Sampsonia Way

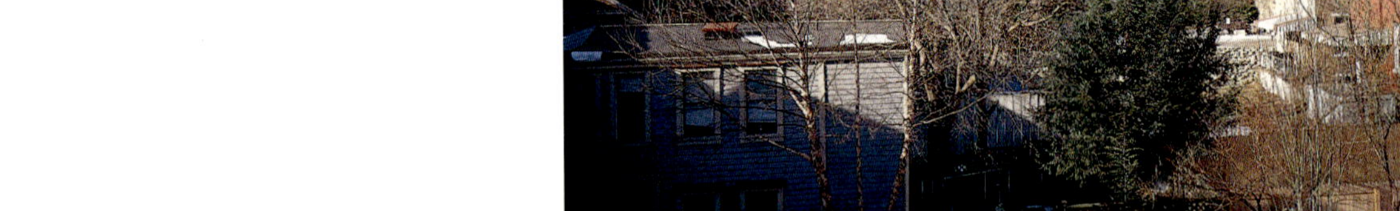

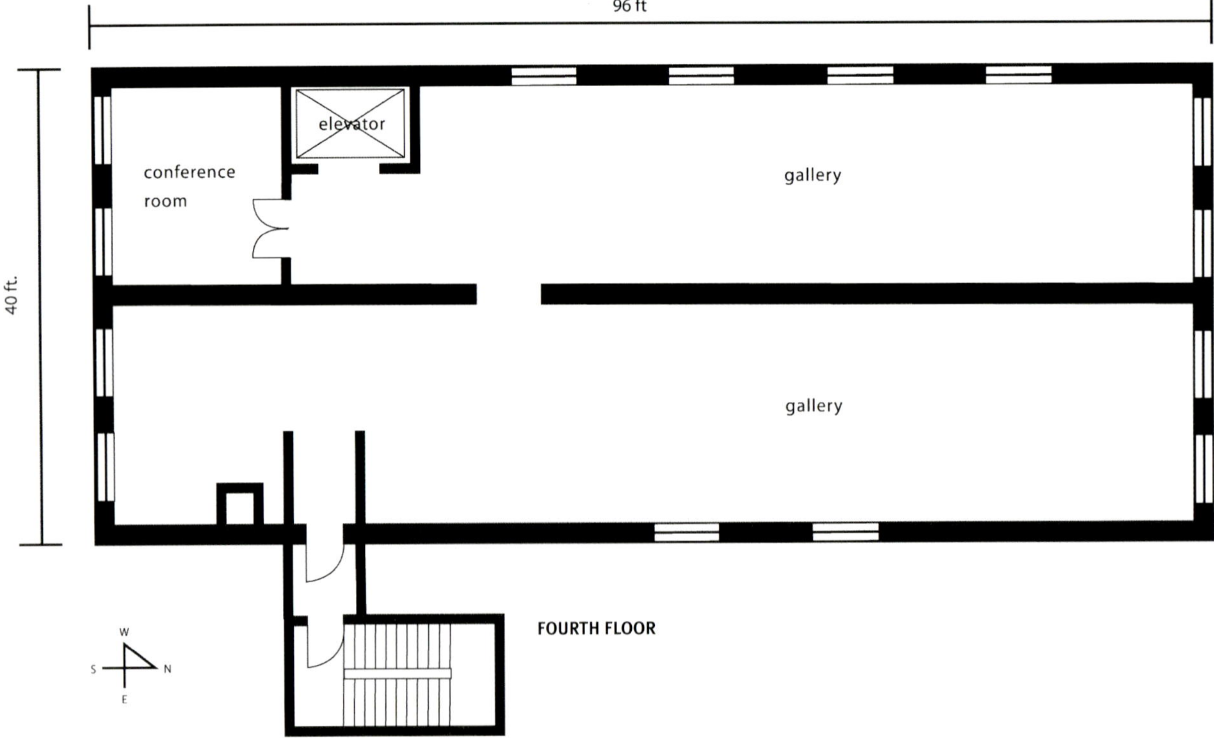

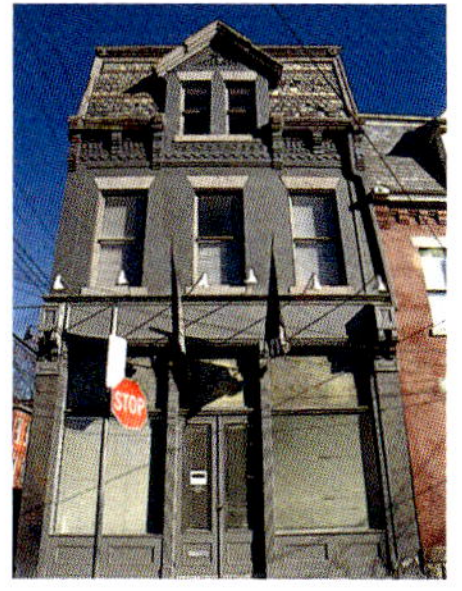

1414 Monterey Street

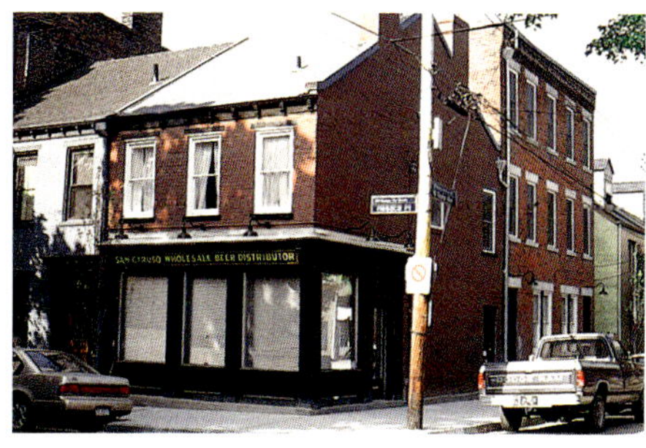

Artists' Residence

503-505 N. Taylor Avenue

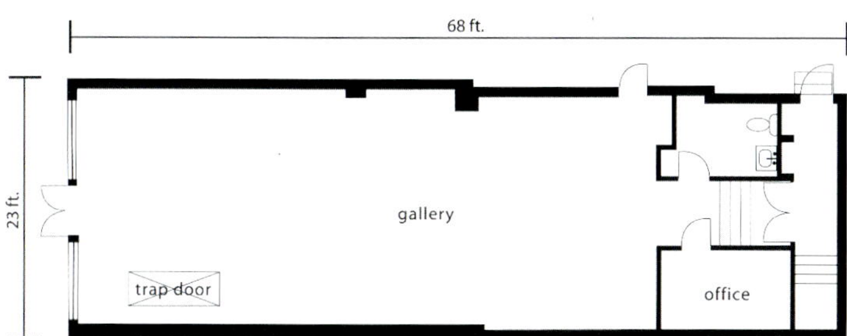


FIRST FLOOR

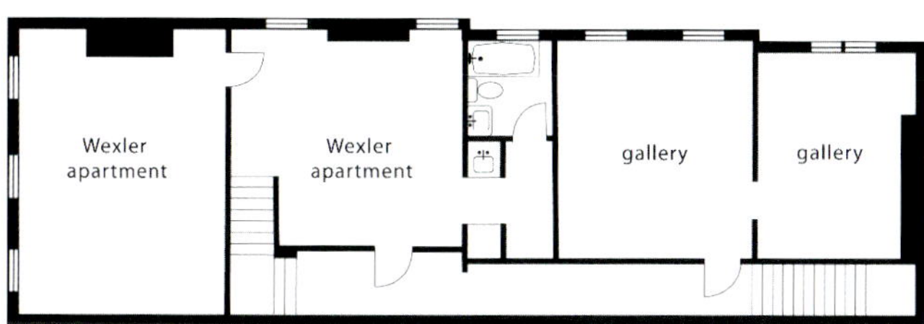


SECOND FLOOR

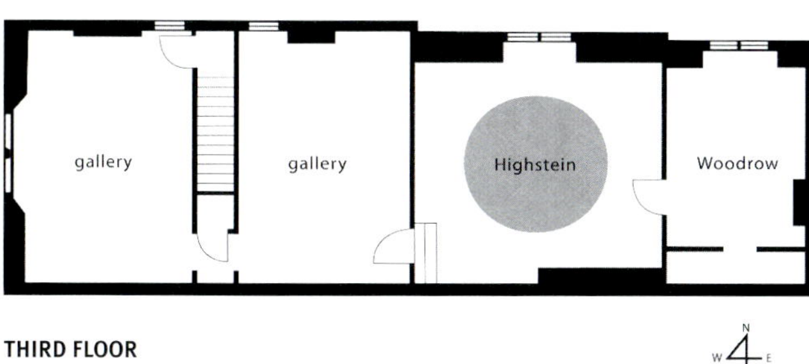


THIRD FLOOR

**Installations, Mattress Factory, 1990–1999**

Designed by Kendra Power Design & Communication, Inc.
Pittsburgh, Pennsylvania

Printed by Superior Printing,
Warren, Ohio

Bound by The Riverside Group,
Rochester, New York

The catalogue is printed on 100# Productolith Dull.

The text is set in Meta Plus Book, Meta Plus Bold and Adobe Garamond.